The Role of Religion in American Life

An Interpretive Historical Anthology
Third Edition
Revised Printing

Robert R. Mathisen
Western Baptist College

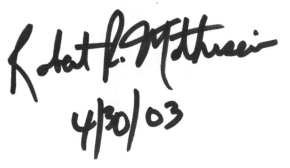

KENDALL/HUNT PUBLISHING COMPANY
4050 Westmark Drive   Dubuque, Iowa 52004

Cover image © 1998 PhotoDisc, Inc.

To

My LS114/124 Students

Contents

Preface

"For the study and understanding of American culture, the recovery of American religious history may well be the most important achievement of the last thirty years." Writing these words in 1964, the eminent historian Henry F. May recognized that "even for those students of American culture who do not find religious thought and practice intrinsically interesting, knowledge of religious history has become a necessity." May realized that "the recovery of American religious history has restored a knowledge of the mode, even the language, in which most Americans, during most of American history, did their thinking about human nature and destiny."

As May has suggested, a knowledge of religion's role in the progress of American history is necessary for a clear understanding of how America has developed. The purpose of the present volume is to provide historical documents which illustrate the role of religion in the emergence of American society. The vehicle used by the editor to achieve this purpose is the perceptive analysis of religion supplied by several sociologists of religion. Particularly helpful is sociology's functional approach to the study of religion which says that religion is not to be considered always as the independent variable that "causes" certain social and cultural developments; nor should religion be thought of as entirely a dependent variable which reflects its social environment. Rather, religion should be looked upon historically as both an independent and a dependent variable. As part of a social structure, it is independent in that it performs certain functions and therefore *acts upon* society as a whole, but it is also dependent in that it is *acted upon* by the society within which it exists.

The documents collected in this volume demonstrate that from the colonial period through the first two-thirds of the nineteenth century, religion as an independent variable was more significant in the shaping of America than was religion as a dependent variable. During the last third of the nineteenth century, however, the trend reversed, so that since that time religion has been influenced by society in more significant ways than it has influenced society. Each of the four parts of this volume focuses on a distinct segment of America's past. As the nation was established by pilgrims in search of a providential destiny, and then expanded by those seeking to quench their thirst for adventure and wealth, it was subsequently energized by forces that challenged the traditional values of America. Evaluation of America's journey thus far is still in progress.

While numerous definitions of religion have been suggested by social scientists, the definition by sociologist Ronald Johnstone is used here. Johnstone has stated that religion is "a system of beliefs and practices by which a group of people interprets and responds to what they feel is supernatural and sacred."

The decisions involved in selecting documents for a reader are never easy; the present volume provided no exceptions. Each of the documents which appears here demonstrates the interaction of religion with other socio-cultural, economic, political, or diplomatic factors. (See diagram on page xi.) It is hoped that the volume will enhance the reader's "knowledge of the mode . . . in which most Americans . . . did their thinking about nature and destiny."

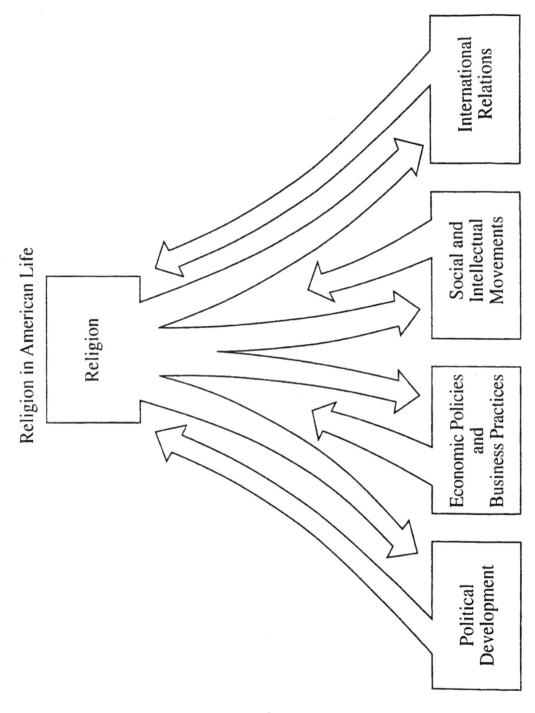

Religion in American Life

Religion

International Relations

Social and Intellectual Movements

Economic Policies and Business Practices

Political Development

Part I   Establishing America
1607-1820

Religion played an important role in the establishment of most of the American colonies during the seventeenth and eighteenth centuries. Particularly noteworthy was the ever present religiously oriented sense of mission which guided people of all ranks to the New World early during the period between 1607 and 1820, and later preserved the nation during a time of philosophical doubt following the American Revolution. For reasons never fully understood, but nevertheless held as truth, a favoring Providence was seen as directing the destiny of His "chosen people" in the abundant wilderness called America.

In no colony is the significance of religion more clearly seen than in Massachusetts. The Pilgrims, the first group of Anglican dissenters who came to America, settled at Plymouth in 1620. Also known as Separatists, they were led by their political "Moses," William Bradford. In his account of Plymouth Plantation he reveals that the economic values and religious practices of the Pilgrims clashed, thus forcing settlers to reevaluate their goals. A short distance to the north from Plymouth, a second group of Anglican malcontents, the Puritans, settled the Bay Colony in 1630. Led by John Winthrop, this group of non-Separatists was urged to build their model society, the "city upon a hill," though as Winthrop indicates, the society would be noted for its divinely fixed social order in which some would be rich and others poor. A model society required model citizens, and some residents of early Massachusetts, like Anne Hutchinson, did not match the requirements.

The Puritanism of the early decades underwent considerable change by the end of the seventeenth century due to both intra-colonial and extra-colonial influences. Much of the vitality and faith of the first Puritans in America was maintained by the next two generations. As the colonial population became increasingly heterogeneous, religious pluralism weakened the prestige of all church groups. Externally, the secular rationalism of the Enlightenment resulted in antagonism between it and Puritan revivalism. When by the early eighteenth century the vast majority of the population was outside of the church, a new approach was needed to revitalize the church and society. What resulted was the Great Awakening, which some, like Jonathan Edwards, defended for positive results, while others, like Charles Chauncy and critics at Harvard, denounced due to what was deemed its emotional excesses.

One of the social effects of the Great Awakening was the elevation of the common man and the advance of lay authority in the church. From this new significance of the individual in the church, it was only natural that the new experience in leadership would find its way to the political sphere where it stimulated the establishment of the United States as a nation. Jonathan Mayhew, who emerged from the Great Awakening as a theological liberal, denounced passive obedience to kings decades before the American Revolution. It is significant to note that the crux of his arguments was debated and disputed until 1776 by many clergy and laity alike, including the English Methodist John Wesley and the American Unitarian Samuel West.

The first several decades of the new, infant nation were fraught with difficulty from without and within. The popular deistic philosophy of the Revolutionary era had been hard on the churches, while the course of the French Revolution, with its excesses of the Reign of Terror, was looked upon by many Americans as the logical outcome of deism. Clergy like Timothy Dwight identified deism as the root of widespread infidelity, a prime target of Second Awakening preachers. The revivalism of the new awakening swept not only the East where it began, but also spread rapidly westward where migrant Americans were establishing new homes. The advance of people to the West was paralleled by the founding of missionary and Bible societies as well as new colleges by the 1840s.

1 Religion and Colonial Massachusetts

You are the light of the world. A city set on a hill cannot be hidden.

—Matt. 5:14

Bradford's History of Plymouth Plantation, 1620-1647
William Bradford

William Bradford (1590-1657) was the leading figure in the founding and early history of the Plymouth colony settled in 1620. His *History of Plymouth Plantation* remains as the most descriptive account of life in early Plymouth, where he served as governor from 1620 until his death. The following account in Bradford's *Of Plymouth Plantation, 1620-1647* describes some of the tensions experienced by the Pilgrim sect of the Puritans as they sought to reconcile their spiritual ideals with troublesome economic realities.

All this while no supply was heard of, neither knew they when they might expect any. So they began to think how they might raise as much corn as they could, and obtain a better crop than they had done, that they might not still thus languish in misery. At length, after much debate of things, the Governor (with the advice of the chiefest amongst them) gave way that they should set corn every man for his own particular, and in that regard trust to themselves; in all other things to go on in the general way as before. And so assigned to every family a parcel of land, according to the proportion of their number, for that end, only for present use (but made no division for inheritance) and ranged all boys and youth under some family. This has very good success, for it made all hands very industrious, so as much more corn was planted than otherwise would have been by any means the Governor or any other could use, and saved him a great deal of trouble, and gave far better content. The women now went willingly in to the field, and took their little ones with them to set corn; which before would allege weakness and inability; whom to have compelled would have been thought great tyranny and oppression.

The experience that was had in this common course and condition, tried sundry years and that amongst godly and sober men, may well evince the vanity of that conceit of Plato's and other ancients applauded by some of later times; that the taking away of property and bringing in community into a commonwealth would make them happy and flourishing; as if they were wiser than God. For this community (so far as it was) was found to breed much confusion and discontent and retard much employment that would have been to their benefit and comfort. For the young men, that were most able and fit for labor and service, did repine that they should spend their time and strength to work for other men's wives and children without any recompense. The strong, or man of parts, had no more in division of victuals and clothes than he that was weak and not able to do a quarter the other could; this was thought injustice. The aged and graver men to be ranked and equalized in labors and victuals, clothes, etc., with the meaner and younger sort, thought it some indignity and disrespect unto them. And for men's wives to be commanded to do service for other men, as dressing their meat, washing their clothes, etc., they deemed it a kind of slavery, neither could many husbands well brook it. Upon the point all being to have alike, and all to do alike, they thought themselves in the like condition, and one as good as another; and so, if it did not cut off those relations that God hath set amongst men, yet it did at least much diminish and take off the mutual respects that should be preserved amongst them. And would have been worse if they had been men of another condition. Let none object this is men's corruption, and nothing to the course itself. I answer, seeing all men have this corruption in them, God in His wisdom saw another course fitter for them.

But to return. After this course settled, and by that their corn was planted, all their victuals were spent and they were only to rest on God's providence; at night not many times knowing where to have a bit of anything the next day. And so, as one well observed, had need to pray that God would give them their daily bread, above all people in the world. Yet they bore these wants with great patience and alacrity of spirit; and that for so long a time as for the most part of two years. Which makes me remember what Peter Martyr writes (in magnifying the Spaniards) in his 5th Decade, page 208. "They" (saith he) "led a miserable life for five days together, with the parched grain of maze only, and that not to saturity"; and then concludes, "that such pains, such labors, and such hunger, he thought none living which is not a Spaniard could have endured."

But alas! these, when they had maize (that is, Indian corn) they thought it as good as a feast and wanted not only for five days together, but some time two or three months together, and neither had bread nor any kind of corn. Indeed, in another place, in his 2nd Decade, page 94, he mentions how others of them were worse put to it, where they were fain to eat dogs, toads and dead men, and died almost all. From these extremities the Lord in his goodness kept these His people, and in their great wants preserved both their lives and healths. Let His name have the praise. Yet let me here make use of his conclusion, which in some sort may be applied to this people:

"That with their miseries they opened a way to these new lands, and after these storms, with what ease other men came to inhabit in them, in respect of the calamities these men suffered; so as they seem to go to a bride feast where all things are provided for them."

Mr. Hatherly came over again this year, but upon his own occasions, and began to make preparation to plant and dwell in the country. He with his former dealings had wound in what money he had in the partnership into his own hands, and so gave off all partnership (except in name) as was found in the issue of things; neither did he meddle or take any care about the same. Only he was troubled about his engagement about the *Friendship*, as will after appear. And now partly about that account in some reckonings between Mr. Allerton and him, and some debts that Mr. Allerton otherwise owed him upon dealing between them in particular, he drew up an account of above £2000 and would fain have engaged the partners here with it, because Mr. Allerton had been their agent. But they told him they had been fooled long enough with such things, and showed him that it no way belonged to them, but he must look to make good his engagement for the *Friendship*, which caused some trouble between Mr. Allerton and him.

Mr. William Peirce did the like, Mr. Allerton being wound into his debt also upon particular dealings, as if they had been bound to make good all men's debts; but they easily shook off these things. But Mr. Allerton hereby ran into much trouble and vexation, as well as he had troubled others, for Mr. Denison sued him for the money he had disbursed for the sixth part of the *White Angel*, and recovered the same with damages.

Though the partners were thus plunged into great engagements and oppressed with unjust debts, yet the Lord prospered their trading, that they made yearly large returns and had soon wound themselves out of it all if yet they had otherwise been well dealt withal as will more appear hereafter.

Also the people of the Plantation began to grow in their outward estates, by reason of the flowing of many people into the country, especially into the Bay of the Massachusetts. By which means corn and cattle rose to a great price, by which many were much enriched and commodities grew plentiful. And yet in other regards this benefit turned to their hurt, and this accession of strength to their weakness. For now as their stocks increased and the increase vendible, there was no longer any holding them together, but now they must of necessity go to their great lots. They could not otherwise keep their cattle, and having oxen grown they must have land for plowing and tillage. And no man now thought he could live except he had cattle and a great deal of ground to keep them, all striving to increase their stocks. By which means they were scattered all over the Bay quickly and the town in which they lived compactly till now was left very thin and in a short time almost desolate.

And if this had been all, it had been less, though too much; but the church must also be divided, and those that had lived so long together in Christian and comfortable fellowship must now part and suffer many divisions. First, those that lived on their lots on the other side of the Bay, called Duxbury, they could not long bring their wives and children to the public worship and church meetings here, but with such burthen as, growing to some competent number, they sued to be dismissed and become a body of themselves. And so they were dismissed about this time, though very unwillingly. But to touch this sad matter, and handle things together that fell out afterward; to prevent any further scattering from this place and weakening of the same, it was thought best to give out some good farms to special persons that would promise to live at Plymouth, and likely to be helpful to the church or commonwealth, and so tie the lands to Plymouth as farms for the same, and there they might keep their cattle and tillage by some servants and retain their dwellings here. And so some special lands were granted at a place general called Green's Harbor, where no allotments had been in the former division, a place very well meadowed and fit to keep and rear cattle good store. But alas, this remedy proved worse than the disease; for within a few years those that had thus got footing there rent themselves away, partly by force and partly wearing the rest with importunity and pleas of necessity, so as they must either suffer them to go or live in continual opposition and contention. And other still, as they conceived themselves straitened or to want accommodation, broke away under one pretense or other, thinking their own conceived necessity and the example of others a warrant sufficient for them. And this I fear will be the ruin of New England, at least of the churches of God there, and will provoke the Lord's displeasure against them.

A Model of Christian Charity
John Winthrop

John Winthrop (1588-1649) was as dominant in the founding and early history of Massachusetts Bay colony as William Bradford was in Plymouth. Moving from London where he had established a law practice, he served as governor of Massachusetts Bay for most of the years from 1630 until his death. The laysermon which follows is taken from the *Winthrop Papers, 1623-1630*, II, 282-295, published by the Massachusetts Historical Society and suggests the blueprint Winthrop wished his fellow passengers to follow as they carried out their mission in building "a city upon a hill" in New England.

A Model Hereof

God Almighty in His most holy and wise providence, hath so disposed of the condition of mankind, as in all times some must be rich, some poor, some high and eminent in power and dignity; others mean and in subjection.

The Reason Hereof

First, to hold conformity with the rest of His works, being delighted to show forth the glory of His wisdom in the variety and difference of the creatures; and the glory of His power, in ordering all these differences for the preservation and good of the whole; and the glory of His greatness, that as it is the glory of princes and to have many officers, so this great King will have many stewards, counting Himself more honored in dispensing His gifts to man by man than if He did it by His own immediate hands.

Secondly, that He might have the more occasion to manifest the work of His Spirit: first upon the wicked in moderating and restraining them, so that the rich and mighty should not eat up the poor, nor the poor and despised rise up against their superiors and shake off their yoke; secondly in the regenerate, in exercising His graces, in them, as in the great ones, their love, mercy, gentleness, temperance, etc.; in the poor and inferior sort, their faith, patience, obedience etc.

Thirdly, that every man might have need of other, and from hence they might be all knit more nearly together in the bonds of brotherly affection. From hence it appears plainly that no man is made more honorable than another or more wealthy, etc., out of any particular and singular respect to himself, but for the glory of his creator and the common good of the creature, man. Therefore God still reserves the property of these gifts to Himself as [in] Ezekiel 16.17. He there calls wealth His gold and His silver. [In] Proverbs 3.9, he claims their service as His due, honor the Lord with thy riches etc. All men being thus (by divine providence) ranked into two sorts, rich and poor; under the first are comprehended all such as are able to live comfortably by their own means duly improved; and all others are poor according to the former distribution.

There are two rules whereby we are to walk one towards another: justice and mercy. These are always distinguished in their act and in their object, yet may they both concur in the same subject in each respect; as sometimes there may be an occasion of showing mercy to a rich man in some sudden danger of distress, and also doing of mere justice to a poor man in regard of some particular contract, etc.

There is likewise a double law by which we are regulated in our conversation one towards another in both the former respects: the law of nature and the law of grace, or the moral law or the law of the Gospel, to omit the rule of justice as not properly belonging to this purpose otherwise than it may fall into consideration in some particular cases. By the first of these laws man as he was enabled so withal [is] commanded to love his neighbor as himself. Upon this ground stands all the precepts of the moral law, which concerns our dealings with men. To apply this to the works of mercy, this law requires two things: first, that every man afford his help to another in every want or distress; secondly, that he performed this out of the same affection which makes him careful of his own goods, according to that of our Savior. Matthew: "Whatsoever ye would that men should do to you." This was practiced by Abraham and Lot in entertaining the Angels and the old man of Gibeah. . . .

Having already set forth the practice of mercy according to the rule of God's law, it will be useful to lay open the grounds of it also, being the other part of the commandment, and that is the affection from which this exercise of mercy must arise. The apos-

tle tells us that this love is the fulfilling of the law, not that it is enough to love our brother and so no further; but in regard of the excellency of his parts giving any motion to the other as the soul to the body and the power it hath to set all the facilities on work in the outward exercise of this duty. As when we bid one make the clock strike, he doth not lay hand on the hammer, which is the immediate instrument of the sound, but sets on work the first mover or main wheel, knowing that will certainly produce the sound which he intends. So the way to draw men to works of mercy, is not by force of argument from the goodness or necessity of the work; for though this course many enforce a rational mind to some present act of mercy, as is frequent in experience, yet it cannot work such a habit in a soul, as shall make it prompt upon all occasions to produce the same effect, but by framing these affections of love in the heart which will as natively bring forth the other, as any cause doth produce effect.

The definition which the Scripture gives us of love is this: "Love is the bond of perfection." First, it is a bond or ligament. Secondly it makes the work perfect. There is not body but consists of parts and that which knits these parts together gives the body its perfection, because it makes each part so contiguous to others as thereby they do mutually participate with each other, both in strength and infirmity, in pleasure and pain. To instance in the most perfect of all bodies: Christ and His church make one body. The several parts of this body, considered apart before they were united, were as disproportionate and as much disordering as so many contrary qualities or elements, but when Christ comes and by His spirit and love knits all these parts to Himself and each to other, it is become the most perfect and best proportioned body in the world. Ephesians 4.16: "Christ, by whom all the body being knit together by every joint for the furniture thereof, according to the effectual power which is in the measure of every perfection of parts," "a glorious body without spot or wrinkle," the ligaments hereof being Christ, or His love, for Christ is love (1 John 4.8). So this definition is right: "Love is the bond of perfection."

If any shall object that it is not possible that love should be bred or upheld without hope of requital, it is granted; but that is not our cause; for this love is always under reward. It never gives, but it always receives with advantage; first, in regard that among the members of the same body, love and affection are reciprocal in a most equal and sweet kind of commerce. Secondly, in regard of the pleasure and content that the exercise of love carries with it, as we may see in the natural body. The mouth is at all the pains to receive and mince the food which serves for the nourishment of all the other parts of the body, yet it hath no cause to complain; for first the other parts send back by several passages a due proportion of the same nourishment, in a better form for the strengthening and comforting the mouth. Secondly, the labor of the mouth is accompanied with such pleasure and content as fare exceeds the pains it takes. So is it all the labor of love among Christians. The party loving, reaps love again, as was showed before, which the soul covets more than all the wealth in the world. Third: Nothing yields more pleasure and content to the soul than when it finds that which it may love fervently, for to love and live beloved is the soul's paradise, both here and in heaven. In the state of wedlock there be many comforts to bear out the troubles of that condition; but let such as have tried the most, say if there be any sweetness in that condition comparable to the exercise of mutual love.

From former considerations arise these conclusions.

First: This love among Christians is a real thing, not imaginary.

Secondly: This love is as absolutely necessary to the being of the body of Christ, as the sinews and other ligaments of a natural body are to the being of that body.

Third: This love is a divine, spiritual nature free, active, strong, courageous, permanent; undervaluing all things beneath its proper object; and of all the graces, this makes us nearer to resemble the virtues of our heavenly father.

Fourth: It rests in the love and welfare of its beloved. For the full and certain knowledge of these truths concerning the nature, use, and excellency of this grace, that which the Holy Ghost hath left recorded, I Corinthians 13, may give full satisfaction, which is needful for every true member of this lovely body of the Lord Jesus, to work upon their hearts by prayer, meditation, continual exercise at least of the special [influence] of this grace, 'til Christ be formed in them and they in him, all in each other, knit together by this bond of love.

It rests now to make some application of this discourse by the present design, which gave the occasion of writing of it. Herein are four things to be propounded: first the persons, secondly the work, third the end, fourth the means.

First, for the persons. We are a company professing ourselves fellow members of Christ, in which respect only though we were absent from each other many miles, and had our employments as far distant, yet we ought to account ourselves knit together by this bond of love, and live in the exercise of it, if we would have comfort of our being in Christ. This was notorious in the practice of the Christians in former times; as is testified of the Waldenses, from the mouth of one of the adversaries *Æneas Sylvius*: "mutuo [ament] pené antequam norunt," they use to love any of their own religion even before they were acquainted with them.

Secondly, for the work we have in hand. It is by a mutual consent, through a special overvaluing providence and a more than ordinary approbation of the Churches of Christ, to seek out a place of cohabitation and consortship under a due form of government both civil and ecclesiastical. In such cases as this, the care of the public must oversway all private respects, by which, not only conscience, but mere civil pol-

icy, doth bind us. For it is a true rule that particular estates cannot subsist in the ruin of the public.

Third. The end is to improve our lives to do more service to the Lord; the comfort and increase of the body of Christ whereof we are members; that ourselves and posterity many be the better preserved from the common corruptions of this evil world, to serve the Lord and work out our salvation under the power and purity of His holy ordinances.

Fourth, for the means whereby this must be effected. They are twofold, a conformity with the work and end we aim at. These we see are extraordinary, therefore we must not content ourselves with usual ordinary means. Whatsoever we did or ought to have done when we lived in England, the same must we do, and more also, where we go. That which the most in their churches maintain as a truth in profession only, we must bring into familiar and constant practice, as in this duty of love. We must love brotherly without dissimulation; we must love one another with a pure heart fervently. We must bear one another's burthens. We must not look only on our own things, but also on the things of our brethren, neither must we think that the Lord will bear with such failings at our hands as he doth from those among whom we have lived; and that for three reasons.

In regard of the more near bond of marriage between Him and us, wherein He hath taken us to be His after a most strict and peculiar manner, which will make Him the more jealous of our love and obedience. So

He tells the people of Israel, you only have I known of all the families of the earth, therefore will I punish you for your transgressions. Secondly, because the Lord will be sanctified in them that come near Him. We know that there were many that corrupted the service of the Lord, some setting up altars before His own, others offering both strange fire and strange sacrifices also; yet there came no fire from heaven or other sudden judgement upon them, as did upon Nadab and Abihu, who yet we may think did not sin presumptuously. Third: When God gives a special commission He looks to have it strictly observed in every article. When He gave Saul a commission to destroy Amaleck, He indented with him upon certain articles, and because he failed in one of the least, and that upon a fair pretense, it lost him the kingdom which should have been his reward if he had observed his commission.

Thus stands the cause between God and us. We are entered into covenant with Him for this work. We have taken out a commission, the Lord hath given us leave to draw our own articles. We have professed to enterprise these actions, upon these and those ends, we have hereupon besought Him of favor and blessing. Now if the Lord shall please to hear us, and bring us in peace to the place we desire, then hath he ratified His covenant and sealed our commission, [and] will expect a strict performance of the articles contained in it; but if we shall neglect the observations of these articles which are the ends we have propounded, and, dissembling with our God, shall fall to embrace this present world and prosecute our carnal intentions, seeking great things for ourselves and our posterity, the Lord will surely break out in wrath against us; be revenged of such a perjured people and make us know the price of the breach of such a covenant.

Now the only way to avoid this shipwreck, and to provide for our posterity, is to follow the counsel of Micah, to do justly, to love mercy, to walk humbly with our God. For this end, we must be knit together in this work as one man. We must entertain each other in brotherly affection, we must be willing to abridge ourselves of our superfluities, for the supply of other's necessities. We must uphold a familiar commerce together in all meekness, gentleness, patience and liberality. We must delight in each other, make other's conditions our own, rejoice together, mourn together, labor and suffer together, always having before our eyes our commission and community in the work, our community as members of the same body. So shall we keep the unity of the spirit in the bond of peace. The Lord will be our God, and delight to dwell among us as His own people, and will command a blessing upon us in all our ways, so that we shall see much more of His wisdom, power, goodness and truth, than formerly we have been acquainted with. We shall find that the God of Israel is among us, when ten of us shall be able to resist a thousand of our enemies; when He shall make us a praise and glory that men shall say of succeeding plantations, "the lord make it like that of *NEW ENGLAND*." For we must consider that we shall be as a city upon a hill. The eyes of all people are upon us, so that if we shall deal falsely with our God in this work we have undertaken, and so cause Him to withdraw His present help from us, we shall be made a story and a by-word through the world. We shall open the mouths of enemies to speak evil of the ways of God, and all professors for God's sake. We shall shame the faces of many of God's worthy servants, and cause their prayers to be turned into curses upon us 'til we be consumed out of the good land whither we are going.

And to shut up this discourse with that exhortation of Moses, that faithful servant of the Lord, in his last farewell to Israel, Deuteronomy 30. Beloved, there is now set before us life and good, death and evil, in that we are commanded this day to love the Lord our God, and to love one another, to walk in His ways and to keep His commandments and His ordinance and His laws, and the articles of our covenant with Him, that we may live and be multiplied, and that the Lord our God may bless us in the land whither we go to possess it. But if our hearts shall turn away, so that we will not obey, but shall be seduced, and worship other Gods, our pleasures and profits, and serve them; it is propounded unto us this day, we shall surely perish out of the good land whither we pass over this vast sea to possess it.

Therefore let us choose life,
that we and our seed
may live by obeying His
voice and cleaving to Him,
for He is our life and
our prosperity.

The First Colonial College

Not wanting their churches to be taken over by uneducated ministers, the founders of the Massachusetts Bay Colony voted in 1636 to provide the necessary funds for the establishing of "a school or college." Shortly before his death in 1638, after only a brief stay in Massachusetts, the Rev. John Harvard arranged to give one half of his estate, along with his library of over 400 books to the college project. What follows is an inside description of the new college as it appeared in *New Englands First Fruits*, an anonymous pamphlet in London in 1643.

After God had carried us safe to New England, and wee had builded our houses, provided necessaries for our livelihood, rear'd convenient places for Gods worship, and setled the Civill Government: One of the next things we longed for, and looked after was to advance Learning, and perpetuate it to Posterity, dreading to leave an illiterate Ministry to the Churches, when our present Ministers shall lie in the Dust. And as wee were thinking and consulting how to effect this great Work; it pleased God to stir up the heart of one Mr. Harvard (a godly Gentleman and a lover of Learning, there living amongst us) to give the one halfe of his Estate (it being in all abot 1700. I.) towards the erecting of a Colledge, and all his Library: after him another gave 300. I. others after them cast in more, and the publique hand of the State added the rest: the Colledge was, by common consent, appointed to be at Cambridge (a place very pleasant and accommodate) and is called (according to the name of the first founder) Harvard Colledge.

The Edifice is very faire and comely within and without, having in it a spacious Hall; (where they daily meet at Commons, Lectures, Exercises) and a large Library with some Bookes to it, the gifts of diverse of our friends, their Chambers and studies also fitted for, and possessed by the Students, and all other roomes of Office necessary and convenient, with all needfull Offices thereto belonging: And by the side of the Colledge a faire Grammar Schoole, for the training up of young Schollars, and fitting of them for Academicall Learning, that still as they are judged ripe, they may be received into the Colledge of this Schoole. Master Corlet is the Mr., who hath very well approved himselfe for his abilities, dexterity and painfulnesse in teaching and education of the youth under him.

Over the Colledge is master Dunster placed, as President, a learned conscionable and industrious man, who has so trained up his Pupills in the tongues and Arts, and so seasoned them with the principles of Divinity and Christianity that we have to our great comfort, (and in truth) beyond our hopes, beheld their progresse in Learning and godliness also; the former of these hath appeared in their publique declamations in Latine and Greeke, and Disputations Logicall and Philosophical, which they have beene wonted (besides their ordinary Exercises in the Colledge-Hall) in the audience of the Magistrates, Ministers, and other Schollars, for the probation of their growth in Learning, upon set dayes, constantly once every moneth to make and uphold: The latter hath been manifested in sundry of them by the savoury breathings of their Spirits in their godly conversation. Insomuch that we are confident, if these early blossomes may be cherished and warmed with the influence of the friends of Learning, and lovers of this pious worke, they will by the help of God, come to happy maturity in a short time.

Over the Colledge are twelve Overseers chosen by the generall Court, six of them are of the Magistrates, the other six of the Ministers, who are to promote the best good of it, and (having a power of influence into all persons in it) are to see that every one be diligent and proficient in his proper place.

2. Rules, and Precepts that are observed in the Colledge.

1. When any Schollar is able to understand Tully, or such like classicall Latine Author extempore, and make and speake true Latine in Verse and Prose, suo ut aiunt Marte; And decline perfectly Paradigim's of Nounes and Verbes in the Greek tongue: Let him then and not before be capable of admission into the Colledge.

2. Let every Student be plainly instructed, and earnestly pressed to consider well, the maine end of his life and studies is, *to know God and Jesus Christ which is eternall life,* Joh. 17. 3. and therefore to lay Christ in the bottome, as the only foundation of all sound knowledge and Learning.

    And seeing the Lord only giveth wisedome, Let every one seriously set himselfe by prayer in secret to seeke it of him *Prov* 2, 3.

3. Every one shall so exercise himselfe in reading the Scriptures twice in a day, that he shall be ready to give such an account of his proficiency therein, both in Theoretticall observations of the Language, and Logick, and in Practicall and spirituall truths, as his Tutor shall require, according to his ability; seeing *the entrance of the word giveth light, it giveth understanding to the simple,* Psalm. 119. 130.

4. That they eschewing all profanation of Gods Name, Attributes, Word, Ordinances, and times of Worship, doe studie with good conscience, carfully to retaine God, and the love of his truth in their mindes else let them know, that (notwithstanding their Learing) God may give them up to strong delusions, and in the end to a reprobate minde, 2 Thes. 2. 11, 12. Rom. 1. 28.

5. That they studiously redeeme the time; observe the generall houres appointed for all the Students, and the speciall houres for their owne Classis: and then dilligently attend the Lectures without any disturbance by word or gesture. And if in any thing they doubt, they shall enquire as of their fellowes, so, (in case of Non satisfaction) modestly of their Tutors.

6. None shall under any pretence whatsoever, frequent the company and society of such men as lead an unfit, and dissolute life.

    Nor shall any without his Tutors leave, or (in his absence) the call of Parents or Guardians, goe abroad to other Townes.

7. Every Schollar shall be present in his Tutors chamber at the 7th. houre in the morning, immediately after the sound of the Bell, at his opening the Scripture and prayer, so also at the 5th. houre at night, and then give account of his owne private reading, as aforesaid in Particular the third, and constantly attend Lectures in the Hall at the houres appointed? But if any (without necessary impediment) shall absent himself from prayer or Lectures, he shall bee lyable to Admonition, if he offend above once a weeke.

8. If any Schollar shall be found to transgresse any of the Lawes of God, or the Schoole, after twice Admonition, he shall be lyable, if not *adultus*, to correction, if *adultus*, his name shall be given up to the Overseers of the Colledge, that he may bee admonished at the publick monethly Act.

3. The times and order of their Studies, unlesse experience shall shew cause to alter.

The second and third day of the weeke, read Lectures, as followeth.

To the first yeare at 8th. of the clock in the morning *Logick*, the first three quarters, *Physicks* the last quarter.

To the second yeare, at the 9th. houre, *Ethicks* and *Politicks*, at convenient distances of time.

To the third yeare at the 10th. *Arithmetick* and *Geometry*, the three first quarters, *Astronomy* the last.

Afternoone.

The first yeare disputes at the second houre.

The 2d. yeare at the 3d. houre.

The 3d. yeare at the 4th. every one in his Art.

The 4th. day reads Greeke.

To the first yeare the *Etymologie* and *Syntax* at the eigth houre.

To the 2d. at the 9th. houre, *Prosodia* and *Dialects.*

Afternoone.

The first yeare at 2d hour practice the precepts of *Grammar* in such Authors as have variety of words.

The 2d. yeare at 3d. houre practice in *Poesy, Nonnus, Duport,* or the like.

The 3d. yeare perfect their *Theory* before noone, and exercise *Style, Composition, Imitation, Epitome,* both in Prose and Verse, afternoone.

The fift day reads Hebrew,
and the Eastern Tongues.

Grammar to the first yeare houre the 8th.

To the 2d. *Chaldee* at the 9th. houre.

To the 3d. *Syriack* at the 10th. houre.

Afternoone.

The first yeare practice in the Bible at the 2d. houre.

The 2d. in *Ezra* and *Danel* at the 3d. houre.

The 3d. at the 4th. houre in *Trostius* New Testament.

The 6th. day reads Rhetorick to
all at the 8th. houre.

Declamations at the 9th. So ordered that every Scholler may declaime once a moneth. The rest of the day *vacat Rhetoricis studiis.*

The 7th. day reads Divinity
Catecheticall at the 8th. houre,
Common places at the 9th. houre.

Afternoone.

The first houre reads history in the Winter,

The nature of plants in the Summer

The summe of every Lecture shall be examined, before the new Lecture be read.

Every Schollar, that on proofe is found able to read the Originalls of the *Old* and *New Testament* into the Latine tongue, and to resolve them *Logically*; withall being of godly life and conversation; And at any publick Act hath the Approbation of the Overseers and Master of the Colledge, is fit to be dignified with his first Degree.

Every Schollar that giveth up in writing a *System*, or *Synopsis*, or summe of *Logick*, Naturall and Morall *Phylosophy*, *Arithmetick*, *Geometry* and *Astronomy*: and is ready to defend his Theses or positions: withall skilled in the Originalls as abovesaid: and of godly life & conversation: and so approved by the Overseers and Master of the Colledge, at any publique *Act*, is fit to be dignified with his 2d. Degree.

2   The Great Awakening

For behold, I create new heavens and a new earth.

—Isa. 65:17

Some Thoughts Concerning the Present Revival of Religion in New England
Jonathan Edwards

Jonathan Edwards (1704–1758), one of the greatest theologians in American history, was a key participant in the Great Awakening. His involvement in the Awakening began in 1734 with a series of sermons he delivered against the growing popularity of Arminianism. These sermons, the leading one of which was concerned with the doctrine of justification by faith, seem to have sparked the Northampton revival in the mid-1730s. In the 1740s much of Edwards' theological writing sought to encourage and defend the Awakening. The following excerpt was taken from a treatise which appeared in the fourth volume of Sereno E. Dwight's edited series of 1830, *The Works of President Edwards with a Memoir of His Life*.

I. Some make Philosophy, instead of the holy scriptures, their rule of judging of this work; particularly the philosophical notions they entertain of the nature of the soul, its faculties and affections. Some are ready to say, "There is but little sober solid religion in this work; it is little else but flash and noise. Religion now all runs out into transports and high flights of passions and affections." In their philosophy, the affections of the soul are something diverse from the will, and not appertaining to the noblest part of the soul. They are ranked among the meanest principles that belong to men as partaking of animal nature, and what he has in common with the brute creation, rather than anything whereby he is conformed to angels and pure spirits. And though they acknowledge that a good use may be made of the affections in religion, yet they suppose that the substantial part of religion does not consist in them, but that they are something adventitious and accidental in Christianity. . . .

If we take the scriptures for our rule, then the greater and higher our exercises of love to God, delight and complacency in him, desires and longings after him, delight in his children, love to mankind, brokenness of heart, abhorrence of sin, and self-abhorrence for it; the more we have of the peace of God which passeth all understanding, and joy in the Holy Ghost, unspeakable and full of glory: the higher our admiring thoughts of God, exulting and glorying in him; so much higher is Christ's religion, or that virtue which he and his apostles taught, raised in the soul.

It is a stumbling to some, that religious affections should seem to be so powerful, or that they should be so violent (as they express it) in some persons. They are therefore ready to doubt whether it can be the Spirit of God; or whether this vehemence be not rather a sign of the operation of an evil spirit. But why should such a doubt arise? What is represented in scripture as more powerful in its effects than the Spirit of God? Which is therefore called "the power of the Highest," . . . So the Spirit is represented by a mighty wind, and by fire, things most powerful in their operation.

II. Many are guilty of not taking the holy scriptures as a sufficient and whole rule, whereby to judge of this work.—They judge by those things which the scripture does not give as any signs or marks whereby to judge one way or the other. viz., the effects that religious exercises and affections of mind have upon the body. Scripture rules respect the state of the mind, moral conduct, and voluntary behavior; and not the physical state of the body. The design of the scripture is to teach us divinity, and not physic and anatomy. Ministers are made the watchmen of men's souls, and not their bodies; and therefore the great rule which God has committed into their hands, is to make them divines, and not physicians. . . . And therefore those ministers of Christ, and overseers of souls, who are full of concern about the involuntary motions of the fluids and solids of men's bodies, and who from thence are full of doubts and suspicions of the cause—when nothing appears but that the state and frame of their minds and their voluntary behavior is good, and agreeable to God's word—go out of the place that Christ has set them in, and leave their proper business, as much as if they should undertake to tell who are under the influence of the Spirit by their looks or their gait. . . .

III. Another thing that some make their rule to judge of this work by, instead of the holy scriptures, is *history*, or former observation. Herein they err two ways:

First, If there be any thing extraordinary in the circumstances of this work, which was not observed in former times, theirs is a rule to reject this work which God has not given them, and they limit God, where he has not limited himself. And this is especially unreasonable in this case: For whosoever has well weighed the wonderful and mysterious methods of divine wisdom is carrying on the work of the new creation . . . may easily observe that it has all along been God's manner to open new scenes, and to bring forth to view things new and wonderful—such as eye had not seen, nor ear heard, nor entered into the heart of man or angels—to the astonishment of heaven and earth, not only in the revelations he makes of his mind and will, but also into the works of his hands. As the old creation was carried on through six days, and appeared all complete, settled in a state of rest on the seventh; so the new creation, which is immensely the greatest and most glorious work, is carried on in a gradual progress, from the fall of man to the consummation of all things. . . .

Secondly, Another way that some err in making history and former observation their rule instead of the holy scripture, is in comparing some external, accidental circumstances of this work, with what has appeared sometimes in enthusiasts.

They find an agreement in some such things, and so they reject the whole work, or at least the substance of it, concluding it to be enthusiasm. Great use has been made of this purpose of many things that are found amongst the Quakers; however totally and essentially different in its nature this work is, and the principles upon which it is built from the whole religion of the Quakers. . . .

IV. I would propose it to be considered, whether or no some instead of making the scriptures their only rule to judge of this work, do not make their own experience the rule, and reject such and such things as are now professed and experienced, because they themselves never felt them. Are there not many, who, chiefly on this ground, have entertained and vented suspicions, if not peremptory condemnations, of those extreme terrors, and those great, sudden, and extraordinary discoveries of the glorious perfections of God, and of the beauty and love of Christ? Have they not condemned such vehement affections, such high transports of love and joy, such pity and distress for the souls of others, and exercises of mind that have great effects, merely, or chiefly, because they knew nothing about them by experience? Persons are very ready to be suspicious of what they have not felt themselves. It is to be feared that many good men have been guilty of this error: which however does not make it the less reasonable.

Another foundation error of those who reject this work, is, their not duly distinguishing the good from the bad, and very unjustly judging of the whole by a part; and so rejecting the work in general, or in the main substance of it, for the sake of some accidental evil in it. . . .

A great deal of noise and tumult, confusion and uproar, darkness mixed with light, and evil with good, is always to be expected in the beginning of something very glorious in the state of things in human society, or the church of God. After nature has long been shut up in a cold dead state, when the sun returns in the spring, there is, together with the increase of the light and heat of the sun, very tempestuous weather, before all is settled calm and serene, and all nature rejoices in its bloom and beauty. It is in the new creation as it was in the old: the Spirit of God first moved upon the face of the waters, which was an occasion of great uproar and tumult. Things were then gradually brought to a settled state, till at length all stood forth in that beautiful, peaceful order, when the heavens and the earth were finished, and God saw every thing that he had made, and behold it was very good. When God is about to bring to pass something great and glorious in the world, nature is in a ferment and struggle, and the world as it were in travail. . . .

Whatever imprudences there have been, and whatever sinful irregularities; whatever vehemence of the passions, and heats of the imagination, transports and ecstacies; whatever error in judgement, and indiscreet zeal; and whatever outcries, faintings, and agitations of body; yet, it is manifest and notorious that there has been of late a very uncommon influence upon the minds of a great part of the inhabitants of New-England, attended with the best effects. . . . Multitudes in all parts of the land, of vain, thoughtless, regardless persons, are quite changed, and become serious and considerate. There is a vast increase of concern for he salvation of the precious soul, and of hat inquiry, "What shall I do to be ived?" . . . They have also been awakened a sense of the shortness and uncertainty of e, and reality of another world and future j gement, and of the necessity of an inter e in Christ. They are more afraid of sin, m e careful and inquisitive that they may kn v what is contrary to the mind and will of d, that they may avoid it, and what he req es of them, that they may do it, more car l to guard against temptations, more wat ul over their own hearts, earnestly desirou f knowing, and of being diligent in the u of the means that God has appointed in his rd, in order to salvation. Many very

stupid, senseless sinners, and persons of a vain mind, have been greatly awakened.

There is a strange alteration almost all over New-England amongst young people: by a powerful invisible influence on their minds, they have been brought to forsake, in a general way, as it were at once, those things of which they were extremely fond, and in which they seemed to place the happiness of their lives, and which nothing before could induce them to forsake; as their frolicking, vain company-keeping, night-walking, their mirth and jollity, their impure language, and lewd songs. . . . It is astonishing to see the alteration there is in some towns, where before there was but little appearance of religion, or any thing but vice and vanity. And now they are transformed into another sort of people; their former vain, worldly, and vicious conversation and dispositions seem to be forsaken, and they are, as it were, gone over to a new world. Their thoughts, their talk, and their concern, affections and inquiries, are now about the favor of God, an interest in Christ, a renewed sanctified heart, and a spiritual blessedness, acceptance, and happiness in a future world.

Now, through the greater part of New-England, the holy Bible is in much greater esteem and use than before. . . . The Lord's day is more religiously and strictly observed. And much has been lately done at making up differences, confessing faults one to another, and making restitution: probably more within two years, that was done in thirty years before. It has been undoubtedly so in many places. And surprising has been the power of this spirit in many instances, to destroy old grudges, to make up long continued breaches, and to bring those who seemed to be in a confirmed irreconcilable alienation, to embrace each other in a sincere and entire amity. . . .

Multitudes in New-England have lately been brought to a new and great conviction of the truth and certainty of the things of the gospel; to a firm persuasion that Christ Jesus is the son of God, and the great and only Savior of the world, and that the great doctrines of the gospel touching reconciliation by his blood, and acceptance in his righteousness, and eternal life and salvation through him, are matters of undoubted truth. . . .

And, under the influences of this work, there have been many of the remains of those wretched people and dregs of mankind, the poor Indians, that seemed to be next to a state of brutality, and with whom, till now, it seemed to be to little more purpose to use endeavors for their instruction and awakening, than with wild beasts. Their minds have now been strangely opened to receive instruction, and been deeply affected with the concerns of their precious souls; they have reformed their lives, and forsaken their former stupid, barbarous and brutish way of living; and particularly that sin to which they have been so exceedingly addicted, their drunkenness. Many of them to appearance brought truly and greatly to delight in the things of God, and to have their souls very much engaged and entertained with the great things of the gospel. And many of the poor Negroes also have been in like manner wrought upon and changed. Very many little children have been remarkably enlightened, and their hearts wonderfully affected and enlarged, and their mouths opened, expressing them-selves in a manner far beyond

their years, and to the just astonishment of those who have heard them. Some of them for many months, have been greatly and delightfully affected with the glory of divine things, and the excellency and love of the Redeemer, with their hearts greatly filled with love to, and joy in him; and they have continued to be serious and pious in their behavior. . . .

It is not unlikely that this work of God's Spirit, so extraordinary and wonderful, is the dawning, or at least a prelude of that glorious work of God, so often foretold in scripture, which, in the progress and issue of it, shall renew the world of mankind. If we consider how long since the things foretold as what should precede this great event, have been accomplished and how long this event has been expected by the church of God, and thought to be nigh by the most eminent men of God, in the church; and withal consider what the state of things now is, and has for a considerable time been, in the church of God, and the world of man-kind; we cannot reasonably think otherwise, than that the beginning of this great work of God must be near. And there are many things that make it probable that his work will begin in America.—It is signified that it shall begin in some very remote part of the world, with which other parts have no communication but by navigation, in Isa. LX.9. "Surely the isles shall wait for me, and the ships of Tarshish first, to bring my sons from far." It is exceeding manifest that this chapter is a prophecy of the prosperity of the church, in its most glorious state on earth, in the latter days; and I cannot think that any thing else can be here intended but America by the isles that are far off, from whence the first-born sons of that glorious day shall be brought. Indeed, by *the isles*, in prophecies of gospel-times, is very often meant Europe . . . But this prophecy cannot have respect to the conversion of Europe, in the time of that great work of God, in the primitive ages of the Christian church; for it was not fulfilled then. The isles and ships of Tarshish, thus understood, did not wait for God first; that glorious work did not begin in Europe, but in Jerusalem, and had for a considerable time been very wonderfully carried on in Asia, before it reached Europe. And as it is not *that* work of God which is chiefly intended in this chapter, but some more glorious work that should be in the latter ages of the Christian church; therefore, some other part of the world is here intended by the isles, that should be, as Europe then was, far separated from that part of the world where the church had before been, and with which it can have no communication but by the ships of Tarshish. And what is chiefly intended is not the British isles, nor any isles near the other continent; they are spoken of as at a great distance from that part of the world where the church had till then been. This prophecy therefore seems plainly to point out America, as the first-fruits of that glorious day.

God has made as it were two worlds here below, two great habitable continents, far separated one from the other: The latter is as it were now but newly created; it has been, till of late, wholly the possession of Satan, the church of God having never been in it, as it has been in the other continent, from the beginning of the world. This new world is probably now discovered, that the new and most glorious state of God's church on earth might commence there; that God might in it begin a new world in a spiritual

respect, when he creates the *new heavens* and *new earth*.

God has already put that honour upon the other continent, that Christ was born there literally, and there made the "purchase of redemption." So, as Providence observes a kind of equal distribution of things, it is not unlikely that the great spiritual birth of Christ, and the most glorious "application of redemption," is to begin in this. . . .

The other continent hath slain Christ, and has from age to age shed the blood of saints and martyrs of Jesus, and has often been as it were, deluged with the church's blood.—God has, therefore, probably reserved the honor of building the glorious temple to the daughter that has not shed so much blood, when those times of the peace, prosperity and glory of the church, typified by the reign of Solomon, shall commence. . . .

The old continent has been the source and original of mankind in several respects. The first parents of mankind dwelt there; and there dwelt Noah and his sons; there the second Adam was born, and crucified, and raised again: And it is probable that, in some measure to balance these things, the most glorious renovation of the world shall originate from the new continent, and the church of God in that respect be from hence. And so it is probable that will come to pass in spirituals, which has taken place in temporals, with respect to America: that whereas, till of late, the world was supplied with its silver, and gold, and earthly treasures from the old continent, now it is supplied chiefly from the new; so the course of things in spiritual respects will be in like manner turned.—And it is worthy to be noted, that

America was discovered about the time of the reformation, or but little before: Which reformation was the first thing that God did towards the glorious renovation of the world, after it had sunk into the depths of darkness and ruin, under the great antichristian apostasy. So that, as soon as this new world stands forth in view, God presently goes about doing some great thing in order to make way for the introduction of the church's latter-day glory—which is to have its first seat in, and is to take its rise from that new world.

It is agreeable to God's manner, when he accomplishes any glorious work in the world, in order to introduce a new and more excellent state of his church, to begin where no foundation had been already laid, that the power of God might be the more conspicuous; that the work might appear to be entirely God's, and be more manifestly a creation out of nothing. . . . When God is about to turn the earth into a paradise, he does not begin his work where there is some good growth already, but in the wilderness, where nothing grows, and nothing is to be seen but dry sand and barren rocks; that the light may shine out of darkness, the world be replenished from emptiness, and the earth watered by springs from a droughty desert: agreeable to many prophecies of scripture. . . . Now as when God is about to do some great work for his church, his manner is to begin at the lower end; so, when he is about to renew the whole habitable earth, it is probable that he will begin in this utmost, meanest, youngest and weakest part of it, where the church of God has been planted last of all: and so the first shall be last, and the last first: and that will be fulfilled in an eminent manner in Isa. xxiv.19. "From the uttermost part of the earth have we heard songs, even glory to the righteous." . . .

. . . And if we may suppose that this glorious work of God shall begin in any part of America, I think, if we consider the circumstances of the settlement of New-England, it must needs appear the most likely, of all American colonies, to be the place whence this work shall principally take its rise. And, if these things be so, it gives more abundant reason to hope that what is now seen in America, and especially in New-England, may prove the dawn of that glorious day; and the very uncommon and wonderful circumstances and events of this work, seem to me strongly to argue that God intends it as the beginning or fore-runner of something vastly great.

I have thus long insisted on this point, because, if these things are so, it greatly manifests how much it behoves us to encourage and promote this work, and how dangerous it will be to forbear so doing. It is very dangerous for God's professing people to lie still, and not to come to the help of the Lord, whenever he remarkably pours out his Spirit, to carry on the work of redemption in the application of it; but above all, when he comes forth to introduce that happy day of God's power and salvation, so often spoken of. . . .

Seasonable Thoughts on the State of Religion in New England

Charles Chauncy

Charles Chauncy (1705-1787), a Boston minister, was the most formidable opponent Jonathan Edwards faced in the debate over the methods and accomplishments of the Great Awakening. In the following selection from Chauncy's *Seasonable Thoughts on the State of Religion in New England* published in 1743 in Boston, Chauncy disputes Edwards' defense of the Awakening in a point by point denunciation of the revival as a resurgence of heresies that had consumed the early Puritans. Chauncy's religious Universalism, an expression of eighteenth century Enlightenment thinking, was particularly critical of the appeal to emotion in revivalism.

———

I have hitherto considered *Ministers* as the Persons, more especially obliged to discountenance the bad Things, prevailing in the Land; and now go on to observe.

That this is the Duty of *all in general*. Not that I would put any upon acting out of their *proper Sphere*. This would tend rather to Confusion than Reformation.—Good Order is the Strength and Beauty of the World.— The Prosperity both of *Church* and *State* depends very much upon it. And can there be Order, where Men transgress the Limits of their Station, and intermeddle in the Business of others? So far from it, that the only effectual Method, under GOD, for the Redress of *general Evils*, is, for *every one* to be faithful, in doing what is *proper* for him in his *own Place*: And even *all* may *properly* bear a Part, in *rectifying the Disorders* of this Kind, at this Day.

Civil Rulers may do a great deal, not only by their *good Example*, but a wise Use of their Authority, in their various Places, for the Suppression of every Thing hurtful to Society, and the Encouragement of whatever has a Tendency to make Men happy in the Enjoyment of their Rights, whether *natural* or Christian. And herein chiefly lies (as I humbly conceive) a Duty of Ruler, at this Day. This true, as *private Men*, they are under the same Obligations with others, to make their Acknowledgements to CHRIST; and doubtless, if HE was visibly and externally (according to the Custom among *Kings and Governors*) to make his solemn Entry into the Land, as their SAVIOR and LORD, "it would be expected they should, as *public Officers*, make their Appearance, and attend him as their *Sovereign* with suitable Congratulations, and Manifestations of Respect and Loyalty; and if they should stand

stand at a Distance, it would be much more taken Notice of, and awaken in Displeasure much more, than such a Behavior in the common People." But the Case is widely different, where his supposed Entry if in this Sense, as that there is a *great Variety of Sentiments* about it, among the *best Sort* of Men, of all Ranks and Conditions: Nor does it appear to me, when the Case is thus circumstanced, that it is either the *Duty of Rulers*, or would be Wisdom in them, by any *authoritative Acts* to determine, whose Sentiments were the most agreeable to Truth. And as to their Appointment of Days of *Thanksgiving, or fasting*, on this Account, there must be an Impropriety in it, so long as that Complaint of God against the *Jews* is to be seen in the *Bible, Behold ye fast for Strife and Debate*! Their *Duty* rather lies in keeping Peace between those, who unhappily differ in their Thoughts about the State of our religious Affairs: And their Care in this Matter ought to be *impartial*. Each Party, without Favor or Affection, should be equally restrained from Out-rage and Insult. Those, who may think themselves Friends to a *Work of god*, should be protected in the Exercise of all their *just Rights*, whether as *Men*, or *Christians*: So on the other Hand, those who may be Enemies to *Error* and *Confusion*, have the same Claim to be protected.

And if, on either Side, they invade the Rights of others, or throw out Slander, at Random, to the Hurt of their Neighbor's Reputation and Usefulness, and the bringing forward a State of Tumult and Disorder; I see not but the civil Arm may justly be stretched forth for the Chastisement of such Persons; and this, though their Abuses should be offered in the Name of the LORD, or under the Pretext of the most flaming Zeal for the REDEEMER'S *Honor*, and serving the Interest of *his Kingdom*: For it ought always to be accounted an Aggravation of Sin of *Slander*, rather than an Excuse for it, its being committed under the *Cloak of Religion*, and Pretense for the *Glory of god*; as it will, under these Circumstances, be of more pernicious Tendency. I am far from thinking, that any Man ought to suffer, either for his *religious Principles*, or *Conduct* arising from them, while he is no Disturber of the *civil Peace*; but when Men, under the Notion of appearing zealous for GOD and *his Truths*, insult their Betters, vilify their Neighbors, and spirit People to Strife and Faction, I know of no Persons more suitable to be taken in Hand by *Authority*: And if they suffer 'tis for their own Follies; nor can they reasonably blame any Body but themselves: Nor am I ashamed, or afraid, to profess it as my Opinion, that it would probably have been of good Service, if those, in these Times, who have been publickly and out-ragiously reviled, has, by their Complaints, put it properly in the *Magistrates* Power, to restrain some Men's *Tongues* with *Bit* and *Bridle*.

Private Christians also, of all Ranks and Conditions, may do something towards the Suppression of these *Errors*, by mourning before the LORD the Dishonor which has hereby been reflected on the Name of CHRIST, an Injury done to Souls; by being much in Prayer to GOD for the out-pouring of his SPIRIT, in all desirable Influences of Light, and Love, and Peace; by taking good Heed that they bent themselves drawn aside, avoiding to this End, the Company and familiar Converse of those, who, by, *good Words* and *fair Speeches*, might be apt to tendance on religious Exercises, where the *Churches* and *Ministry* are freely declaimed against by those who have gone out from them, under the vain Pretence of being more holy than they; and in fine, by a faithful Performance of those Duties, which arise from the various Relations they sustain towards each other: As thus, if they are *Children*, by hearkening to the Advice of their *Parents*, by counseling, reproving, warning, restraining, and commanding their *Children*, as there may be Occasion: If they are *Servants*, by pleasing their *Masters* well in all Things, not defrauding them of their Time and Labor, but accounting them worthy of all Honor, that the Name of GOD be not blasphemed; and, if they are *Master*, not only by providing for their *Servants* Things honest and good, but by keeping them within the Rules of Order and Decorum, not suffering them to neglect the Religion of the Family at home, under Pretence of carrying it on elsewhere; especially, when they continue abroad 'till late in the Night, and so as to unfit themselves for the Services of the following Day.

In these, and such like Ways, *all* may exert themselves in making a Stand against the Progress of Error: And all are oblig'd to do so; and for this Reason, among others I han't Room to mention, because the *last Days* are particularly mark'd in the *Prophecies of Scripture*, as the Times wherein may be expected, the Rise of SEDUCERS.

'This true, we read of the coming on of a *glorious State* of Things in the LAST DAYS: Nor will the *Vision fail*.—We may rely upon it, the Prophesies, foretelling the Glory of the REDEEMER'S *Kingdom* will have their Accomplishment to the making this Earth of *Paradise*, in Compare with what it now is. But for the *particular Time* when this will be, it *is not for us to know it, the Father having put it in his own Power*: And whoever pretend to such Knowledge, they are wise above what is written; and tho' they may think they know much, they really know nothing as to this Matter.

It may be suggested, that "the Work of GOD'S SPIRIT that is so extraordinary and wonderful, is the *dawning*, or at least, a *Prelude* of that glorious *Work of* GOD, so often foretold in Scripture, which, in the Progress and Issue of it, shall renew the whole world." But what are such Suggestions, but the Fruit of Imagination? Or at best, uncertain Conjecture? And can any good End be answered in endeavoring, upon Evidence absolutely precarious, to instill into the Minds of People a Notion of the *millennium* State, as what is now going to be introduced; yea, and of AMERICA, as that Part of the World, which is pointed out in the *Revelations* of GOD for the Place, where this glorious Scene of Things, "will, probably, first begin?" How often, at other Times, and in other Places, has the Conceit been propagated among People, as if the Prophecies touching the Kingdom of CHRIST, in the *latter Days*, were NOW to receive their Accomplishment? And what has been the Effect, but their running wild? So it was in GERMANY, in the Beginning of the Reformation. The *extraordinary* and wonderful Things in that Day, were look'd upon by the Men then thought to be most under the SPIRIT'S *immediate Direction*, as "the Dawning of that glorious Work of GOD, which should renew the whole World"; and the Imagination of the Multitude being fired with this Notion, they were soon persuaded, that the Saints with this Notion, they were soon persuaded, that the Saints were now to reign on Earth, and the Dominion to be given into their Hands: And it was under the Influence of this vain Conceit (in which they were strengthened by *Visions, Raptures, and Revelations*) that they took up Arms against the lawful *Authority*, and were destroy'd, at one Time and another, to the Number of an HUNDRED THOUSAND. . . .

And 'tis well known, that this same Pretence of the near Approach of the MILLENNIUM, the promised Kingdom of the MESSIAH, was the *Foundation-Error of the French Prophets*, and those in their Way, no longer ago than the Beginning of this Century: And so infatuated were they at last, as to publish it to the World, that the glorious Times they spake of, *would be manifest over the whole Earth, within the Term of* THREE YEARS. And what Set of Men have ever yet appear'd in the Christian World, whose Imaginations have been thorowly warmed, but they have, at length, wrought themselves up to a *full Assurance*, that NOW was the Time for the Accomplishment of the Scriptures, and the Creation of the *new Heavens*, and the *new Earth*? No one Thing have they more unitedly concurred in, to their own shameful Disappointment, and the doing unspeakable Damage to the Interest of Religion.—A sufficient Warning, one would think, to keep Men modest; and restrain them from Endeavors to lead People into a Belief of that, of which they have no sufficient *Evidence*; and in which, they may be deceived by their vain *Imaginations*, as Hundreds and Thousands have been before them.

There are unquestionably many Prophesies concerning CHRIST, and the *Glory of his Kingdom*, still to be fulfilled; and it may be of good Service to labor to beget in People a Faith in these Things; or, if they have Faith, to quicken and strengthen it: But it can answer no good End to lead People into the Belief of any *particular* Time, as the Time *appointed* of GOD for the Accomplishment of these Purposes of his Mercy; because this is one of those Matters, his Wisdom had thought fit to keep conceal'd from the Knowledge of Man. Our own Faith therefore upon this Head can be founded only on *Conjecture*; and as 'tis only the like *blind Faith* we can convey to others, we should be cautious, lest their Conduct should be agreeable to their Faith. When they have imbib'd from us the Thought, as if the glorious Things, spoken of in Scripture, were to come forward in their Day, they will be apt (as has often been the Case) to be impatient, and from their *Officiousness* in tendering their Help where it is not needed, to disserve the Interest of the Redeemer.

The Testimony of Harvard College Against George Whitefield

The Great Awakening gave birth to sharp hostilities in many parts of the colonies. The center of many of these controversies was the preacher, George Whitefield, who more than any other person was responsible for fanning the revival sparks started by others into a single flame. The religious cleavages which had emerged in New England, as seen in Edwards' and Chauncy's writings, intensified when Whitefield denounced the spiritual condition of Harvard College in terms which caused the school to oppose his planned return from England to America in 1744. The 1744 Harvard pamphlet which follows is one of the clearest criticisms leveled against The Great Awakening.

In regard of the Danger which we apprehend the People and Churches of this Land are in, on the Account of the Rev. Mr. *George Whitefield*, we have tho't ourselves oblig'd to bear our Testimony, in this public Manner, against him and his Way of Preaching, as tending very much to the Detriment of Religion and the entire Destruction of the Order of these Churches of Christ, which our Fathers have taken such Care and Pains to settle, as by the Platform, according to which the Discipline of the Churches of *New England* is regulated: And we do therefore hereby declare, That we look upon his going about, in an Itinerant Way, especially as he hath so much of an enthusiastic Turn, utterly inconsistent with the Peace and Order, if not the very Being of these Churches of Christ.

And now, inasmuch as by a certain Faculty he hath of raising the Passions, he hath been the Means of rousing many from their Stupidity, and setting them on thinking, whereby some may have been made really better, on which Account the People, many of them, are strongly attach'd to him (tho' it is most evident, that he hath not any superior Talent at instructing the Mind, or shewing the Force and Energy of those Arguments for a religious Life, which are directed to in the everlasting Gospel). Therefore, that the People who are thus attach'd to him, may not take up an unreasonable Prejudice against this our testimony, we think it very proper to give some Reasons for it, which we shall offer, respecting the Man himself, and then his Way and Manner of Preaching.

First, as to the Man himself, whom we look upon as an Enthusiast, a censorious, uncharitable Person, and a Deluder of the People; which Things, if we can make out, all reasonable Men will doubtless excuse us, tho' some such, thro' a fascinating Curiosity, may still continue their Attachment to him.

First then, we charge him, with Enthusiasm. Now that we may speak clearly upon this Head, we mean by an Enthusiast, one that acts, either according to Dreams, or some sudden Impulses and Impressions upon his Mind, which he fondly imagines to be from the Spirit of God, perswading and inclining him thereby to such and such Actions, tho' he hath no Proof that such

Perswasions or Impressions are from the holy Spirit: For the perceiving a strong Impression upon our Minds, or a violent Inclination to do any Action, is a very different Thing from perceiving such Impressions to be from the Spirit of God moving upon the Heart: For our strong Faith and Belief, that such a Motion on the Mind comes from God, can never be any Proof of it; and if such Impulses and Impressions be not agreeable to our Reason, or to the Revelation of the Mind of God to us, in his Word, nothing can be more dangerous than conducting ourselves according to them; for otherwise, if we judge not of them by these Rules, they may as well be the Suggestions of the evil Spirit: And in what Condition must that People be, who stand ready to be led by a Man that conducts himself according to his Dreams, or some ridiculous and unaccountable Impulses and Impressions on his Mind?

But we proceed to mention one Piece of *Enthusiasm* of a very uncommon Turn, which shews to what a great Length this unhappy pernicious Disposition of the Mind may carry a Man. When on Pag. 32 of his Life, he personates our blessed Lord himself, when in his Passion, says he, *It was suggested to me, that when Jesus cried out, I thirst, his Sufferings were near at an end; upon this I threw myself upon the Bed, crying out, I thirst, I thirst: Soon after I felt my Load go off—, and knew what it was truly to rejoice in the Lord.* And certainly it is easy enough to conceive, from what Spirit such a *Suggestion* must come. To mention but one Instance more, tho' we are not of such Letter-learned as deny, that there is such an Union of Believers to Christ, whereby *they are one in him, as the Father and he are One*, as the Evangelist speaks, or rather the Spirit of God by him; yet so Letter-learned we are, as to say, that that Passage in Mr. W——'s Sermon of the *Indwelling of the Spirit*, p. 311: vol. of Sermons, contains the true Spirit of Enthusiasm, where he says, *to talk of any having the Spirit of God without feeling of it, is really to deny the Thing.* Upon which we say, That the Believer may have a Satisfaction, that he hath the Assistance of the Spirit of God with him, in so continual and regular a Manner, that he may be said to dwell in him, and yet have no feeling of it; for the Metaphor is much too gross to express this (however full) Satisfaction of the Mind, and has led some to take the Expression literally, and hath (we fear) given great Satisfaction to many an Enthusiast among us since the Year 1740, from the swelling of their Breasts and Stomachs in their religious Agitations, which they have tho't to be *feeling the Spirit*, in its Operations on them. But it is no way necessary to instance any further upon this Head; for the aforesaid Compositions are full of these Things.

The whole tends to perswade the World (and it has done so with respect to many) that Mr. W. hath as familiar a Converse and Communion with God as any of the Prophets and Apostles, and such as we all acknowledge to have been under the Inspiration of the Holy Ghost.

In the next Place, we look upon Mr. W. as an uncharitable, censorious and slanderous Man; which indeed is but a natural Consequence of the heat of Enthusiasm, by which he has so evidently acted; for this Distemper of the Mind always puts a Man into a vain Conceit of his own Worth and Excellency, which all his Pretenses to Humility will never hide, as long as he evidently shews, that he would have the World think he hath a greater Familiarity with God than other Men, and more frequent Communications from his Holy Spirit. Hence such a Man naturally assumes an Authority to dictate to others, and a Right to direct their Conduct and Opinions; and hence if any act not according to his Directions, and the Model of Things he had form'd in his own heated Brain, he is presently apt to run into slander, and stigmatize them as *Men of no Religion, unconverted*, and *Opposers of the Spirit of God*: And that such hath been the Behavior of Mr. W. is also sufficiently evident. . . .

Again, We think it highly proper to bear our Testimony against Mr. W. as we look upon him a *Deluder of the People*. How he designs to manage in this Affair now, we know not: but we mean, that he hath much deluded them, and therefore suppose we have Reason in this respect to guard against him. And here we mean more especially as to the Collections of Money, which, when here before, by an extraordinary mendicant Faculty, he almost *extorted* from the People. As the Argument he then used was, the Support and Education of his dear Lambs at the Orphan-House, who (he told us, he hop'd) might in Time preach the Gospel to us or our Children; so it is not to be doubted, that the People were greatly encouraged to give him largely of their Substance, supposing they were to be under the immediate Tuition and Instruction of himself, as he then made them to believe; and had not this been their Tho't, it is, to us, without all Peradventure, they would never have been perswaded to any considerable Contribution upon that Head; and this, notwithstanding, he hath scarce seen them for these four Years; and besides hath left the Care of them with a Person, whom these Contributors know nothing of, and we ourselves have Reason to believe is little better than a *Quaker*; so that in this Regard we think the People have been greatly deceiv'd.

Secondly, We have as much Reason to dislike and bear Testimony against the *Manner* of his Preaching; and this in Two respects, both as an *Extempore* and as an *Itinerant* Preacher.

And first, as this his *extempore* Manner of preaching; this we think by no means proper, for that it is impossible that any Man should be able to manage any Argument with that Strength, or any Instruction with that Clearness in an *extempore* Manner, as he may with Study and Meditation. Besides, it is observable that your *extempore* Preachers give us almost always the same Things in the applicatory Part of their Sermons, so that it is often very little akin to their Text, which is just open'd in a cursory, and not seldom in a perverted Manner, and then comes the same kind of Harangue which they have often used before, as an *Application*; so that this is a most lazy Manner, and the Preacher offers that which cost him nothing, and is accordingly little Instructive to the Mind, and still less cogent to the reasonable Powers. Now Mr. W. evidently shows, that he would have us believe his Discourses are *extempore*, and indeed from the Rashness of some of his Expressions, as well as from the dangerous Errors vented in them, it is very likely; Hence, no doubt, were the many unguarded Expressions in his Sermons when he was here before; and since he has come again, he hath told us, "That Christ loves unregenerate Sinners with a *Love of Complacency*:" Nay, he hath gone rather further, and said, "*That God loves Sinners as Sinners*;" which, if it be not an unguarded Expression, must be a thousand times worse: For we cannot look upon it as much less than Blasphemy, and shows him to be stronger in the *Antinomian* Scheme than most of the Professors of that *Heresy* themselves; and that this is not unlikely, is to be suspected, because the Expression was repeated, and when he was tax'd with it, by a certain Gentleman, he made no Retractions.

But, *lastly*, We think it our Duty to bear our strongest Testimony against that *Itinerant* Way of preaching which this Gentleman was the first promoter of among us, and still delights to continue in: For if we had nothing against the *Man*, either as an *Enthusiast*, an *uncharitable* or *delusive* Person, yet we apprehend this Itinerant Manner of preaching to be of the worst and most pernicious Tendency.

Now by an *Itinerant* Preacher, we understand One that hath no particular Charge of his own, but goes about from Country to Country, or from Town to Town, in any Country, and stands ready to Preach to any Congregation that shall call him to it; and such an one is Mr. W. for it is but trifling for him to say (as we hear he hath) That he requires in order to his preaching any where, that the Minister also should invite him to it; for he knows the Populace have such an Itch after him, that when they generally desire it, the Minister (however diverse from their's, his own Sentiments may be) will always be in the utmost Danger of his People's quarrelling with, if not departing from him, shou'd he not consent to their impetuous Desires. Now as it is plain, no Man will find much Business as an *Itinerant* Preacher, who hath not something in his Manner, that is (however trifling, yea, and erroneous too, yet) very taking and agreeable to the People; so when this is the Case, as we lately unhappily seen it, it is then in his Power to raise the People to any Degree of Warmth he pleases, whereby they stand ready to receive almost any Doctrine he is pleased to broach; as hath been the Case as to all the Itinerant Preachers who have followed Mr. W's. Example, and thrust themselves into Towns and Parishes, to the Destruction of all Peace and Order, whereby they have to the great impoverishment of the Community, taken the People from their Work and Business, to attend their Lectures and Exhortations, always fraught with Enthusiasm, and other pernicious Errors: But, *which is worse, and it is the natural Effect of these Things*, the People have been thence ready to despise their own Ministers, and their usefulness among them, in too many Places, hath been almost destroy'd.

Indeed, if there were any thing leading to this manner of Management in the Directions and Instructions given, either by our Saviour or his Apostles, we ought to be silent, and so wou'd a Man of any Modesty, if (on the other hand) there be nothing in the N. Testament leading to it. And surely Mr. W. will not have the Face to pretend he acts now as an *Evangelist*, tho' he seems to prepare for it in Journ. from N.E. to *Falmouth* in *England*, p. 12. where he says, *God seems to shew me it is my Duty to Evangelize, and not to fix in any particular Place*: For the Duty of that Officer certainly was not to go preaching of his own Head from one Church to another, where Officers were already settled, and the Gospel fully and faithfully preached. And it is without Doubt, that the Mind and Will of Christ, with respect to the Order of his Churches, and the Business of his Ministers in them, is plainly enough to be understood in the N. Testament; and yet Mr. W. has said of late, in one of his Sermons, he thinks that an Itinerant Manner of preaching many be very convenient for the furtherance of the good of the Churches, if it were under a good Regulation. Now we are apt to imagine, if such an Officer wou'd have been useful, Christ himself wou'd have appointed him; and therefore (under Favour) this is to *be wise about what is written*, and supposes either that our Lord did not know, or that he neglected to appoint all such Officers in the Ministry, as wou'd further in the best man-

ner the Truths of the Gospel: And it is from such Wisdom as this, that all the Errors of *Popery* have come into the *Christian Church*, while the Directions of the Word of God were not strictly adhered to, but one tho't this Way or that Ceremony was very convenient and significant and another another, till they have dress'd up the Church in such a monstrous heap of Appendages, that at this Day it can hardly be discern'd to be a Church of Christ.

And now, upon the whole, having, we think, made it evident to every one that is not prejedic'd on his Side (for such as are so, we have little hope to convince) that Mr. W. is chargeable with that *Enthusiasm, Censoriousness and delusive Management* that we have tax'd him with; and since also he seems resolv'd for that Itinerant Way of preaching, which we think so destructive to the Peace of the Churches of Christ; we cannot but bear our faithful Testimony against him, as a Person very unfit to preach about as he has done heretofore, and as he has now begun to do.

And we wou'd earnestly, and with all due respect, recommend it to the Rev. Pastors of these Churches of Christ, to advise with each other in their several Associations, and consider whether it be not high Time to make a stand against the Mischiefs, which we have here suggested as coming upon the Churches.

Harvard College, Dec. 28, 1744.

Edward Holyoke, *President. . .*

3 The Coming of the American Revolution

Submit yourselves for the Lord's sake to every human institution, whether to a king as the one in authority, or to governors as sent by him for the punishment of evildoers and the praise of those who do right.

—I Pet. 2:13-14

Discourse Concerning Unlimited Submission
Jonathan Mayhew

Jonathan Mayhew (1720-1766), one of the boldest exponents of the Enlightenment in America during the pre-Revolution years, was well known in the Boston area for his theological liberalism. Along with Charles Chauncy, Mayhew leveled a heavy attack against the traditional doctrines of Calvinism. Both men held that revelation must be validated by human reason. Thus for Mayhew, the use of Romans 13 to support the giving of passive obedience to kings under all conditions was unreasonable. *The Discourse Concerning Unlimited Submission*, from which the following excerpt is selected, was published in Boston twenty-six years before the Americans declared their independence from England. It was a clear foreshadowing of the arguments which were voiced by clergy of many theological persuasions on the eve of the American Revolution.

If we calmly consider the nature of the thing itself, nothing can well be imagined more directly contrary to <u>common sense</u> than to suppose that millions of people should be subjected to the arbitrary, precarious pleasure of one single man (who has naturally no superiority over them in point of authority), so that their estates and everything that is valuable in life, and even their lives also, shall be absolutely at his disposal, if he happens to be wanton and capricious enough to demand them. What unprejudiced man can think that God made all to be thus subservient to the lawless pleasure and frenzy of one, so that it shall always be a sin to resist him! Nothing but the most plain and express revelation from heaven could make a sober impartial man believe such a monstrous, unaccountable doctrine, and, indeed, the thing itself appears so shocking—so out of all proportion—that it may be questioned whether all the miracles that ever were wrought, could make it credible, that this doctrine really came from God. At present, there is not the least syllable in scripture which gives any countenance to it. The hereditary, indefeasible, divine right of kings, and the doctrine of non-resistance which is built upon the supposition of such a right, are altogether as fabulous and chimerical as transubstantiation or any of the most absurd reveries of ancient or modern visionaries. These notions are fetched neither from divine revelation nor human reason; and if they are derived from neither of those sources, it is not much matter from whence they come, or whither they go. Only it is a pity that such doctrines should be propagated in society, to raise factions and rebellions, as we see they have, in fact, been both in the last and in the present reign.

But then, if unlimited submission and passive obedience to the higher powers, in all possible cases, be not a duty, it will be asked, "How far are we obliged to submit? If we may innocently disobey and resist in some cases, why not in all? Where shall we stop? What is the measure of our duty? This doctrine tends to the total dissolution of civil government; and to introduce such scenes of wild anarchy and confusion as are more fatal to society than the worst of tyranny."

After this manner, some men object; and, indeed, this is the most plausible thing that can be said in favor of such an absolute submission as they plead for. But the worst (or rather the best) of it is that there is very little strength or solidity in it. For similar difficulties may be raised with respect to almost every duty of natural and revealed religion. To instance only in two, both of which are near akin, and indeed exactly parallel, to the case before us: it is unquestionably the duty of children to submit to their parents, and of servants to their masters. But no one asserts that it is their duty to obey and submit to them in all supposable cases; or universally a sin to resist them. Now does this tend to subvert the just authority of parents and masters? Or to introduce confusion and anarchy into private families? No. How then does the same principle tend to unhinge the government of that larger family, the body politic? We know, in general, that children and servants are obliged to obey their parents and masters respectively. We know also, with equal certainty, that they are not obliged to submit to them in all things, without exception, but may, in some cases reasonably, and therefore innocently, resist them. These principles are acknowledged upon all hands, whatever difficulty there may be in fixing the exact limits of submission. Now there is at least as much difficulty in stating the measure of duty in these two cases as in the case of rulers and subjects. So that this is really no objection, at least no reasonable one, against resistance to the higher powers. Or, if it is one, it will hold equally against resistance in the other cases mentioned.

It is indeed true, that turbulent, vicious-minded men may take occasion from this principle, that their rulers may in some cases be lawfully resisted, to raise factions and disturbances in the state; and to make resistance where resistance is needless and therefore sinful. But is it not equally true that children and servants of turbulent, vicious minds, may take occasion from this principle, that parents and masters may in some cases be lawfully resisted, to resist when resistance is unnecessary and therefore criminal? Is the principle in either case false in itself, merely because it may be abused and applied to legitimate disobedience and resistance in those instances, to which it ought not to be applied? According to this way of arguing, there will be no true principles in the world; for there are none but what may be wrested and perverted to serve bad purposes, either through the weakness or wickedness of men.

A people, really oppressed to a great degree by their sovereign, cannot well be insensible when they are so oppressed. And such a people (if I may allude to an ancient fable) have, like the hesperian fruit, a dragon for their protector and guardian. Nor would they have any reason to mourn if some Hercules should appear to dispatch him. For a nation thus abused to arise unanimously, and to resist their prince, even to the dethroning him, is not criminal, but a reasonable way of vindicating their liberties and just rights; it is making use of the means, and the only means, which God has put into their power, for mutual and self-defense. And it would be highly criminal in them not to make use of this means. It would be stupid tameness and unaccountable folly for whole nations to suffer one unreasonable, ambitious and cruel man to wanton and riot in their misery. And in such a case it would, of the two, be more rational to suppose that they that did not resist, than that they who did, would receive to themselves damnation.

A Calm Address to Our American Colonies
John Wesley

John Wesley (1703-1791), the founder of Methodism and the most popular evangelical preacher of the day, first came to America in 1735, when he accompanied James Ogelthorpe to Georgia as a missionary to the Indians. He returned to England in 1738, and shortly thereafter joined George White-field in his open-air preaching. In "A Calm Address to Our American Colonies" which was first published in 1775 in London, Wesley calls upon the Americans to "fear God and honour the King."

The grand question which is now debated (and with warmth enough on both sides) is this, Has the English Parliament power to tax the American colonies?

In order to determine this, let us consider the nature of our Colonies. An English Colony is a number of persons to whom the King grants a charter, permitting them to settle in some far country as a corporation, enjoying such powers as the charter grants, to be administered in such a manner as the charter prescribes. As a corporation they make laws for themselves: but as a corporation subsisting by a grant from higher authority, to the control of that authority, they still continue subject.

Considering this, nothing can be more plain, than that the supreme power in England has a legal right of laying any tax upon them for any end beneficial to the whole empire.

But you object, "It is the privilege of a Freeman and an Englishman to be taxed only by his own consent. And this consent is given for every man by his representative in parliament. But we have no representation in parliament. Therefore we ought not to be taxed thereby."

I answer, This argument proves too much. If the parliament cannot tax you, because you have no representation therein, for the same reason it can make no laws to bind you. If a freeman cannot be taxed without his own consent, neither can he be punished without it: for whatever holds with regard to taxation, holds with regard to all other laws. Therefore he who denies the English Parliament the power of taxation, denies it the right of making any laws at all. But this power over the Colonies you have never disputed: you have always admitted statutes, for the punishment of offenses, and for the preventing or redressing of inconveniences. And the reception of any law draws after it by a chain which cannot be broken, the necessity of admitting taxation.

But I object to the very foundation of your plea. That "every freeman is governed by laws to which he has consented," as confidently as it has been asserted, it is absolutely false. In wide-extended dominions, a very small part of the people are concerned in making laws. This, as all public business, must be done by delegation, the delegates are chosen by a select number. And those that are not electors, who are for the greater part, stand by, idle and helpless spectators.

The case of electors is little better. When they are near equally divided, almost half of them must be governed, not only without, but even against their own consent.

And how has any man consented to those laws, which were made before he was born? Our consent to these, may and to the laws now made even in England, is purely passive. And in every place, as all men are born the subjects of some state or other, so they are born, passively, as it were consenting to the laws of that state. Any other than this kind of consent, the condition of civil life does not allow.

But you say, You *are intitled to life, liberty and property by nature: and that you have never ceded to any sovereign power, the right to dispose of these without your consent.*

While you speak as the naked sons of nature, this is certainly true. But you presently declare, Our *ancestors at the time they settled these Colonies, were intitled to all the rights of natural-born subjects, within the realm of England.* This likewise is true: but when this is granted, the boast of original rights is at an end. You are no longer in a state of nature, but sink down to Colonists, governed by a charter. If your ancestors were subjects, they acknowledged a Sovereign: if they had a right to English privileg-

es, they were accountable to English laws, and had *ceded* to the King and Parliament, *the power of disposing without their consent, of both their lives, liberties and properties.* And did the Parliament cede to them, a dispensation from the obedience, which they owe as natural subjects? Or any degree of independence, not enjoyed by other Englishmen?

They did not indeed, as you observe, *by emigration forfeit any of those privileges: but they were, and their descendants now are intitled to all such as their circumstances enable them to enjoy.*

That they who form a Colony by a lawful charter, forfeit no privilege thereby, is certain. But what they do not forfeit by any judicial sentence, they may lose by natural effects. When a man voluntarily comes in to America, he may lose what he had when in Europe. Perhaps he has a right to vote for a knight or burgess: by crossing the sea he did not *forfeit* this right. But it is plain, he has made the exercise of it no longer possible.

He has reduced himself from a voter to one of the innumerable multitude that have no votes.

But you say, *As the Colonies are not represented in the British Parliament, they are entitled to a free power of legislation. For they inherit all the rights which their ancestors had of enjoying all the privileges of Englishmen.*

They do inherit all the privileges which their ancestors had: but they can inherit no more. Their ancestors left a country where the representatives of the people were elected by men particularly qualified, and where those who wanted that qualification were bound by the decisions of men whom they had not deputed. You are the descendants of men who either had no votes, or resigned them by emigration. You have therefore exactly what your ancestors left you: not a vote in making laws, nor a chusing legislators, but the happiness of being protected by laws, and the duty of obeying them.

What your ancestors did not bring with them, neither they nor their descendants have acquired. They have not, by abandoning their right in one legislature, acquired a right to constitute another: any more than the multitudes in England who have no vote, have a right to erect a Parliament for themselves.

However the *Colonies have a right to all the privileges granted them by royal charters, or secured to them by provincial laws.*

The first clause is allowed: they have certainly a right to all the privileges granted them by royal charters. But as to the second there is a doubt: provincial laws may grant privileges to individuals of the province. But surely no province can confer provincial privileges on itself! They have a right to all which the King has given them; but not to all which they have given themselves.

A corporation can no more assume to itself privileges which it had not before, than a man can, by his own act and deed, assume titles or dignities. The legislature of a colony may be compared to the vestry of a large parish: which may lay a cess on its inhabitants, but still regulated by the law: and

which (whatever be its internal expenses) is still liable to taxes laid by superior authority.

The charter of Pennsylvania has a clause admitting, in express terms, taxation by Parliament. If such a clause be not inserted in other charters, it must be omitted as not necessary; because it is manifestly implied in the very nature of subordinate government: all countries which are subject to laws, being liable to taxes.

It is true, the first settlers in *Massachusetts Bay* were promised *an exemption from taxes for seven years.* But does not this very exemption imply they were to pay them afterwards?

If there is in the charter of any Colony a clause exempting them from taxes for ever, then undoubtedly they have a right to be so exempted. But if there is no such clause, then the English Parliament has the same right to tax them as to tax any other English subjects.

All that impartially consider what has been observed, must readily allow, that the English Parliament has undoubted right to tax all the English Colonies.

But whence then is all this hurry and tumult? Why is America all in an uproar? If you can yet give yourselves time to think, you will see, the plain case is this.

A few years ago, you were assaulted by enemies, whom you were not well able to resist. You represented this to your Mothercountry, and desired her assistance. You were largely assisted, and by that means wholly delivered from all your enemies.

After a time, your Mother-country, desiring to be reimbursed for some part of the large expense she had been at, laid a small tax (which she had always a right to do) on one of her Colonies.

But how is it possible, that the taking of this reasonable and legal step, should have set all America in a flame?

I will tell you my opinion freely; and perhaps you will not think it improbable. I speak the more freely, because I am unbiassed: I have nothing to hope or fear from either side. I gain nothing either by the Government or by the Americans, and probably never shall. And I have no prejudice to any man in America: I love you as my brethren and countrymen.

My opinion is this. We have a few men in England, who are determined enemies to Monarchy. Whether they hate his present Majesty on any other ground, then because he is a King, I know not. But they cordially hate his office, and have for some years been undermining it with all diligence, in hopes of erecting their grand idol, their common wealth upon its ruins. I believe they have let very few into their design: (although many forward it, without knowing any thing of the matter), but they are steadily pursuing it, as by various other means, so in particular by inflammatory papers, which are industriously and continually dispersed, throughout the town and country: by this method they have already wrought thousands of the people, even to the pitch of madness. By the same, only varied according to your circumstances, they have likewise inflamed America. I make no doubt, but these very men are the original cause of the present breach between England and her Colonies. And they are still pouring oil into the flame, studiously incensing each against the other, and opposing under a variety of pretenses, all measures of accommodation. So that although the Americans, in general, love the English, and the English, in general, love the Americans (all, I mean that are not yet cheated and exasperated by these artful men), yet the rupture is growing wider every day, and none can tell where it will end.

These good men hope it will end, in the total defection of North America from England. If this were effected, they who trust the English, in general, would be so irreconcilably disgusted, that they should be able, with or without foreign assistance, entirely to overturn the government: especially while the main of both the English and Irish forces are at so convenient a distance.

But, my brethren, would this be any advantage to *you*? Can *you* hope for a more desirable form of government, either in England or America, than that which you now enjoy? After all the vehement cry for liberty, what more liberty can you have? What more religious liberty can you desire, than that which you enjoy already? May not every one among you worship God according to his own conscience? What civil liberty can you desire, which you are not already possessed of? Do not you sit without restraint, every man under his own vine? Do you not, every one, high or low, enjoy the fruit of your labour? This is real, rational liberty, such as is enjoyed by Englishmen alone; and not by any other people in the inhabitable world. Would the being independent of England make you more free? Far, very far from it. It would hardly be possible for you to steer clear, between anarchy and tyranny. But suppose, after numberless dangers and mischiefs, you should settle into one or more Republics: would a republican government give you more liberty, either religious or civil? By no means. No governments under heaven are so despotic as the Republican: no subjects are governed in so arbitrary a manner, as those of a Commonwealth. If any one doubt of this, let him look at the subjects of Venice, of Genoa, or even of Holland. Should any man talk or write of the Dutch government as every cobbler does of the English, he would be laid in irons, before he knew where he was. And then woe be to him! Republics shew no mercy.

"But if we submit to one tax, more will follow." Perhaps so, and perhaps not. But if they did; if you were taxed (which is quite improbable), equal with Ireland or Scotland, still were you to prevent this by renouncing connection with England, the remedy would be worse than the disease. For O! what convulsions must poor America feel, before any other government was settled? Innumerable mischiefs must ensue, before any general form could be established. And the grand mischief would ensue, when it was established; when you had received a yoke, which you could not shake off.

Brethren, open your eyes! Come to yourselves! Be no longer the dupes of designing men. I do not mean any of your countrymen in America: I doubt whether any of these are in the secret. The designing men, the Ahithophels are in England; those who have laid their scheme so deep, and covered it so well, that thousands who are ripening it, suspect nothing at all the matter. These well-meaning men, sincerely believing that they are serving their country, exclaim against grievances, which either never existed, or are aggravated above measure, and thereby inflame the people more and more, to the wish of those who are behind the scene. But be not you duped any longer: do not ruin yourselves for them that owe you no good will, that now employ you only for their own purposes, and in the end will give you no thanks. They love neither England nor America, but play one against the other, in subserviency to their grand design, of overturning the English government. Be warned in time. Stand and consider before it is too late; before you have entailed confusion and misery on your latest posterity. Have pity upon your mother country! Have pity upon your own! Have pity upon yourselves, upon your children, and upon all that are near and dear to you! Let us not bite and devour one of another, lest we be consumed one of another! O let us follow after peace! Let us put away our sins; the real ground of all our calamities! Which never will or can be thoroughly removed, till we fear God and honour the King.

1776 Election Sermon
Samuel West

Samuel West (1730-1807), a graduate of Harvard in 1754, was a preacher of a theology that would later be known as Unitarianism. Shortly after the battle of Bunker Hill, he joined the American army as a chaplain, a position he held for several months. On the eve of the signing of the Declaration of Independence, he delivered a sermon to mark the anniversary of the election of the honorable council in Massachusetts.

[In 1 Peter 2:13,14, we hear] "Submit yourselves to every ordinance of man," — or as the words ought to be rendered from the Greek, submit yourselves to every human creation; or human constitution,—"for the Lord's sake, whether it be to the king, or unto governors,—for the punishment of evil-doers, and for the praise of them that do well." Here we see that the apostle asserts that magistrates are of human creation that is, that magistrates have no power or authority but what they derive from the people; that this power they are to exert for the punishment of evil-doers, and for the praise of them that do well.

The only reason assigned by the apostle why magistrates should be obeyed . . . is because they punish the wicked and encourage the good; it follows, that when they punish the virtuous we have a right to refuse yielding any submission to them; whenever they act contrary to the design of their institution, they forfeit their authority to govern the people, and the reason for submitting to them immediately ceases. . . . Hence we see that the apostle, instead of being a friend to

tyranny . . ., turns out to be a strong advocate for the just rights of mankind.

David, the man after God's own heart, makes piety a necessary qualification in a ruler: "He that ruleth over men must be just, ruling in the fear of God."

To despise government, and to speak evil of dignitaries is represented in Scripture as one of the worst of characters; and it is an injunction of Moses, "Thou shalt not speak evil of the ruler . . ." Great mischief may ensue upon reviling the character of good rulers; for the unthinking herd of mankind are very apt to give ear to scandal, and when it falls upon men in power, it brings their authority into contempt, lessens their influence, and disheartens them from doing service.

But though I would recommend to all Christians to treat rulers with proper honor and respect, none can reasonably suppose that I mean that rulers ought to be flattered in their vices, or honored and caressed while they are seeking to undermine and ruin the state; for this would be wickedly betraying our just rights, and we should be guilty of our own destruction.

It is with a particular view to the present unhappy controversy . . . that I chose to discourse upon the nature and design of government . . . so that we stand firm in our opposition to tyranny, while at the same time we pay all proper obedience to our lawful magistrates; while we are contending for liberty, may we avoid running into licentiousness . . . I acknowledge that I have undertaken a difficult task; but, it appears to me, the present state of affairs loudly calls for such a discourse. Need I upon this occasion descend to particulars? Can any one be ignorant what the things are of which we complain? . . . And, after all this wanton exertion of arbitrary power, is there any man who is not fired with a noble indignation against such merciless tyrants. . . .

Let us treat our rulers with all that honor and respect which the dignity of their station requires, but let it be such an honor and respect as is worthy of the sons of freedom to give. Let us ever abhor the base arts used by fawning parasites and cringing courtiers, who by their flatteries obtain offices which they are unqualified to sustain. Often times they have a greater number of places assigned them than any one person of the greatest abilities can properly fill . . . and the community becomes greatly injured . . . so many an important trust remains undischarged.

. . . In order to avoid this evil, I hope our legislators will always despise flattery as something below the dignity of a rational mind, and that that they will ever scorn the man that will be corrupted . . . And let us all

resolve with ourselves that no motives of interest, nor hopes of preferment, shall ever induce us to flattering men in power. Let the honor and respect which we show our superiors be simple and genuine. . . . Tyrants have been flattered in their vices, and have often had an idolatrous reverence paid them. The worse princes have been the most flattered and adored and many such, in the pagan world, assumed the title of gods, and had divine honors paid them. This idolatrous reverence has ever been the inseparable concomitant of arbitrary power and tyrannical government; even Christian rulers, if they have not been adored as gods, yet the titles given them strongly savor of blasphemy, and the reverence paid them is idolatrous. What right has a poor sinful worm of the dust to claim the title of his most sacred Majesty? Most sacred certainly belongs only to God alone, — yet how common is it to see this title or ones like it given to rulers! And how often have we been told that the ruler can do no wrong! Even though he should be so foolish and wicked as hardly capable of ever being in the right, yet still it must be asserted and maintained that it is impossible for him to do wrong! The cruel, savage disposition of tyrants, and the idolatrous reverence paid them, are both most beautifully exhibited to view by the apostle John in Revelation, thirteenth chapter. . .

The apostle gives description of a horrible wild beast which he saw rise out of the sea, having seven heads and ten horns, and upon his heads the names of blasphemy. By heads are to be understood forms of government, and by blasphemy, idolatry; so that it seems implied that there will be a degree of idolatry in every form of tyrannical government. This beast is represented as having the body of a leopard, the feet of a bear, and the mouth of a lion; i.e., a horrible monster, possessed of the rage and fury of the lion, the fierceness of the bear, and the swiftness of the leopard to seize and devour its prey. Can words more strongly point out, or exhibit in more lively colors, the exceeding rage, fury, and impetuosity of tyrants, destroying and making havoc of mankind? To this beast we find the dragon gave his power . . ., this is to denote that tyrants are the ministers of Satan.

Such a horrible monster, we should have thought, would have been abhorred and detested of all mankind, . . . that all nations would have joined their power and forces together to oppose and utterly destroy him from off the face of the earth; but, so far are they from doing this, that, on the contrary, they are represented as worshipping him (verse 8): "And all that dwell on the earth shall worship him"—all those "whose names are not written in the Lamb's book of life;" . . . Those who pay an undue and sinful veneration to tyrants are properly the servants of the devil. . . . Hence that terrible denunciation of divine wrath against the worshippers of the beast . . .: "If any man worship the beast . . . the same shall drink the wine of the wrath of God." . . . We have here set forth in the clearest manner, God's abhorrence of tyranny, tyrants, and the idolatrous reverence that their subjects are wont to pay them . . . Does it not, then, highly concern us all to stand fast in the liberty wherewith Heaven hath made us free, to strive to get the victory over the beast and his image—over every species of tyranny? Let us look upon a freedom from the power of tyrants as a blessing that cannot be purchased too dear, and let us bless God that he had delivered us from that idolatrous reverence which men are so apt to pay to arbitrary tyrants. Let not the powers of earth and hell prevail against liberty.

Honored fathers, we look up to you, in this day of calamity as the guardians of our invaded rights, and the defenders of our liberties against tyranny. You are called to save your country from ruin . . .

My reverend fathers and brethren in the ministry will remember that according to our text, it is part of the work of a gospel minister to teach his hearers the duty they owe to magistrates. Let us, then, endeavor to explain the nature of their duty faithfully, and show them the difference between liberty and licentiousness; and let us animate them to oppose tyranny and arbitrary power; and let us inculcate upon them the duty of yielding due obedience to lawful authority.

To conclude: While we are fighting for liberty, and striving against tyranny, let us remember to fight the good fight of faith, and earnestly seek to be delivered from that bondage of corruption which we are brought in to by sin, and that we may be made partakers of the glorious liberty of the sons and children of God: which may the Father of Mercies grant us all, through Jesus Christ. "AMEN."

4 Sources and Impact of the Second Awakening

And this is the judgment, that the light is come into the world, and men loved the darkness rather than the light; for their deeds were evil.

—John 3:19

Attack on Infidelity
Timothy Dwight

Timothy Dwight (1752-1817), grandson of the famous theologian, Jonathan Edwards, has been referred to by some historians as "the father of the Second Awakening." After graduation from Yale in 1769, he remained there as a tutor, only to be greatly disappointed at not being named president of the college in 1777. Instead, he entered the army chaplaincy, serving during the Revolutionary War for a little over a year. For the next decade and a half, he divided his time between preaching, teaching, and writing poetry and hymns. In 1795, he was invited to become president of Yale. As president of the college, he was also pastor of the college church, where his solid doctrinal sermons attacked the skepticism rampant in the student body and defended the authenticity of the Bible, identifying "infidelity" as the enemy of faith. The following selection is taken from *A Discourse, on Some Events of the Last Century, delivered in the Brick Church in New Haven, on Wednesday, January 7, 1801* (New Haven, 1801), pp. 17-23, 28-30, 32-4, 45-47.

In the course of this period, God has, in various instances, been pleased to revive his glorious work of sanctification, and to extend it through many parts of the land. I know that a number of men, and some of much respectability, have entertained unfavorable ideas of what are called revivals of religion; but I cannot help thinking their opinions of this subject rather formed in the closet than derived from facts, or warranted by the scriptures. Seasons of enthusiasm about various subjects have indeed often existed, and probably in every civilized country. In these seasons the human kind

51

has not infrequently exhibited many kinds and degrees of weakness, error, and deformity. Hence, perhaps, sober men have, in some instances, been led to believe that wherever enthusiasm exists, these evils exist also. As therefore revivals of religion have frequently been more or less accompanied by enthusiasm, they have, I think sufficient grounds, determined, that all which existed was enthusiasm, and that nothing would flow from it but these evils.

That the mind under the first clear, strong, and solemn views of its own sins should be deeply affected, and greatly agitated, is to be expected from the nature of man. He is always thus affected by the first strong view, taken of any object deeply interesting, and always thus agitated when such an object is seen in an uncertain, suspended state. No object can be so interesting, or more entirely suspended, than the state of the soul in the case specified.

When these emotions, thus excited by objects of such immense importance, and in so absolute a state of suspense, as the guilt, the condemnation, and the salvation, of an immortal mind, are attended with some degree of enthusiasm and extravagance; when they are followed by seasons of deep despondence, and successive transport; nothing takes place, but that, which sound philosophy must presuppose; as similar emotions are, in all similar cases, followed, especially in ardent minds, by the same consequences. All this, however, will go no length towards proving, that nothing exists beyond enthusiasm; and that, amid several irregular and excessive exertions of the mind, there is not to be found a real change of the disposition, a real assumption of piety. To me it is evident,

that revivals of religion are often what they are called, if not always; and that the proof abundantly exists (where alone it ought to be looked for) in the real and permanent melioration of the moral character of multitudes, who then become serious and professedly religious.

Of the last of these revivals of religion, that which still extensively exists, it ought to be observed, that it has absolutely, or at least very nearly, been free from every extravagance, enthusiasm, and superstition, with them. But no man of common candor can hesitate to admit, that vice is not the only sober and rational state of a moral being; and that impiety is an unhappy proof of a real wisdom. In this great and auspicious event of which I have spoken, thousands have been already happily concerned, and thousands more will, it is hoped, hereafter claim a share.

But, with the rest of mankind, we have abused our blessings. Loose opinions and loose practices have found their place here also. The first considerable change in the religious character of the people of this country was accomplished by the war, which began in 1755. War is at least as fatal to morals, as to life, or happiness. The officers and soldiers of the British armies, then employed in this country, although probably as little corrupted as those of most armies, were yet loose patterns of opinion and conduct, and were unhappily copied by considerable numbers of our own country-men, united with them in military life. These, on their return, spread the infection through those around them. Looser habits of thinking began then to be adopted, and were followed, as they always are, by looser conduct. The American war increased these evils. Peace had not, at the commencement of this war, restored the purity of life, which existed before the preceding war. To the depravation still remaining was added a long train of immoral doctrines and practices, which spread into every corner of the country. The profanation of the Sabbath, before unusual, profaneness of language, drunkenness, gambling, and lewdness, were exceedingly increased; and, what is less commonly remarked, but is perhaps not less mischievous, than any of them, a light, vain method of thinking, concerned sacred things, a cold, contemptuous indifference toward every moral and religious subject. In the mean time, that enormous evil, a depreciating currency gave birth to a new spirit of fraud, and opened numerous temptations, and a boundless field for its operations; while a new and intimate correspondence with corrupted foreigners introduced a multiplicity of loose doctrines, which were greedily embraced by licentious men, as the means of palliating and justifying their sins.

At this period Infidelity began to obtain, in this country, an extensive currency and reception. As this subject constitutes far the most interesting and prominent characteristics of the past Century, it will not be amiss to exhibit it with some degree of minuteness, and to trace through several particulars the steps of its progress.

Infidelity has been frequently supposed to be founded on an apprehended deficiency of the evidence, which supports a divine Revelation. No opinion can be more erroneous than this. That solitary instances may have existed, in which men did not believe the scriptures to be the word of God, because

they doubted of the evidence in their possession, I am ready to admit; but that this has been the common fact, is, at least, in my view, a clear impossibility.

Our Savior informs us, that "This is the condemnation, that light is come into the world, and men loved darkness rather than light, because their deeds were evil:" and subjoins, that "he who doth evil hateth the light, neither cometh to the light, lest his deeds should be reproved." Here one of the two great causes of Infidelity is distinctly and exactly alleged, viz. The opposition of a heart, which loves sin, and dreads the punishment of it, to that truth, which with infinite authority, and under an immense penalty, demands of all men a holy life. The other great cause of Infidelity is frequently mentioned by the inspired writers, particularly St. Paul, St. Peter, and St. Jude. In the following passages of St. Peter it is exhibited with peculiar force. "For when they speak great swelling words of vanity, they allure through the lusts of the flesh, through much wantonness, them that were clean escaped from them, that live in error. While they promise them liberty, they themselves are the servants (bond-slaves) of corruption." "there shall come in the last days scoffers, walking after their own lusts, and saying, Where is the promise of his coming? For since the fathers fell asleep, all things continue as they were from the beginning of the creation."

The Infidels, here referred to, are plainly philosophists; the authors of vain and deceitful philosophy; of science falsely so called; always full of vanity in their discourses: Scoffers, walking after their own lusts, and alluring others, through the same lusts, to follow them; promising them liberty, as their reward, and yet being themselves, and making their disciples, the lowest and most wretched of all slaves, the slaves of corruption. Philosophical pride, and the love of sinning in security and peace, are, therefore, the two great causes of Infidelity, according to the scriptures.

A more exact account of this subject, as existing in fact, could not even now be given. Infidelity has been assumed because it was loved, and not because it was supported by evidence; and has been maintained and defended, to quiet the mind of sin, and to indulge the pride of talents and speculation.

The form, which it has received, has varied in the hands of almost every distinguished Infidel. It was first Theism, or natural Religion, then mere Unbelief, then Animalism, then Skepticism, then partial, and then total Atheism. Yet it has, in three things at least, preserved a general consistency; opposition to Christianity, devotion of sin and lust, and a pompous profession of love to Liberty. To a candid and logical opposition to Christianity, consisting of facts fairly stated and justly exhibited, no reasonable objection can be made. It is to be wished, that this had been the conduct of the opposition actually made; but nothing has been more unlike that conduct. The war has been the desultory attack of a barbarian, not of a civilized soldier; and onset of passion, pride, and wit; a feint of conjectures and falsified facts; an incursion of sneers, jests, gross banter, and delicate ridicule; a parade of hints and insinuations; and a vigorous assault on fancy, passion, and appetite. These were never the weapons of sober conviction; this was never the conduct of honest men.

In the earlier periods of this controversy there were, however, more frequent efforts at argumentation, on the part of Infidels. For the last twenty or thirty years they seem to have despaired of success in this field, and have betaken themselves to that of action and influence. In this field they have wrought with a success totally unprecedented. Nor is this at all to be wondered at, if we consider the opportunity of succeeding presented to them, during the latter half of the last Century, by the state of society in Europe. The excessive wealth of that division of the eastern Continent has generated an enormous luxury, the multiplied enjoyments of which have become not only the ruling objects of desire, and the governing motives of action, but, in the view of a great part of the inhabitants, the necessary means of even a comfortable existence. On these life is employed, ambition fastened, order exhausted, and energy spent. Voluptuousness and splendour, formed on the Asiatic scale, engross men in public and private stations, in the university, the camp, the shop, and the desk, as well as the court and the cabinet. To glitter with diamonds, to roll in pomp, to feast on dainties, to wanton in amusements, to build palaces, and to fashion wildernesses of pleasure, are the supreme objects of millions, apparently destined to the grave, still, and humble walks of life, as well as of those, who were high born, and highly endowed. Science toils, ingenuity is stretched in the rack, and art is wearied through all her refinements, to satisfy the universal demand for pleasure; the mines of Golconda are ransacked, the caverns of Mexico emptied, and the mountains of Potosi transported across the ocean.

Of this universal devotion to pleasure and shew, modern Infidels have availed themselves to the utmost. To a mind, to a nation, dissolved in sloth, enervated by pleasure, and fascinated with splendour, the Gospel is preached, and heaven presented, in vain. The eye is closed, the ear stopped, and the heart rendered gross and incapable of healing. The soul is of course, unconscious of danger, impatient of restraint, and insensible to the demands of moral obligation. It is, therefore, prepared to become an Infidel, without research, and without conviction. Hence, more sagacious than their predecessors, the later Infidels have neither laboured, nor wished, to convince the understanding, but have bent all their efforts to engross the heart.

In the mean time other events, highly favourable to their designs, have taken place both in America and Europe. The American Revolution, an august, solemn, and most interesting spectacle, drew towards it at this time the eyes of mankind. The novelty of the scene, the enchanting sound of Liberty, to which the pulse of man instinctively beats, the sympathy ever excited for the feebler and suffering party, embarked deeply in the American cause a great part of the civilized world. Benevolent men, of all countries, hoped, when the contest was ended prosperously for us, and ardent men boldly pronounced, that a new era had arrived in human things, that "the iron rod of the oppressor was broken," and that "the oppressed would soon be universally set free."

Among the agents in the American Revolution, were many natives of France; men, in numerous instances, or ardent minds, and daring speculation; who either imbibed here new sentiments of liberty, or ripened those, which they had already adopted at home. These men, returning to their own country, diffused extensively the enthusiasm, which they had cherished here, and thus hastened the crisis, to which France was otherwise approaching. . . .

In this great moral convulsion Royalty and Christianity sunk in the kingdom of France. Emboldened beyond every fear by this astonishing event, Infidelity, which anciently had hid behind a mask, walked forth in open day, and displayed her genuine features to the sun. Without a blush she now denied the existence of moral obligation, annihilated the distinction between virtue and vice, challenged and authorized the indulgence of every lust, strode down the barriers of truth, perjured herself daily in the fight of the universe, lifted up her front in the face of heaven, denied the being, and dared the thunder, of the Almighty. Virtue and truth, her native enemies, and the objects of all her real hatred, she hunted from every cell and solitude; and, whenever they escaped her fangs, she followed them with the execrations of malice, the finger of derision, and the hisses of infamy.

Elevated now, for the first time to the chair of dominion, she ushered forth her edicts with the gravity of deliberation and the authority of law, and executed them by the oppressive hand of the jailor, the axe of the executioner, and the sword of the warrior. All rights fell before her, all interests were blasted by her breath, and happiness and hope were together swept away by her bosom of destruction.

In the midst of all this effrontery, Infidels forgot not their arts and impositions. As occasion dictated, or ingenuity whispered, they availed themselves of every disguise, and of every persuasive. As if they had designed to give the last wound to virtue, they assumed all her titles and challenged all her attributes to their own conduct. Daily forsworn, and laughing at the very distinction between right and wrong, they proclaimed themselves the assertors of justice, and the champions of truth. While they converted a realm into a Bastile, they trumpeted their inviolable attachment to liberty; while they "cursed their God, and looked upward," they announced themselves worshippers of the Supreme Being. With a little finger, thicker than the loins of both the monarchy and the hierarchy, encircled with three millions of corpses, and in the center of a kingdom changed into a stall of slaughter, they hung themselves over with labels of philanthropy. Nay, they have far outgone all this. Two of their philosophers, independently of each other, have declared, that, to establish their favourite system, the sacrifice of all the existing race of man would be a cheap price: an illustrious instance of Infidel benevolence, and of the excellence of their darling maxim, that "the end sanctifies the means."

These however, are but a small portion of their arts. They have, as the state of things required, disguised their designs; disavowed them; doubted their existence; wondered at those, who believed them real; ridiculed the belief; and professed themselves amazed at such credulity. This conduct has been reduced to a system, and taught and enjoined on their followers, as a code of policy, and as being often the most effectual means of spreading their opinions.

Nor have they less frequently resorted to the aid of obscure, unsuspected, and apparently undesigned communication. Their doctrines have, with great success, been propagated by remote hints; by soft and gentle insinuations; by half started doubts, and half proposed objections; and by the suggestion of a train of thoughts in which those doctrines are taken for granted, and considered as being so plain, and so generally received, that no person can be imagined to disbelieve, or even to doubt. The reader himself is presupposed to have long since admitted them, as the only doctrines of truth or common sense; as being too rational and candid to hesitate about things so clear and acknowledged; as unquestionably lifted above the reception of the contrary pitiful absurdities; and as thus prepared to act, as all other sensible and liberal persons have already acted. Thus their opinions steal upon his mind in methods equally unsuspected and imposing. . . .

Such is the astonishing state of moral things; in several parts of Europe, which, within a short time, has opened upon the view of our countrymen. The strong sympathy which, unhappily, and on no rational grounds, prevailed here towards those, who were leaders in the French Revolution, and towards the Revolution itself, prepared us to become the miserable dupes of their principles and declarations. They were viewed merely as human beings, embarked deeply in the glorious cause of liberty; and not at all as Infidels, as the abettors of falsehood, and the enemies of Righteousness, of Truth, and of God. Hence all their concerns were felt, and all their conduct covered with the veil of charity. They were viewed as having adventured, and suffered, together with ourselves, and as now enlisted for the support of a kindred cause. The consequences of these prejudices were such, as would naturally be expected. A general and unexampled confidence was soon felt, and manifested, by every licentious man. Every Infidel, particularly, claimed a new importance, and treated religion with enhanced contempt. The graver ones, indeed, through an affected tenderness for the votaries of christianity, adopted a more decent manner of despising it; but all were secure of a triumph and satisfied, that talents, character, and the great world, were on their side. The young, the ardent, the ambitious, and the voluptuous, were irresistibly solicited to join a cause, which harmonized with all their corruptions, pointed out the certain road to reputation, and administered the necessary opiates to conscience; and could not refuse to unite themselves with men, who spoke great swelling words of vanity, who allured them through much wantonness, and promised them the unbounded liberty of indulging every propensity to pleasure. The timid at the same time were terrified, the orderly let loose, the sober amazed, and the religious shocked beyond example; while the floating part of our countrymen, accustomed to swim with every tide, moved onward on obedience to the impulse. Thus principles were yielded, useful habits were relaxed, and a new degree of irreligion extensively prevailed.

Happily for us, the source, when these peculiar evils flowed, furnished us in some degree with a remedy. It was soon discovered, that the liberty of Infidels was not the liberty of New England; that France, instead of being free, merely changed through a series of tyrannies, at the side of which all former despotisms whitened into moderation and humanity; and that of the immeasurable evils, under which she and her neighbors agonized, Infidelity was the genuine source; the Vesuvius, from whose mouth issued those rivers of destruction, which deluged and ruined all things in their way. It was seen, that man, unrestrained by law and religion, is a mere beast of prey that licentiousness, although adorned with the graceful name of liberty, is yet the spring of continual alarm, bondage, and misery; and that the restraints, imposed by equitable laws, and by the religion of the scriptures, were far less burdensome and distressing than the boasted freedom of Infidels.

Even sober Infidels began to be alarmed for their own peace, safety, and enjoyments; and to which, that other men might continue still to be christians; while christians saw with horror their God denied, their Savior blasphemed, and war formally declared against Heaven.

To all this was added a complete development of the base and villainous designs of the French government against our country, their piratical plunder of our property, and their inhuman treatment of our seamen. Persons, who thought nothing, who felt nothing, concerning religion, felt these things exquisitely; and rationally concluded, that men, who could do these things, could, and would, do every thing else, that was evil and unjust; and that their moral principles, which produced, and sanctioned, these crimes, could not fail to merit contempt and detestation. Such persons, therefore, began now to lean towards the side of christianity, and to seek in it a safety and peace, which they beheld Infidelity destroy.

Thus having in the midst of these enormous dangers obtained help of God, we continue until the present time; and this part of our country, at least, has escaped not only tributary bondage, but the infinitely more dreadful bondage of Infidelity, corruption, and moral ruin.

It ought, here, and forever, to be remembered with peculiar gratitude, that God has, during the past Century, often and wonderfully interposed in our behalf, and snatched us from the jaws of approaching destruction. The instances of this interposition are too numerous to be now recounted, and are happily too extraordinary to be either unknown or forgotten. We have been frequently on the brink of destruction; but although cast down, we have not been destroyed. Perhaps we have so often been, and are still, suffered to stand on this precipice, that we may see, and feel, and acknowledge, the hand of our Preserver. . . .

In the mean time, let me solemnly warn you, that if you intend to accomplish anything, if you mean not to labour in vain, and to spend your strength for nought, you must take your side. There can be here no halting between two opinions. You must marshall yourselves, finally, in your own defense, and in the defense of all that is dear to you. You must meet face to face the bands of disorder, of falsehood, and of sin. Between them and you there is, there can be, no natural, real, or lasting harmony. What communion hath light with darkness? What concord hath Christ with Belial? Or what part hath he that believeth with an Infidel? From a connection with them what can you gain? What will you not lose? Their neighborhood is contagious; their friendship is a blast;

their communion is death. Will you imbibe their principles? Will you copy their practices? Will you teach your children, that death is an eternal sleep? that the end sanctifies the means? that moral obligation is a dream? Religion a farce? and your Savior the spurious offspring of pollution? Will you send your daughters abroad in the attire of a female Greek? Will you enrol your sons as conscripts for plunder and butchery? Will you make marriage the mockery of a registers' office? Will you become the rulers of Sodom, and the people of Gomorrah? Shall your love to man vanish in a word, and evaporate on the tongue? Shall it be lost in a tear, and perish in a sigh? Will you enthrone a Goddess of Reason before the table of Christ? Will you burn your Bibles? Will you crucify anew your Redeemer? Will you deny your God?

COME out, therefore, from among them, and be ye separate, saith the Lord, and touch not the unclean thing; and I will receive you, and will be a father to you: And ye shall be my sons and daughters, saith the Lord almighty.

To this end you must coolly, firmly, and irrevocably make your determination, and resolve, that Jehovah is your God, and that you will serve him only. His enemies are the enemies of yourselves, and of your children; of your peace, liberty, and happiness; of your religion, virtue, and salvation,—Their principles abhor; their practices detest. Before your steady indignation, and firm contempt, they will fall of course. No falsehood can bear the sunbeams of truth; no vice can withstand the steady current of virtue. The motives to this opposition are infinite. Your all, your children's all, is at stake. If you contend manfully, you will be more than conquerors; if you yield, both you and they are undone. You are endeared by a thousand ties. Your common country is a land of milk and honey: In it a thousand churches are vocal with the praise of your Creator; and four thousand schools receive your children to their bosom, and nurse them to wisdom and piety. In this country you all sprang from one stock, speak one language, have one system of manners, profess one religion, and wear one character. Your laws, your institutions, your interests, are one. No mixture weakens, no strangers divide you. You have fought and bled, your fathers have fought and died, together. Together they worshipped God; together they sat around the table of the Redeemer; together they ascended to heaven; and together they now unite in the glorious concert of eternal praise. With such an interest at hazard, with such bonds of union, with such examples, you cannot separate; you cannot fear.

Let me at the same time warn you, that your enemies are numerous, industrious, and daring, full of subtlety, and full of zeal. Nay, some of them are your own brethren, and endeared to you by all of the ties of nature. The contest is, therefore, fraught with hazard and alarm. Were it a war of arms, you would have little to dread. It is a war of arts, of temptations; of enchantments; a war against the magicians of Egypt; in which no weapons will avail, but "the rod of God." In this contest you may be left alone. Fear not; "they that be for you will even then be more than they that are against you." Almighty power will protect, Infinite wisdom will guide, and Unchangeable goodness will prosper you. The Christian world rises daily in prayer to heaven for your faithfulness and success; the host of sleeping saints calls to you from the grave, and bids you God speed. The spirits of your fathers lean from yonder skies to survey the conflict, and your children of many generations, will rise up, and call you blessed.

Forming the American Bible Society

The advent of the Second Awakening sparked the growing interest in and demand for the distribution of Bibles. All along the east coast, local and state Bible societies were organized during the first fifteen years of the nineteenth century. Then in May 1816, sixty representatives of these scattered societies met in New York, where they established the American Bible Society. The primary figure in the movement was Samuel J. Mills, who was spiritually a child of the Second Awakening. The organization, deploring "local feelings, party prejudices, sectarian jealousies," called for cooperation in the great work of Bible distribution. In less than four years it had sent out approximately a hundred thousand Bibles. The following statement which describes the purpose of the organization appeared in the *Panoplist and Missionary Magazine*, XII (1816), 271-73.

Every person of observation has remarked that the times are pregnant with great events. The political world has undergone changes stupendous, unexpected, and calculated to inspire thoughtful men with the most boding anticipations.

That there are in reserve, occurrences of deep, of lasting, and of general interest, appears to be the common sentiment. Such a sentiment has not been excited without a cause, and does not exist without an object. The cause is to be sought in that Providence, which adapts, with wonderful exactitude, means to ends; and the object is too plain to be mistaken by those who carry a sense of religion into their speculations upon the present and the future condition of our afflicted race.

An excitement, as extraordinary as it is powerful, has roused the nations to the importance of spreading the knowledge of the one living and true God, as revealed in his Son, the Mediator between God and men,

Christ Jesus. This excitement is the more worthy of notice, as it has followed a period of philosophy falsely so called, and has gone in the track of those very schemes which, under the imposing names of reason and liberality, were attempting to seduce mankind from all which can bless the life that is, or shed a cheering radiance on the life that is to come.

We hail the reaction, as auspicious to whatever is exquisite in human enjoyment, or precious to human hope. We would fly to the aid of all that is holy, against all that is profane; of the purest interest of the community, the family, and the individual, against the conspiracy of darkness, disaster and death—to help on the mighty work of Christian charity—to claim our place in the age of Bibles.

We have, indeed, the secondary praise, but still the praise, of treading in the footsteps of those who have set an example without a parallel—an example of the most unbounded benevolence and beneficence: and it cannot be to us a source of any pain, that it has been set by those who are of one blood with most of ourselves; and has been embodied in a form so noble and so Catholic, as *"The British and Foreign Bible Society."*

The impulse which that institution, ten thousand times more glorious than all the exploits of the sword, has given to the conscience of Europe, and to the slumbering hope of millions in the region and shadow of death, demonstrates to Christians of every country what they *cannot* do by insulated zeal; and what they *can* do by co-operation.

In the United States we want nothing but concert to perform achievements astonishing to ourselves, dismaying to the adversaries of truth and piety; and most encouraging to every evangelical effort, on the surface of the globe.

No spectacle can be so illustrious in itself, so touching to man, or so grateful to God, as a nation pouring forth its devotion, its talent, and its treasures, for that kingdom of the Savior which is righteousness and peace.

If there be a single measure which can overrule objection, subdue opposition, and command exertion, this is the measure. That all our voices, all our affections, all our hands, should be joined in the grand design of promoting "peace on earth and good will toward men"—that they should resist the advance of misery—should carry the light of instruction into the dominions of ignorance; and the balm of joy to the soul of anguish; and all this by diffusing the oracles of God—addresses to the understanding an argument which cannot be encountered; and

to the heart an appeal which its holiest emotions rise up to second.

Under such impressions, and with such views, fathers, brethren, fellow-citizens, the *American Bible Society* has been formed. Local feelings, party prejudices, sectarian jealousies, are excluded by its very nature. Its members are leagued in that, and in that alone, which calls up every hallowed, and puts down every unhallowed, principle—the dissemination of the Scriptures in the received versions where they exist, and in the most faithful where they may be required. In such a work, whatever is dignified, kind, venerable, true, has ample scope: while sectarian littleness and rivalries can find no avenue of admission.

The only question is, whether an object of such undisputed magnitude can be best obtained by a national Society, or by independent associations in friendly understanding and correspondence.

Without entering into the details of this inquiry, we may be permitted to state, in a few words, our reasons of preference to a national Society supported by local Societies and by individuals throughout our country.

Concentrated action is powerful action. The same powers, when applied by a common direction, will produce results impossible to their divided and partial exercise. A national object unites national feeling and concurrence. Unity of a great system combines energy of effect with economy of means. Accumulated intelligence interests and animates the public mind. And the Catholic efforts of a country, thus harmonized, give her a place in the moral convention of the world; and enable her to act directly upon the universal plans of happiness which are now pervading the nations.

It is true, that the prodigious territory of the United States—the increase of their population, which is gaining every day upon their moral cultivation—and the dreadful consequences which will ensue from a people's outgrowing the knowledge of eternal life; and reverting to a species of heathenism, which shall have all the address and profligacy of civilized society, without any religious control, present a sphere of action, which may for a long time employ and engross the cares of this Society, and of all the local Bible Societies of the land.

In the distinct anticipation of such an urgency, one of the main objects of the *American Bible Society*, is, not merely to provide a sufficiency of well printed and accurate editions of the Scriptures; but also to furnish great districts of the American continent with well executed Stereotype plates, for their cheap and extensive diffusion throughout regions which are now scantily supplied, at a discouraging expense; and which, nevertheless, open a wide and prepared field for the reception of revealed truth.

Yet, let it not be supposed, that geographical or political limits are to be the limits of the *American Bible Society*. That designation is meant to indicate, not the restrictions of their labor, but the source of its emanation. They will embrace, with thankfulness and pleasure, every opportunity of raying out, by means of the Bible, according to their ability, the light of life and immortality, to such parts of the world, as are destitute of the blessing, and are within their reach. In this high vocation, their ambition is to be fellow-workers with them who are fellow-workers with God.

People of the United States;

Have you ever been invited to an enterprise of such grandeur and glory? Do you not value the Holy Scriptures? Value them as containing your sweetest hope; your most thrilling joy? Can you submit to the thought that you should be torpid in your endeavors to disperse them, while the rest of Christendom is awake and alert? Shall you hang back, in heartless indifference, when Princes come down from their thrones, to bless the cottage of the poor with the Gospel of peace; and Imperial Sovereigns are gathering their fairest honors from spreading abroad the oracles of the Lord your God? Is it possible that *you* should not see, in this state of human things, a mighty motion of Divine Providence? The most Heavenly charity treads close upon the march of conflict and blood! The world is at peace! Scarce has the soldier time to unbind his helmet, and to wipe away the sweat from his brow, ere the voice of mercy succeeds to the clarion of battle, and calls the nations from enmity to love! Crowned heads bow to the head which is to wear "many crowns;" and, for the first time since the promulgation of Christianity, appear to act in unison for the recognition of its gracious principles, as being fraught alike with happiness to man and honor to God.

What has created so strange, so beneficent an alteration? This is no doubt the doing of the Lord, and it is marvelous in our eyes. But what instrument has he thought fit chiefly to use? That which contributes, in all latitudes and climes, to make Christians feel their unity, to rebuke the spirit of strife, and to open upon them the day of brotherly concord—the Bible! the Bible!—through Bible societies!

Come then, fellow-citizens, fellow-Christians, let us join in the sacred covenant. Let no heart be cold; no hand be idle; no purse reluctant! Come, while room is left for us in the ranks whose toil is goodness, and whose recompense is victory. Come cheerfully, eagerly, generally. Be it impressed on your souls, that a contribution, saved from even a cheap indulgence, may send a Bible to a desolate family; may become a radiatory point of "grace and truth" to a neighborhood of error and vice; and that a number of such contributions made at really no expense, may illumine a large tract of country, and successive generations of immortals, in that celestial knowledge, which shall secure their present and their future felicity.

But whatever be the proportion between expectation and experience, this much is certain: we shall satisfy our conviction of duty—we shall have the praises of high endeavors for the highest ends—we shall minister to the blessedness of thousands, and tens of thousands, of whom we may never see the faces, nor hear the names. We shall set forward a system of happiness which will go on with accelerated motion and augmented vigor, after we shall have finished our career; and confer upon our children, and our children's children, the delight of seeing the wilderness turned into a fruitful field, by the blessing of God upon that seed which their father's sowed, and themselves watered. In fine we shall do our part toward that expansion and intensity of light divine, which shall visit, in its progress, the palaces of the great, and the hamlets of the small, until the whole "earth be full of the knowledge of Jehovah, as the waters cover the sea."

The Need for Western Colleges

Under the pressure of denominational rivalries which in part resulted from the Second Awakening, numerous church colleges were founded during the decades prior to the Civil War. The era has been termed by some as "the era of the church college." Many of these institutions did not survive for long, however, due to inadequate financial support and lack of sound planning. The former problem was particularly acute during the period of national economic distress in the late 1830s. To deal with the situation, the Society for the Promotion of Collegiate and Theological Education at the West was organized in 1843 in New York City. Shortly thereafter the society printed the following report to answer the question as to why colleges were needed in the West.

The considerations advanced in my last article go to show, that Colleges are a necessity of every extensive community, marked by nature as a social unity. We are now to look at some reasons why they are peculiarly needed at the West. First, then, we find such a reason in the fact that Rome is at this time making unprecedented efforts to garrison this valley with her seminaries of education. She claims already to have within it between fifteen and twenty colleges and theological schools; and this number is rapidly increasing.

To these permanency is ensured by the steadfastness of her policy, the constancy of her receipts from Catholic Europe, yearly increasing under the stimulating reports of her missionaries, and by her exacting despotism, moral if nor ecclesiastic, over the earnings of her poor in this country. They are among the enduring formative forces in western society; and the causes which sustain them, will constantly add to their number. These institutions, together with numerous grades, under the conduct of their Jesuits and various religious orders, are offering (what professes to be) education almost as a gratuity, in many places in the West. Whatever other qualities her education may lack, we may be sure it will not want a subtle and intense proselytism, addressing not the reason but the senses, the taste, the imagination, and the passions; applying itself diversely to the fears of the timid, the enthusiasm of the ardent, the credulity of the simple, the affections of the young, and to that trashy sentiment and mawkish charity to which all principles are the same. Now the policy of Rome in playing upon all these elements through her educational enginery, is steadfast and profoundly sagacious. Her aim, in effect, is at the whole educational interest. The college is naturally the heart of the whole. The lower departments necessarily draw life from that. If Rome then grasps the college in the system of Western education, she virtually grasps the common school; she distills out the heart of the whole, if not a putrid superstition, at least that covert infidelity of which she is still more prolific.

Now a system so deep and so persistent, must be met by a correspondent depth and persistency of policy. Protestantism can no more counteract it by temporary and spasmodic efforts, than she could stop the Mississippi with a whirlwind. She can encounter it only by a system of permanent and efficient Protestant colleges. And this for two reasons. First, the Catholic seminaries in this country seem to meet a great and deeply felt social want, and can be displaced only by a supply for this want from another quarter. And secondly, in the nature of things, a college alone can counteract a college. The college acts upon the public mind in a manner so peculiar, through such ages and classes, and through influences so various and subtle, so constant, noiseless and profound, that it can be successfully combated only by a similar institution. Place efficient Protestant colleges in the proximity of the Catholic, and the latter will wither. For all purposes of severe intellectual discipline or masculine reason, their education is soon found to be a sham. A spiritual despotism dare not, cannot, teach true history or a free and manly philosophy. Again, other facts, which constitute a peculiar necessity for colleges in the West, are found in the circumstances and character of its population. First, the West is in its formative state. Never will impressions be made so easily and so enduringly for good or evil. Never will it be so important that its architect-minds—its plastic forces—should be endued with a broad and liberal intelligence. According to the elements now thrown in, it will soon permanently crystalize into dark and unshapely forms, or into order and beauty.

Another peculiar demand for colleges, may be found in the immense rapidity of our growth, and in the character of that growth, being a representative of almost every clime, opinion, sect, language, and social institute, not only of this country but of Christian Europe. Never was a more intense power of intellectual and moral fusion requisite to prevent the utter disorganization of society. Never was a people put to such a perilous proof of its power of assimilation, or required to incorporate with itself so rapidly such vast masses. We have in this fact, as well as in that of the Catholic aggression, dangers and trials put upon us, which our fathers never knew. Society here is new yet vast, and with all its forces in insulation or antagonism. Never was a community in more urgent need of those institutions, whose province it is profoundly to penetrate a people with a burning intelligence that shall fuse it into a unity with those great principles which are the organic life and binding forces of all society.

Again, in consequence of the incoherency of this element in a population thus hetero-geneous, and broken off from the fixtures of old communities, without time to form new ones, all the social forces are shifting and mutable, and yield like the particles of liquid to the last force impressed. This quality of western society, combined with the bold, prompt, energetic and adventurous temperament impressed generally on it by common influences in the life of the emigrant, exposes it to vehement and brief excitements, to epidemic delusion and agitation. Upon this sea of incoherent and vehement mind, every wind of opinion has been let loose, and is struggling for the mastery; and the mass heaves restlessly to and fro under the thousand different forces impressed. The West is, therefore, peculiarly perturbed with demagogism and popular agitation, not only in politics, but in religion, and all social interests. Amid these shifting social elements, we want principles of stability, we want a system of permanent forces, we want deep, strong and constant influences, that shall take from the change-fulness and excitability of the western mind, by giving it the tranquillity of depth, and shall protect it from delusive and fitful impulses, by enduing it with a calm, profound and pure reason.

Thus, while society with us has on the one hand to contend against a masked and political spiritual despotism entrenching itself in the educational interest, and on the other against a demagogic agitation, urged on too often by avarice, or ruffianism, or faction, or a sophistical but specious skepticism, or by fanatical or superstitious or shallow religionisms and socialisms of every hue, we find our defence against both to be the same, a thorough popular enlightenment and belief, anchored by permanent institutions gradually pervading the mass with great and tranquil and guardian truths, and adjusting the system to the fixed laws of intellectual and moral gravitation. It may perhaps be asked, "Why not, in such a community, immediately proceed by opposing to agitation for evil, agitation for good?" This may at times be expedient, but cannot be relied on permanently. First, because popular agitation, unless based on deep-wrought intellectual convictions, can only palliate, it cannot cure any evil. In the second place, in the germ of popular agitation, a freedom from the restraints of conscience and truth and honor, often gives a decisive advantage, and agitating movements springing forth immediately from the people to be moved, and possessing a quiet

sympathy with its feeling, and a shrewd tact in dealing with its passions and prejudices, must ever out-general any counter-movements originating from a different source. Especially, movements of this kind from abroad are liable to find themselves forestalled—the popular ear and mind preoccupied—arguments closed— opposing tracts already in the hands of the people—and the Bible itself, under their elected interpreters, made to preach another gospel.

The above exigencies of Western society cannot be met without colleges. I am far from undervaluing over [other?] movements of Christian philanthropy towards the country. I am most grateful for them. I bless God for his Word broadcast by the American Bible Society amid this people; I am thankful for the interest the American Tract Society are directing hitherward, and hail with pleasure all the living truth and hallowed thought brought by it into contact with the popular mind. The attitude and history of the American Home Missionary Society in relation to the West, fill my mind with a sentiment of moral sublimity, and give it rank among the noblest and most sagacious schemes in the records of Christian benevolence. It will stand in history invested, to a great extent, with the moral grandeur of a civilizer and evangelizer of a new empire. But these are far from excluding the scheme of colleges. The permanency of their benefits can be grounded only on a thorough and liberal popular enlightenment. The educational interest, then, must underlie them all. But the only way in which the East can lay a controlling grasp on this, is by the establishment among us of permanent educational institutions. In a population, one tenth at least of which cannot read, it is plain that education is an essential prerequisite to bringing a large class—and that most necessary to be reached—within the influence of truth through the press. And no system of foreign supply of ministers, teachers or educated men, can obviate the necessity of institutions that shall constantly send forth those that shall be the educators of this people, in the school, the pulpit, the legislature, and the various departments of social life. Artificial irrigation cannot take the place of living waters. We are grateful for streams from abroad, but we feel there is need of opening fountains of life in the bosom of the people itself. The supplies from abroad we cannot rely on long. They are every day becoming more inadequate in numbers, and must to some extent be deficient in adaptation to our wants; a deficiency that often for years, sometimes for life, shuts one out from the people.

The common exigencies, then, of every extensive society, require colleges within itself. The peculiar evils to which that of the West is exposed, obviously cannot be permanently and successfully met by other means. The question then recurs in every aspect of this subject, Will the East assist the West in establishing a Protestant system of home education, or will she leave her to grapple single-handed with Romanism, and the other peculiar dangers to which she is exposed, in addition to the necessities that cluster around every infant community, or will she attempt by palliatives addressed to the symptoms, to heal a disease seated in the heart? A dangerous malady is on the patient. The peril is imminent and requires promptitude. Shall remedies be adapted to the disease or the symptoms, or with such fearful chances against it, shall the patient be abandoned to the conflict betwixt nature and death? Let the East remember the life thus hazarded involves her own—it is to her the brand of Meleager.

Part II   Expanding America
1820-1865

The period from 1820 to 1865 was a time of unprecedented expansion not only for the American nation geographically, but also for religion as the churches confronted the problems and opportunities of the rapidly changing American society. The results of the Second Awakening included the establishing of new religious institutions in western areas recently populated by eastern migrants. These institutions—churches, schools, and missionary societies—would have to face the problems which would accompany the westward movement.

During the first twenty years of the nineteenth century, many voluntary societies emerged that channeled the energy emitted by Second Awakening revivals into missionary, educational, and reform causes. In the years which followed, this activity was aided by changes in theology which placed greater emphasis on man's freedom to improve the human situation, as well as by a general atmosphere of optimism that favored the activism of the reform movement. With a touch of millennial expectancy, Charles G. Finney, the leading revivalist of the period, challenged the church to take the lead in cleaning up America's social sins. Revivalist Phoebe Palmer contended that personal holiness was a prerequisite to a life of social activism. The coming of the millennium would be hastened through the reforming of people's diet, argued health reformer Sylvester Graham.

Of the problems facing the country in 1820, none presented a greater challenge than the institution of slavery. Since slavery influenced everything it touched, the church could not escape its impact, nor did slavery go unaltered when faced by the church. Such was the case long before 1820, however. For as early as the seventeenth century, and continuing through the eighteenth, churchmen argued the case and preached sermons which both supported and opposed human bondage. When the massive assault led by the abolitionists was leveled against slavery in the 1830s, those on both sides of the issue made new efforts in defense of their case. In the heat of the verbal battles which ensued, slaveowners were called "sinners," while their opponents were considered "biblical infidels." To no one's surprise, numerous individual churches and entire denominations experienced divisions. Antagonists like Theodore D. Weld and James H. Hammond, presented opinions on slavery which provided the basis for the ecclesiastical involvement in the slavery struggle. Former slave, Frederick Douglass, calls upon the churches to reject their support of slavery.

In this period of expansion, it was not uncommon for churchmen to provide theological arguments for the concept of American destiny. Such ideas lingered from seventeenth century

New England Puritans who considered themselves God's chosen people, and continued to draw strength in the era of the Revolution when clergymen insisted God was conceiving a new nation to serve Him. During the decades just prior to the Civil War, this same God was expanding America's power so it could bring blessing to the world. If a journalist like John O'Sullivan could talk about America's "manifest destiny," certainly a seasoned politician like John Quincy Adams might expect a sympathetic hearing of his scriptural argument for American expansion. The growing home missions enterprise welcomed the attention focused on the national movement westward, as is suggested by the veteran medical missionary Marcus Whitman. Militarist Robert F. Stockton illustrates how the idealism of destiny was always in danger of being confused with opportunism.

When the Civil War came, the religious beliefs of those cloaked in both blue and gray led each to behave as though God were on their side in this "holy war." The aura of self-righteousness which exuded over the slavery issue during the antebellum years intensified during the war. Individuals, as well as groups of religious people, like those gathered at Richmond in 1863, insisted they were right. Toward the end of the war, President Lincoln found little reason for rejoicing, though clergyman Henry Ward Beecher detected numerous positive results from it.

5 The Age of Revivalism and Reform

For I am the Lord your God. Consecrate yourselves therefore, and be holy; for I am holy.

—Lev. 11:44

The Church Must take Right Ground
Charles G. Finney

Charles G. Finney (1792-1875), the greatest antebellum revivalist in the nation, often linked religion with antislavery and other reforms in his sermons and lectures. At first a Presbyterian preacher, he later became a Congregationalist, serving as president of Oberlin College from 1851 to 1866. He was particularly influential in inspiring many other men and women to support the antislavery cause. In his view, America would experience a religious revival only when it abandoned sin in all forms. This abandonment of sin was a necessary prerequisite to Christ's second coming and the beginning of the millennial period of peace and justice. In a series of *Lectures on Revivals of Religion* which he delivered in 1835, Finney indicated the relationship between revivalism and reform. The following lecture, published in 1868 in Oberlin, Ohio was part of that series.

I proceed to mention things *which ought to be done* to continue this great and glorious revival of religion, which has been in progress for the last ten years.

There should be great and deep repentings on the part of ministers. WE, my brethren, must humble *ourselves* before God. It will not do for us to suppose that it is enough to call on the *people* to repent. We must repent, we must take the lead in repentance, and then call on the churches to follow. . . .

The church must take right ground in regard to politics. Do not suppose, now, that I am going to preach a political sermon, or that I wish to have you join and get up a *Christian party* in politics. No, you must not believe that. But the time has come that Christians must vote for honest men, and take consistent ground in politics, or the Lord will curse them. They must be honest men themselves, and instead of voting for a man because he belongs to their party, bank or anti-bank, Jackson or anti-Jackson, they must

73

find out whether he is honest and upright, and fit to be trusted. They must let the world see that the church will uphold no man in office who is known to be a knave, or an adulterer, or a Sabbath-breaker, or a gambler. Such is the spread of intelligence and the facility of communication in our country, that every man can know for whom he gives his vote. And if he will give his vote only for honest men, the country will be obliged to have upright rulers. All parties will be compelled to put up honest men as candidates. Christians have been exceedingly guilty in this matter. But the time has come when they must act differently, or God will curse the nation, and withdraw his Spirit. As on the subjects of slavery and temperance, so on this subject, the church must act right, or the country will be ruined. God cannot sustain this free and blessed country, which we love and pray for, unless the church will take right ground. Politics are a part of religion in such a country as this, and Christians must do their duty to the country as a part of their duty to God. It seems sometimes as if the foundations of the nation were becoming rotten: and Christians seem to act as if they thought God did not see what they do on politics. But I tell you, he does see it; and he will bless or curse this nation, according to the course they take.

The churches must take right ground on the subject of slavery. And here the question arises, what is right ground? And *first*, I will state some of the things that should be avoided.

1. First of all a *bad spirit* should be avoided. Nothing is more calculated to injure religion, and to injure the slaves themselves, than for Christians to get into an angry controversy on the subject. It is a subject upon which there needs to be no angry controversy among Christians. Slave-holding professors, like rumselling professors, may endeavor to justify themselves, and may be angry with those who press their consciences, and call upon them to give up their sins. Those proud professors of religion, who think a man to blame, or think it is a shame to have a black skin, may allow their prejudices so far to prevail, as to shut their ears, and be disposed to quarrel with those who urge the subject upon them. But I repeat it, the subject of slavery is a subject upon which Christians, praying men, *need not* and *must not* differ.

2. Another thing to be avoided is *an attempt to take neutral ground* on this subject. Christians can no more take neutral ground on this subject, since it has come up for discussion, than they can take neutral ground on the subject of the sanctification of the Sabbath. It is a great national sin. It is a sin of the church. The churches, by their silence, and by permitting slave-holders to belong to their communion, have been consenting to it. All denominations have been more or less guilty; although the Quakers have, of late years, washed their hands of it. It is in vain for the churches to pretend it is merely a political sin. I repeat it, it is the sin of the church, to which all denominations have consented. They have virtually declared that it is lawful. The very fact of suffering slave-holders quietly to remain in good standing in their churches, is the strongest and most public expressions of their views that it is not sin. For the church, therefore, to pretend to take neutral ground on the subject, is perfectly

absurd. The fact is that she is not on neutral ground at all. While she tolerates slave-holders in her communion *she justifies* the practice! And as well might an enemy of God pretend that he was neither a saint nor a sinner, that he was going to take neutral ground, and pray, "good Lord and good devil," because he did not know which side would be the most popular.

3. Great care should be taken *to avoid a censorious spirit on both sides*. It is a subject on which there has been, and probably will be for some time to come, a difference of *opinion* among Christians, as to the best method of disposing of the question: and it ought to be treated with great forbearance on both sides. A denunciatory spirit, impeaching each other's motives, is unchristian, calculated to grieve away the Spirit of God, and to put down revivals, and is alike injurious to the church, and to the slaves themselves.

In the *second* place, I will mention several things, that, in my judgment, the church is imperatively called upon to do, on this subject:

1. Christians, of all denominations, should lay aside prejudice, and *inform themselves* on this subject, without any delay. Vast multitudes of professors of religion have indulged prejudice to such a degree, as to be unwilling to read and hear, and come to a right understanding of the subject. But Christians cannot pray in this state of mind. I defy any one to possess the spirit of prayer, while he is too prejudiced to examine this, or any other question of duty. If the light did not shine, Christians might remain in the dark upon this point, and still possess the spirit of prayer. But if they *refuse to come to the light*, they cannot pray. Now, I call upon all you who are here present, and who have examined this subject because you were indisposed to examine it, to say whether you have the spirit of prayer. Where ministers, individual Christians, or whole churches, *resist truth* upon this point now, when it is so extensively diffused and before the public mind, I do not believe they will or can enjoy a revival of religion.

2. Writings, containing temperate and judicious discussions on this subject, and such developments of facts as are before the public, should be quietly and extensively circulated, and should be carefully and prayerfully examined by the whole church. I do not mean by this, that the attention of the church should be so absorbed by this, as to neglect the main question of saving souls in the midst of them. I do not mean that such premature movements on this subject should be made, as to astound the Christian community, and involve them in a broil; but that praying men should act judiciously, and that, as soon as sufficient information can be diffused through the community, the churches should meekly, but *firmly*, take decided ground on the subject, and express, before the whole nation and the world, their abhorrence of this sin.

The anti-masonic excitement which prevailed a few years since, made such desolations in the churches, and produced so much alienation of feeling and ill-will among ministers and people, and the first introduction of *this* subject has been attended with such commotions, that many good ministers, who are themselves entirely opposed to slavery, dread to introduce the subject among their people, through fear that their churches have not religion enough to take it up, and consider it calmly, and decide upon it in the spirit of the gospel. I know there is danger of this. But still, the subject must be presented to the churches. And if introduced with discretion, and with great prayer, there are very few churches that have enjoyed revivals, and that are at the present time anywhere near a revival spirit, which may not be brought to receive the truth on this subject.

Perhaps no church in this country has had a more severe trial upon this subject, than this. They were a church of young, and for the most part, inexperienced Christians. And many circumstances conspired, in my absence, to produce confusion and wrong feeling among them. But so far as I am now acquainted with the state of feeling in this church, I know of no ill-will among them on this subject. The Lord has blessed us, the Spirit has been distilled upon us, and considerable numbers added to our communion every month since my return. There are doubtless in this church those who feel on this subject in very different degrees: and yet I can honestly say that I am not aware of the least difference *in sentiment* among them. We have from the beginning, *previous* to my going on my foreign tour, taken the same ground on the subject of slavery, that we have on temperance. We have excluded slave-holders, and all concerned in the traffic, from our communion. By some, out of this church, this course has been censured as unwarrantable and uncharitable, and I would by no means make my own judg-

ment, or the example of this church, a rule for the government of other ministers and churches. Still, I conscientiously believe, that the time is not far distant, when the churches will be united in this expression of abhorrence against this sin. If I do not baptize slavery by some soft and Christian name, if I call it SIN, both consistency and conscience conduct to the inevitable conclusion, that while this sin is persevered in, its perpetrators cannot be fit subjects for Christian communion and fellowship.

To this it is objected, that there are *many ministers* in the Presbyterian church, who are slave-holders. And it is said to be very inconsistent that we should refuse to suffer slaveholders to come to our communion, and yet belong to the same church with them, sit with them in ecclesiastical bodies, and acknowledge them as ministers. To this I answer, that I have not the power to deal with those ministers, and certainly I am not to withdraw from the church because some of its ministers or members are slave-holders. My duty is to belong to the church, even if the devil belong to it. Where I *have authority*, I exclude slave-holders from the communion, and I always will as long as I live. But where I have no authority, if the table of Christ be spread, I will sit down to it, in obedience to his commandment, whoever else may sit down or stay away.

I do not mean, by any means, to denounce all those slave-holding ministers and professors as hypocrites, and to say that they are not Christians. But this I say, that while they continue in that attitude, the cause of Christ and of humanity demands that they should not be recognized as such, unless we mean to be partakers of other men's sins. It is no more inconsistent to exclude slave-holders because they belong to the Presbyterian church, than it is to exclude persons who drink or sell ardent spirits; for there are a great many rumsellers belonging to the Presbyterian church.

I believe the time has come, and although I am no prophet, I believe it will be found to have come, that the revival in the United States, will continue and prevail no further and faster than the church takes right ground upon this subject. The churches are God's witnesses. The fact is, that slavery is, pre-eminently, *the sin of the church*. It is the very fact that ministers and professors of religion of different denominations hold slaves, which sanctifies the whole abomination in the eyes of ungodly men. Who does not know that on the subject of temperance, every drunkard in the land will skulk behind some rum-selling deacon, or wine-drinking minister? It is the most common objection and refuge of the intemperate, and of moderate drinkers, that it is practiced by professors of religion. It is *this* that creates the imperious necessity for excluding traffickers in ardent spirit, and rum-drinkers, from the communion. Let the churches of all denominations speak out on the subject of temperance, let them close their doors against all who have anything to do with the death-dealing abomination, and the cause of temperance is triumphant. A few years would annihilate the traffic. Just so with slavery.

It is the church that mainly supports this sin. Her unified testimony upon the subject would settle this question. Let Christians of all denominations meekly, but firmly, come forth, and pronounce their verdict, let them clear their communions, and wash their hands of this thing, let them give forth and write on the head and front of this great abomination, SIN! and in three years, a public sentiment would be formed that would carry all before it, and there would not be a shackled slave, nor a bristling, cruel slave-driver, in this land.

Still it may be said, that in many churches, this subject *cannot* be introduced, without creating confusion and ill-will. This may be. It has been so on the subject of temperance, and upon the subject of revivals too. In some churches, neither temperance nor revivals can be introduced without producing dissension. Sabbath schools, and missionary operations, and everything of the kind, have been opposed, and have produced dissensions in many churches. But is this a sufficient reason for excluding these subjects? And where churches have excluded these subjects for fear of contention, have they been blessed with revivals? Everybody knows that they have not. But where churches have taken firm grounds on these subjects, although individuals, and sometimes numbers, have opposed, still they have been blessed with revivals. Where any of these subjects are carefully and prayerfully introduced, where they are brought forward with a right spirit, and the true relative importance is attached to each of them, if in such cases, there are those who will make disturbance and resist, *let the blame fall where it ought*. There are some individuals, who are *themselves* disposed to quarrel with this subject, who are always ready to exclaim, "Do not introduce these things into the church, they will create opposition." And if the minister and praying people feel it their duty to bring the matter forward, they will themselves create a disturbance, and then say, "There, I told you so;

now see what your introducing this subject has done; it will tear the church all to pieces." And while they are themselves doing all they can to create a division, they are charging the division upon the subject, and not upon themselves. There are some such people in many of our churches. And neither Sabbath schools, nor missions, nor revivals, nor anti-slavery, nor anything else that honours God or benefits the souls of men, will be carried in the churches, without these careful souls being offended by it.

These things, however, have been introduced, and carried, one by one, in some churches with more, and others with less opposition at all. And as sure as God is the God of the church, as certain as that the world must be converted, this subject must be considered and pronounced sin by the church. There might infinitely better be no church in the world, than she should attempt to remain neutral, or give a false testimony on a subject of such importance as slavery, especially since the subject has come up, and it is impossible from the nature of the case, that her testimony should not be in the scale, on the one side or the other.

Do you ask, "What shall be done; shall we make it the all-absorbing topic of conversation, and divert attention from the all-important subject of the salvation of souls in the midst of us?" I answer, No. Let a church express her opinion upon the subject, and be at peace. So far as I know, *we* are entirely at peace upon this subject. We have expressed our opinion, we have closed our communion against slave-holders, and are attending to other things. I am not aware of the least un-

healthy excitement among us on this subject. And where it has become an absorbing topic of conversation in a place, in most instances, I believe it has been owing to the pertinacious and unreasonable opposition of a few individuals against even granting the subject a hearing.

If the church wishes to promote revivals, *she must sanctify the Sabbath*. There is a vast deal of Sabbath-breaking in the land. Merchants break it, travellers break it, the government breaks it. A few years ago an attempt was made in the western part of this state, to establish and sustain a Sabbath-keeping line of boats and stages. But it was found that the *church* would not sustain the enterprise. Many professors of religion would not travel in these stages, and would not have their goods forwarded in canal boats that would be detained from travelling on the Sabbath. At one time, Christians were much engaged in petitioning Congress to suspend the Sabbath mails, and now they seem to be ashamed of it. But one thing is most certain, that unless something be done, and done speedily, and done effectually, to promote the sanctification of the Sabbath by the church, the Sabbath will go by the board, and we shall not only have our mails running on the Sabbath, and post-offices open, but, by and by, our courts of justice, and halls of legislation, will be kept open on the Sabbath. And what can the church do, what will this nation do, *without any Sabbath*?

The church must take right ground on the subject of temperance, and moral reform, and all the subjects of practical morality which come up for discussion from time to time.

There are those in the churches who are standing aloof from the subject of moral reform, and who are as much afraid to have anything said in the pulpit against lewdness, as if a thousand devils had got up into the pulpit. On this subject, the church need not expect to be permitted to take neutral ground. In the providence of God, it is up for discussion. The evils have been exhibited; the call has been made for reform. And what is to reform mankind but the truth? And who shall present the truth if not the church and the ministry? Away with the idea, that Christians can remain neutral, and yet enjoy the approbation and blessing of God.

In all such cases, the minister who holds his peace is counted among those on the other side. Everybody knows that it is so in a revival. It is not necessary for a person to rail out against the work. If he only keep still and take neutral ground, the enemies of the revival will all consider him as on their side. So on the subject of temperance. It is not needful that a person should rail at the cold-water society, in order to be on the best terms with drunkards and moderate drinkers. Only let him plead for the moderate use of wine, only let him continue to drink it as a luxury, and all the drunkards account him on their side. If he refuse to give his influence to the temperance cause, he is claimed, of course, by the other side, as a friend. On all these subjects, when they come up, the churches and ministers must take the right ground, and take it openly and stand to it, and carry it through, if they expect to enjoy the blessing of God in revivals. They must cast out from their communions such members, as, in contempt of the light that is shed upon them, continue to drink or traffic in ardent spirits.

There must be more done for all the great objects of Christian benevolence. There must be much greater effort for the cause of missions, and education, and the Bible, and all the other branches of religious enterprise, or the church will displease God. Look at it. Think of the mercies we have received, of the wealth, numbers, and prosperity of the church. Have we rendered unto God according to the benefits we have received, so as to show that the church is bountiful, and willing to give their money, and to work for God? No. Far from it. Have we multiplied our means and enlarged our plans, in proportion as the church has increased? Is God satisfied with what has been done, or has he reason to be? Such a revival as has been enjoyed by the churches of America for the last ten years! We ought to have done ten times as much as we have for missions, Bibles, education, tracts, free churches, and in all the ways designed to promote religion and save souls. If the churches do not wake up on this subject, and lay themselves out on a larger scale, they may expect that the revival in the United States will cease.

The Way of Holiness
Phoebe Palmer

Phoebe Palmer (1807-1874) was a Methodist lay revivalist, humanitarian, writer (*The Way of Holiness,* 1845), and hymnologist ("The Cleansing Wave"). By the mid-1830s she was active in a "Tuesday Meeting for the Promotion of Holiness," which established the groundwork for her modified version of John Wesley's perfectionism, or "entire sanctification." Her "altar theology," based on the belief that God sanctifies (makes holy) those who consecrate (set apart) themselves entirely to Him, was later adapted by Holiness denominations such as the Wesleyan Methodists, the Free Methodists, the Church of the Nazarene, and the Salvation Army. Though a feminist who promoted the cause of women's ministries, she penned *The Way of Holiness* in the third person, calling herself "a sister."

Section I.

"Be always ready to give an answer to every man that asketh you a reason of the hope that is within you, with meekness and fear."
—*Peter.*

"I HAVE thought," said one of the children of Zion to the other, as in love they journeyed onward in the way cast up for the ransomed of the Lord to walk in; "I have thought," said he, "whether there is not a *shorter way* of getting into this way of holiness than some of our . . . brethren apprehend?"

"Yes," said the sister addressed, who was a member of the denomination alluded to; "Yes, brother, THERE IS A SHORTER WAY! O! I am sure this long waiting and struggling with the powers of darkness is not necessary. There is a shorter way." And then, with a solemn feeling of responsibility, and with a realizing conviction of the truth ut-

tered, she added, "But, brother, there is but one way."

Days and even weeks elapsed, and yet the question, with solemn bearing, rested upon the mind of that sister. She thought of the affirmative given in answer to the inquiry of the brother—examined yet more closely as the Scriptural foundation upon which the truth of the affirmation rested—and the result of the investigation tended to add still greater confirmation to the belief, that many sincere disciples of Jesus, by various needless perplexities, consume much time in endeavoring to get into this way, which might, more advantageously to themselves and others, be employed in making progress in it, and testifying, from experimental knowledge, of its blessedness.

How many, whom Infinite Love would long since have brought into this state, instead of seeking to be brought into the possession of the blessing at once, are seeking a preparation for the reception of it! They feel that their *convictions* are not deep enough to warrant an approach to the throne of grace, with the confident expectation of receiving the blessing *now*. Just at this point some may have been lingering months and years. Thus did the sister, who so confidently affirmed "there is a shorter way." And here, dear child of Jesus, permit the writer to tell you just how that sister found the "shorter way."

On looking at the requirements of the word of God, she beheld the command, "Be ye holy." She then began to say in her heart, "Whatever my former deficiencies may have been, God requires that I should *now* be holy. Whether *convicted,* or otherwise, *duty is plain.* God requires *present* holiness." On coming to this point, she at once apprehended a simple truth before unthought of, i.e., *Knowledge is conviction.* She well knew that, for a long time, she had been assured that God required holiness. But she had never deemed this knowledge a sufficient plea to take to God—and because of present need, to ask a present bestowment of the gift.

Convinced that in this respect she had mistaken the path, she now, with renewed energy, began to make use of the knowledge already received, and to discern a "shorter way."

Another difficulty by which her course had been delayed she found to be here. She had been accustomed to look at the blessing of holiness as such a high attainment, that her general habit of soul inclined her to think it almost beyond her reach. This erroneous impression rather influenced her to rest the

matter thus:—"I will let every high state of grace, in name, alone, and seek only to be *fully conformed to the will of God, as recorded in his written word.* My chief endeavors shall be centered in the aim to be an humble *Bible Christian.* By the grace of God, all my energies shall be directed to this one point. With this single aim, I will journey onward, even though my faith may be tried to the uttermost by those manifestations being withheld, which have previously been regarded as essential for the establishment of faith."

On arriving at this point, she was enabled to gain yet clearer insight into the simplicity of the way. And it was by this process. After having taken the Bible as the rule of life, instead of the opinions and experience of professors, she found, on taking the blessed word more closely to the companionship of her heart, that no one declaration spoke more appealing to her understanding than this: "Ye are not your own, ye are bought with a price, therefore glorify God in your body and spirit which are his."

By this she perceived the duty of *entire consecration* in a stronger light, and as more sacredly binding, than ever before. Here she saw God as her Redeemer, claiming, by virtue of the great price paid for the redemption of body, soul, and spirit, the *present and entire service* of all these redeemed powers.

By this she saw that if she lived constantly in the entire surrender of all that had been thus dearly purchased unto God, she was but an unprofitable servant; and that, if less than all was rendered, she was worse than unprofitable, inasmuch as she would be guilty of keeping back part of that price which had been purchased unto God: "Not with corruptible things, such as silver and gold, but by the precious blood of Jesus." And after so clearly discerning the will of God concerning her, she felt that the sin of Ananias and Sapphira would be less culpable in the sight of Heaven than her own, should she not at once resolve on living in the *entire* consecration of all her redeemed powers to God.

Deeply conscious of past unfaithfulness, she now determined that the time past should suffice; and with a humility of spirit, induced by a consciousness of not having lived in the performance of such a "reasonable service," she was enabled, through grace, to resolve, with firmness of purpose, that entire devotion of heart and life to God should be the absorbing subject of the succeeding pilgrimage of life.

Section II.

"We by his Spirit prove,
    And know the things of God,
The things which freely of his love
He hath on us bestow'd."

AFTER having thus resolved on devoting the entire service of her heart and life to God, the following questions occasioned much serious solicitude:—How shall I know when I have consecrated all to God? And how ascertain whether God accepts the sacrifice— and how know the manner of its acceptance? Here again the blessed Bible, which she had now taken as her counselor, said to her heart, "We have received not the spirit of the world, but the Spirit which is of God, that we might know the things freely given to us of God."

It was thus she became assured that it was her privilege to know when she had consecrated all to God, and also to know that the sacrifice was *accepted*, and the resolve was solemnly made that the subject should not cease to be absorbing until this knowledge was obtained.

Feeling it a matter of no small importance to stand thus solemnly pledged to God, conscious that sacred responsibilities were included in these engagements, a *realization* of the fact, that neither body, soul, nor spirit, time, talent, nor influence, were, even for one moment, at her own disposal, began to assume the tangibility of living truth to her mind, in a manner not before apprehended.

From a sense of responsibility thus imposed, she began to be more abundant in labors, "instant in season and out of season."

While thus engaged in active service, another difficulty presented itself. How much of self in these performances? said the accuser. For a moment, almost bewildered at being thus withstood, her heart began to sink. She felt most keenly that she had no certain standard to raise up against this accusation?

It was here again that the blessed word sweetly communed with her heart, presenting the marks of the way, by a reference to the admonition of Paul: "Therefore, my beloved brethren, be ye steadfast and unmovable, always abounding in the work of the Lord, forasmuch as ye know that your labor is not in vain in the Lord."

These blessed communings continued thus. If the primitive Christians had the assurance that their labors were in the Lord; and thus enjoyed the heart-inspiring *confidence* that their labors were *not in vain*, because performed in the might of the Spirit, then it is also your privilege to *know* that your labor is in the Lord. It was at this point in her experience that she first perceived the *necessity*, and also the *attainableness* of the witness of *purity of intention*—which, in her petition to God, as most expressive of her peculiar need, she denominated, "The witness that the spring of every motive is pure."

It was by the word of the Lord she became fully convinced that she needed this heart-encouraging confidence in order to insure success in her labors of love. The next step taken was to resolve, as in the presence of the Lord, not to cease importuning the throne of grace until the witness was given "that the spring of every motive was pure."

On coming to this decision, the blessed Word, most encouragingly, yea, and also assuringly said to her heart, "Stand still, and see the salvation of God."

Section III.

"Here, in thine own appointed way,
I wait to learn thy will;
Silent I stand before thy face,
And hear thee say, 'Be still!
Be still! and know that I am God:'
'Tis all I wish to know,
To feel the virtue of thy blood,
And spread its praise below."

THUS admonished, she began to anticipate, with longings unutterable, the fulfillment of the word upon which she had been enabled to rest her hope.

These exercises, though so deep as to assure the heart, most powerfully and permanently, that the word of the Lord is quick and powerful, and sharper than any two-edged sword, piercing to the dividing asunder of the soul and spirit, and of the joints and marrow, and is a discerner of the thoughts and intents of the hear," were not of that distressing character which, according to her preconceived opinions, were necessary, preparatory to entering into a state of holiness.

So far from having those overwhelming perceptions of guilt, on which she afterward saw she had been too much disposed to place reliance, as somewhat meritorious, she was constantly and *consciously* growing in grace daily—yea, even hourly her heavenward progress seemed marked as by the finger of God.

No gloomy fears that she was *not a child of God* dimmed her spiritual horizon, presenting fearful anticipation of impending wrath. There had been a period in her experience, some time previous to that under present consideration, from which she had not *one lingering doubt of her acceptance with God, as a member of the household of faith.* But, conscious that she had *not the witness of entire consecration to God*, neither the assurance that the great deep of her heart, the fountain from whence action emanates, was pure, which at this time stood before the vision of her mind as two distinct objects (yet which, as she afterward perceived, most clearly merged in *one*), and impelled onward also by such an intense desire to be *fruitful in every good work*, the emotions of her spirit could not perhaps be more clearly expressed than in the nervous language of the poet—

> "My heart strings groan with deep
> complaint.
> My flesh lies panting, Lord, for
> thee;
> And every limb, and every joint
> Stretches for perfect purity"

And yet, to continue poetic language, it was a "sweet distress," for the *word of the Lord* continually said to her heart, "The Spirit helpeth our infirmities;" and conscious that she had submitted herself to the dictations of the Spirit, a sacred conviction took possession of her mind that she was being led into all truth.

"Stand still, and see the salvation of God," was now the listening attitude in which her soul eagerly waited before the Lord, and it was but a few hours after the above encouraging admonition had been spoken to her heart that she set apart a season to wait before the Lord, especially for the bestowment of the object, or rather the two distinct objects previously stated.

On first kneeling, she thought of resolving that she would continue to wait before the Lord until the desire of her heart was granted. But the adversary, who had stood ready to withstand every progressive step, suggested, "Be careful, God may disappoint your expectations; and suppose you should be left to wrestle all night; ay, and all the morrow too?"

She had ever felt it a matter of momentous import to say, either with the language of the heart or lip, "I have lifted my hand to God;" and for a moment she hesitated whether she should really determine to continue in a waiting attitude until the desire of her heart was fulfilled; but afterward concluded to rest the matter thus: One duty can never, in the order of God, interfere with another; and, unless necessarily called away by surrounding circumstances, I will, in the strength of grace, wait till my heart is assured, though it may be all night, and all the morrow too.

And here most emphatically could she say, she was led by a "way she knew not;" so simple, so clearly described, and urged by the word of the Lord, and yet so often overlooked, for want of that child-like simplicity which, without reasoning, takes God at his word. It was just while engaged in the act of preparing the way, as she deemed, to some great and undefinable exercise, that the Lord, through the medium of faith in his *written word,* led her astonished soul directly into the "way of holiness," where, with unutterable delight, she found the comprehensive desires of her soul blended and satisfied in the fulfillment of the command, *"Be ye holy."*

It was thus, waiting child of Jesus, that this traveler in the King's highway was directed onward, through the teachings of the word of God and induced so confidently to affirm, in reply to the brother, *"There is a shorter way."*

Human Aliment and the Wines of Scripture
Sylvester Graham

Sylvester Graham (1794-1851) was a Presbyterian minister and health reformer who in his own day was widely regarded as a "wild-eyed fanatic and crank." Ralph Waldo Emerson called him "the prophet of bran bread and pumpkins." Graham believed that the source of America's antebellum problems lay not in slavery but in diet. He wished to "purge the souls of his generation by cleansing their debauched bodies." The culmination of his popular lectures on temperance and physiology in the 1830s was his work *The Science of Human Life* (1839) in which he explained his "Graham System" of vegetarianism and the use of his graham bread. His posthumously edited work *The Philosophy of Sacred History Considered in Relation to Human Aliment and the Wines of Scripture* (1855) showed the relationship between his system and the teachings of the Bible. Ellen G. White of Seventh-day Adventism made reference to Graham's writings in her own works.

Having clearly and fully ascertained the true nature and character of God; the real nature and constitutional character, condition and relations of man; the primary purpose of God, in the creation and earthly existence of man; the great, paramount purpose of God, concerning man, in the economy of grace; and, in a general manner, the causes which render man, as a moral agent, incapable of being so acted on by the moral and spiritual power of God, as to be kept from sin with conscious freedom of choice and action, and which there by hinder the accomplishment of the great purposes of Divine benevolence, and prevent man's being brought into the spiritual kingdom of God, I now proceed to inquire more particularly,—

First, what effects the use of flesh as food, and of wine or alcoholic liquor of any kind, as a drink, have on the condition, character and actions of man, as a subject of the moral and spiritual government of God, with reference to the fulfillment of the great purposes of Divine benevolence, and,

Second, what are the bearings or teachings of the Bible, as a whole, in relation to these points: or, in other words, how far the Sacred Scriptures may, by accurate interpretation, be shown to be in harmony with the true revelations of God, in the volume of Nature.

It is evident that the first of these particular subjects of investigation, is mainly a question of natural Science, and as such, must be solved by the revelations of God in the volume of Nature. For, we have seen that, every law and principle, and property of Nature, is an institution of the Divine will,—that Nature is, in truth, the first great

Volume of Divine Revelation, in which the deeply written will of God lies ever ready to be disclosed to the human mind by the true developments of science, and by accurate experience,—that the Revealed Word is but a Supplement to this first great Volume, and, in strictness, as a pure revelation, contains, principally, Divine instructions concerning moral and spiritual things, which Nature speaks not of, or but faintly implies, or dimly indicates; and that the truth of Nature and the true meaning of the Revealed Word, must be in harmony; and, consequently, it is impossible that the true meaning of the Revealed Word can, as a permanent law, be contrary to the laws of Nature. The truth of natural science, therefore, is the truth of God, and always comes with Divine authority to man:—and the Bible, as the revealed word of God, must, when accurately interpreted, be perfectly consistent with what is true in chemistry, and mineralogy, and botany, and zoology, and astronomy, and every other natural science. Yet the Bible was not given to teach us the natural sciences; and no correct philosopher thinks of going to the Bible to study these sciences. To ascertain what is true in these, he goes to the Volume of Nature as the primary and irreversible code of the omniscient and omnipotent Creator and Ruler of all things: And, in regard to his Bible, he is satisfied if he finds nothing in it, which is apparently incompatible with the demonstrations of natural science; and pleased if he finds it confirmed by scientific truth: knowing that the truth of Nature must stand, whether the apparent meaning of any particular portion of the Sacred Scriptures, agrees with it or not. He, therefore, who truly loves and reverences the Bible as the revealed word of God, will not be forward to

introduce it into controversies of a scientific nature, and oppose his interpretations of it to the demonstrations of science, in such a manner as to make it appear that the Bible and the truths of natural science, are at variance: for he knows that this must only serve to invalidate his Bible, and not the truth of science. But, the true philosopher, who cordially and understandingly loves and reverences his Bible, will, as a scientific man, in all his investigations, and researches, pursue the truth for the truth's sake; and when he has fully ascertained the truth of science, if he finds any *apparent* want of agreement between this and his Bible, he will, with the spirit of truth still ruling his soul, honestly set about such an examination of the matter, as will enable him to show that the disagreement is only *apparent*, and that when accurately understood, the Bible perfectly harmonizes with scientific truth; or at least, that, the true meaning of the Revealed Word is not incompatible with the truth of natural science. . . .

In this manner only, can the particular question now before us, be correctly met and accurately solved. I affirm that the use of flesh as food, and alcoholic liquor as a drink, is incompatible with the highest and best state of human nature. But immediately, a multitude of voices are heard vociferating—"You are wrong, Sir! you are wrong! The Bible explicitly declares that God gave Noah and his family permission to eat every moving thing that liveth; and that, Abraham the chosen of God, gave the angels of the Lord flesh to eat; and that, God commanded the children of Israel to eat flesh at the supper of the passover, and miraculously supplied them with flesh to eat in the wilderness; and that, Moses, under Divine inspiration, permitted the Jews to eat flesh, and commanded them to supply the priests with it for food; and that, God caused the ravens to carry flesh to the prophet Elijah for his food; and that, our Saviour and his inspired apostles ate animal food; and Paul declared that 'every creature of God is good and nothing to be refused, if it be received with thanksgiving.' And the Bible also, expressly permits the use of wine as a drink; and speaks of it as a blessing;—and Christ drank it and gave it to his disciples; and made it for others to drink; and instituted it in the sacramental supper, as a perpetual memorial of his blood shed for a sinful race; and Paul ordered Timothy to drink it; and the primitive Christians drank it under the apostolic sanction."—I reply to this multitude of gain sayers, I cannot enter into any controversy with you, in regard to what the Bible, according to your understanding of it, teaches on this subject.—I shall not dispute with you about the meaning of words. For, I regard such controversies and disputes, as fruitful of no good, and as serving in no measure to the clear and satisfactory ascertainment of truth. The question before us, is not a question of Revelation, but of natural science; and as such, I have fairly met it, and thoroughly examined it, and fully solved it, in my Lectures, on the Science of Human Life.—In those lectures, I have clearly and incontrovertibly shown that, all the evidence of comparative anatomy, when correctly apprehended and accurately estimated, goes to prove conclusively, that man is naturally, in no measure a flesh-eating animal, but is organized to subsist wholly on the products of the vegetable kingdom. And with equal conclusiveness, I have also shown that all the evidence of physiology in relation to the matter, concurs in the demon-

stration of the same truth: that, taking man as a species extending through all generations, rather than as an individual in particular circumstances, and, taking the most perfect state of the human constitution, as the true criterion or point of departure and reference in all reasoning on this subject, flesh-meat, in comparison with the best vegetable food, is much more stimulating in proportion to the nourishment which it actually imparts to the body—renders the general physiological action of the organic system more rapid and intense,—accelerates all the vital functions, and deteriorates all the functional results,—increases the expenditure of the vital properties of the tissues and functional powers of the organs, and more rapidly wears out the vital constitution;—that, it is not so conducive to the healthy growth, and full development, and true proportions, and perfect symmetry and beauty of the body;—that, it is not so conducive to suppleness, activity, agility and strength; and will not sustain man so well and so long in hard labor and under fatigue, and exposure to changes of weather and of climate;—that, it tends to induce acute and chronic disease, diminishes the vital power of the body to resist the action of disturbing and morbific causes and noxious agents; and, therefore, is neither so well adapted to preserve health and prevent disease, nor to enable the diseased body to recover health; nor is it so conducive to long life and true bodily comfort and enjoyment;—that, it diminishes the sensorial power of the nervous system, impairs the special senses, and the powers of perception and reflection, and renders the mind less active, clear and vigorous and spiritual;—that it increases the influences of the animal appetites, desires and propensities, on the intellectual, moral and religious faculties and renders man more sensual, passionate and brutish,— more immoral, vicious and criminal, and less able to perceive and understand and obey moral and religious truth.,—In short, that, the use of flesh as food, serves to deteriorate the whole complex nature of man,— to multiply disease and suffering, and error and wickedness in the human world, and abbreviate the period of human life, and increase the power of the animal over the intellectual and moral and religious man, and render man less able to understand the true nature and character of God, and the true relations between God and man, and less able to be actuated by any other than selfish and sensual motives, and thus serves to sink man into a deeper and darker and more brutally savage state of barbarian heathenism.

Again, I have shown in my Lectures on the Science of Life, that, alcohol is a destructive poison to the vital constitution of man; and always immediately impairs the vital properties of the tissues on which it acts; and, when concentrated to a pure state, a small quantity of it in the human stomach, almost instantaneously destroys life. And, however diluted the form, the poisonous or *anti-vital* character of alcohol always remains; and, to the extent of its energy, immediately impairs the vital properties and tends to the destruction of the vital constitution of the parts on which it acts: and, by causing a vital reaction or antagonism, preternaturally excites the whole organic system; and, in proportion to its quantity, throws the organs into a violent action,— disturbs all the functions and deteriorates all the functional results,— increases the exhaustion of the constitutional powers,—abbreviates the period of life, and so acts on the whole complex nature of man, as to tend to every kind of disease and suffering in the body, and to every kind of injury and wickedness, and the greatest misery in the soul, and to the utter destruction of every organic, and animal, and intellectual, and moral, and religious, and social faculty, and power.—I have also shown that, alcohol is not produced by any formative process in nature, but by a process of decay or destruction, called, by the chemists, "vinous fermentation," in which the saccharine matter or sugar which is produced by the vital economy of organized bodies, and which is an organic element, is resolved to chemical elements and, at the same time, in consequence of confinement, by human art, some of these chemical elements, as they are set free, or produced by the destruction of the saccharine constitution, enter into the alcoholic constitution by a combination peculiar to this process. The deadly poison called alcohol, is, therefore, entirely a result of fermentation, and in no measure, of distillation; and has precisely the same nature and properties wherever it is found;— precisely the same, whether in rum, brandy, gin, whiskey, wine, beer, cider or any other kind of distilled or fermented liquors. And although when taken in small quantities and in a diluted form, its pernicious effects are exceedingly insidious, and the progress of its work of death is by imperceptible degrees, yet however diluted the form and however small the quantity, its immediate and direct effect on the living tissues of the human body, is, from constitutional necessity, always pernicious; and from the same necessity, its pernicious energy always simultaneously assails the whole complex nature of man. So that, in the day man drinks of it, he "*begins to die,*" in the fullest import of the language of the primal prohibition.—

The direct and certain tendency of alcoholic liquor as a drink, therefore, like that of flesh as food, but in a vastly greater degree, is to sensualize, debase and destroy man's whole nature; to increase the power of the animal over the intellectual, and moral and religious man, to render man less able to understand the true nature and character of God, and the true relations between God and man—less able to perceive and understand and obey moral and religious truth.—In short, its direct and powerful tendency is to sink man in spirit and soul and body, into the lowest and most brutalized state of human degradation and perdition.

The use of flesh as food, and wine or any other kind of alcoholic liquor as a drink, therefore, is utterly incompatible with the highest and best and happiest state of man's complex organic, animal, intellectual, moral and religious nature;—serves to keep man out of the spiritual kingdom of God,—to prevent the success of the Divine economy of grace,—to retard the development of the moral and spiritual government of God in the human world, and thus to hinder the accomplishment of the great purposes of Divine benevolence.

Let it be clearly understood, however, that I do not place flesh-meat in the same category with alcohol, as a poison. I do not affirm that flesh-meat is in any degree, an actual poison to the human constitution; nor that, the habitual dietetic use of it, in moderate quantities and under proper regulations, is, in all conditions and circumstances, a source of more immediate and permanent evil than good to man as an individual. On the contrary, I freely admit, that, man, as an individual, may be brought into such a condition and placed in such circumstances as will render it both necessary and proper,—nay, even best to eat flesh. But if there is any truth in anatomical and physiological science, and in the demonstrations of human history, I have fully and conclusively shown, in my lectures on the Science of Human Life, that the use of flesh as food is not conducive to the highest and best state of the complex nature of man as a species, extending through all generations. Human experience has fully and largely confirmed the doctrine of the Sacred Scriptures that man has the constitutional capability of deriving nourishment from "every moving thing that liveth;" and that, he may habitually use flesh as food, from generation to generation, and still, as a species, retain sufficient constitutional power to perpetuate himself, and in a measure, fulfill the relations and duties of individual and social life. Yet it is none the less true that he cannot attain to the highest and best state of which his nature is capable, while he continues to eat flesh.

Do my opposers still persist in asserting their Bible authority for the dietetic use of flesh and wine? Then, I reply to them, your pertinacity is blind and mischievous: for it is infinitely easier for you to bring the authority of your Bible into discredit, in such a controversy, than to shake these scientific demonstrations. You may just as well tell me, at this day, that you have Bible authority for the doctrine that the earth stands still, and the sun moves round it once in twenty-four hours, as to tell me that you have Bible authority for the doctrine that the use of flesh as food, and wine or any other kind of alcohol liquor as a drink, is compatible with the highest and best state of which human nature is capable: for the later proposition is quite as credible as the other, to an accurately informed mind.—Do they captiously answer, "O that is just the way of all you vain speculators who become 'wise above what is written!' The Bible and every thing else must give way to make room for your favorite theories?"—I respectfully say to them, I trust that I love and reverence the Bible as truly and as much as you do. But it is not the print and paper and binding of the Book that I reverence.—I love and reverence the Divine truth and spirit of the Bible. And now, I am ready to take the Bible and sit down with you, and, in the light of the scientific demonstrations before us, carefully and prayerfully study it from beginning to end; and show you that every part of the Bible, when accurately interpreted, is perfectly consistent with these scientific demonstrations. And when I have done this, if you assert that I have not succeeded in *proving, to your satisfaction*, from the Bible, that the use of flesh as food, and alcoholic liquor as a drink is incompatible with the highest and best state of which human nature is capable, then I shall say I undertook no such thing!—the proposition before us, does not belong to Revelation, but to natural science, and therefore it is impossible to prove either the affirmative or negative of it from the Bible, so conclusively as to satisfy all minds, and put an end to controversy concerning it. But it must forever remain an unsettled and vexed question, so long as the reasoning in regard to it, is founded on evidence drawn from the Scriptures.—I have fully demonstrated its truth on its own legitimate ground, as a proposition in natural science; and I went with you to the Bible, not to prove from it, the truth of the same proposition; but, to show you that the Bible may, upon correct principles of interpretation, be made to har-

monize perfectly, with those demonstrations of natural science; and if I have not satisfied you on that point, you had better endeavor to harmonize the Bible with those demonstrations, in a manner more satisfactory to yourselves; for while the constitutional laws which God has established in the nature of things, remain in their integrity, the truth of those scientific demonstrations must, of necessity remain. And, let it also be remembered that, inasmuch as the great economy of Divine benevolence embraces man's whole nature, and aims as truly at the health and happiness of his body as of his soul, the Bible, though it does not explicitly teach the science of physiology, does, in its moral and spiritual precepts and requirements, implicitly demand that man should, to the full extent of his capabilities, and opportunities and means, acquire that knowledge of the nature and properties of things, which will enable him in the greatest degree, to maintain the highest well-being of his whole nature, and relations. . . .

But what do the Scriptures mean when they affirm that without holiness no man shall see the Lord? and what has this sentiment to do with the use of flesh and wine? The Scriptures mean that, in the very nature of things, without spiritual cleanness no man can have a true perception of spiritual things, and therefore cannot see the Lord; or, in other words, that state of things in which all the passions, lusts, exercises, operations, desires, propensities, and appetites of the whole animal, intellectual, and moral nature of man, are brought into conformity to the Holy Spirit, is essentially necessary in order to a true spiritual perception of the divine nature and character of the Lord; and wine-drinking necessarily, to the full extent of its effects on the human system, increases the power with which "the flesh lusteth against the spirit," and consequently is calculated to increase the influence of the carnal appetites, propensities, desires, and passions on the operations of the intellectual and moral faculties, and thus, in a spiritual and moral sense, darken the understanding, and deprave the con-science: so that they who are wedded to their lusts are neither able to perceive the beauty of holiness nor the loathsome deformity of their own uncleanness. And hence it is that they who are given up to these strong delusions, feel themselves injured and even persccutcd when any efforts are made to sanctify them from their abominable pollutions. "Let us alone. What have we to do with thee?" &c., is always the cry of these deluded beings in all parts and ages of the world, whenever the true Spirit of Christ moves any one to preach to them the sanctifying truth of God. Nevertheless, Jesus, with infinite benevolence for abused humanity, cast out such evil spirits, and promised that his true and faithful followers should do even greater works than he did, by the instrumentality of his Spirit and his truth.

Flesh-eating, though by no means to be compared, in any respect, to the use of wine and other intoxicating substances, yet, as we have already seen, tends more than a well-chosen vegetable diet to the development and depravity of the animal propensities and passions, diminishes the sensorial power of the nervous system, impairs the intellectual and moral faculties, and increases the influence of the carnal nature of man over his mental and moral nature: or, to use the language of Paul, "it increases the power of the law of sin in our members."

But we shall lose much of the force of our argument if we do not continually keep in view the incontrovertible truth, that the health and happiness of the body of man is as truly a final cause of the gospel economy as the salvation of the soul; and that such is the compound nature and complicated structure of man, that the highest and best interests of the soul cannot be secured while the true interests of the body are violated or neglected: and therefore, the effects of intoxicating substances and of flesh-meat on the human body, in causing or aggravating the disorders and diseases which it suffers, and in producing is premature death, are fully to be taken into the account in the gospel view of the subject. And that we may the more accurately appreciate the extent of these evils, we should bear in mind that the same prophets who, speaking as they were moved by the Holy Spirit, foretold the coming of Christ and the introduction and effects of the gospel dispensation, clearly specified, among other legitimate results of the genuine operations of that dispensation, that the evil and rancorous passions of mankind should be subdued, and men should become peaceful and gentle, and kind and benevolent, and philanthropic and holy; and that all disease should be removed from among them, and human life should be greatly prolonged. These things, it is true, are generally supposed to refer more particularly to the Millennium. But what is the Millennium, other than that state of things on earth in which the gospel principles are fully understood and obeyed in the spirit?—for this would be the reign of Christ. And so perfectly is the gospel adapted to all the laws and conditions and relations of human nature, that it only needs to be thus universally understood and obeyed, to produce, as a natural and necessary consequence, all the blessings promised in the Millennium. And be assured, that until the gospel shall be regarded and obeyed as a scheme of divine benevolence, adapted to and embracing the whole nature of man, and aiming as really at the welfare of his body as of his soul, and as truly fitted and designed to secure his happiness in time as in eternity, the Millennium of our prayers and expectations will never be realized on earth.

6 Slavery

You shall not covet your neighbor's house; you shall not covet your neighbor's wife or his male servant or his female servant or his ox or his donkey or anything that belongs to your neighbor.

—Ex. 20:17

The Bible Against Slavery
Theodore D. Weld

Theodore D. Weld (1803-1895) was perhaps the most famous of the converts of Charles Finney. Immediately upon his conversion in 1825, Weld came under the influence of numerous lay workers who devoted much of their time to various social reforms. One of these was James G. Birney, a prominent lawyer and planter, with whom he exchanged views on slavery in 1832. About this time the newly formed Lane Seminary in Cincinnati gained the famed Lyman Beecher as its president, a move which led Weld to enter Lane in the fall of 1833. He soon converted Lane into a hotbed of abolitionism and would gain a reputation for his radical anti-slavery crusades. In 1837 he wrote one of abolitionism's most powerful tracts, *The Bible Against Slavery*, which was published the next year by the American Anti-Slavery Society in New York.

The spirit of slavery never seeks refuge in the Bible on its own accord. The horns of the altar are its last resort—seized only in desperation, as it rushes from the terror of the avenger's arm. Like other unclean spirits, it "hateth the light, neither cometh to the light, lest its deeds should be reproved." Goaded to frenzy in its conflicts with conscience and common sense, denied all quarter, and hunted from every covert, it vaults over the sacred inclosure and courses up and down the Bible, "seeking rest, and finding none." THE LAW OF LOVE, glowing on every page, flashes around it an omnipresent anguish and despair. It shrinks from the hated light, and howls under the consuming touch, as demons quailed before the Son of God, and shrieked, "Torment us not." At last, it slinks away under the types of the Mosaic system, and seeks to burrow out of sight among their shadows. Vain hopes! Its asylum is its sepulchre; its city of refuge, the city of destruction. It flies from light into the sun; from heat, into devouring fire; and from the voice of God into the thickest of His thunders.

Definition of Slavery

If we would know whether the Bible sanctions slavery, we must determine *what slavery is*. An element, is one thing; a relation, another; an appendage, another. Relations and appendages presuppose other things to which they belong. To regard them as the things themselves, or as constituent parts of them, leads to endless fallacies. Mere political disabilities are often confounded with slavery; so are many relations, and tenures, indispensable to the social state. We will specify some of these.

1. **Privation of Suffrage**. Then minors are slaves.

2. **Ineligibility to Office**. Then females are slaves.

3. **Taxation Without Representation**. Then slaveholders in the District of Columbia are slaves.

4. **Privation of One's Oath in Law**. Then atheists are slaves.

5. **Privation of Trial by Jury**. Then all in France are slaves.

6. **Being Required to Support a Particular Religion**. Then the people of England are slaves.

7. **Apprenticeship**. The rights and duties of master and apprentice are correlative. The *claim* of each upon the other results from his *obligation* to the other. Apprenticeship is based on the principle of equivalent for value received. The rights of the apprentice are secured, equally with those of the master. Indeed while the law is *just* to the former it is *benevolent* to the latter; its main design being rather to benefit the apprentice than the master. To the master it secures a mere compensation—to the apprentice, both a compensation and a virtual gratuity in addition, he being of the two in greatest favor. The law not only recognizes the *right* of the apprentice of a reward for his labor, but appoints the wages, and enforces the payment. The master's claim covers only the *services* of the apprentice. The apprentice's claim covers *equally* the services of the master. Neither can hold the other as property; but each holds property in the services of the other, and BOTH EQUALLY. Is this slavery?

8. **Filial Subordination and Parental Claims**. Both are nature's dictates, and intrinsic elements of the social state; the natural affections which blend parent and child in one, excite each to discharge those offices incidental to the relation, and are a shield for mutual protection. The parent's legal claim to the child's services is a slight return for the care and toil of his rearing exclusively of outlays for support and education. This provision, is, with the mass of mankind, indispensable in the preservation of the family state. The

child, in helping his parents, helps himself—increases a common stock, in which he has a share; while his most faithful services do but acknowledge a debt that money cannot cancel.

9. **Claims of Government on Subjects**. Governments owe their subjects protection: subjects owe just governments allegiance and support. The obligations of both are reciprocal, and the benefits received by both are mutual, equal, and voluntarily rendered.

10. **Bondage for Crime**. Must innocence be punished because guilt suffers penalties? True, the criminal works for the government without pay; and well he may. He owes the government. A century's work would not pay its drafts on him. He will die a public defaulter. Because laws make men pay their debts, will those be forced to pay who owe nothing? The law makes no criminal, PROPERTY. It restrains his liberty, and makes him pay something, a mere penny in the pound, of his debt to the government; but it does not make him a chattel. Test it. To own property, is to own its product. Are children born of convicts, government property? Besides, can *property* be guilty? Can *chattels* deserve punishment?

11. **Restraints Upon Freedom**. Children are restrained by parents, pupils by teachers, patients by physicians, corporations by charters, and legislatures by constitutions. Embargoes, tariffs, quarantine, and all other laws, keep men from doing as they please. Restraints are the web of civilized society, warp and woof. Are they slavery; then a government of LAW is the climax of slavery!

12. **Involuntary or Compulsory Service**. A juryman is impanelled against his will, and sit he *must*. A sheriff orders his posse; bystanders *must* turn in. Men are *compelled* to remove nuisances, pay fines and taxes, support their families, and "turn to the right as the law directs," however much against their wills. Are they therefore slaves? To confound slavery with involuntary service is absurd. Slavery is a *condition*. The slave's *feelings* toward it cannot alter its nature. Whether he desires or detests it, the condition remains the same. The slave's willingness to be a slave is no palliation of the slave-holder's guilt. Suppose he should really believe himself a chattel, and consent to be so regarded by others, would that *make* him a chattel, or make those guiltless who *hold* him as such? I may be sick of life, and I tell the assassin so that stabs me; is he any the less a murderer? Does my consent to his crime, atone for by my partnership in his guilt, blot out his part of it? The slave's willingness to be a slave, so far from lessening the guilt of his "owner," aggravates it. If slavery has so palsied his mind that he looks upon himself as a chattel, and consents to be one, actually to hold him as such falls in with his delusion, and confirms the impious falsehood. These very feelings and convictions of the slave (if such were possible) increase a hundredfold the guilt of the master, and call upon him in thunder, immediately

to recognize him as a MAN, and thus break the sorcery that cheats him out of his birthright—the consciousness of his worth and destiny.

Many of the foregoing conditions are *appendages* of slavery, but no one, nor all of them together, constitute its intrinsic unchanging element.

ENSLAVING MEN IS REDUCING THEM TO ARTICLES OF PROPERTY—making free agents, chattels—converting *persons* into *things*—sinking immortality into *merchandise*. A *slave* is one held in this condition. In law, "he owns nothing, and can acquire nothing." His right to himself is abrogated. If he say *my* hands, *my* body, *my* mind, *myself*, they are figures of speech. To *use himself* for his own good, is a *crime*. To keep what he earns, is *stealing*. To take his body into his own keeping, is *insurrection*. In a word, the profit of his master is made the END of his being, and he, a *mere means* to that end—a mere means to an end into which his interests do not enter, of which they constitute no portion. MAN, sunk to a *thing*! the intrinsic element, the *principle* of slavery; MEN, bartered, leased, mortgaged, bequeathed, invoiced, shipped in cargoes, stored as goods, taken on executions, and knocked off at a public outcry! Their *rights*, another's conveniences; their interests, wares on sale; their happiness, a household utensil; their personal inalienable ownership, a serviceable article or a plaything, as best suits the humour of the hour; their deathless nature, conscience, social affectations, sympathies, hopes—marketable commodities! We repeat it, THE REDUCTION OF PERSONS TO THINGS! Not robbing a man of privileges, but of *himself*; not loading him with burdens, but making him a *beast of burden*; not restraining liberty, but subverting it; not curtailing rights, but abolishing them; not inflicting personal cruelty, but annihilating *personality*; not exacting involuntary labor, but sinking man into an *implement* of labor; not abridging human comforts, but abrogating human *nature*; not depriving an animal of immunities, but despoiling a rational being of attributes—uncreating a MAN, to make room for a *thing*!

That this is American slavery, is shown by the laws of slave states. Judge Stroud, in his "Sketch of the Laws relating to Slavery," says, "The cardinal principle of slavery, that the slave is not to be ranked among sentient beings, but among *things*—obtains an undoubted law in all of these [the slave] states." The law of South Carolina says, "Slaves shall be deemed, held, taken, reputed, and adjudged in law to be chattels personal in the hands of their owners and possessors, and their executors, administrators, and assigns, to ALL INTENTS, CONSTRUCTIONS, AND PURPOSES WHATSOEVER." *Brev. Dig., 229*. In Louisiana, "A slave is one who is in the power of a master to whom he belongs; the master may sell him, dispose of his person, his industry, and his labor; he can do nothing, possess nothing, nor acquire any thing, but what must belong to his master." *Civ. Code*, Art. 35.

This is American slavery. The eternal distinction between a person and a thing, trampled under foot—the crowning distinction of all others—alike the source, the test, and the measure of their value—the rational, immortal principle, consecrated by God to universal homage in a baptism of glory and honor, by the gift of his Son, his Spirit, his word, his presence, providence, and power; his shield, and staff, and sheltering wing; his opening heavens, and angels ministering, and chariots of fire, and songs of morning stars, and a great voice in heaven proclaiming eternal sanctions, and confirming the word with signs following.

Having stated the *principle* of American slavery, we ask, does THE BIBLE SANCTION SUCH A PRINCIPLE?" "To the *law* and the testimony!"

The Moral Law Against Slavery

Just after the Israelites were emancipated from their bondage in Egypt, while they stood before Sinai to receive the law, as the trumpet waxed louder, and the mount quaked and blazed, God spake the ten commandments from the midst of clouds and thunderings. *Two* of those commandments deal death to slavery. "THOU SHALT NOT STEAL," or, "thou shalt not take from another what *belongs* to him." All man's powers are God's gift to HIM. Each of them is a part of himself, and all of them together constitute himself. All else that belongs to him, because the principal does; the product is his, because he is the producer. Ownership of any thing, is ownership of its *use*. The right to use according to will, is *itself* ownership. The eighth commandment presupposes and assumes the right of every man to his powers, and their product. Slavery robs of both. A man's right to himself, is the only right absolutely original and intrinsic—his

right to anything else is merely *relative* to this, is derived from it, and held only by virtue of it. SELF-RIGHT is the *foundation right*—the *post in the middle*, to which all other rights are fastened. Slave-holders, when talking about their RIGHT to their slaves, always assume their own right to them-selves. What slave-holder ever undertook to prove his right to himself? He knows it to be a self-evident proposition, that a *man belongs to himself*—that the right is intrinsic and absolute. In making out his own title, he makes out the title of every human being. As the fact of being *a man* is itself the title, the whole human family have one common title deed. If one man's title is valid, all are valid. If one is worthless, all are. To deny the validity of the *slave's* title is to deny the validity of *his own*; and yet in the act of making a man a slave, the slave-holder *asserts* the validity of his own title, while he seizes him as his property who has the *same* title. Further, in making him a slave, he does not merely disfranchise of humanity *one* individual, but UNIVERSAL MAN. He destroys the foundations. He annihilates *all rights*. He attacks not only the human race, but *universal being*, and rushes upon JEHOVAH. For rights are *rights*; God's are no more—man's are no less.

The eighth commandment forbids the taking of *any part* of that which belongs to another. Slavery takes the *whole*. Does the same Bible which prohibits the taking of any thing from him, sanction the taking of *every* thing? Does it thunder wrath against the man who robs his neighbor of a *cent*, yet commission him to rob his neighbor of *himself*? Slaveholding is the highest possible violation of the eighth commandment. To take from a man his earnings, is theft. But to take the earner, is a compound, life-long theft—supreme robbery that vaults up the climax at leap—the dread, terrific, giant robbery, that towers among other robberies a solitary horror. The eighth commandment forbids the taking away, and the tenth adds, "Thou shalt not *covet* any thing that is thy neighbor's"; thus guarding every man's right to himself and property, by making not only the actual taking away a sin, but even that state of mind which would *tempt* to it. Who ever made human beings slaves, without *coveting* them? Why take from them their time, labor, liberty, right of self-preservation and improvement, their right to acquire property, to worship according to conscience, to search the Scriptures, to live with their families, and their right to their own bodies, if they do not *desire* them? They COVET them for purposes of gain, convenience, lust of dominion, of sensual gratification, of pride and ostentation. THEY break the tenth commandment, and pluck down upon their heads the plagues that are written in the book. Ten commandments constitute the brief compound of human duty. *Two* of these brand slavery as sin.

What to the Slave is the Fourth of July?
Frederick Douglass

Frederick Douglass (1818-1895) was born a slave in Maryland, living his first twenty years on several slave plantations. He escaped from slavery in Baltimore in 1838 and fled to the North to live out his vision of freedom. The next year he purchased his first copy of William Lloyd Garrison's radical abolitionist newspaper, the *Liberator*, his first step towards his transformation into an abolitionist leader. In 1841, when the Massachusetts Anti-Slavery Society asked Douglass to join it as an agent, he committed his life to the "great work" of abolition and black liberation. He became well known for both his writing and speaking against the practice of slavery. His speeches were powerful and moving accounts of his experiences as a slave. On July 5, 1852, he delivered an address in Rochester, New York, "What to the Slave is the Fourth of July?" In the excerpts of the address which follow, he distinguished between true and false Americans and Christians, assuming the role of prophet called to warn American society against the error of its ways.

. . . Fellow Citizens, I am not wanting in respect for the fathers of this republic. The signers of the Declaration of Independence were brave men. They were great men too— great enough to give fame to a great age. It does not often happen to a nation to raise, at one time, such a number of truly great men. The point from which I am compelled to view them is not, certainly, the most favorable; and yet I cannot contemplate their great deeds with less than admiration. They were statesman, patriots and heroes, and for the good they did, and the principles they contended for, I will unite with you to honor their memory. They loved their country better than their own private interests; and, though this is not the highest form of human excellence, all will concede that it is a rare virtue, and that when it is exhibited, it ought to command respect. He who will, intelligently, lay down his life for his country, is a man whom it is not in human nature to despise. Your fathers staked their lives, their fortunes, and their sacred honor, on the cause of their country. In their admiration of liberty, they lost sight of all other interests.

They were peace men; but they preferred revolution to peaceful submission to bondage. They were quiet men; but they did not shrink from agitating against oppression. They showed forbearance; but that they knew its limits. They believed in order; but not in the order of tyranny. With them, nothing was "*settled*" that was not right. With them, justice, liberty and humanity were "*final*"; not slavery and oppression. You may well cherish the memory of such men. They were great in their day and generation. Their solid manhood stands out the more as we contrast it with these degenerate times.

How circumspect, exact and proportionate were all their movements! How unlike the politicians of an hour! Their statesmanship looked beyond the passing moment, and stretched away in strength into the distant future. They seized upon eternal principles, and set a glorious example in their defence. Mark them!

Fully appreciating the hardship to be encountered, firmly believing in the right of their cause, honorably inviting the scrutiny of an on-looking world, reverently appealing to heaven to attest their sincerity, soundly comprehending the solemn responsibility they were about to assume, wisely measuring the terrible odds against them, your fathers, the fathers of this republic, did, most deliberately, under the inspiration of a glorious patriotism, and with a sublime faith in the great principles of justice and freedom, lay deep the corner-stone of the national superstructure, which has risen and still rises in grandeur around you.

Of this fundamental work, this day is the anniversary. Our eyes are met with demonstrations of joyous enthusiasm. Banners and pennants wave exultingly on the breeze. The din of business, too, is hushed. Even Mammon seems to have quitted his grasp on this day. The ear-piercing fife and the stirring drum unite their accents with the ascending peal of a thousand church bells. Prayers are made, hymns are sung, and sermons are preached in honor of this day; while the quick martial tramp of a great and multitudinous nation, echoed back by all the hills, valleys and mountains of a vast continent, bespeak the occasion one of thrilling and universal interest—a nation's jubilee.

Friends and citizens, I need not enter further into the causes which led to this anniversary. Many of you understand them better than I do. You could instruct me in regard to them. That is a branch of knowledge in which you feel, perhaps, a much deeper interest than your speaker. The causes which led to the separation of the colonies from the British crown have never lacked for a tongue. They have all been taught in your common schools, narrated at your firesides, unfolded from your pulpits, and thundered from your legislative halls, and are as familiar to you as household words. They form the staple of your national poetry and eloquence.

I remember, also, that, as a people, Americans are remarkably familiar with all facts which make in their own favor. This is esteemed by some as a national trait— perhaps a national weakness. It is a fact, that whatever makes for the wealth or for the reputation of Americans, and can be had *cheap*! will be found by Americans. I shall not be charged with slandering Americans, if I say I think the American side of any question may be safely left in American hands.

I leave, therefore, the great deeds of your fathers to other gentlemen whose claim to have been regularly descended will be less likely to be disputed than mine!

The Present

My business, if I have any here to-day, is with the present. The accepted time with God and his cause is the ever-living now.

"Trust no future, however pleasant,
Let the dead past bury its dead;
Act, act in the living present,
Heart within, and God overhead."

We have to do with the past only as we can make it useful to the present and to the future. To all inspiring motives, to noble deeds which can be gained from the past, we are welcome. But now is the time, the important time. Your fathers have lived, died, and have done much of it well. You live and must die, and you must do your work. You have no right to enjoy a child's share in the labor of your fathers, unless your children are to be blest by your labors. You have no right to wear out and waste the hard-earned fame of your fathers to cover your indolence. Sydney Smith tells us that men seldom eulogize the wisdom and virtues of their fathers, but to excuse some folly or wickedness of their own. This truth is not a doubtful one. There are illustrations of it near and remote, ancient and modern. It was fashionable, hundreds of years ago, for the children of Jacob to boast, we have "Abraham to our father," when they had long lost Abraham's faith and spirit. That people contented themselves under the shadow of Abraham's great name, while they repudiated the deeds which made his name great. Need I remind you that a similar thing is being done all over this country to-day? Need I tell you that the Jews are not the only people who built the tombs of the prophets, and garnished the sepulchres of the righteous?

Washington could not die till he had broken the chains of his slaves. Yet his monument is built up by the price of human blood, and the traders in the bodies and souls of men, shout—"We have Washington to be *our father*." Alas! that it should be so; yet so it is.

"The evil that men do, lives after them,
The good is oft' interred with their bones."

Fellow-citizens, pardon me, allow me to ask, why am I called upon to speak here to-day? What have I, or those I represent, to do with your national independence? Are the great principles of political freedom and of natural justice, embodied in that Declaration of Independence, extended to us? and am I, therefore, called upon to bring our humble offering to the national altar, and to confess the benefits and express devout gratitude for the blessings resulting from your independence to us?

Would to God, both for your sakes and ours, that an affirmative answer could be truthfully returned to these questions! Then would my task be light, and my burden easy and delightful. For *who* is there so cold, that a nation's sympathy could not warm him? Who so obdurate and dead to the claims of gratitude, that would not thankfully acknowledge such priceless benefits? Who so stolid and selfish, that would not give his voice to swell the hallelujahs of a nation's jubilee, when the chains of servitude had been torn from his limbs? I am not that man. In a case like that, the dumb might eloquently speak, and the "lame man leap as an hart."

But, such is not the state of the case. I say it with a sad sense of the disparity between us.

I am not included within the pale of this glorious anniversary! Your high independence only reveals the immeasurable distance between us. The blessings in which you, this day, rejoice, are not enjoyed in common. The rich inheritance of justice, liberty, prosperity and independence, bequeathed by your fathers, is shared by you, not by me. The sunlight that brought life and healing to you, has brought stripes and death to me. This Fourth [of] July is *yours*, not *mine*. *You* may rejoice, *I* must mourn. To drag a man in fetters into the grand illuminated temple of liberty, and call upon him to join you in joyous anthems, were inhuman mockery and sacrilegious irony. Do you mean, citizens, to mock me, by asking me to speak to-day? If so, there is a parallel to your conduct. And let me warn you that it is dangerous to copy the example of a nation whose crimes, towering up to heaven, were thrown down by the breath of the Almighty, burying that nation in irrecoverable ruin! I can to-day take up the plaintive lament of a peeled and woe-smitten people!

"By the rivers of Babylon, there we sat down. Yea! we wept when we remembered Zion. We hanged our harps upon the willows in the midst thereof. For there, they that carried us away captive, required of us a song; and they who wasted us required of us mirth, saying, Sing us one of the songs of Zion. How can we sing the Lord's song in a strange land? If I forget thee, O Jerusalem, let my right hand forget her cunning. If I do not remember thee, let my tongue cleave to the roof of my mouth."

Fellow-citizens; above your national, tumultuous joy, I hear the mournful wail of millions! whose chains, heavy and grievous yesterday, are, to-day, rendered more intolerable by the jubilee shouts that reach them. If I do forget, if I do not faithfully remember those bleeding children of sorrow this day, "may my right hand forget her cunning, and may my tongue cleave to the roof of my mouth!" To forget them, to pass lightly over their wrongs, and to chime in with the popular theme, would be treason most scandalous and shocking, and would make me a reproach before God and the world. My subject, then fellow-citizens, is AMERICAN SLAVERY. I shall see, this day, and its popular characteristics, from the slave's point of view. Standing, there, identified with the American bondman, making his wrongs mine, I do not hesitate to declare, with all my soul, that the character and conduct of this nation never looked blacker to me than on this 4th of July! Whether we turn to the declarations of the past or to the professions of the present, the conduct of the nation seems equally hideous and revolting. America is false to the past, false to the present, and solemnly binds herself to be false to the future. Standing with God and the crushed and bleeding slave on this occasion, I will, in the name of humanity which is outraged, in the name of liberty which is fettered, in the name of the constitution and the Bible, which are disregarded and trampled upon, dare to call in question and to denounce, with all the emphasis I can command, everything that serves to perpetuate slavery—the great sin and shame of America! "I will not equivocate; I will not excuse"; I will use the severest language I can command; and yet not one word shall escape me that any man, whose judgement is not blinded by prejudice, or who is not at heart a slaveholder, shall not confess to be right and just.

But I fancy I hear some one of my audience say, it is just in this circumstance that you and your brother abolitionists fail to make a favorable impression on the public mind. Would you argue more, and denounce less, would you persuade more, and rebuke less, your cause would be more likely to succeed. But, I submit, where all is plain there is nothing to be argued. What point in the anti-slavery creed would you have me argue? On what branch of the subject do the people of this country need light? Must I undertake to prove that the slave is a man? That point is conceded already. Nobody doubts it. The slaveholders themselves acknowledge it in the enactment of law, for their government. They acknowledge it when they punish disobedience on the part of the slave. There are seventy-two crimes in the State of Virginia, which, if committed by a black man (no matter how ignorant he be), subject him to the punishment of death; while only two of the same crimes will subject a white man to the like punishment. What is this but the acknowledgement that the slave is a moral, intellectual and responsible being? The manhood of the slave is conceded. It is admitted in the fact that Southern statute books are covered with enactments forbidding, under severe fines and penalties, the teaching of the slave to read or to write. When you can point to any such laws, in reference to the beasts of the field, then I may consent to argue the manhood of the slave. When the dogs in your streets, when the fowls of the air, when the cattle on your hills, when the fish of the sea, and the reptiles that crawl, shall be unable to distinguish the slave from a brute, *then*, will I argue with you that the slave is a man!

For the present, it is enough to affirm the equal manhood of the negro race. Is it not astonishing that, while we are ploughing, planting and reaping, using all kinds of mechanical tools, erecting houses, constructing bridges, building ships, working in metals of brass, iron, copper, silver and gold; that, while we are reading, writing and cyphering, acting as clerks, merchants and secretaries, having among us lawyers, doc-tors, ministers, poets, authors, editors, orators and teachers; that, while we are engaged in all manner of enterprises common to other man, digging gold in California, capturing the whale in the Pacific, feeding sheep and cattle on the hill-side, living, moving, acting, thinking, planning, living in families as husbands, wives and children, and, above all, confessing and worshipping the Christian's God, and looking hopefully for life and immorality beyond the grave, we are called upon to prove that we are men!

Would you have me argue that man is entitled to liberty? that he is the rightful owner of his own body? You have already declared it. Must I argue the wrongfulness of slavery? Is that a question for Republicans? Is it to be settled by the rules of logic and argumentation, as a matter beset with great difficulty, involving a doubtful application of the principle of justice, hard to be understood? How should I look to-day, in the presence of Americans, dividing, and subdividing a discourse, to show that men have a natural right to freedom? speaking of it relatively, and positively, negatively, and affirmatively. To do so, would be to make myself ridiculous, and to offer an insult to your understanding. There is not a man beneath the canopy of heaven, that does not know that slavery is wrong *for him*.

What, am I to argue that it is wrong to make men brutes, to rob them of their liberty, to work them without wages, to keep them ignorant of their relations to their fellow men, to beat them with sticks, to flay their flesh with the lash, to load their limbs with irons, to hunt them with dogs, to sell them at auction, to sunder their families, to knock out their teeth, to burn their flesh, to starve them into obedience and submission to their masters? Must I argue that a system thus marked with blood, and stained with pollution, is *wrong*? No! I will not. I have better employments for my time and strength, than such arguments would imply.

What, then, remains to be argued? Is it that slavery is not divine; that God did not establish it; that our doctors of divinity are mistaken? There is blasphemy in the thought. That which is inhuman, cannot be divine! *Who* can reason on such a proposition? They that can, may; I cannot. The time for such argument is past.

At a time like this, scorching irony, not convincing argument, is needed. O! had I the ability, and could reach I the nation's ear, I would, to-day, pour out a fiery stream of biting ridicule, blasting reproach, withering sarcasm, and stern rebuke. For it is not light that is needed, but fire; it is not the gentle shower, but thunder. We need the storm, the whirlwind, and the earthquake. The feeling of the nation must be quickened; the conscience of the nation must be roused; the propriety of the nation must be startled; the hypocrisy of the nation must be exposed; and its crimes against God and man must be proclaimed and denounced.

What, to the American slave, is your 4th of July? I answer: a day that reveals to him, more than all other days in the year, the gross injustice and cruelty to which he is the constant victim. To him, your celebration is a sham; your boasted liberty, an unholy license; your national greatness, swelling vanity; your sounds of rejoicing are empty and heartless; your denunciations of tyrants, brass fronted impudence; your shouts of liberty and equality, hollow mockery; your prayers and hymns, your sermons and thanksgivings, with all your religious parade, and solemnity, are, to him, mere bombast, fraud, deception, impiety, and hypocrisy—a thin veil to cover up crimes which would disgrace a nation of savages. There is not a nation on the earth guilty of practices, more shocking and bloody, than are the people of these United States, at this very hour.

Go where you may, search where you will, roam through all the monarchies and despotisms of the old world, travel through South America, search out every abuse, and when you have found the last, lay your facts by the side of the everyday practices of this nation, and you will say with me, that, for revolting barbarity and shameless hypocrisy, America reigns without a rival.

The Internal Slave Trade

. . . Fellow-citizens, this murderous traffic is, to-day, in active operation in this boasted republic. In the solitude of my spirit, I see clouds of dust raised on the highways of the South; I see the bleeding footsteps; I hear the doleful wail of fettered humanity, on the way to the slave-markets, where the victims are to be sold like *horses, sheep,* and *swine,* knocked off to the highest bidder. There I see the tenderest ties ruthlessly broken, to gratify the lust, caprice and rapacity of the buyers and sellers of men. My soul sickens at the sight.

"Is this the land your Fathers loved,
The freedom which they toiled to win?
Is this the earth whereon they moved?
Are these the graves they slumber in?"

But a still more inhuman, disgraceful, and scandalous state of things remains to be presented.

By an act of the American Congress, not yet two years old, slavery has been nationalized in its most horrible and revolting form. By that act, Mason & Dixon's line has been obliterated; New York has become as Virginia; and the power to hold, hunt, and sell men, women, and children as slaves remains no longer a mere state institution, but is now an institution of the whole United States. The power is co-extensive with the star-spangled banner and American Christianity. Where these go, may also go the merciless slave-hunter. Where these are, man is not sacred. He is a bird for the sportsman's gun. By that most foul and fiendish of all human decrees, the liberty and person of every man are put in peril. Your broad republican domain is hunting ground for *men. Not* for thieves and robbers, enemies of society, merely, but for men guilty of no crime. Your lawmakers have commanded all good citizens to engage in this hellish sport. Your President, your Secretary of State, your *lords, nobles*, and ecclesiastics, enforce, as a duty you owe to your free and glorious country, and to your God, that you do this accursed thing. Not fewer than forty Americans have, within the past two years, been hunted down and, without a moment's warning, hurried away in chains, and consigned to slavery and excruciating torture. Some of these have had wives and children, dependent on them for bread; but of this, no account was made. The right of the hunter to his prey stands superior to the right of marriage, and to *all* rights in this republic, the rights of God included! For black men there are neither law, justice, humanity, nor religion. The Fugitive Slave *Law* makes MERCY TO THEM, A CRIME; and bribes the judge who tries them. An American JUDGE GETS TEN DOLLARS FOR EVERY VICTIM HE CONSIGNS to slavery, and five, when he fails to do so. The oath of any two villains is sufficient, under this hell-black enactment, to spend the most pious and exemplary black man into the remorseless jaws of slavery! His own testimony is nothing. He can bring no witnesses for himself. The minister of American justice is bound by the law to hear but *one* side; and *that* side, is the side of the oppressor. Let this damning fact be perpetually told. Let it be thundered around the world, that, in tyrant-killing, king-hating, people-loving, democratic, Christian America, the seats of justice are filled with judges, who hold their offices under an open and palpable *bribe*, and are bound, in deciding in the case of a man's liberty, *to hear only his accusers!*

In glaring violation of justice, in shameless disregard of the forms of administering law, in cunning arrangement to entrap the defenseless, and in diabolical intent, this Fugitive Slave Law stands alone in the annals of tyrannical legislation. I doubt if there be another nation on the globe, having the brass and the baseness to put such a law on the statute-book. If any man in this assembly thinks differently from me in this matter, and feels able to disprove my statements, I will gladly confront him at any suitable time and place he may select.

Religious Liberty

I take this law to be one of the grossest infringements of Christian Liberty, and, if the churches and ministers of our country were not stupidly blind, or most wickedly indifferent, they, too, would so regard it.

At the very moment that they are thanking God for the enjoyment of civil and religious liberty, and for the right to worship God according to the dictates of their own consciences, they are utterly silent in respect to a law which robs religion of its chief significance, and makes it utterly worthless to a world lying in wickedness. Did this law concern the *"mint, anise, and cummin"*—abridge the right to sing psalms, to partake of the sacrament, or to engage in any of the ceremonies of religion, it would be smitten by the thunder of a thousand pulpits. A general shout would go up from the church, demanding *repeal, repeal, instant repeal!* And it would go hard with that politician who presumed to solicit the votes of the people without inscribing this motto on his banner. Further, if this demand were not complied with, another Scotland would be added to the history of religious liberty, and the stern old Covenanters would be thrown into the shade. A John Knox would be seen at every church door, and heard from every pulpit, and Fillmore would have no more quarter than was shown by Knox, to the beautiful, but treacherous Queen Mary of Scotland. The fact that the church of our country (with

fractional exceptions), does not esteem "the Fugitive Slave Law" as a declaration of war against religious liberty, implies that that church regards religion simply as a form of worship, an empty ceremony, and *not* a vital principle, requiring active benevolence, justice, love and good will towards man. It esteems sacrifice above mercy; psalm-singing above right doing; solemn meetings above practical righteousness. A worship that can be conducted by persons who refuse to give shelter to the houseless, to give bread to the hungry, clothing to the naked, and who enjoin obedience to a law forbidding these acts of mercy, is a curse, not a blessing to mankind. The Bible addresses all such persons as "scribes, pharisees, hypocrites, who pay the tithe of *mint, anise,* and *cummin*, and have omitted the weightier matters of the law, judgement, mercy and faith."

The Church Responsible

But the church of this country is not only indifferent to the wrongs of the slave, it actually takes sides with the oppressors. It has made itself the bulwark of American slavery, and the shield of American slave-hunters. Many of its most eloquent Divines, who stand as the very lights of the church, have shamelessly given the sanction of religion and the Bible to the whole slave system. They have taught that man may, properly, be a slave; that the relation of master and slave is ordained of God; that to send back an escaped bondman to his master is clearly the duty of all the followers of the Lord Jesus Christ; and this horrible blasphemy is palmed off upon the world for Christianity.

For my part, I would say, welcome infidelity! welcome atheism! welcome anything! in preference to the gospel, *as preached by those Divines*! They convert the very name of religion into an engine of tyranny, and barbarous cruelty, and serve to confirm more infidels, in this age, than all the infidel writings of Thomas Paine, Voltaire, and Bolingbroke, put together, have done! These ministers make religion a cold and flinty-hearted thing, having neither principles of right action, nor bowels of compassion. They strip the love of God of its beauty, and leave the throne of religion a huge, horrible, repulsive form. It is a religion for oppressors, tyrants, man-stealers, and *thugs*. It is not that *"pure and undefiled religion"* which is from above, and which is *"first pure, then peaceable, easy to be entreated,* full of mercy and good fruits, *without partiality, and without hypocrisy."* But a religion which favors the rich against the poor; which exalts the proud above the humble; which divides mankind into two classes, tyrants and slaves; which says to the man in chains, *stay there*; and to the oppressor, *oppress on*; it is a religion which may be professed and enjoyed by all the robbers and enslavers of mankind; it makes God a respecter of persons, denies his fatherhood of the race, and tramples in the dust the great truth of the brotherhood of man. All this we affirm to be true of the popular church, and the popular worship of our land and nation—a religion, a church, and a worship which, on the authority of inspired wisdom, we pronounce to be an abomination in the sight of God. In the language of Isaiah, the American church might be well addressed, "Bring no more vain oblations; incense is an abomination unto me; the new moons and Sabbaths, the calling of assemblies, I cannot away with; it is iniquity, even the solemn meeting. Your new moons and your appointed feasts my soul hateth. They are a trouble to me; I am weary to bear them; and when ye spread forth your hands I will hide mine eyes from you. Yea! when ye make many prayers, I will not hear. YOUR HANDS ARE FULL OF BLOOD; cease to do evil, learn to do well; seek judgement; relieve the oppressed; judge for the fatherless; plead for the widow."

The American church is guilty, when viewed in connection with what it is doing to uphold slavery; but it is superlatively guilty when viewed in connection with its ability to abolish slavery.

The sin of which it is guilty is one of omission as well as of commission. Albert Barnes but uttered what the common sense of every man at all observant of the actual state of the case will receive as truth, when he declared that "There is no power out of the church that could sustain slavery an hour, if it were not sustained in it."

Let the religious press, the pulpit, the Sunday school, the conference meeting, the great ecclesiastical, missionary, Bible and tract associations of the land array their immense powers against slavery and slaveholding; and the whole system of crime and blood would be scattered to the winds; and that they do not do this involves them in the most awful responsibility of which the mind can conceive.

In prosecuting the anti-slavery enterprise, we have been asked to spare the church, to spare the ministry; but *how*, we ask, could such a thing be done? We are met on the threshold of our efforts for the redemption of the slave, by the church and ministry of the country, in battle arrayed against us; and we are compelled to fight or flee. From what *quarter*, I beg to know, has proceeded a fire so deadly upon our ranks, during the last two years, as from the Northern pulpit? As the champions of oppressors, the chosen men of American theology have appeared— men, honored for their so-called piety, and their real learning. The LORDS of Buffalo, the SPRINGS of New York, the LATHROPS of Auburn, the COXES and SPENCERS of Brooklyn, the GANNETS and SHARPS of Boston, the DEWEYS of Washington, and other great religious lights of the land, have, in utter denial of the authority of *Him*, by whom they professed to be called to the ministry, deliberately taught us, against the example of the Hebrews and against the remonstrance of the Apostles, they teach *"that we ought to obey man's law before the law of God."*

My spirit wearies of such blasphemy; and how such men can be supported, as the "standing types and representatives of Jesus Christ," is a mystery which I leave others to penetrate. In speaking of the American church, however, let it be distinctly understood that I mean the *great mass* of the religious organizations of our land. There are exceptions, and I thank God that there are. Noble men may be found, scattered allover these Northern States, of whom Henry Ward Beecher of Brooklyn, Samuel J. May of Syracuse, and my esteemed friend on the platform, are shining examples; and let me say further, that upon these men lies the duty to inspire our ranks with high religious faith and zeal, and to cheer us on in the great mission of the slave's redemption from his chains.

Religion in England and Religion in America

One is struck with the difference between the attitude of the American church towards the anti-slavery movement, and that occupied by the churches in England towards a similar movement in that country. There, the church, true to its mission of ameliorating, elevating, and improving the condition of mankind, came forward promptly, bound up the wounds of the West Indian slave, and restored him to his liberty. There, the question of emancipation was a high[ly] religious question. It was demanded, in the name of humanity, and according to the law of the living God. The Sharps, the Clarksons, the Wilberforces, the Buxtons, and Burchells and the Knibbs, were alike famous for their piety, and for their philanthropy. The anti-slavery movement *there* was not an anti-church movement, for the reason that the church took its full share in prosecuting that movement: and the anti-slavery movement in this country will cease to be an anti-church movement, when the church of this country shall assume a favorable, instead of a hostile position towards that movement.

Americans! your republican politics, not less than your republican religion, are flagrantly inconsistent. You boast of your love of liberty, your superior civilization, and your pure Christianity, while the whole political power of the nation (as embodied in the two great political parties), is solemnly pledged to support and perpetuate the enslavement of three millions of your countrymen. You hurl your anathemas at the crowned headed tyrants of Russia and Austria, and pride yourselves on your Democratic institutions, while you yourselves consent to be the mere *tools* and *body-guards* of the tyrants of Virginia and Carolina. You invite to your shores fugitives of oppression from abroad, honor them with banquets, greet them with ovations, cheer them, toast them, salute them, protect them, and pour out your money to them like water; but the fugitives from your own land you advertise, hunt, arrest, shoot and kill. You glory in your refinement and your universal education; yet you maintain a system as barbarous and dreadful as ever stained the character of a nation—a system begun in avarice, supported in pride, and perpetuated in cruelty. You shed tears over fallen Hungary, and make the sad story of her wrongs the theme of your poets, statesmen and orators, till your gallant sons are ready to fly to arms to vindicate her cause against her oppressors; but, in regard to the ten thousand wrongs of the American slave, you would enforce the strictest silence, and would hail him as an enemy of the nation who dares to make those wrongs the subject of public discourse! You are all on fire at the mention of liberty for France or for Ireland; but are as cold as an iceberg at the thought of liberty for the enslaved of America. You discourse eloquently on the dignity of labor; yet, you sustain a system which, in its very essence, casts a stigma upon labor. You can bare your bosom to the storm of British artillery to throw off a threepenny tax on tea; and yet wring the last hard-earned farthing from the grasp of the black laborers of your country. You profess to believe "that, of one blood, God made all nations of men to dwell on the face of all the earth," and hath commanded all men, everywhere to love one another; yet you notoriously hate (and glory in your hatred), all men whose skins are not colored like your own. You declare, before the

world, and are understood by the world to declare, that you *"hold these truths to be self evident, that all men are created equal; and are endowed by their Creator with certain inalienable rights; and that, among these are, life, liberty, and the pursuit of happiness;"* and yet, you hold securely, in a bondage which, according to your own Thomas Jefferson, *"is worse than ages of that which your fathers rose in rebellion to oppose,"* a *seventh part* of the inhabitants of your country.

Fellow-citizens! I will not enlarge further on your national inconsistencies. The existence of slavery in this country brands your republicanism as a sham, your humanity as a base pretence, and your Christianity as a lie. It destroys your moral power abroad; it corrupts your politicians at home. It saps the foundation of religion; it makes your name a hissing, and a byword to a mocking earth. It is the antagonistic force in your government, the only thing that seriously disturbs and endangers your *Union*. It fetters your progress; it is the enemy of improvement, the deadly foe of education; it fosters pride; it breeds insolence; it promotes vice; it shelters crime; it is a curse to the earth that supports it; and yet, you cling to it, as if it were the sheet anchor of all your hopes. Oh! be warned! be warned! a horrible reptile is coiled up in your nation's bosom; the venomous creature is nursing at the tender breast of your youthful republic; *for the love of God, tear away,* and fling from you the hideous monster, and *let the weight of twenty million crush and destroy it forever!* . . .

Allow me to say, in conclusion, notwithstanding the dark picture I have this day presented of the state of the nation, I do not despair of this country. There are forces in operation, which must inevitably work the downfall of slavery. *"The arm of the Lord is not shortened,"* and the doom of slavery is certain. I, therefore, leave off where I began, with *hope*. While drawing encouragement from the Declaration of Independence, the great principles it contains, and the genius of American Institutions, my spirit is also cheered by the obvious tendencies of the age. Nations do not now stand in the same relation to each other that they did ages ago. No nation can now shut itself up from the surrounding world, and trot round in the same old path of its fathers without interference. The time *was* when such could be done. Long established customs of hurtful character could formerly fence themselves in, and do their evil work with social impunity. Knowledge was then confined and enjoyed by the privileged few, and the multitude walked on in mental darkness. But a change has now come over the affairs of mankind. Walled cities and empires have become unfashionable. The arm of commerce has borne away the gates of the strong city. Intelligence is penetrating the darkest corners of the globe. It makes its pathway over and under the sea, as well as on earth. Wind, steam, and lightning are its chartered agents. Oceans no longer divide, but link nations together. From Boston to London is now a holiday excursion. Space is comparatively annihilated. Thoughts expressed on one side of the Atlantic are distinctly heard on the other.

The far off and almost fabulous Pacific rolls in grandeur at our feet. The Celestial Empire, the mystery of ages, is being solved. The fiat of the Almighty, *"Let there be Light,"* has not yet spent its force. No abuse, no outrage whether in taste, sport or avarice, can now hide itself from the all-pervading light. The iron shoe, and crippled foot in China must be seen, in contrast with nature. *Africa must rise and put on her yet unwoven garment. "Ethiopia shall stretch out her hand unto God."* In the fervent aspirations of William Lloyd Garrison, I say, and let every heart join in saying it:

> God speed the year of jubilee
> 　　The wide world o'er!
> When from their galling chains set free,
> Th' oppress'd shall vilely bend the knee,
> And wear the yoke of tyranny
> 　　Like brutes no more.
> That year will come, and freedom's reign,
> To man his plundered rights again
> 　　Restore.
>
> God speed the day when human blood
> 　　Shall cease to flow!
> In every clime be understood,
> The claims of human brotherhood,
> And each return for evil, good,
> 　　Not blow for blow;
> That day will come all feuds to end,
> And change into faithful friend
> 　　Each foe.

God speed the hour, the glorious hour,
    When none on earth
Shall exercise a lordly power,
Nor in a tyrant's presence cower;
But all to manhood's stature tower,
    By equal birth!
THAT HOUR WILL COME, to each, to all,
And from his prison-house, the thrall
    Go forth.

Until that year, day, hour, arrive,
With head, and heart, and hand I'll strive,
To break the rod, and rend the gyve,
The spoiler of his prey deprive—
    So witness Heaven!
And never from my chosen post,
Whate'er the peril or the cost,
    Be driven.

Letters on Slavery
James H. Hammond

During the years prior to the Civil War, the accusation that slaveholders were sinful was resented by many Southerners. The South was a stronghold of orthodox religion, and slaveholding church members argued that the Bible defended their actions. James H. Hammond, a Christian owner of slaves from South Carolina, claimed it was presumptuous for those who attacked slavery to claim Divine support. His argument is taken from his "Letters on Slavery," *The Pro-Slavery Argument* (Charleston, S.C., 1852), pp. 104-9.

If you were to ask me whether I am an advocate of Slavery in the abstract, I should probably answer, that I am not, according to my understanding of the question. I do not like to deal in abstractions. It seldom leads to any useful ends. There are few universal truths. I do not now remember any single moral truth universally acknowledged. We have no assurance that it is given to our finite understanding to comprehend abstract moral truth. Apart from revelation and the inspired writings, what ideas should we have even of God, salvation and immortality? . . . I might say that I am no more in favor of Slavery in the abstract, than I am of poverty, disease, deformity, idiocy, or any other inequality in the condition of the human family; that I love perfection, and think I should enjoy a millennium such as God has promised. But what would it amount to? A pledge that I would join you to set about eradicating those apparently inevitable evils of our nature, in equalizing the condition of all mankind, consummating the perfection of our race, and introducing the millennium? By no means. To effect these things, belongs exclusively to a higher power-er. And it would be well for us to leave the Almighty to perfect his own works and fulfil his own covenants. . . . On Slavery in the abstract, then, it would not be amiss to have as little as possible to say. Let us contemplate it as it is. And thus contemplating it, the first question we have to ask ourselves is, whether it is contrary to the will of God, as revealed to us in his Holy Scriptures—the only certain means given to us to ascertain his will. If it is, then Slavery is a sin. And I admit at once that every man is bound to set his face against it, and to emancipate his slaves, should he hold any.

Let us open these Holy Scriptures. In the twentieth chapter of Exodus, seventeenth verse, I find the following words: "Thou shalt not covet thy neighbor's house, thou shalt not covet thy neighbor's wife, nor his man-servant, nor his maid-servant, nor his ox, nor his ass, nor anything that is thy neighbor's"—which is the tenth of those commandments that declare the essential principles of the great moral law delivered to Moses by God himself. Now, discarding all technical and verbal quibbling as wholly unworthy to be used in interpreting the Word of God, what is the plain meaning, undoubted intent, and true spirit of this commandment? Does it not emphatically and explicitly forbid you to disturb your neighbor in the enjoyment of his property; and more especially of that which is here specifically mentioned as being lawfully, and by this commandment made sacredly his? Prominent in the catalogue stands his "man-servant and his maid-servant who are thus distinctly *consecrated as his property*, and guaranteed to him for his exclusive benefit, in the most solemn manner. . . .

You cannot deny that there were among the Hebrews "bondmen forever." You cannot deny that God especially authorized his chosen people to purchase "bondmen for-ever" from the heathen, as recorded in the twenty-fifth chapter of Leviticus, and that they are there designated by the very Hebrew word used in the tenth commandment. Nor can you deny that a "BONDMAN FOREVER" is a "SLAVE;" yet you endeavor to hang an argument of immortal consequence upon the wretched subterfuge, that the precise word "slave" is not to be found in the *translation* of the Bible. As if the translators were canonical expounders of the Holy Scriptures, and *their words*, not *God's meanings*, must be regarded as his revelation.

It is vain to look to Christ or any of his Apostles to justify such blasphemous perversions of the word of God. Although Slavery in its most revolting form was everywhere visible around them, no visionary notions of piety or philanthropy ever tempted them to gainsay the LAW, even to mitigate the cruel severity of the existing system. On the contrary, regarding Slavery as an *established*, as well as *inevitable conditions of human society*, they never hinted at such a thing as its termination on earth, any more than that "the poor may cease out of the land," which God affirms to Moses shall never be: and they exhort "all servants under the yoke" to "count their masters as worthy of all honor:" "to obey them in all things according to the flesh; not with eye-service as men-pleasers, but in singleness of heart, fearing God;" "not only the good and gentle, but also the forward:" "For what glory is it if when ye are buffeted for your faults ye shall take it patiently, but if when ye do well and suffer for it ye take it patiently, this is acceptable of God." St. Paul actually apprehended a runaway slave, and sent him to his master! Instead of deriving from the Gospel any sanction for the work you have undertaken, it would be difficult to imagine sentiments and conduct more strikingly in contrast, than those of the Apostles and the abolitionists. . . .

I think, I may safely conclude, and I firmly believe, that American Slavery is not only not a sin, but especially commanded by God through Moses, and approved by Christ through his apostles. And here I might close its defence; for what God ordains, and Christ sanctifies, should surely command the respect and toleration of man. But I fear there has grown up in our time a transcendental religion, which is throwing even transcendental philosophy into the shade—a religion too pure and elevated for the Bible; which seeks to erect among men a higher standard of morals than the Almighty has revealed, or our Saviour preached; and which is probably destined to do more to impede the extension of God's kingdom on earth than all the infidels who have ever lived. Error is error. It is as dangerous to deviate to the right hand as the left. And when man, professing to be holy man, and who are by numbers regarded, declare those things to be sinful which our Creator has expressly authorized and instituted, they do more to destroy his authority among mankind than the most wicked can effect, by proclaiming that to be innocent which was forbidden. To this self-righteous and self-exalted class belong all the abolitionists whose writings I have read. With them it is no end of the argument to prove your propositions by the text of the Bible, interpreted according to its plain and palpable meaning, and as understood by all mankind for three thousand years before their time. They are more ingenious at construing and interpolating to accommodate it to their new-fangled and etherial [*sic*] code of morals, than ever were Voltaire and Hume in picking it to pieces, to free the world from what they considered a delusion. When the abolitionists proclaim "man-stealing" to be a sin, and show me that it is so written down by God, I admit them to be right, and shudder at the idea of such a crime. But when I show them that to hold "bondmen forever" is ordained by God, *they deny the Bible, and set up in its place a law of their own making.* I must then cease to reason with them on this branch of the question. Our religion differs as widely as our manners. The great judge in our day of final account must decide between us.

7 Manifest Destiny

And God blessed them; and God said to them, "Be fruitful and multiply, and fill the earth and subdue it."

—Gen 1:28

Justification by Scripture
John Quincy Adams

John Quincy Adams (1767-1848), son of President John Adams, served as secretary of state in the Monroe administration. While occupying that office, he was responsible for the Adams-Onis Treaty of 1819 by which the United States acquired the Floridas and Spanish claims to the Oregon region. In 1823 he was the guiding force behind the presidential statements that became known as the Monroe Doctrine. Following his term as president from 1825 to 1829, he was elected to the House of Representatives in 1831, where he served until his death in 1848. While serving in the House, his vision of a United States spanning the North American continent, with a sphere of influence extending throughout South America, drew him into the congressional debate over the American claim to Oregon. On February 9, 1846, in his well known address before the House, Adams insisted the American claim to Oregon was superior to the British claim in that the former nation would utilize the land in ways more excellent than the latter nation.

. . . Sir, there has been so much said on the question of title in this case, that I believe it would be a waste of time for me to say anything more about it, unless I refer to a little book you have there upon your table, which you sometimes employ to administer a solemn oath to every member of this House to support the Constitution of the United States. If you have it, be so good to pass it to the Clerk, and I will ask him to read what I conceive to be the foundation of our title.

If the Clerk will be so good as to read the 26th, 27th, and 28th verses of the 1st chapter of Genesis, the committee will see what I consider to be the foundation of the title of the United States.

The Clerk read accordingly as follows:

"26.   And God said, Let us make man in our image, after our likeness; and let them have dominion over the fish of the sea, and over the fowl of the air, and over the cattle, and over all the earth, and over every creeping thing that creepeth upon the earth.

"27.   So God created man in his own image, in the image of God created he him: male and female created he them.

"28.   And God blessed them, and God said unto them, Be fruitful and multiply, and replenish the earth, and subdue it; and have dominion over the fish of the sea, and over the fowl of the air, and over every living thing that moveth upon the earth."

That, sir (continued Mr. A), in my judgment, is the foundation not only of our title to the territory of Oregon, but the foundation of all human title to all human possessions. It is the foundation of the title by which you occupy that chair; it is the territory of Oregon; and we cannot do it without putting a close to any agreement which we have made with Great Britain that we will not occupy it.

And here I beg leave to repeat an idea that I have already expressed before, and that is, that there is a very great misapprehension of the real merits of this case founded on the misnomer which declares that convention to be a convention of joint occupation. Sir, it is not a convention of joint occupation. It is a convention of non-occupation—a promise on the part of both parties that neither of the parties will occupy the territory for an indefinite space; first for ten years, then until the notice shall be given from one party to the other that the convention shall be terminated—that is to say, that the restriction, the fetter upon our hands shall be thrown off, which prevents occupation, and prevents the carrying into execution the law of God, which the Clerk has read from the Holy Scriptures. How, if this controversy in relation to the territory of Oregon was with any other than a Christian nation, I could not cite that book. With the Chinese, and all nations who do not admit the canon of Scripture, it would be quite a different question. It would be a different question between us and the Indian savages, who occupy that country as far as there is any right of occupation, for they do not believe this book. I suppose the mass of this House believe this book. I see them go up and take their oath of office upon it; and many of the southern members kiss the book in token, I suppose, of their respect for it. It is between Christian nations that the foundation of title to land is laid in the first chapter of Genesis, and it is in this book that the title to jurisdiction, to eminent domain, to individual property, had its foundation—all of which flow from other sources subsequent to that which the Clerk read.

Now I will ask the Clerk to read another passage of that book; and that is, I think the 8th verse of the 2nd Psalm.

The Clerk read:

> "8. Ask of me, and I shall give thee the heathen for thine inheritance, and the uttermost parts of the earth for thy possession."

If the Clerk will read a verse or two before that which he has just read it will be seen to whom it is said He will give them.

The Clerk read:

> "6. Yet have I set my king upon my holy hill of Zion.
>
> "7. I will declare the decree: the Lord hath said unto me, Thou art my son; this day have I begotten thee.
>
> "8. Ask of me, and I shall give thee the heathen for thine inheritance, and the uttermost parts of the earth for thy possession."

That (continued Mr. A) is the Personage to whom the promise was made of giving the heathen for his inheritance, and the uttermost parts of the earth for his possession. Now, the promise contained in that verse was understood by all commentators upon the Bible, and by the Christian nations of all denominations, certainly before the reformation of another, to apply to the Lord Jesus Christ. Then, sir, without entering into any long historical detail, by the Christians and Christian nations (for he spoke now of international law), the Pope, or the Bishop of Rome, was considered as the representative of Christ upon earth; and this verse from the Psalm promising the heathen for his inheritance and the uttermost parts of the earth for his possession, together with another verse at the close of one of the gospels (which he would not detain the committee by asking the Clerk to read at the desk), in which the Lord Jesus Christ, after rising from the dead, said to his disciples (in substance), "Go forth and preach to all nations my Gospel; and I will be with you to the end of the world." From these three several passages of the Scriptures, the Pope of Rome asserted, and for many ages it was admitted he had, the power of giving to any king or sovereign to whom he pleased, the power of going and subduing all barbarous nations, and subduing and conquering all territory, either not subdued at all, or subdued by barbarous nations, for the purpose of converting them to Christianity. At the time of the discovery of the continents of North and South America by Christopher Columbus, this was the law of nations between Christians, recognized, acknowledged, admitted; and when Christopher Columbus came, under a commission from Ferdinand and Isabella, King and Queen of Castile, Leon, and Aragon—when he came and made his discovery, which he did in October, 1492, in the next year, some time in the month of March or April, 1493, the Pope of Rome—at that time authorized, according to all international law between Christians to do it—gave to Ferdinand and Isabella the whole continents of North and South America. He authorized the drawing of a line from pole to pole, to Ferdinand and Isabella, King and Queen of Castile, Leon, and Aragon. Now, do I intend to say that that is one of our titles? I must say it, although I think, perhaps, as little of it as any member of this House. But it was a good title when it was given. It was the understanding, the faith, the belief of all the Christian nations of Europe, that the Pope had his power; and it was acquiesced in by them all for a time. That same Pope at that time was in the custom of giving away not only barbarous nations, but civilized nations. He dethroned sovereigns, put them under interdict, and excommunicated them from intercourse with all other Christians: and it was submitted to. And now, sir, the Government of Great Britain—the nation of Great Britain—holds the island of Ireland on no other title. Three hundred years before that time, Pope Adrian of Rome gave, by that same power, to Henry I of England the island of Ireland, and England has held it from that day to this under that title, and no other. That is, no other, unless by conquest; (for it has been in a continued state of rebellion ever since, and now the question is, whether Ireland shall ever become an independent kingdom. If we come to a war with Great Britain, she will find enough to do to maintain that island.) I do not think it of very great value; though I think it does not go for nothing. Now, that general authority given to man to increase, multiply, and replenish the earth, and subdue it, was a grant from the Creator to man as man; it was a grant to every individual of the human race in his individual capacity. But, then, the portion that belongs to the individual, and was given thereby, was a matter for the whole human race to accommodate amoung themselves. That is to say, in communities, communities were to agree together what should be the metes and bounds of that portion of the earth given them by the general grant from the Creator. When communities were formed, it became a matter of legislation among them to whom any particular property—e.g., a lot of land on which to build a house—should belong. Any territorial right whatever, as between individuals, was to be regulated by legislation, as between nations it was to be regulated by consent, by convention; and in that way the laws of nations, as they are called (which are nothing more than the customs of nations), and the treaties and conventions of nations, have regulated how every spot, every inch of land, shall be occupied. And among the rest, it is by these laws and regulations—internal among communities and international among nations—that you hold that seat (referring to the Speaker's seat), and I do not, because you have it, elevated to it by the laws of the country, and no other man can take, except by permission, so long as your right continues.

Well, sir, our title to Oregon stands on the same foundation. When this discovery of Columbus came to be a matter of great importance among the nations of the earth, other nations took into their heads to plant colonies on this continent, and then came the question of controversy between them, which never has been settled to this day. Our question now with Great Britain is one of the consequences of that state of things. There never has been any agreement between the nations of the earth how these points shall be settled.

There have been titles derived from treaty, from agreement, from conquest; there have been sources from which they have derived title to territory. We have been told here that our title to the Columbia river and all the territory that is drained by it, is in consequence of discovery and exploration. Well, sir, that has been partially an agreement between the nations that they will say they consider that where a nation discovers the mouth of a river, and explores that river to its source, then that nation is entitled, and has been generally allowed, to maintain their authority. But that is not the foundation of any of our titles. . . .

Coming down to this pretended principle, that the discovery of the mouth of a river gives title to all the land watered by that river and its tributaries—and this is the ground on which we contend that the Mississippi valley, among the rest, belongs to us—that title is a parcel of the rights by which you hold that seat, and by which all property is held. This charter of Charles I, to the colony of Massachusetts Bay, gives from 40 to 48 degrees of latitude, without reference to any rivers. The kings of England, following the example of the Pope of Rome, undertook to grant lands all over this continent, and upon such terms as they thought proper. When they found the mouth of a river, and it was for their interest to claim the territory watered by that river, they claimed it. Louis XIV gave to Crozart—and that is the title by which we still hold that country—he gave him no land, but gave him merely the power to trade with the Mississippi river and all its tributaries, because that river had been discovered by French subjects many years before coming from Canada.

All these titles are imperfect. Discovery is, therefore, no title of itself. The discovery of a river and of land is no title of itself. Exploration comes next. That gives something more of a title. Continuity and contiguity both concur to give a title. They are none of them perfect in themselves. There is nothing complete in the way of title, but actual possession; and that is the only thing we now want, to have a perfect, clear, indisputable, and undoubted right to the territory of Oregon. It is possession; it is occupation, if you please. . . .

. . . She herself [Great Britain] admits that she has no title there; she pretends that she has none. But what does she say? She says that it is an open country; that it is one of those countries occupied, as far as it is occupied at all, only by barbarous nations—that it is a country which is open to all parties. She does not claim exclusive jurisdiction. I promise you she will, if you suffer her to do it, before she has done, not only to what you choose to give her, but to the whole territory. But at this day she claims no exclusive jurisdiction over the whole country. She claims, and by virtue of this convention, to have the country free and open—that is, to keep it in a savage and barbarous state for her hunters—for the benefit of the Hudson Bay Company for hunting. Now, she knows that it would have no value to her at all from the day that it is settled by tillers of her ground. It is abolished from that time by the nature of things. And therein consists the difference between her claims and our claims. We claim that country—for what? To make the wilderness blossom as the rose, to establish laws, to increase, multiply, and subdue the earth, which we are commanded to do by the first behest of God Almighty. That is what we claim it for. She claims to keep it open for navigation, for her hunters to hunt wild beasts; and of course she claims for the benefit of the wild beasts, as well as of the savage nations. There is the difference between our claims.

Letter to Rev. L. P. Judson
Marcus Whitman

Marcus Whitman (1802-1847), a medical doctor, and Rev. Henry Spalding were appointed by the American Board of Commissioners for Foreign Missions in 1836 as the board's first missionaries to Oregon. Along with their wives, who were the first white women to cross the Rocky Mountains, Whitman and Spalding carried on religious, medical, agricultural, and educational efforts among the Cayuse Indians for over a decade. Whitman's letter to his brother-in-law which follows indicates his interest in the development of civilization in Oregon and the role of the missionary in that development. He was troubled by some of the contemporary religious developments which he believed detracted from the work of spreading Protestantism and allowed Catholicism to infiltrate the Northwest. About a year after he wrote the letter, Whitman, his wife, their two adopted children, and ten others were massacred by the Cayuse, who believed Whitman was responsible for a series of epidemics among them.

Waiilatpu, Nov. 5th, 1846

Rev. L. P. Judson, My Dear Brother:

I have a last moment to spare in writing, and I have resolved to write to you, inasmuch as you have given me the hint by the note you appended to a family letter from Mrs. Whitman's friends. I am going to write plainly to you, for we love you and do not like to see your influence and usefulness abridged. I have known you long and well—better perhaps than you me. I esteem you for your warm affections and ardent temperament, but although these are amiable qualities, they are like the health of an infant, of so high and excitable a nature that it is but a step between them and derangement or disease. Mental disease is not suspected by the person who is the subject of it. But do not be surprised at what I am intimating. There are but few who are possessed of perfectly balanced minds. I have felt and acted with you on points to which the public mind was not awake, nor ready for action. It is well to be awake on all important points of duty and truth, but it can do no good to be ultra on any of these points. Why part friends for an opinion only, and that, too, when nothing is to be gained for truth and principle, and much lost of confidence, love, usefulness, enjoyment, and interest.

Why trouble those you cannot convince with any peculiarity of your own sentiment, especially if it is likely to debar you from the opportunity of usefulness to them. By one part of your own confession let me confute your ultra perfectionism; that is, you complain of not being perfect and pray for more sanctification. Now, brother, let that suffice that as long as you have to pray for sanctification you are not perfect, and that as long as you live you will pray for it and then conclude you will be perfect when "this mortal shall put on in corruption," and not till then; and then let us cry, grace; grace unto it. Do not think of being an ultra perfectionist until you could bear to hear a man say, I have already attained and am already perfect, and to use only thanksgiving to God for his having attained to and being perfect, instead [of] praying for more sanctification. If you could arrive at the point where you felt you were perfect, of course you would no longer pray for sanctification, and what would be your prayer after that? Let the thought awe you, for such cannot be the prayer of mortals in the flesh. Prayer becomes us, and we shall not be fitted in this life to join in the song of praise triumphant, of Moses and the Lamb.

And now for Millerism. I was in Boston when the famous time came for the end of the world, but I did not conclude that as the time was so short I would not concern myself to return to my family. But I did conclude that inasmuch as you had adopted such sentiments, you were not prepared for any work calling for time in its execution, and thinking the work of time so short with you that it would be in vain to call forth any principle to your mind that would involve length of time for its execution, I was contented to pass you in silence. For to my mind all my work and plans involved time and distance, and required confidence in the stability of God's government and purpose to give the heathen to his Son for an inheritance, and among them those uttermost parts of the earth for his possession.

I had adopted Oregon as my country, as well as the Indians for my field of labour, so that I must superintend the immigration of that year, which was to lay the foundation for the speedy settlement of the country if prosperously conducted and safely carried through; but if it failed and became disastrous, the reflex influence would be to discourage for a long time any further attempt to settle the country across the mountains, which would be to see it abandoned altogether. Now, mark the difference between the sentiments of you and me. Since that time you have allowed yourself to be laid aside from the ministry, and have parted with tried friends for an opinion only, and that opinion has done you nor no one else any good. Within the same time, I have returned to my field of labour, and in my return brought a large immigration of about one thousand individuals safely through the long and the last part of it an untried route to the western shores of the continent. Now that they were once safely conducted through, three successive immigrations have followed after them, and two routes for wagons are now open into the Willamette valley. Mark; had I been of your mind I should have slept, and now the Jesuit Papists would have been in quiet possession of this the only spot in the western horizon of America not before their own. They were fast fixing themselves here, and had we missionaries had no American population to come in to hold on and give stability, it would have been but a small work for them and the friends of English interests, which they had also fully avowed, to have routed us, and then the country might have slept in their hands forever.

Time is not so short yet but it is quite important that such a country as Oregon should not on the one hand fall into the exclusive hands of the Jesuits, nor on the other under the English government. In all the business of this world we require time. And now let us redeem it, and then we shall be ready, and our Lord will not come upon us unawares. Come, then, to Oregon, resume your former motto, which seemed to be onward and upward—that is in principle, action, duty and attainments, and in holiness. Dismiss all ultraism, and then you will be cooperative and happy in the society of acting and active Christians. I say again, come to Oregon; but do not bring principles of discord with you.

This is a country requiring devoted, pious labourers in the service of our Lord. There are many and great advantages offered to those who select and that of the best of land, and in a near proximity to a vast ocean and in a mild climate where stock feed out all winter, is not a small boon. Nor should men of piety and principle leave it all to be taken by worldlings and worldly men.

A man of your stamp can do much by coming to this country, if you adopt correct principles and action. Should you come, the best way is to take a raft at Olean, if you are near Cuba at the time of starting. You will need to bring bedding with you for the journey, so that you can come on a raft, and also take a deck passage on the steamboat if you wish to be saving of money. A piece of cloth painted suitable to spread under a bed will be most useful. Do not bring feathers, but let your bed be made of blankets, quilts, etc. If you want any goods after you get into the country, be sure and have them come around by water, if you do not like to trust the shippers in the country. A train of oxen

will be the best with a light wagon; no loading except provisions. Good sheep are excellent stock to drive, and travel well. Some sheep we imported from the Sandwich Islands in 1838, have increased one hundred and twenty-five per cent in eight years. Think of what a few good men could do to come together into the country. On the way they could make a party of their own and so rest on the Sabbath. With 640 acres of land as bounty, they could, by mutual consent, set apart a portion for the maintenance of the gospel and for schools and learning in such form as they felt disposed.

A large country to the south as far as the California line is now open by the new wagon route made this fall. You have a good faculty to be a pioneer and lead out a colony; that is to start people to come. But when once on the way do not overpersuade the mind but remember that the best of men and women when fatigued and anxious by the way will be very jealous of all their rights and privileges and must be left to take their own way if possible. Restraint will not be borne under such circumstances.

As I do not know where to send to reach you, I will direct this to the care of Father Prentiss [the father of Judson's wife], who will forward it to you, after reading it himself.

The Indians are doing very well we think in their way and their habits of civilization. A good attention is paid to religious instruction. Morning and evening worship is quite general in their lodges, and a blessing is strictly regarded as being a duty to be asked upon taking food.

I do not think you can be ignorant of the advantages of this country, nor of its disadvantages. I wrote a letter of Father Hotchkin, which I hope was copied and sent to Father Prentiss, which you may have seen. That applies to this section and climate. The country best suited for settlement are the Willamette valley and the coast west. Then the valley of the Umpqua on the south, and still south the Klamath which takes you south to the California line.

North of the Columbia, you know, is in dispute between the British and the States; you may early learn the result. The greatest objection to the country west of the Cascade range is the rains of winter. But that is more than overbalanced by the exemption from the care and labour of feeding stock. It is not that so much rain falls, but that it rains a great many days from November to April or May. People that are settled do not find it so rainy as to be much of an objection. It is a climate much like England in that respect.

I hope you will excuse the freedom with which I have written. If we shall see each other, we can better bring our thoughts to harmonize.

Narcissa's health is on the gain, and is now pretty good. She joins me in love to yourself and wife, hoping to see you both in due time.

In the best of bonds,

Yours truly,
Marcus Whitman

Redeem Mexico from Misrule and Civil Strife
Robert F. Stockton

Robert F. Stockton (1795-1866), who served in the U.S. Navy for nearly forty years, was well known in the 1840s for his military exploits against the Mexicans in the gaining of California for the United States. In a speech he delivered at a dinner held in his honor in Philadelphia on December 30, 1847, Stockton boasted of America's unlimited military success in Mexico and called upon American officials to extend further the blessings of American civilization. It was Stockton's opinion that the United States' great mission to humanity was to be enhanced by "redeeming Mexico from misrule and civil strife." His speech which follows was published in *Niles' National Register*, LXXIII (January 22, 1848).

No thoughtful observer of the progress of the U. States, can fail to be impressed with the conviction that we enjoy a degree of happiness and prosperity never heretofore vouchsafed to the nations of mankind. With an unexampled measure of political liberty; unbroken social order; extraordinary growth of the arts and sciences—philanthropic and benevolent institutions, the fair offspring of the Christian faith, extending their blessed agency, in all directions—unbounded religious toleration, heaven's best gift; for which our fathers risked and suffered most—with all these rich endowments, do we not indeed present an example of the beneficent care of Providence for which we can find no parallel in the history of man? And now when engaged in war, find ourselves, followed by the same blessed influences. Wherever our soldiers have carried our arms, victory has awaited them. We see them rushing against walls, bristling with bayonets and artillery, and lined with legions of armed men—we see our youthful heroes precipitating themselves from parapet to parapet, and charging from bastion to bastion—we hear the crash of grape and canister, and amid the smoke and thunder of the battle we behold the flag of our country, waiving—[*the remainder of the sentence was lost in the tremendous cheering which here burst forth from the assemblage.*] We behold the flag of civil and religious freedom waiving over what had been regarded as unpregnable fortresses and the remains of armies fleeing to the mountains.

Gentlemen, how has all this been accomplished? Whence those achievements? I speak to intellectual men. All in the hearing of my voice entertain, I doubt not, a just and abiding sense of their deep responsibility not only on this earth, but in time hereafter. I ask you, then, how has all this happened? Is it to be attributed exclusively to the wisdom of our cabinet and the powers of our armies? These are all well—admittable well. But our successes have overleaped the bounds of all human calculating and the most sanguine hope. Therefore we must look beyond all this for the secret of our successes and the source of our remarkable prosperity. It is because the spirit of our pilgrim fathers is with us.—It is because of the God of armies and Lord of hosts is with us. [*Tremendous applause.*] And how is it with poor, unfortunate, wretched Mexico? Ever since the day of the last of the Montezumas, intestine broils have disturbed her peace. Her whole territory has been drenched with the blood of her own children. Within the last quarter of a century revolution has succeeded revolution. Now in the encounter with us she has been beaten in every field. She has been driven from fortress to fortress—from town to town, until the scattered remnants of her broken armies are fleeing to the mountains and calling upon the rocks to hide them. [*Applause.*] Is it not, therefore, in this disposition of public affairs, proper to rise superior to the consideration of party influence, and in true philosophical spirit and patriotic fidelity, take an honest view of our condition, in the sight of God and beneath the scrutiny of the christian and civilized world?

What you may think of it, I know not; and you must permit me to add, I care not; but for myself I speak not to you as a party man. Remember, gentlemen, that I go for my country. I cannot be bound, I cannot be kept within the restraints of party discipline when my country calls me forth. [*Tremendous cheering, which lasted several minutes.*] I go for my country—my whole country and nothing but my country. I desire to address you now in the spirit of the father of a large family, desirous to transmit to his latest posterity the blessings of civil and religious liberty. I speak to you as a Christian man—as a son, perhaps an unworthy son of this great republic, but one whose heart burns with an ardent desire to transmit, not only to his own immediate descendants, the blessings of which I speak, but to extend them to our neighbors on this continent. [*Great applause.*]

But do not mistake me. Do not misunderstand me. I am no propagandist in the common reception of the term. In my judgment, principles depend much upon relations and circumstances, and that which in the abstract may be well enough, often wastes itself in fanaticism. All things must bide their time.

I have no respect for the man or set of men who will recklessly disturb the social order of my community and produce civil war for the purpose of hastening such a result, no matter how beneficial in the abstract it may seem to be. [*Cheers.*] And I am bound to say farther, that I have quite as little respect for the man or set of men, who have in the Providence of God been placed in stations, when the great questions of civil and religious liberty are to be determined, who will shrink from the responsibilities of that station. [*Cheers.*] In the application of these principles to the future policy of this country, let it not be supposed for a moment that I would presume to censure the great men of this nation. —Nor would I attempt to instruct the most humble of my country-men. I present these views merely for the purpose of rendering more distinct and clear the remarks which I have offered, and which I may not have stated with sufficient explicitness.

I suppose the war with Mexico was caused by the repeated insults which time after time had been heaped upon this nation. [*Great applause*.] I regard this much talked of indemnity as merely collateral or incidental, arising out of the circumstances of the war. In my opinion, that question will be set aside, if not wholly lost sight of in the pressure of the great considerations which are to grow out of the high responsibilities and delicate duties crowding upon us, and the unexampled victories which have attended our arms. [*Cheer*.] In pursuing a legitimate object of war—in the providence of God we are placed, or are likely to be placed, in a position where by a fair and legitimate construction of the law of nations, the fate of Mexico and the peace of this continent, to a greater or less extent, will devolve upon the virtue, the wisdom, and the humanity of our rulers. [*Applause*.] In these rulers I have the greatest confidence, and for them I entertain the most profound respect. [*Applause*.]

I tell you again gentlemen, this matter of indemnity, in money or any thing else, will be secondary, altogether secondary, in comparison with the considerations which I have no doubt will be presented to this nation in the farther prosecution of this war. The insults have been resented—nobly resented—they have been wiped out—they have been washed out with blood. [*Enthusiastic applause*.] If, then indemnity, means money, any financier will tell you that if *that* is what you seek as the only object of the war, you had better withdraw your troops as soon as possible, and you will save money. [A laugh.]

But indemnity is not the object of the war. No man here or elsewhere will consent to weigh blood against money. [*Great applause*.] I do not care who presents the proposition—when it is presented; or to whom it is presented, whig or democrat, no man will weigh blood for money. [*Loud applause*.]

But this is not, I repeat, our condition. Higher and nobler objects present them-selves for the attainment of which you must increase your armies in Mexico, cost what it may. [*Great applause*.] Let me then state the objects for the attainment of which, in my judgment, this augmentation of our force in Mexico is required.

Mexico is poor and wretched. Why? Misgovernment—insatiable avarice— unintermitted wrong, unsparing cruelty and unbending insolence—these have inflicted their curse on the unhappy country, and made her what she is. But as the darkest hour is that which just precedes the advent of the morning sun, so let us hope that a better and happier day is now about to dawn upon fortunate Mexico. Be it ours, now to forgive her all her trespasses, and returning good for evil, make her free and happy!—

If I were now the sovereign authority as I was once the viceroy—[*laughter*]—I would prosecute this war for the express purpose of redeeming Mexico from misrule and civil strife. If, however, such a treaty were offered me as that offered to the government of the United States, before God, I would consider it my bounden duty to reject it. [*Loud applause*.]—I would say to them, we can pay the indemnity ourselves. But we have a duty before God which we cannot— we must not evade. The priceless bond of civil and religious liberty has been confided to us as trustees—[*cheers*]—I would insist, if the war were to be pro-longed for fifty years, and cost money enough to demand from each year the half of all that we possess, I would still insist that the inestimable blessings of civil and religious liberty should be guaranteed to Mexico. We must not shrink from it. We cannot lose sight of the great truth that nations are accountable as well as individuals, and that they too must meet the stern responsibilities of their moral character—they too must encounter the penalty of violated law in the more extended sphere adapted to their physical condition.

Let the solemn question come home to the bosom and business of every citizen of this great republic: "What have I done—what has this generation done for the advancement of civil and religious liberty!"—[Applause.]

It is in view of this responsibility—of our obligations to the infinite source of all our peace, prosperity and happiness—of our duty to fulfil the great mission of liberty committed to our hands, that I would insist, cost what it may, on the establishment of a permanent, independent republic in Mexico.—[Cheers] I would insist that the great principle of religious toleration should be secured to all—that the Protestant in Mexico should be guaranteed the enjoyment of all the immunities and privileges enjoyed by Mexicans in the United States: [Loud cheers.] These great and benevolent objects I would accomplish by sending into Mexico a force adequate to maintain all the posts which we now occupy, to defend them against any assaults that might be made against them, and to keep open our communications. I would seize upon Paredes, Arista, and other military chieftains, and send them to St. Helena, if you please. [Laughter and applause.] I would declare an armistice; and the executive should be called upon to issue a proclamation, and send six or more commissioners to meet Mexico in a liberal and generous spirit.

We have vanquished Mexico. She is prostrate at our feet—we can afford to be magnaminous. Let us act so that we need not fear the strictest scrutiny of the Christian and civilized world. I would with a magnaminous and kindly hand gather these wretched people within the fold of republicanism. [Loud applause.] This I would accomplish at any cost.—"Oh!" but it is said, "this will bring us to direct taxation." Well, let it come. We must not shrink from our responsibility. We have ample means. — Throwing aside long financial reports which nobody understands, [Laughter] let us in a manly, upright and philanthropic spirit meet every emergency which we may be called upon to encounter in the discharge of duty. . . .

8   Religion and the Civil War

Woe to the world because of its stumbling blocks! For it is inevitable that stumbling blocks come; but woe to that man through whom the stumbling block comes!

—Matt. 18:7

An Address to Christians Throughout the World

During the heat of Civil War battles, churches and denominations continued their debates and discussions in regard to slavery and states' rights, much like they had done during antebellum years. But now during the war the wearers of blue and gray would also challenge each other on the rightfulness and wrongfulness of the internecine struggle. Again, the religious community participated in the verbal barrages that tore apart numerous religious institutions. The address which follows was delivered at a convention of Confederate ministers assembled at Richmond, Virginia in April 1863. The tone of the speech, however, was reflective of similar sentiments to be found within Union borders.

Christian Brethren:—In the name of our holy Christianity we address you in this form, respecting matters of great interest to us, which we believe deeply concern the cause of our Blessed Master, and to which we invoke your serious attention.

We speak not in the spirit of controversy, not by political inspiration, but as servants of the Most High God, we speak the "truth in love," concerning things which make for peace.

In the midst of war—surrounded by scenes that pain the souls of all good men—deploring the evils which are inseparable from national contention—we feel most deeply impressed by the conviction that, for our own sake, for the sake of our posterity, for the sake of humanity, for the sake of the truth, above all for the sake of our Redeemer's kingdom, it behooves us to testify of certain things in our beloved land which seem neither to be understood nor appreciated by our enemies, nor yet clearly appreciated by Christians of other nations.

We put forth this address, after much prayer, solemnly invoking the blessing of Almighty God, and committing what we say to that

Providence by which we trust we are directed, and by whose authority and power the governments of the earth stand or fall. If we were moved to make this address by any fears of the final issue of the war in which our country is now engaged, by any inclination to meddle with political questions, by any desire to resume controversy in respect to matters which have been referred to the arbitration of the sword; if, indeed, anything that compromised the simplicity, dignity and purity of Christian duty moved us to issue this address, we should deserve to have it despised by you, and could hope for no blessing of God to rest upon it. But for all we say in the following declarations, we are willing to be judged by succeeding generations, and to answer in that day when the secrets of all hearts shall be made known.

We do not propose to discuss the causes of the war. They are matters of recent history, easily known and read of all men. To discuss them would obviously involve much more than, as Christian ministers, we feel it our province to argue. We submit for your consideration, as the first point of our testimony and ground of protest:

> That the war waged against our people, in principle and in fact, proposes to achieve that which, in the nature of the case, it is impossible to accomplish by violence.

The war proposes the restoration of the Union. We can rationally suppose a war for conquest, or to expel an invader, or to compel respect for stipulations of peace and international intercourse which have been violated; but how measures of violence can reunite independent States, restore their broken fellowship, reestablish equality of representative rights, or coerce a people to brotherly kindness, unity and devotion to each other, is utterly beyond our conception.

But if our enemies be disingenuous in their professions; if they fight not to recover seceded States, but to subjugate them, what promise do men find in the numbers, intelligence, courage, resources and moral energies of the millions who inhabit the Confederate States, that such a people can ever become profitable or happy, as subordinate to mere military force? If subjugation, therefore, were possible, is it desirable? Would the United States gain anything? Would Christian civilization gain anything? Said a great British statesman, in 1775, when arguing in favor of adopting conciliatory measures in respect to the revolted colonies of America—colonies, not seceding States—that were in actual rebellion against their sovereign: "The use of force is but temporary. It may subdue for a moment, but it does not remove the necessity for subduing again; and a nation is not governed which is perpetually to be conquered. My next objection is its uncertainty. Terror is not always the effect of force, and an armament is not a victory. . . . A further objection is that you impair the object by your very endeavors to preserve it. The thing you fought for is not the thing you recover." Christian brethren, could the hand of violence win you to desire fellowship with a people while it destroyed your peace, polluted your sanctuaries, invaded the sacred precincts of your homes, robbed you of your property, slaughtered your noble sons, clothed your daughters in grief, filled your land with sorrow, and employed its utmost strength to reduce your country to the degradation of a subjugated province? Would it not rather animate you to prefer death—honorable—the patriot's alternative, the Christian's martyrdom?

As an excuse for violence, our enemies charge that the Confederate States have attempted to overthrow *"the best government on earth,"* and call us "traitors," "rebels." We deny the charge, and as to the epithets, if they defined our position, under the circumstances we should glory in them as do the people of God persecuted for truth and conscience' sake. But we regard such terms as gratuitously assuming the very point at issue. If employed sincerely, we will not complain; but we are persuaded that many have uttered these expressions, under the influence of resentful feelings, who would not otherwise assert the political doctrines they imply. We are not disposed to engage in angry retort, and only mention these things to show that we appreciate them. It will appear singular, when men reflect upon it, that so many intelligent and Christian people should desire to withdraw from *"the best government on earth."* And we need not discuss the kindness of those who so generously propose to confer on us, *by force of arms,* "the best government." No attempt has been made to overthrow the government of the United States, unless by the fanatical party which now administers its affairs. The South never entertained such an idea. If that government fall for lack of Southern support, let men discriminate between the downfall of an oppression when the oppressed have escaped, and a wanton effort to break up a good government. So Pharaoh fell, but not by the hand of Israel. The dismemberment of the Union by secession was not a blow at the government. It was for our own deliverance. It was an election of the people, only hastened, and

rendered in some cases imperative, by the violent movements of the Executive of the United States. Virginia may be referred to as an illustration. The state was not willing to secede hastily; but the demand of President Lincoln that she furnish troops to fight her sister States ended all hesitation. At once she took position with the Confederacy, preferring to battle in defence of liberty rather than, in opposition to all her principles, to invade to suffer the invasion of the South. So far, therefore, from desiring to destroy the United States government, the great object of those States which *first* seceded was to secure their own rights and their tranquillity; while the *immediate* object of the States which *last* seceded was to place themselves as barriers in the way of a fanatical administration, and if possible, stay the bloody effort to coerce independent States to remain in the Union, when their constitutional rights would not be respected, and when the very purpose to coerce them showed a readiness to sacrifice the loves of citizens to the demands of sectional hostility. The South would never vote in favor of annexing or retaining a Northern State by force of arms. Instead, therefore, of waging war for the overthrow of the United States, the Confederate States simply defend themselves.

The war is forced upon us. We have always desired peace. After a conflict of opinions between the North and the South, in Church and State, of more than thirty years, growing more bitter and painful daily, we withdraw from them to secure peace—they send troops to compel us into reunion! Our proposition was peaceful separation, saying, "we are *actually* divided, our *nominal* union is only a platform in strife." The answer is a call for *seventy-five thousand* troops to force submission to a government whose character, in the judgment of the South, had been sacrificed to sectionalism. From the speech of Mr. Burke, already referred to, the following language may be quoted as not inappropriate to our position in respect to peace: "The proposition is peace. Not peace through the medium of war; not peace to be hunted through the labyrinth of intricate and endless negotiation; not peace to arise out of universal discord, fomented from principle, in all parts of the empire, not peace to depend on the judicial determination of perplexing questions, or the precise marking of the shadowy boundaries of a complex government. It is simple peace, sought in the spirit of peace and laid in principles purely pacific." Such a proposition of peace was clearly the appropriate duty of a Christian people. The South can point out on the pages of history the names, and refer to the earnest and repeated efforts of her commissioners of peace. But our foes preferred war—violence—and by violence the end they aimed at was unattainable, as the purpose was unworthy of a Christian nation. *Against this violence*, upon principle, and in the light of all the facts of the case, we, as servants of God and ministers of peace, testify and solemnly protest. The second general point which we submit for your Christian consideration is:

> *The separation of the Southern States is universally regarded by our people as final, and the formation of the Confederate States government as a fixed fact, promising in no respect a restoration of the former Union.*

Politically and ecclesiastically the line has been drawn between North and South. It has been done distinctly, deliberately, finally, and in most solemn form. The Confederacy claims to possess all the conditions and essential characteristics of an independent government. Our institutions, habits, tastes, pursuits and religion suggest no wish for reconstruction of the Union. We regard the Confederacy, in the wise providence of the Almighty, as the result of causes which render its independent existence a moral and political necessity, and its final future independence of the United States not a matter that admits of the slightest doubt.

Among all the indefensible acts growing out of the inexcusable war waged against us, we will refer to one especially, in regard to which, for obvious reasons, we would speak, and as becometh us, plainly and earnestly:

> *The recent proclamation of the President of the United States, seeking the emancipation of the slaves of the South, is in our judgment, a suitable occasion for solemn protest on the part of the people of God throughout the world.*

First, upon the hypothesis that the proclamation could be carried out in its design, we have no language to describe the bloody tragedy that would appall humanity. Christian sensibilities recoil from the vision of a struggle that would inevitably lead to the slaughter of tens of thousands of poor deluded insurrectionists! Suppose their owners suffered; in the nature of things the slaves would suffer infinitely more. Make it absolutely necessary for the public safety that the slaves be slaughtered, and he who would write the history of that event would record the darkest chapter of human woe yet written.

But, *secondly*, suppose the proclamation—as indeed we esteem it in the South—a mere political document, devised to win favor among the most fanatical of the Northern people, uttering nothing that has not already been attempted practically, but in vain, by the United States; suppose it to be worth no more than the paper on which its bold iniquity is traced, nevertheless, it is an avowal of a principle, the declaration of a wish, the deliberate attempt of the chief magistrate of a nation to do that which, as a measure of war, must be repugnant to civilization, and which we calmly denounce as worthy of universal reprobation, and against which Christians in the name of humanity and religion ought to protest. What shall sound Christianity say to that one idea of philanthropy which, in the name of an *imaginary* good, in blind fury rushes upon a thousand *unquestionable* evils? If it were the time for such an argument, we should not fear the issue of a full discussion of this whole question of slavery.

We fear no investigation, we decline no debate; but we would not, at an hour like this and in an address which is chiefly a protest, invoke the spirit of controversy. We content ourselves with what we regard as infinitely more solemn; we stand before the world, while war silences the voices of disputants, and men in deadly contention wrestle in fields of blood, protesting against the crimes that, in the name of liberty and philanthropy, are attempted. Let it go forth from our lips while we live; let it be recorded of us when we are dead, that we—ministers of our Lord Jesus Christ, and members of his holy Church, with our hands upon the Bible, at once the sacred chart of our liberties and the foundation of our faith, call heaven and earth to record that, in the name of Him whose we are and whom we serve, we protest! No description we can give of this measure of the Executive of the United States, even though indignation alone inspired us to utter it, would exaggerate what we regard as an unholy infatuation, a ruthless persecution, a cruel and shameful device, adding severity and bitterness to a wicked and reckless war.

When it is remembered that, in the name of a *"military necessity,"* this new measure was adopted, we may pass by the concession of weakness implied in this fact, and content ourselves with calling attention to the *immortality* of a necessity created by a needless war of invasion. "Military necessity" an excuse not for self-defense— not for self-preservation—but for violating the rules of civilized warfare, and attempting a barbarity. If "military necessity" be the inspiration to attempt emancipation, how shall men praise it as philanthropy? Are other nations uninterested in such conduct? Proclaim the right first to invade and subjugate independent States, exhaust all resources, and then avow the principle of "military necessity" as an excuse to add severity to a wrong, as a plea upon which to project a scheme violative of every manly, honorable and Christian sentiment! Suppose an invader happens to be too weak to conquer upon any other plan, has he therefore the right to proclaim that poison and the indiscriminate slaughter of women and children shall be his legal method? The common cause of humanity and the common hope of Christian civilization, as they appeal to every nation, cry out against this wretched subterfuge. If the "military necessity" of *weakness* may righteously adopt any measure that an invader's ingenuity can invest, or his malice suggest, what laws, what principles of justice and equity shall nations at war respect? At one time the world is told that "the rebellion is weak and will be crushed out in sixty days;" at another, "Union men abound in the South, and will welcome the United States troops as deliverers;" and *now* the invader is so hopeless of his task that it is a "military necessity" that he obtain the help of slaves!

May it not pertinently be asked what that is creditable to this invasion, ought men to believe, and to what end is this deceitful war waged?

When this last resort, like all the enemy's preceding schemes shall signally fail, as it certainly will, to achieve the ruin of the South, what is promised? Nothing but war, cruel, relentless, desperate war! Because the President, by his scheme, violates the Constitution, we might condemn him; though the constitutionality of his acts be less important to us than to the people over whom he presides: because he has violated his word, his *special promise*, and even his solemn oath of office, we might abhor his act; though that is a matter which may chiefly concern his conscientiousness, and illustrate the character of that officer whom Southerners refused to salute as their President: because of the diabolical *mischief intended* we might, in the name of heaven, indignantly denounce his proclamation; though no weapon formed against us be, practically, more harmless. But these are not the considerations which move us to protest; we solemnly protest *because, under the guise of philanthropy and the pretext of doing good, he would seek the approbation of mankind upon a war that promises to humanity only*

evil and that continually. Let philanthropists observe, even according to its own terms, this measure is in no proper sense an act of mercy to the slave, but of malice toward the master. It provides for freeing *only the slaves of those who fight* against the United States. The effort is not to relieve that government of slavery, where the philanthropy has full opportunity for displaying its generosity, and the power to exercise it in respect to slavery, if it exist at all, can be indulged; but the effort is simply to invoke slavery as an agent against the South, reckless of the consequences to the slaves themselves. Shall a pretext at once so weak and so base mislead intelligent men, and make them imagine that Abraham Lincoln is a philanthropist? His position ought to be offensive to every sincere abolitionist, as well as disgusting to every sincere friend of the slave, of every shade of opinion on the question of slavery. How does it affect the cause of the Confederacy? If to awaken a deeper resentment than ever inflamed the people of the South before; if to quench the last sentiment of respect that lingered in their breasts for the United States government; if to unite them more resolutely than ever, and to make it to the individual interest of every person in the bounds of the Confederacy to sustain and strengthen it with every dollar and every arm, and every prayer, and every energy of manly virtue and Christian encouragement—be to advance the invader's interest and give him hope of success, then has the proclamation furnished him opportunity of congratulating himself.

We submit further: *That the war against the Confederate States has achieved no good result, and we find nothing in the present state of the struggle that gives promise of the United States accomplishing any good by its continuance.* Though hundreds of thousands of lives have been lost, and many millions of treasure spent: though a vast amount of valuable property has been destroyed, and numbers of once happy homes made desolate: though cities and towns have been temporarily captured, and aged men and helpless women and children have suffered such things as it were even a shame to speak of plainly: though sanctuaries have been desecrated, and ministers of God been dragged from sacred altars to loathsome prisons: though slaves have been instigated to insurrection, and every measure has been adopted that the ingenuity of the enemy could devise or his ample resources afford by sea and by land: yet we aver, without fear of contradiction, that the only possession which the United States holds in the Confederate States is the ground on which United States troops pitch their tents; and that whenever those troops withdraw from a given locality in our territory, the people resident therein testify a warmer devotion to the Confederate cause than even before their soil was invaded. Nothing is therefore conquered—no part of the country is subdued; the civil jurisdiction of the United States, the real test of their success, *has not been established by any force of arms.* Where such civil jurisdiction exists at all along the border, it has existed all the while, was not obtained by force, and is not the fruit of conquest. This fact is submitted by our enemies themselves.

It is worthy of special notice, that notwithstanding the gigantic exertions of the United States, they have not been able to secure the return of a single county, or section of a county, much less a single State that has se-

ceded. No civil order and peace spring up in the track of their armies. All in front of them is resolute resistance, and behind them when they have entered our territory, is a deep, uncompromising opposition, over which only military force can for a moment be trusted. Thus the civilized world is called upon to observe an invasion which has lasted for nearly two years, and achieved nothing but cruelty. Before it a people ready to die, but neither ready to submit, nor weak enough to be conquered; and for its gloomy prospect an interminable war, growing more bitter and unfeeling every day, because more hopeless to them that by it have sought things impossible as well as unrighteous. In the name of the great Prince of Peace, has Christianity, has civilization, nothing to say to such an awful tragedy? Such is the war for the *Union*! Yet every day our foes are deepening and widening that river of blood which divides us from them forever!

The only change of opinion among our people since the beginning of the war, that is of material importance to the final issue, has been the change from all lingering attachment to the former Union to a more sacred and reliable devotion to the Confederate government. The sentiments of the people are not alterable in any other respects by force of arms. If the whole country were occupied by United States troops, it would merely exhibit a military despotism, against which the people would struggle in perpetual revolutionary effort while any Southrons remained alive. Extermination of the inhabitants could alone realize civil possession of their soil. Subjugation is therefore clearly impossible. Is extermination desired by Christians?

The moral and religious interests of the South ought to be appreciated by Christians of all nations.

These interests have realized certainly no benefit from the war. We are aware that in respect to the moral aspects of the question of slavery, we differ from those who conceive of emancipation as a measure of benevolence, and on that account we suffer much reproach which we are conscious of not deserving. With all the facts of the system of slavery in its practical operations before us, "as eye-witnesses and ministers of the word, having had perfect understanding of all things" on this subject of which we speak, we may surely claim respect for our opinions and statements. Most of us have grown up from childhood among the slaves; all of us have preached to and taught them the word of life; have administered to them the ordinances of the Christian Church; sincerely love them as souls for whom Christ died; we go among them freely and know them in health and sickness, in labor and rest, from infancy to old age. We are familiar with physical and moral condition, and alive to all their interests; and we testify in the sight of God, that the relation of master and slave among us, however we may deplore abuses in this, as in other relations of mankind, is not incompatible with our holy Christianity, and that the presence of the Africans in our land is an occasion of gratitude on their behalf, before God; seeing that thereby Divine Providence has brought them where missionaries of the cross may freely proclaim to them the word of salvation, and the work is not interrupted by agitating fanaticism. The South has done more than any people on earth for the Christianization of the African race. The condition of the slave here is not wretched, as Northern fictions would have men believe, but prosperous and happy, and would have been yet more so but for the mistaken zeal of the abolitionists. Can emancipation obtain for them a better portion? The practicable plan for benefiting the African race must be the Providential plan—the Scriptural plan. We adapt that plan in the South, and while the States would seek by wholesome legislation to regard the interest of master and slave, we, as ministers would preach the word to both as we are commanded of God. This war has not benefited the slaves. Those that have been encouraged or compelled by the enemy to leave their masters, have gone, and we aver can go, to no state of society that offers them any better things than they have at home, either in respect to their temporal or eternal welfare. We regard abolitionism as an interference with the plans of Divine Providence. It has not the signs of the Lord's blessing. It is a fanaticism which puts forth no good fruit; instead of blessing, it has brought forth cursing; instead of love, hatred; instead of life, death; bitterness and sorrow, and pain, and infidelity, and moral degeneracy follow its labors. We remember how the apostle has taught the minister of Jesus upon this subject, saying: "Let as many servants as are under the yoke, count their own masters worthy of all honor that the name of God and his doctrine be not blasphemed. And they that have believing masters, let them not despise them because they are brethren; but rather do them service because they are faithful and beloved, partakers of the benefit. *These things teach and exhort.* If any man teach otherwise, and consent not to wholesome words, even the words of our Lord Jesus Christ, and to the doctrine which is according to godliness, he is proud, knowing nothing, but doting about questions and strifes of words, whereof cometh envy, strife, railings, evil surmisings, perverse disputings of men of corrupt minds, and destitute of the truth, supposing that gain is godliness: from such withdraw thyself."

This is what we teach, and obedient to the last verse of the text, from men that "teach otherwise"—hoping for peace—we "withdraw" ourselves.

The Christians of the South, we claim, are pious, intelligent and liberal. Their pastoral and missionary works have points of peculiar interest. There are hundreds of thousands here, both white and colored, who are not strangers to the blood that bought them. We rejoice that the great Head of the Church has not despised us. We desire, as much as in us lieth, to live peaceably with all men, and though reviled, to revile not again.

Much harm has been done to the religious enterprises of the Church by the war; we will not tire you by enumerating particulars. We thank God for the patient faith and fortitude of our people during these days of trial.

Our soldiers were before the war our fellow citizens, and many of them are of the household of faith, who have carried to the camp so much of the leaven of Christianity, that amid all the demoralizing influence of army life, the good work of salvation has gone forward there.

Our President, some of our most influential statesmen, our commanding General, and an unusual proportion of the principal Generals, as well as scores of other officers, are prominent and we believe consistent members of the Church. Thousands of our soldiers are men of prayer. We regard our success in the war as due to divine mercy, and our government and people have recognized the hand of God in the normal and humble celebration of his goodness. We have no fear in regard to the future. If the war continues for years, we believe God's grace sufficient for us.

In conclusion, we ask for ourselves, our churches, our country, the devout prayers of all God's people—"the will of the Lord be done."

Christian brethren, think on these things and let your answer to our address be the voice of an enlightened Christian sentiment going forth from you against war, against persecution for conscience' sake, against the ravaging of the Church of God by fanatical invasion. But if we speak to you in vain, nevertheless we have not spoken in vain in the sight of God: for we have proclaimed the truth—we have testified in behalf of Christian civilization—we have invoked charity—we have filed our solemn protest against a cruel and useless war. And our children shall read it and honor our spirit, though in much feebleness we may have borne our testimony.

"Charity beareth all things, believeth all things, hopeth all things, endureth all things." We desire to "follow after charity"; and "as many as walk according to this rule, peace be on them and mercy, and upon the Israel of God."

Second Inaugural Address
Abraham Lincoln

President Abraham Lincoln (1809-1865) gave his Second Inaugural Address on Saturday, March 4, 1865. This was six weeks before his death and less than five weeks before the end of the war. His short speech of 701 words, 505 of which are of one syllable, did not include any battle cries or predictions of triumph. The first paragraph, which is devoid of celebration or self-congratulation, sets the tone for the total document. The distinctive feature of the second paragraph is its balanced treatment of the two sides, as is seen with the words *all* and *both*. Lincoln did have an interpretation, however, of the cause of the war, which he states in the third paragraph. The final paragraph, which consists of only one sentence, contains his call for and anticipation of the war's end.

Fellow Countrymen:

At this second appearing to take the oath of the presidential office, there is less occasion for an extended address than there was at the first. Then a statement, somewhat in detail, of a course to be pursued, seemed fitting and proper. Now, at the expiration of four years, during which public declarations have been constantly called forth on every point and phase of the great contest which still absorbs the attention, and engrosses the energies of the nation, little that is new could be presented. The progress of our arms, upon which all else chiefly depends, is as well known to the public as to myself; and it is, I trust, reasonably satisfactory and encouraging to all. With high hope for the future, no prediction in regard to it is ventured.

On the occasion corresponding to this four years ago, all thoughts were anxiously directed to an impending civil-war. All dreaded it—all sought to avert it. While the inaugural address was being delivered from this place, devoted altogether to *saving* the Union without war, insurgent agents were in the city seeking to *destroy* it without war—seeking to dissolve the Union, and divide effects, by negotiation. Both parties deprecated war; but one of them would *make* war rather than let the nation survive; and the other would *accept* war rather than let it perish. And the war came.

One-eighth of the whole population were colored slaves, not distributed generally over the Union, but localized in the Southern part of it. These slaves constituted a peculiar and powerful interest. All knew that this interest was, somehow, the cause of the war. To strengthen, perpetuate, and extend this interest was the object for which the insurgents would rend the Union, even by war; while the government claimed no right to do more than to restrict the territorial enlargement of it. Neither party expected for the war, the magnitude, or the duration, which it has already attained. Neither anticipated that the *cause* of the conflict might cease with, or even before, the conflict itself should cease. Each looked for an easier triumph, and a result less fundamental and astounding. Both read the same Bible, and pray to the same God; and each invokes His aid against the other. It may seem strange that any men should dare to ask a just God's assistance in wringing their bread from the sweat of other men's faces; but let us judge not that we be not judged. The prayers of both could not be answered; that of neither has been answered fully. The Almighty has His own purposes. "Woe unto the world because of offences! for it must needs be that offences come; but woe to that man by whom the offence cometh!" If we shall suppose that American Slavery is one of those offences which, in the providence of God, must needs come, but which, having continued through His appointed time, He now wills to remove, and that He gives to both North and South, this terrible war, as the woe due to those by whom the offence came, shall we discern therein any departure from those divine attributes which the believers in a Living God always ascribe to Him, Fondly do we hope—fervently do we pray—that this mighty scourge of war may speedily pass away. Yet, if God wills that it continue, until all the wealth piled by the bond-men's two hundred and fifty years of unrequited toil shall be sunk, and until every drop of blood drawn with the lash, shall be paid by another drawn with the sword, as was said three thousand years ago, so still it must be said "the judgments of the Lord, are true and righteous altogether."

With malice toward none; with charity for all; with firmness in the right, as God gives us to see the right, let us strive on to finish the work we are in; to bind up the nation's wounds; to care for him who shall have borne the battle, and for his widow, and his orphan—to do all which may achieve and cherish a just, and a lasting peace, among ourselves, and with all nations.

Address at the Raising of the Union Flag over Fort Sumter
Henry Ward Beecher

Henry Ward Beecher (1813-1887), son of Lyman Beecher and brother of Harriet Beecher Stowe, was one of America's most influential preachers during the nineteenth century. His unconventional preaching style was characterized by showmanship and punctuated with humor because he believed it was necessary to appeal to his audience emotionally. Prior to the Civil War he expressed consistently his opposition to slavery, which he contended would eventually die out as an institution if it were limited to the South. At the conclusion of the war he was invited by the Union government to deliver an address at Charleston, South Carolina on the anniversary of the fall of Fort Sumter. It was later published in *Patriotic Addresses in America and England, from 1850 to 1855* (New York: Ford, Howard, and Hulbert, 1891), pp. 676-97.

Ladies and Gentlemen:

On this solemn and joyful day, we again lift to the breeze our fathers' flag, now again the banner of *the United States*, with the fervent prayer that God would crown it with honor, protect it from treason, and send it down to our children, with all the blessings of civilization, liberty, and religion. Terrible in battle, may it be beneficent in peace. Happily, no bird or beast of prey has been inscribed upon it. The stars that redeem the night from darkness, and the beams of red light that beautify the morning, have been united upon its folds. As long as the sun endures, or the stars, may it wave over a nation neither enslaved or enslaving. Once, and but once, has treason dishonored it. In that insane hour, when the guiltiest and bloodiest rebellion of time hurled their fires upon this fort, you, Sir, [turning to General Anderson] and a small heroic band, stood within these now crumbled walls, and did gallant and just battle for the honor and defense of the nation's banner. . . .

Hail to the flag of our fathers, and our flag! Glory to the banner that has gone through four years black with tempests of war, to pilot the nation back to peace without dismemberment! And glory be to God, who, above all hosts and banners, hath ordained victory, and shall ordain peace!

Wherefore have we come hither, pilgrims from distant places? Are we come to exult that Northern hands are stronger than Southern? No, but to rejoice that the hands of those who defend a just and beneficent government are mightier than the hands that assaulted it! Do we exult over fallen cities? We exult that a nation has not fallen. We sorrow with the sorrowful. We sympathize with the desolate. We look upon this shattered fort, and yonder dilapidated city, with sad eyes, grieved that men should have committed such treason, and glad that God hath set such a mark upon treason that all ages shall dread and abhor it.

We exult, not for a passion gratified, but for a sentiment victorious; not for temper, but for conscience; not as we devoutly believe that *our* will is done, but that God's will hath been done. We should be unworthy of that liberty entrusted to our care, if, on such a day as this, we sullied our hearts by feelings of aimless vengeance; and equally unworthy, if we did not devoutly thank Him who hath said, *Vengeance is mine, I will repay, saith the Lord*, that he hath set a mark upon arrogant Rebellion, ineffaceable while time lasts! . . .

We raise our fathers' banner that it may bring back better blessings than those of old; that it may cast out the devil of discord; that it may restore lawful government, and a prosperity purer and more enduring than that which it protected before; that it may win parted friends from their alienation; that it may inspire hope, and inaugurate universal liberty; that it may say to the sword, "Return to thy sheath," and to the plow and sickle, "Go forth'; that it may heal all jealousies, unite all policies, inspire a new national life, compact our strength, purify our principles, ennoble our national ambitions, and make this people great and strong, not for aggression and quarrelsomeness, but for the peace of the world, giving to us the glorious prerogative of leading all nations to juster laws, to more humane policies, to sincerer friendship, to rational, instituted civil liberty, and to universal Christian brotherhood.

Reverently, piously, in hopeful patriotism, we spread this banner on the sky, as of old the bow was planted on the cloud; and, with solemn fervor, beseech God to look upon it, and make it the memorial of an everlasting covenant and decree that never again on this fair land shall a deluge of blood prevail. . . .

When God would prepare Moses for Emancipation, he overthrew his first steps, and drove him for forty years to brood in the wilderness. When our flag came down, four years it lay brooding in darkness. It cried to the Lord, "Wherefore am I deposed?" Then arose before it a vision of its sin. It had strengthened the strong, and forgotten the weak. It proclaimed liberty, but trod upon slaves.

In that seclusion it dedicated itself to liberty. Behold, to-day it fulfills its vows! When it went down, four million people had no flag. To-day it rises, and four million people cry out, "Behold *our* banner!" Hark! they murmur. It is the Gospel that they recite in sacred words: "It is a Gospel to the poor, it heals our broken hearts, it preaches deliverance to captives, it gives sight to the blind, it sets at liberty them that are bruised." Rise up, then, glorious Gospel Banner, and roll out these messages of God. Tell the air that not a spot now sullies thy whiteness. The red is not the blush of shame, but the flush of joy. Tell the dews that wash thee that thou art as pure as they. Say to the night, that thy stars lead toward the morning; and to the morning, that brighter day arises with healing in its wings. And then, O glorious flag, bid the sun pour light on all they folds with double brightness, whilst thou art bearing around and round the world the solemn joy—a race set free, a nation redeemed!

The mighty hand of Government, made strong in war by the favor of the God of Battles, spreads wide to-day the banner of liberty that went down in darkness, that rose in light; and there it streams, like the sun above it, neither parceled out nor monopolized, but flooding the air with light for all mankind. Ye scattered and broken, ye wounded and dying, bitten by the fiery serpents of oppression, everywhere, in all the world, look upon this sign lifted up, and live! And ye homeless and houseless slaves, look, and ye are free! At length you, too, have part and lot in this glorious ensign, that broods with impartial love over small and great, the poor and the strong, the bond and the free! In this solemn hour, let us pray for the quick coming of reconciliation and happiness, under this common flag!

But we must build again, from the foundations, in all these now free Southern States. No cheap exhortation "to forgetfulness of the past, to restore all things as they were" will do. God does not stretch out his hand, as he has for four dreadful years, that men may easily forget the might of his terrible acts. Restore things as they were? What, the alienations and jealousies? The discords and contentions, and the causes of them? No. In that solemn sacrifice on which a nation has offered up for its sins so many precious victims, loved and lamented, let our sins and mistakes be consumed utterly and forever.

No. Never again shall things be restored as before the war. It is written in God's decree of events fulfilled, "Old things are passed away." That new earth, in which dwelleth righteousness, draws near. . . .

I charge the whole guilt of this war upon the ambitious, educated, plotting, political leaders of the South. They have shed this ocean of blood. They have desolated the South. They have poured poverty through all her towns and cities. They have bewildered the imagination of the people with phantasms, and led them to believe that they were fighting for their homes and liberty, whose homes were unthreatened, and whose liberty was in no jeopardy.

These arrogant instigators of civil war have renewed the plagues of Egypt, not that the oppressed might go free, but that the free might be oppressed. A day will come when God will reveal judgment, and arraign at his bar these mighty miscreants; and then every orphan that their bloody game has made, and every widow that sits sorrowing, and every maimed and wounded sufferer, and every bereaved heart in all the wide regions of this land, will rise up and come before the Lord to lay upon these chief culprits of modern history their awful testimony. And from a thousand battle-fields shall rise up armies of airy witnesses, who, with the memory of their awful sufferings, shall confront these miscreants with shrieks of fierce accusation, and every pale and starved prisoner shall raise his skinny hand in judgment. Blood shall call out for vengeance, and tears shall plead for justice, and grief shall silently beckon, and love, heart-smitten, shall wail for justice. Good men and angels will cry out, "How long, O Lord, how long, wilt thou not avenge!"

And, then, these guiltiest and most remorseless traitors, these high and cultured men with might and wisdom, used for the destruction of their country; these most accursed and detested of all criminals, that have drenched a continent in needless blood, and moved the foundations of their times with hideous crimes and cruelty, caught up in black clouds full of voices of vengeance and lurid with punishment, shall be whirled aloft and plunged downward forever and forever in an endless retribution; while God shall say, "Thus shall it be to all who betray their country"; and all in heaven and upon the earth will say, "Amen!" . . .

I now pass to the considerations of benefits that accrue to the South in distinction from the rest of the nation. At present the South reaps only suffering, but good seed lies buried under the furrows of war, that peace will bring to harvest.

1. Deadly doctrines have been purged away in blood. The subtle poison of secession was a perpetual threat of revolution. The sword has ended that danger. That which reason has affirmed as a philosophy, the people have settled as a fact. Theory pronounces, "There can be no permanent government where each integral particle has liberty to fly, off." Who would venture upon a voyage on a ship, each plank and timber of which might withdraw at its pleasure? But the people have reasoned by the logic of the sword and of the ballot, and they have declared that States are inseparable parts of national government. They are not sovereign. State *rights* remain; but *sovereignty* is a right higher than all others; and that has been made into a common stock for the benefit of all. All further agitation is ended. This element must be cast out of our political prob-

lems. Henceforth that poison will not rankle in the blood.

2. Another thing has been learned: the rights and duties of minorities. The people of the whole nation are of more authority than the people of any section. These United States are supreme over Northern, Eastern, Western, and Southern States. It ought not to have required the awful chastisement of this war to teach that a minority must submit the control of the nation's government to a majority. The army and the navy have been good political schoolmasters. The lesson is learned. Not for many generations will it require further illustration.

3. No other lesson will be more fruitful of peace than the dispersion of those conceits of vanity, which, on either side, have clouded the recognition of the manly courage of all Americans. If it be a sign of manhood to be able to fight, then Americans are men. The North certainly are in no doubt whatever of the soldierly qualities of Southern men. Southern soldiers have learned that all latitudes breed courage on this continent. Courage is a passport to respect. The people of all the regions of this nation are likely hereafter to cherish generous admiration of each other's prowess. The war has bred respect, and respect will breed affection, and affection peace and unity.

4. No other event of the war can fill an intelligent Southern man of candid nature with more surprise than the revelation of the capacity, moral and military, of the black race. It is a revelation, indeed.

No people were ever less understood by those most familiar with them. They were said to be lazy, lying, impudent, and cowardly wretches, driven by the whip alone to the tasks needful to their own support, and the functions of civilization. They were said to be dangerous, blood-thirsty, liable to insurrection; but four years of tumultuous distress and war have rolled across the area inhabited by them, and I have yet to hear of one authentic instance of the misconduct of a colored man. They have been patient and gentle and docile in the land, while the men of the South were away in the army, they have been full of faith and hope and piety; and when summoned to freedom they have emerged with all the signs and tokens that freedom will be to them what it was to be—the swaddling band that shall bring them to manhood. And after the Government, honoring them as men, summoned them to the field, when once they were disciplined and had learned the art of war, they proved themselves to be not second to their white brethren in arms. And when the roll of men that have shed their blood is called in the other land, many and many dusky face will rise, dark no more, when the light of eternal glory shall shine upon it from the throne of God.

5. The industry of the Southern States is regenerated and now rests upon a basis that never fails to bring prosperity. Just now industry is collapsed; but it is not dead. It sleepeth. It is vital yet. It will spring like mown grass from the roots, that need but showers and heat and time to bring them forth. Though in many districts not a generation will see wanton wastes of self-invoked war repaired, and many portions may lapse again to wilderness; yet, in our life-time we shall see States, as a whole, raised to a prosperity, vital, wholesome and immovable.

6. The destruction of class interests, working with a religion which tends towards true democracy in proportion as it is pure and free, will create a new era of prosperity for the common laboring people of the South. Upon them has come the labor, the toil, and the loss of this war. They have fought for a class that sought their degradation, while they were made to believe that it was for their own homes and altars. Their leaders meant a supremacy which would not long have left them political liberty, save in name. But their leaders are swept away. The sword has been hungry for the ruling classes. It has sought them out with remorseless zeal. New men are to rise up; new ideas are to bud and blossom; and there will be men with different ambition and altered policy.

7. Meanwhile, the South, no longer a land of plantations, but of farms; no longer tilled by slaves, but by freemen, will find no hindrance to the spread of education. Schools will multiply. Books and papers will spread. Churches will bless every hamlet. There is a good day coming for the South. Through darkness and tears, and blood she has sought it. It has been an unconscious *Via Dolorosa*. But, in the end, it will be worth all it has cost. Her institutions before were deadly. She nourished death in her bosom.

The greater her secular prosperity, the more sure was her ruin. Every year of delay but made the change more terrible. Now, by an earthquake, the evil is shaken down. Her own historians, in a better day, shall write that from the day the sword cut off the cancer she began to find her health.

What, then, shall hinder the rebuilding of this republic? The evil spirit is cast out: why should not this nation cease to wander among tombs, cutting itself? Why should it not come, clothed in its right mind, to "sit at the feet of Jesus?" Is it feared that the Government will oppress the conquered States? What possible motive has the Government to narrow the base of that pyramid on which its own permanence stands? . . .

From this pulpit of broken stone we speak forth our earnest greeting to all our land.

We offer to the President of these United States our solemn congratulations that God has sustained his life and health under the unparalleled burdens and sufferings of four bloody years, and permitted him to behold this auspicious consummation of that national unity for which he has waited with so much patience and fortitude, and for which he has labored with such disinterested wisdom.

To the members of the Government associated with him in the administration of perilous affairs in critical times: to the Senators and Representatives of the United States who have eagerly fashioned the instruments by which the popular will might express and enforce itself, we tender our grateful thanks.

To the officers and men of the army and navy, who have so faithfully, skillfully, and gloriously upheld their country's authority, by suffering, labor, and sublime courage, we offer here a tribute beyond the compass of words.

Upon those true and faithful citizens, men and women, who have borne up with unflinching hope in the darkest hour, and covered the land with the labors of love and charity, we invoke the divinest blessing of Him whom they have so truly imitated.

But chiefly to Thee, God of our fathers, we render thanksgiving and praise for that wondrous providence that has brought forth, from such a harvest of war, the seed of so much liberty and peace.

We invoke peace upon the North. Peace be to the West. Peace be upon the South!

In the name of God, we lift up our banner, and dedicate it to Peace, Union, and Liberty, now and forevermore. Amen.

Part III Energizing America
1865-1920

The energy unleashed with the rise of industrial capitalism, mechanization, and urbanization between 1865 and 1920 brought many social and economic changes to America. But the intellectual and cultural transformations produced by the scientific thought of evolutionary naturalism were of a different kind, which cannot be measured in dollars or percentages. The very presuppositions of traditional Christianity upon which the American society rested in 1865 were undermined by the doctrine of the evolution of species popularized by Charles Darwin in his 1859 publication of *The Origin of Species*.

It was during this time of transition when religion became less an independent variable, and in turn, became more a dependent variable. After 1865 leaders in science, education, industry, and other areas replaced religious leaders as dominant spokesmen in American society. Although the secularization of America was moving gradually across the social and intellectual landscape long before 1865, from 1865 to 1920 the process accelerated at an unprecedented rate. In the words of historian Paul A. Carter, America experienced a "spiritual crisis" during the last third of the nineteenth century. In part this is what Arthur M. Schlesinger had in mind when he referred to this period as "a critical period in American religion."

Within organized religion evolution raised issues and problems that threatened the traditional beliefs as well as practices of most Americans. The emerging conflict within Protestantism between liberals and fundamentalists was paralleled by equally significant power struggles within Catholicism and Judaism. Little did Darwin know in 1859 that his ideas would have such far-reaching religious influence, but by the 1870s the battle lines were drawn between the scientific and religious supporters of the evolutionary naturalism tenets and its opponents. Works by scientist James Woodrow and theologians Charles Hodge and Henry Ward Beecher suggest how some thinkers responded to Darwin's ideas, while the writings of clergymen Theodore T. Munger, Washington Gladden, and Walter Rauschenbusch explain the new theology of liberalism.

The implications of naturalistic evolution went far beyond the biological and theological realms. If the evolutionary process expounded by Darwin were to be applied to socio-economic relationships, might not an inevitable progress automatically follow there also? Many businessmen like Andrew Carnegie believed and behaved as though it were so, for reasons he explained in his 1889 essay, "Wealth." Churchmen William Lawrence and Russell H. Conwell concurred and then added their own religious perspectives to Carnegie's secular ideals.

Not all naturalists agreed, however, that inevitable progress was a function of evolutionary forces. The reformer evolutionists asserted that man's ability to think must be used to direct the evolutionary process into socially desirable channels. Among the reformers was the social gospeler Washington Gladden who, along with clergymen James Cardinal Gibbons and Charles M. Sheldon, believed it was essential for man to remold society into something better.

During the late nineteenth century the energy and ambition of America were loosened in a mighty expansionist thrust abroad, a result in part of the adherence to evolutionary precepts. Josiah Strong, Albert J. Beveridge, and William Jennings Bryan discuss the rise of the United States to world power stature as the nation entered the twentieth century.

9 Science and Religion

In the beginning God created the heavens and the earth.

—Gen. 1:1

What is Darwinism?
Charles Hodge

Charles Hodge (1797-1878), a foremost Presbyterian theologian of the nineteenth century, taught at Princeton Seminary for more than a half century. In the 1870s he emerged as a staunch conservative opponent of Darwinism. While some antagonists of the evolutionary doctrines used ridicule in their efforts to laugh evolutionary theories out of serious consideration, Hodge engaged a much more reasoned approach in his analysis of Darwin's propositions. In his orthodox repudiation, *What is Darwinism?*, he appropriately identified natural selection as the essential factor and promptly pronounced it to be a contradiction of the doctrine of an omnipotent, omniscient Creator. The excerpted essay which follows was taken from *What is Darwinism?* (New York: Scribner, Armstrong and Company, 1874), *passim.*

This is a question which needs an answer. Great confusion and diversity of opinion prevail as to the real views of the man whose writings have agitated the whole world, scientific and religious. If a man says he is a Darwinian, many understand him to avow himself virtually an atheist; while another understands him as saying that he adopts some harmless form of the doctrine of evolution. This is a great evil.

It is obviously useless to discuss any theory until we are agreed as to what that theory is. The question, therefore, What is Darwinism? must take precedence of all discussion of its merits.

The great fact of experience is that the universe exists. The great problem which has ever pressed upon the human mind is to account for its existence. What was its origin? To what causes are the changes we witness around us to be referred? As we are a part of the universe, these questions concern ourselves. What are the origin, nature, and destiny of man?... Mr. Darwin undertakes to answer these questions. He proposes a solution of the problem which thus deeply concerns every living man. Darwinism is, therefore, a theory of the universe, at least so far as the living organisms on earth are concerned. . . .

The Scriptural solution of the problem of the universe is stated in words equally simple and sublime: "In the beginning God created the heavens and the earth." We have here, first, the idea of God. The word God has in the Bible a definite meaning. It does not stand for an abstraction, for mere force, for law or ordered sequence. God is a spirit, and as we are spirits, we know from consciousness that God is, (1) A Substance; (2) That He is a person; and, therefore, a self-conscious, intelligent, voluntary agent. He can say I; we can address Him as thou; we can speak of Him as He or Him. This idea of God pervades the Scriptures. It lies at the foundation of natural religion. It is involved in our religious consciousness. It enters essentially into our sense of moral obligation. It is inscribed ineffaceably, in letters more or less legible, on the heart of every human being. The man who is trying to be an atheist is trying to free himself from the laws of his being. He might as well try to free himself from liability to hunger or thirst.

The God of the Bible, then, is a Spirit, infinite, eternal, and unchangeable in his being, wisdom, power, holiness, goodness, and truth. As every theory must begin with some postulate, this is the grand postulate with which the Bible begins. This is the first point.

The second point concerns the origin of the universe. It is not eternal either as to matter of form. It is not independent of God. It is not an evolution of his being, or his existence form. He is extramundane as well as antemundane. The universe owes its existence to his will.

Thirdly, as to the nature of the universe; it is not a mere phenomenon. It is an entity, having real objective existence, or actuality. This implies that matter is a substance endowed with certain properties, in virtue of which it is capable of acting and of being acted upon. These properties being uniform and constant, are physical laws to which, as their proximate causes, all the phenomena of nature are to be referred.

Fourthly, although God is extramundane, He is nevertheless everywhere present. That presence is not only a presence of essence, but also of knowledge and power. He upholds all things. He controls all physical causes, working through them, with them, and without them, as He sees fit. As we, in our limited spheres, can use physical causes to accomplish our purposes, so God everywhere and always cooperates with them to accomplish his infinitely wise and merciful designs.

Fifthly, man a part of the universe, is, according to the Scriptures, as concerns his body, of the earth. So far, he belongs to the animal kingdom. As to his soul, he is a child of God, who is declared to be the Father of the spirit of all men. God is a spirit, and we are spirits. We are, therefore, of the same nature with God. We are God-like; so that in knowing ourselves we know God. No man conscious of his manhood can be ignorant of his relationship to God as his Father.

The truth of the theory of the universe rests, in the first place, so far as it has been correctly stated, on the infallible authority of the word of God. In the second place, it is a satisfactory solution of the problem to be solved: (1) It accounts for the origin of the universe. (2) It accounts for all the universe contains, and gives a satisfactory explanation of the marvelous contrivances which abound in living organisms, of the adaptations of these organisms to conditions external to themselves, and for those provisions for the future, which on any other assumption are utterly inexplicable. (3) It is in conflict with no truth of reason and with no fact of experience. (4) The Scriptural doctrine accounts for the spiritual nature of man, and meets all his spiritual necessities. It gives him an object of adoration, love, and confidence. It reveals the Being on whom his indestructible sense of responsibility terminates. The truth of this doctrine, therefore, rests not only on the authority of the Scriptures, but on the very constitution of our nature. The Bible has little charity for those who reject it. It pronounces them to be either derationalized or demoralized, or both. . . .

We have not forgotten Mr. Darwin. It seemed desirable, in order to understand his theory, to see its relation to other theories of the universe and its phenomena, with which it is more or less connected. His work on the "Origin of Species" does not purport to be philosophical. . . . Darwin does not speculate on the origin of the universe, on the nature of matter, or of force. He is simply a naturalist, a careful and laborious observer;

skillful in his descriptions, and singularly candid in dealing with the difficulties in the way of his peculiar doctrine. He set before himself a single problem, namely, How are the fauna and flora of our earth to be accounted for? In the solution of this problem, he assumes: (1) The existence of matter, although he says little on the subject. Its existence however, as a real entity, is everywhere taken for granted. (2) He assumes the efficiency of physical causes, showing no disposition to resolve them into mind-force, or into the efficiency of the First Cause. (3) He assumes also the existence of life in the form of one or more primordial germs. He does not adopt the theory of spontaneous generation. What life is he does not attempt to explain. . . . (4) To account for the existence of matter and life, Mr. Darwin admits a Creator. This is done explicitly and repeatedly. Nothing, however, is said of the nature of the Creator and of his relation to the world, further than is implied in the meaning of the word. (5) From the primordial germ or germs (Mr. Darwin seems to have settled down to the assumption of only one primordial germ), all living organisms, vegetable and animal, including man, on our globe, through all the stages of its history, have descended. (6) As growth, organization, and reproduction are the functions of physical life, as soon as the primordial germ began to live, it began to grow, to fashion organs, however simple, for its nourishment and increase, and for the reproduction, in some way, of living forms like itself. How all living things on earth, including the endless variety of plants, and all the diversity of animals—insects, fishes, birds, the ichthyosaurus, the mastodon, the mammoth, and man—have descended from the primordial animalcule, he thinks, may be accounted for by the operation of the following natural laws:

> First, the law of Heredity, or that by which like begets like. The offspring are like the parent.
>
> Second, the law of Variation, that is, while the offspring are, in all essential characteristics, like their immediate progenitor, they nevertheless vary more or less within narrow limits, from their parent and from each other. Some of these variations are indifferent, some deteriorations, some improvements, that is, they are such as enable the plant or animal to exercise its functions to greater advantage.
>
> Third, the law of Over Production. All plants and animals tend to increase in a geometrical ratio; and therefore tend to overrun enormously the means of support. . . . Hence of necessity arises a struggle for life. Only a few of the myriads born can possibly live.
>
> Fourth, here comes in the law of Natural Selection, or the Survival of the Fittest. That is, if any individual of a given species of plant or animal happens to have a slight deviation from the normal type, favorable to its success in the struggle for life, it will survive. This variation, by the law of heredity, will be transmitted to its offspring, and by them again to theirs. Soon these favored ones gain the ascendancy, and the less favored perish; and the modification becomes established in the species. After a time another and another of

such favorable variations occur, with like results. Thus very gradually, great changes of structure are introduced, and not only species, but genera, families, and orders in the vegetable and animal world, are produced. Mr. Darwin says he can set no limit to the changes of structure, habits, instincts, and millions or milliards of centuries may bring into existence. He says, "we cannot comprehend what the figures 60,000,000 really imply, and during this, or perhaps a longer roll of years, the land and waters have everywhere teemed with living creatures, all exposed to the struggle for life, and undergoing change." . . . Years in this connection have no meaning. We might as well try to give the distance of the fixed stars in inches. As astronomers are obliged to take the diameter of the earth's orbit as the unit of space, so Darwinians are obliged to take a geological cycle as their unit of duration. . . .

We have not reached the heart of Mr. Darwin's theory. The main idea of his system lies in the word "natural." He uses that word in two senses: first, as antithetical to the word artificial. Men can produce very marked varieties as to structure and habits of animals. This is exemplified in the production of the different breeds of horses, cattle, sheep, and dogs; and specifically, as Mr. Darwin seems to think, in the case of pigeons. . . . If, then he argues, man, in a comparatively short time, has by artificial selection produced all these varieties, what might be accomplished on the boundless scale of nature, during the measureless ages of the geologic periods?

Secondly, he uses the word natural as antithetical to supernatural. Natural selection is a selection made by natural laws, working without intention and design. It is, therefore, opposed not only to artificial selection, which is made by the wisdom and skill of man to accomplish a given purpose, but also to supernatural selection, which means either a selection originally intended by a power higher than nature; or which is carried out by such power. In using the expression Natural Selection, Mr. Darwin intends to exclude design, or final causes. All the changes in structure, instinct, or intelligence, in the plants or animals, including man, descended from the primordial germ, or animalcule, have been brought about by unintelligent physical causes. On this point he leaves us in no doubt. It is affirmed that natural selection is the operation of natural laws, analogous to the action of gravitation and of chemical affinities. It is denied that it is a process originally designed, or guided by intelligence, such as the activity which foresees an end and consciously selects and controls the means of its accomplishment. Artificial selection, then, is an intelligent process; natural selection is not.

There are in the animal and vegetable worlds innumerable instances of at least apparent contrivance, which have excited the admiration of men in all ages. There are three ways of accounting for them. The first is the Scriptural doctrine, namely, that God is a Spirit, a personal, self-conscious, intelligent agent; that He is infinite, eternal, and unchangeable in his being and perfections; that He is ever present; that this presence is a presence of knowledge and power. In the external world there is always and everywhere indisputable evidence of the activity of two kinds of force: the one physical, the other mental. The physical belongs to matter, and is due to the properties with which it has been endowed; the other is the everywhere present and ever acting mind of God. To the latter are to be referred all the manifestations of design in nature, and the ordering of events in Providence. This doctrine does not ignore the efficiency of second causes; it simply asserts that God overrules and controls them. Thus the Psalmist says, "I am fearfully and wonderfully made. . . . My substance was not hid from thee, when I was made in secret, and curiously wrought. . . . in the lower parts of the earth. Thine eyes did see my substance yet being imperfect; and in thy book all my members were written, which in continuance were fashioned, when as yet there were none of them." . . . He sends rain, frost, and snow. He controls the winds and the waves. He determines the casting of the lots, the flight of an arrow, and the falling of a sparrow. This universal and constant control of God is not only one of the most patent and pervading doctrines of the Bible, but it is one of the fundamental principles of even natural religion.

The second method of accounting for contrivances in nature admits that they were foreseen and purposed by God, and that He endowed matter with forces which He foresaw and intended should produce such results. But here his agency stops. He never interferes to guide the operation of physical causes. He does nothing to control the course of nature, or the events of history. . . . Paley indeed says, that if the construction of a watch be an undeniable evidence of design it would be a still more wonderful manifestation of skill, if a watch could be made to produce other watches; and, it may be added, not only other watches, but all kinds of time pieces in endless variety. So it has been asked, if man can make a telescope, why cannot God make a telescope which produces others like itself? This is simply asking, whether matter can be made to do the work of the mind? The idea involves a contradiction. For a telescope to make a telescope, supposes it to select copper and zinc in due proportions and fuse them into brass; to fashion that brass into interentering tubes; to collect and combine the requisite materials for the different kinds of glass needed; to melt them, grind, fashion, and polish them, adjust their densities and focal distances, etc., etc. A man who can believe that brass can do all this, might as well believe in God. . . .

This banishing God from the world is simply intolerable, and, blessed be his name, impossible. An absent God who does nothing is, to us, no God. Christ brings God constantly near to us. . . . It may be said that Christ did not teach science. True, but He taught the truth; and science, so called, when it comes in conflict with truth, is what man is when he comes in conflict with God.

The advocates of these extreme opinions protest against being considered irreligious. Herbert Spencer says, that his doctrine of an inscrutable, unintelligent, unknown force, as the cause of all things, is a much more religious doctrine than that of a personal, intelligent, and voluntary Being of infinite power and goodness. Matthew Arnold holds that an unconscious "power which makes for right," is a higher idea of God than the Jehovah of the Bible. Christ says, God is a Spirit. . . .

The third method of accounting for the contrivances manifested in the organs of plants and animals, is that which refers them to the blind operation of natural causes. They are not due to the continued cooperation and control of the divine mind, nor to the original purpose of God in the constitution of the universe. This is the doctrine of the Materialists, and to this doctrine, we are sorry to say, Mr. Darwin, although himself a theist, has given in his adhesion. It is on this account the Materialists almost deify him.

From what has been said, it appears that Darwinism includes three distinct elements. First evolution, or the assumption that all organic forms, vegetable and animal, have been evolved or developed from one, or a few, primordial living germs; second, that this evolution has been effected by natural selection, or the survival of the fittest; and third, and by far the most important and only distinctive element of his theory, that this natural selection is without design, being conducted by unintelligent physical causes. . . .

It is however neither evolution nor natural selection, which gives Darwinism its peculiar character and importance. It is that Darwin rejects all teleology, or the doctrine of final causes. He denies design in any of the organisms in the vegetable or animal world. He teaches that the eye was formed without any purpose of producing an organ of vision. . . . It is the distinctive doctrine of Mr. Darwin, that species owe their origin, not to the original intention of the divine mind; not to special acts of creation calling new forms into existence at certain epochs; not to the constant and everywhere operative efficiency of God, guiding physical causes in the production of intended effects; but to the gradual accumulation of unintended variations of structure and instinct, securing some advantage to their subjects. . . .

All the innumerable varieties of plants, all the countless forms of animals, with all their instincts and faculties, all the varieties of men with their intellectual endowments, and their moral and religious nature, have, according to Darwin, been evolved by the agency of the blind, unconscious laws of nature. . . . The grand and fatal objection to Darwinism is this exclusion of design in the origin of species, or the production of living organisms. . . .

The conclusion of the whole matter is, that the denial of design in nature is virtually the denial of God. Mr. Darwin's theory is virtually atheistical; his theory, not he himself. He believes in a Creator. But when that Creator, millions on millions of ages ago, did something—called matter and a living germ into existence— and then abandoned the universe to itself to be controlled by chance and necessity, without any purpose on his part as to the result, or any intervention or guidance, then He is virtually consigned, so far as we are concerned, to nonexistence. . . . This is the vital point. The denial of final causes is the formative idea of Darwin's theory, and therefore no teleologist can be a Darwinian. . . .

We have thus arrived at the answer to our question, What is Darwinism? It is Atheism.

Evolution
James Woodrow

James Woodrow (1828-1907), the uncle of President Woodrow Wilson, was Professor of Natural Sciences in Connection with Divinity at the Presbyterian Seminary in Columbia, South Carolina. In appointing him to the position, the seminary called upon him "to evince the harmony of science with the records of our faith, and to refute the objections of infidel scientists." After years of opposition to the evolutionary hypothesis, Woodrow modified his view and came to hold that theistic evolution—what he called "mediate creation"—was probably true. In 1884 he delivered the address which follows when asked by the seminary's governing board to state his position on the evolution question. It resulted in the loss of his professorship and sparked a controversy between pro- and anti-Darwinian Presbyterian ministers in the South.

At the same time that you honored me with an invitation to deliver an address before you on this occasion, the Board of Directors at the Theological Seminary, in view of the fact that "Scepticism in the world is using alleged discoveries in science to impugn the word of God," requested me "to give fully my views, as taught in this institution, upon Evolution, as it respects the world, the lower animals and man." Inasmuch as several members of the Board are also members of this Association, and both Board and Association feel the same interest in the Seminary, I have supposed that I could not select a subject more likely to meet with your approval than the one suggested to me by the Directors. . . . As is intimated in the Board's request, I may assume that your chief interest in the topic is not in its scientific aspects, but in relations it may bear to the word of God; and therefore I will speak mainly of these relations. . . .

Before entering on the discussion of the specific subject of Evolution in itself and in its relations to the Sacred Scriptures, it may be well to consider the relations subsisting between the teachings of the Scriptures and the teachings of natural science generally. We hear much of the harmony of science and Scripture, of their reconciliation, and the like. Now, is it antecedently probable that there is room for either agreement or disagreement? We do not speak of the harmony of mathematics and chemistry, or of zoology and astronomy, or the reconciliation of physics and metaphysics. Why? Because the subject matter of each of these branches of knowledge is so different from the rest. It is true we may say that some assertion made by astronomy cannot be correct, because it contradicts some known truth of mathematics or of physics. But yet, in such a case, we would not proceed to look for harmony or reconciliation; we would confine ourselves to the task of removing the contradiction by seeking the error which caused it, and which it proved to exist; for we know that, as truth is one, two contradictions cannot both be true.

May it not be that we have here a representation of the probable relations between the Bible and science—that their contents are so entirely different that it is vain and misleading to be searching for harmonies; and that we should confine our efforts to the examination of real or seeming contradictions which may emerge, and rest satisfied, without attempting to go farther, when we have discovered that there is no contradiction, if it was only seeming, or have pointed out the error that caused it, if real?

Let us test this point by examining special cases which have arisen, and with regard to which conclusions satisfactory to all believers in the Bible have now been reached.

In Genesis i.16, the Bible speaks of the two great lights, the sun and the moon, and of the stars as if these were of comparatively insignificant size and importance. It says further, Joshua x.13, that "the sun stood still, and the moon stayed"; "the sun stood still in the midst of the heaven, and hastened not to go down about a whole day." In these and other passages the Bible has been thought to teach that the sun and the moon are larger than any of the stars, and that sun, moon, and stars, having been created for the benefit of man, revolve around the earth as a centre. On the scientific side, two forms of astronomy have been presented: the Ptolemaic, teaching that the earth is the centre of the universe; the Copernican, teaching that the sun is the centre of our planetary system. Those who asked for harmony between science and the Bible found wonderful confirmation of the Bible in the Ptolemaic astronomy, and of the Ptolemaic astronomy in the Bible. But gradually it came to be seen and admitted that, whatever might be its teachings on other subjects, the Bible was at least not intended to teach astronomy; and for centuries general assent has been given to the words of Calvin: "Moses does not speak with philosophical acuteness on occult mysteries, but relates those things which are everywhere observed, even by the uncultivated. . . . He who would learn astronomy, and other recondite arts, let him go elsewhere." . . . The Bible does not teach science; and to take its language in a scientific sense is grossly to pervert its meaning.

As in the example above given, so in all other cases of supposed contradiction of the Bible by science, I have found that the fair honest application of such principles has caused the contradiction to disappear. I have found nothing in my study of the Holy Bible and of natural science that shakes my firm belief in the divine inspiration of every word of that Bible, and in the consequent absolute truth, the absolute inerrancy, of every expression which it contains, from beginning to end. While there are not a few things which I confess myself wholly unable to understand, yet I have found nothing which contradicts other known truth. It ought to be observed that this is a very different thing from saying that I have found everything in the Sacred Scriptures to be in harmony with natural science. To teach this result it would be necessary to know the exact meaning of every part of the Scriptures, and the exact amount of truth in each scientific proposition. But to show that in any case there is no contradiction, all that is needed is to show that a reasonable supposition of what the passage in question may mean does not contradict the proved truth in science. . . .

After these preliminary observations, I proceed to discuss the main subject of this address.

Before answering the question, What do you think of Evolution? I must ask, What do you mean by Evolution?

When thinking of the origin of anything, we may inquire, Did it come into existence just as it is? or did it pass through a series of changes from a previous state in order to reach its present condition? For example, if we think of a tree, we can conceive of it as having come immediately into existence just as we see it; or, we may conceive of it as having begun its existence as a minute cell in connexion with a similar tree, and as having reached its present condition by passing through a series of changes, continually approaching and at length reaching the form before us. Or thinking of the earth, we can conceive of it as having come into existence with its present complex character; or we may conceive of it as having begun to exist in the simplest possible state, and as having reached its present condition by passing through a long series of stages, each derived from its predecessor. To the second of these modes, we apply the term "Evolution." It is evidently equivalent to "derivation"; or, in the case of organic beings, to "descent."

This definition or description of Evolution does not include any reference to the power by which the origination is effected; it refers to the mode, and to the mode alone. So far as the definition is concerned, the immedi-

ate existence might be attributed to God or to chance; the derived existence to inherent uncreated law, or to an almighty personal Creator, acting according to laws of his own framing. It is important to consider this distinction carefully, for it is wholly inconsistent with much that is said and believed by both advocates and opponents of Evolution. It is not unusual to represent Creation and Evolution as mutually exclusive, as contradictory: Creation meaning the immediate calling out of non-existence by divine power; Evolution, derivation from previous forms or states by inherent, self-originated or eternal laws, independent of all connexion with divine personal power. Hence, if this is correct, those who believe in Creation are theists; those who believe in Evolution are atheists. But there is no propriety in thus mingling in the definition two things which are so completely different. . . .

The definition now given, which seems to me the only one which can be given within the limits of natural science, necessarily excludes the possibility of the questions whether the doctrine is theistic or atheistic, whether it is religious or irreligious, moral or immoral. It would be as plainly absurd to ask these questions as to inquire whether the doctrine is white or black, square or round, light or heavy. In this respect it is like every other hypothesis or theory in science. These are qualities which do not belong to such subjects. The only question that can rationally be put is, Is the doctrine true or false? If this statement is correct—and it is almost if not quite self-evident—it should at once end all disputes not only between Evolution and religion, but between natural science and religion universally. To prove that the universe, the earth, and the organic beings upon the earth, had once been in a different condition from the present, and had gradually reached the state which we now see, could not disprove or tend to disprove the existence of God or the possession by him of a single attribute ever thought to belong to him. How can our belief in this doctrine tend to weaken or destroy our belief that he is infinite, that he is eternal, that he is unchangeable, in his being, or his wisdom, or his power, or his holiness, or his justice, or his goodness, or his truth? Or how can our rejection of the doctrine either strengthen or weaken our belief in him? Or how can either our acceptance or rejection of Evolution affect our love to God, or our recognition of our obligation to obey and serve him—carefully to keep all his commandments and ordinances?

True, when we go outside the sphere of natural science, and inquire whence this universe, questions involving theism forthwith arise. Whether it came into existence immediately or mediately is not material; but what or who brought it into existence? Did it spring from the fortuitous concurrence of eternally-existing atoms? Are the matter and the forces which act upon it in certain definite ways eternal; and is the universe, as we behold it, the result of their blind unconscious operation? Or, on the other hand, was the universe in all its orderly complexity brought into existence by the will of an eternal, personal, spiritual God, one who is omniscient, omnipresent, omnipotent? These questions of course involve the very foundations of religion and morality; but they lie wholly outside of natural science; and are, I repeat, not in the least affected by the decision of that other question, Did the universe come into its present condition immediately or mediately; instantly, in a moment, or gradually, through a long series of intermediate stages? They are not affected by, nor do they affect, the truth or falsehood of Evolution.

But, admitting that the truth of Theism is not involved in the question before us, it may fairly be asked, Does not the doctrine of Evolution contradict the teachings of the Bible? This renders it necessary to inquire whether the Bible teaches anything whatever as to the mode in which the world and its inhabitants were brought into their present state; and if so, what that teaching is.

It does not seem to be antecedently probable that there would be any specific teaching there on the subject. We have learned that "the Scriptures principally teach what man is to believe concerning God, and what duty God requires of man"; and that "the whole counsel of God, concerning all things necessary for his own glory, man's salvation, faith, and life, is either expressly set down in Scripture, or by good and necessary consequence may be deducted from Scripture." But this does not include the principles of natural science in any of its branches. We have already seen that it certainly does not include the teaching of astronomy or geography; it does not include anatomy or physiology, zoology or botany—a scientific statement of the structure, growth, and classification of animals and plants. Is it any more likely that it includes an account of the limits of the variation which the kinds of plants and animals may undergo, or the circumstances and conditions by which such variation may be affected? We would indeed expect to find God's relation to the world and all its inhabitants set forth; but he is equally the Creator and Preserver, however it may have pleased him, through his creating and preserving power, to have brought the universe into its present state. He is as really and truly your Creator, though you are the descendant of hundreds of ancestors, as he was of the first particle of matter which he called into being, or the first plant or animal, or the first angel in heaven.

So much at least seems clear—that whatever the Bible may say touching the mode of creation, is merely incidental to its main design, and must be interpreted accordingly. Well may we repeat with Calvin, "He who would learn astronomy and other recondite arts, let him go elsewhere."

It is further to be observed, that whatever may be taught is contained in the first part of the oldest book in the world, in a dead language, with a very limited literature; that the record is extremely brief, compressing an account of the most stupendous events into the smallest compass. Now the more remote from the present is any event recorded in human language, the more completely any language deserves to be called dead, the more limited its contemporaneous literature, the briefer the record itself, the more obscure must that record be—the more difficult it must be to ascertain its exact meaning, and especially that part of its meaning which is merely incidental to its main design. . . .

The actual examination of the sacred record seems to me to show that the obscurity exists which might have been reasonably anticipated. It is clear that God is there represented as doing whatever is done. But whether in this record the limitless universe to the remotest star or nebula is spoken of,

or only some portion of it, and if the latter, what portion, I cannot tell. And if there is an account of the methods according to which God proceeded in his creative work, I cannot perceive it. It is said *that* God created; but, so far as I can see, it is not said *how* he created. We are told nothing that contradicts the supposition, for example, that, in creating our earth and the solar system of which it forms a part, he brought the whole into existence very much in the condition in which we now see the several parts; or, on the other hand, that he proceeded by the steps indicated in what is called the nebular hypothesis. Just as the contrary beliefs of Calvin and ourselves touching the centre of the solar system fail to contradict a single word in the Bible, so the contrary beliefs of those who accept and those who reject the nebular hypothesis fail to contradict a single word of the Bible.

I regard the same statements as true when made respecting the origin of the almost numberless species of organic beings which now exist and which have existed in the past. In the Bible I find nothing that contradicts the belief that God immediately brought into existence each form independently; or that contradicts the contrary belief that God immediately brought into existence each form independently; or that contradicts the contrary belief that, having originated one or a few forms, he caused all the others to spring from these in accordance with the laws which he ordained and makes operative. . . .

When we reach the account of the origin of man, we find it more detailed. In the first narrative there is nothing that suggests the mode of creating any more than in the case of the earth, or the plants and animals. But in the second, we are told that "the Lord God formed man of the dust of the ground, and breathed into his nostrils the breath of life; and man became a living soul." Here seems to be a definite statement utterly inconsistent with the belief that man, either in body or soul, is the descendant of other organised beings. At first sight the statement, that "man was formed of the dust of the ground," seems to point out with unmistakable clearness the exact nature of the material of which man's body was made. But further examination does not strengthen this view. For remembering the principles and facts already stated, and seeking to ascertain the meaning of "dust of the ground" by examining how the same words are employed elsewhere in the narrative, the sharp definiteness which seemed at first to be so plainly visible somewhat disappears. For example, we are told in one place that the waters were commanded to bring forth the moving creature that hath life, and fowl that may fly above the earth; and the command was obeyed. And yet, in another place we are told that out of the ground the Lord God formed every beast of the field, and every fowl of the air. Now as both these statements are true, it is evident that there can be no intention to describe the material employed. There was some sort of connexion with the water, and some with the ground; but beyond this nothing is clear. Then further, in the sentence which God pronounced upon Adam, he says: "Out of the ground wast thou taken; for dust thou art, and unto dust shalt thou return." And in the curse uttered against the serpent, it was said: "Dust shalt thou eat all the days of thy life." Now Adam, to whom God was speaking, was flesh and blood and bone; and the food of serpents then as now consisted of the same substances, flesh and blood. The only proper conclusion in view of these facts seems to be that the narrative does not intend to distinguish in accordance with chemical notions different kinds of matter, specifying here inorganic in different states, and there organic, but merely to refer in a general incidental way to previously existing matter, without intending or attempting to describe its exact nature. . . .

As regards the soul of man, which bears God's image, and which differs so entirely not merely in degree but in kind from anything in the animals, I believe that it was immediately created, that we are here so taught; and I have not found in science any reason to believe otherwise. Just as there is no scientific basis for the belief that the doctrine of derivation or descent can bridge over the chasms which separate the non-existent from the existent, and the inorganic from the organic, so there is no such basis for the belief that this doctrine can bridge over the chasm which separates the mere animal from the exalted being which is made after the image of God. The mineral differs from the animal in kind, not merely in degree; so the animal differs from man in kind; and while science has traced numberless transitions from degree to degree, it has utterly failed to find any indications of transition from kind to kind in this sense. . . .

Believing, as I do, that the Scriptures are almost certainly silent on the subject, I find it hard to see how any one can hesitate to prefer the hypothesis of mediate creation to the hypothesis of immediate creation. . . .

I cannot take time to discuss at length objections which have been urged against this hypothesis, but may say that they do not seem to me of great weight. It is sometimes said that, if applied to man, it degrades him to regard him as in any respect the descendant of the beast. We have not been consulted on the subject, and possibly our desire for noble origin may not be able to control the matter; but, however that may be, it is hard to see how dirt is nobler than the highest organisation which God had up to that time created on the earth. And further, however it may have been with Adam, we are perfectly certain that each one of us has passed through a state lower than that of the fish, then successively through states not unlike those of the tadpole, the reptile, and the quadruped. Hence, whatever nobility may have been conferred on Adam by being made of dust has been lost to us by our passing through these low animal stages.

It has been objected that it removes God to such a distance from us that it tends to atheism. But the doctrine of descent certainly applies to the succession of men from Adam up to the present. Are we any farther from God than were the earlier generations of the antediluvians? Have we fewer proofs of his existence and power than they had? It must be plain that, if mankind shall continue to exist on the earth so long, millions of years hence the proofs of God's almighty creative power will be as clear as they are today.

It has been also objected that this doctrine excludes the idea of design in nature. But if the development of an oak from an acorn in accordance with laws which God has ordained and executes, does not exclude the ideas of design, I utterly fail to see how the development of our complex world, teeming with co-adaptations of the most striking character, can possibly exclude that idea.

I have now presented briefly, but as fully as possible in an address of this kind, my views as to the method which should be adopted in considering the relations between the Scriptures and natural science, showing that all that should be expected is that it shall be made to appear by interpretations which may be true that they do not contradict each other; that the contents and aims of the Scriptures and of natural science are so different that it is unreasonable to look for agreement or harmony; that terms are not and ought not to be used in the Bible in a scientific sense, and that they are used perfectly truthfully when they convey the sense intended; that on these principles all alleged contradictions of natural science by the Bible disappear; that a proper definition of Evolution excludes all reference to the origin of the forces and laws by which it works, and therefore that it does not and cannot affect belief in God or in religion; that, according to not unreasonable interpretations of the Bible, it does not contradict anything there taught so far as regards the earth, the lower animals, and probably man as to his body; that there are many good grounds for believing that Evolution is true in these respects; and lastly, that the reasons urged against it are of little or no weight.

I would say in conclusion, that while the doctrine of Evolution in itself, as before stated, is not and cannot be either Christian or anti-Christian, religious or irreligious, theistic or atheistic, yet viewing the history of our earth and inhabitants, and of the whole universe, as it is unfolded by its help, and then going outside of it and recognising that it is God's PLAN OF CREATION, instead of being tempted to put away thoughts of him, as I contemplate this wondrous series of events, caused and controlled by the power and wisdom of the Lord God Almighty, I am led with profounder reverence and admiration to give glory and honor to him that sits on the throne, who liveth for ever and ever; and with fuller heart and a truer appreciation of what it is to create, to join in saying, Thou art worthy, O Lord, to receive glory and honor and power; for thou hast created all things, and for thy pleasure they are and were created.

Evolution and Religion
Henry Ward Beecher

Henry Ward Beecher (1813-1887), minister at Brooklyn's Plymouth Church for many years, provided a significant boost to the acceptance of evolution among Protestants with his efforts to accommodate theism with Darwinism. In 1885 he delivered a series of sermons on evolution in which he discussed the bearing of evolution on the fundamental doctrines of orthodox Christianity. Beecher insisted he had no problem with divine design in the light of evolution, stating that he hailed the "evolutionary philosophy with joy." The following excerpt taken from his *Evolution and Religion* (New York: Ford, Howard, and Hulbert, 1886), pp. 112-17, illustrates why he could identify himself as a Christian evolutionist.

The law of cause and effect is fundamental to the every existence of science, and, I had almost said, to the very operation of the human mind. So, then, we gain nothing by excluding divine intelligence, and to include it smooths the way to investigation, and is agreeable to the nature of the human mind. It is easier to conceive of the personal divine being with intelligence, will and power, than it is to conceive of a world of such vast and varied substance as this, performing all the functions of intelligence and will and power. That would be giving to miscellaneous matter the attributes which we denied to a personal God.

The doctrine of Evolution, at first sight, seems to destroy the theory of intelligent design in creation, and in its earlier states left those who investigated it very doubtful whether there was anything in creation but matter, or whether there was a knowable God.

So sprang up the Agnostic school, which includes in it some of the noblest spirits of our day. "God may exist, but we do not know it." That is what the Bible says from the beginning to end; that is what philosophy is now beginning to explain. We cannot understand the divine nature, so exalted above everything that has yet been developed in human consciousness, except it dawns upon us when we are ourselves unfolding and rising to such a higher operation of our minds as does not belong to the great mass of the human race. God is to be seen only by those faculties that verge upon the divine nature, and to them only when they are in a state of exaltation. Moral intuitions are not absolute revelations, but they are as sure of higher truths as the physical senses are of material truths.

But the question of design in creation, which has been a stable argument for the proof of the existence of God and his attributes, seems to have been shaken from its former basis. It is being restored in a larger and grander way, which only places the fact upon a wider space, and makes the outcome more wonderful. Special creation, and the adaptation in consequence of it, of structure to uses in animals, and in the vegetable kingdom to their surroundings, has always been an element of God's work regarded as most remarkable. How things fit to their places; how regular all the subordinations and developments that are going on; how fit they are to succeed one another! Now the old theory conceived God as creating things for special uses, When the idea of the lily dawned on him, he smiled and said: "I will make it"; and he made it to be just as beautiful as it is. And when the rose was to be added, like an artist God thought just how it should be all the way through. That is the old view that some plants were made to do without water and could live in parched sands; and that some could live only in the tropics; and thus God adapted all his creation to the climate and the soil and the circumstances, and it was a beautiful thing to see how things did fit, by the divine wisdom, the place where they were found.

Then comes Evolution and teaches that God created through the mediation of natural laws; that creation, in whole or detail, was a process of slow growth, and not an instantaneous process; that plants and animals alike were affected their surrounding circumstances favorably or unfavorably; and that, in the long run, those which were best adapted to their environment survived, and those perished which could not adapt themselves to the conditions of soil, climate, moisture, cold or heat which in the immeasurable periods of creation befell them. The adaptation then of plants to their condition

did not arise from the direct command of the Great Gardener; but from the fact that, among these infinite gradations of plants, only those survived and propagated themselves which were able to bear the climate and soil in which they found themselves; all others dwindled and perished. Of course there would be a fine adjustment of the plant to its condition; it came to this by a long preparation of ancestral influences.

How beautiful it is to see a plant growing right under the cheek of a precipice or snow bed, or by the edges of winter through the year! Men say how beautiful the thought was that God should create in vegetables and flowers right alongside the snow, as it were, to cheer the bosom of winter: whereas it turned out that everything that could live there died; and, by and by, there were some plants so tough that they could live there, and they did; and the adaptation was the remainder after a long series of perishings. Men say, What a remarkable instance of divine design that the cactus can live on arid deserts, where water scarcely falls more than once or twice a year; and what a special creation and adaptation it was on the part of God that he should make such plants as that! But the Evolutionist says that all the plants were killed in succession until it came about, in the endless variations of the vegetable kingdom, that a plant developed whose structure was covered, as it were, with an india rubber skin, and whose leaves were substantially little cisterns, which drank up all the water they wanted to use through the summer, and so continued to live in spite of their dry surroundings, when others could not live because they could not adapt themselves. So the argument for special design, as we used to hold it, fails there.

Through long periods all things intended to vary more or less from their original forms, and adapted themselves to their necessary conditions; and what could not do this perished; for the theory of Evolution is as much a theory of destruction and degradation as of development and building up. As the carpenter has numberless shavings, and a vast amount of wastage of every log which he would shape to some use, so creation has been an enormous waste, such as seems like squandering, on the scale of human life, but not to Him that dwells in Eternity. In bringing the world to its present conditions, vast amounts of things have lived for a time and were unable to hold on, and let go and perished. We behold the onflowing, through immeasurable ages of creation, of this peculiar tendency to vary, and in some cases to improve. The improvement is transmitted; and in the battle of life, one thing conflicting with another, the strong or the best adapted crowd out the weak, and these continue to transmit their qualities until something better yet shall supplant them.

Vast waste and the perishing of unfit things is one of the most striking facts in the existence of this world; for while life is the consummation, death seems to be the instrument by which life itself is supplied with improvement and advancement. Death prepares the way for life. Things are adapted thus to their condition, to their climate, to their food; or by their power of escape from their adversaries, or their power of establishing themselves and of defending their position, they make it secure. The vast universe, looked at largely, is moving onward and upward in determinate lines and directions, while on the way the weak are perishing. Yet, there is an unfolding process that is car-

rying creation up to higher planes and upon higher lines, reaching more complicated conditions in structure, in function, in adaptation, with systematic and harmonious results, so that the whole physical creation is organizing itself for a sublime march toward perfectness.

If single acts would evince design, how much more a vast universe, that by inherent laws gradually builded itself, and then created its own plants and animals, a universe so adjusted that it left by the way the poorest things, and steadily wrought toward more complex, ingenious, and beautiful results! Who designed this mighty machine, created matter, gave to it its laws, and impressed upon it that tendency which has brought forth the almost infinite results on the globe, and wrought them into a perfect system? Design by wholesale is grander than design by retail.

You are familiar with the famous illustration of Dr. Paley, where a man finds a watch, and infers irresistibly that that watch was made by some skillful, thoughtful watchmaker. Suppose that a man, having found a watch, should say to himself, "Somebody thought this out, somebody created this; it was evidently constructed and adapted exactly to the end in view the keeping of time." Suppose, then, that some one should take him to Waltham, and introduce him into that vast watch factory, where watches are created in hundreds of thousands by machinery; and suppose the question should be put to him, "What do you think, then, about the man who created this machinery, which of itself goes on cutting out wheels, and springs, and pinions, and everything that belongs to making a watch? If it be an argument of design that there is a man existing who could create a manufactory turning out millions of watches, and machinery too, so that the human hand has little to do but to adjust the parts already created by machines?" If it be evidence of design in creation that God adapted one single flower to its place and functions, is it not greater evidence if there is a system of such adaptations going on from eternity to eternity? Is not the Creator of the system a more sublime designer than the creator of any single act?

Or, let me put down before you an oriental rug, which we all know has been woven by women squatting upon the ground, each one putting in the color that was wanted to form the figure, carrying out the whole with oriental harmony of color. Looking upon that, you could not help saying, "Well, that is a beautiful design, and these are skillful women that made it, there can be no question about that." But now behold the power loom where not simply a rug with long, drudging work by hand is being created, but where the machine is creating carpets in endless lengths, with birds, and insects, and flowers, and scrolls, and every elements of beauty. It is all being done without a hand touching it. Once start the engine, and put the perforated papers above the loom, and that machine turns out a carpet that puts to shame the beauty of these oriental rugs. Now the question is this: It is an evidence of design in these women that they turn out such work, and is it not evidence of a higher design in the man who turned out that machine—that loom—which could carry on this work a thousandfold more magnificently than human fingers did?

It may be safely said, then, that Evolution, instead of obliterating the evidence of divine Design, has lifted it to a higher plane, and made it more sublime than it ever was contemplated to be under the old reasonings.

10 The Gospel of Wealth and Big Business

He who is faithful in a very little thing is faithful also in much; and he who is unrighteous in a very little thing is unrighteous also in much.

—Luke 16:10

Wealth
Andrew Carnegie

Andrew Carnegie (1835-1919) was the son of a poor Scottish weaver who emigrated to America with his family in 1848. During his early years in America, Andrew worked as a bobbin boy in a cotton mill and then as an engine tender. In 1853 he gained a job with the Pennsylvania Railroad, where he stayed until 1865. After the Civil War he entered business for himself, and in 1868 founded Union Iron Mills. Over the course of the next thirty years he became so successful that his company was turning out the bulk of American steel. Along with the amassing of a large personal fortune, Carnegie was concerned with the ethical responsibilities of the person of wealth, whom he believed must see to it that his private fortune was used for the public welfare. Before he died he disposed of 90 percent of his wealth by endowing more than 2,500 libraries, donating pipe organs and public buildings, and creating numerous foundations. The following selection, "Wealth," *North American Review*, 148 (June, 1889), 653-64, presents his personal viewpoints concerning wealth.

The problem of our age is the proper administration of wealth, so that the ties of brotherhood may still bind together the rich and poor in harmonious relationship. The conditions of human life have not only been changed, but revolutionized, within the past few hundred years. In former days there was little difference between the dwelling, dress, food, and environment of the chief and those of his retainers. The Indians are today where civilized man then was. When visiting the Sioux, I was led to the wigwam of the chief. It was just like the others in external appearance, and even within the difference was trifling between it and those of the poorest of his braves. The contrast between

179

the palace of the millionaire and the cottage of the laborer with us today measures the change which has come with civilization.

This change, however, is not to be deplored, but welcomed as highly beneficial. It is well, nay, essential for the progress of the race, that the houses of some should be homes for all that is highest and best in literature and the arts, and for all the refinements of civilization, rather than that none should be so. Much better this great irregularity than universal squalor. Without wealth there can be no Maecenas. The "good old times" were not good old times. Neither master nor servant was as well situated then as today. A relapse to old conditions would be disastrous to both—not the least so to him who serves and would sweep away civilization with it. But whether the change be for good or ill, it is upon us, beyond our power to alter, and therefore to be accepted and made the best of. It is a waste of time to criticize the inevitable. . . .

The price we pay for this salutary change is, no doubt, great. We assemble thousands of operatives in the factory, in the mine, and in the counting-house, of whom the employer can know little or nothing, and to whom the employer is little better than a myth. All intercourse between them is at an end. Rigid Castes are formed, and, as usual, mutual ignorance breeds mutual distrust. Each Caste is without sympathy for the other, and ready to credit anything disparaging in regard to it. Under the law of competition, the employer of thousands is forced into the strictest economies, among which the rates paid to labor figure prominently, and often there is friction between the employer and the employed, between capital and labor, between

rich and poor. Human society loses homogeneity.

The price which society pays for the law of competition, like the price it pays for cheap comforts and luxuries, is also great; but the advantages of this law are also greater still, for it is to this law that we owe our wonderful material development, which brings improved conditions in its train. But, whether the law be benign or not, we must say of it, as we say of the change in the conditions of men to which we have referred: It is here; we cannot evade it; no substitutes for it have been found; and while the law may be sometimes hard for the individual, it is best for the race, because it insures the survival of the fittest in every department. We accept and welcome, therefore, as conditions to which we must accommodate ourselves, great inequality of environment, the concentration of business, industrial and commercial, in the hands of a few, and the law of competition between these, as being not only beneficial, but essential for the future progress of the race. Having accepted these, it follows that there must be great scope for the exercise of special ability in the merchant and in the manufacturer who has to conduct affairs upon a great scale. That this talent for organization and management is rare among men is proved by the fact that it invariably secures for its possessor enormous rewards, no matter where or under what laws or conditions. The experienced in affairs always rate the man whose services can be obtained as a partner as not only the first consideration, but such as to render the question of his capital scarcely worth considering, for such men soon create capital; while, without the special talent required, capital soon takes wings. Such men become interested in firms or corporations using millions; and estimating only simple interest to be made upon the capital invested, it is inevitable that their income must exceed their expenditures, and that they must accumulate wealth. Nor is there any middle ground which such men can occupy, because the great manufacturing or commercial concern which does not earn at least interest upon its capital soon becomes bankrupt. It must either go forward or fall behind: to stand still is impossible. It is a condition essential for its successful operation that it should be thus far profitable, and even that, in addition to interest on capital, it should make profit. It is a law, as certain as any of the others named, that men possessed of this peculiar talent of affairs, under the free play of economic forces, must, of necessity, soon be in receipt of more revenue than can be judiciously expended upon themselves; and this law is as beneficial for the race as the others.

Objections to the foundations upon which society is based are not in order, because the condition of the race is better with these than it has been with any others which have been tried. Of the effect of any new substitutes proposed we cannot be sure. The Socialist or Anarchist who seeks to overturn present conditions is to be regarded as attacking the foundation upon which civilization itself rests, for civilization took its start from the day that the capable, industrious workman said to his incompetent and lazy fellow, "If thou dost not sow, thou shalt not reap," and thus ended primitive Communism by separating the drones from the bees. One who studies this subject will soon be brought face to face with the conclusion that upon the sacredness of property civilization itself depends—the right of the laborer to his hundred dollars in the savings bank, and equally the legal right of the millionaire to his millions. To those who propose to substitute Communism for this Individualism the answer, therefore is: The race has tried that. All progress from that barbarous day to the present time has resulted from its displacement. Not evil, but good, has come to the race from the accumulation of wealth by those who have the ability and energy that produce it. But even if we admit for a moment that it might be better for the race to discard its present foundation, Individualism,—that it is a nobler ideal that man should labor, not for himself alone, but in and for a brotherhood of his fellows, and share with them all in common, realizing Swedenborg's idea of Heaven, where as he says, the angels derive their happiness, not from laboring for self, but for each other,— even admit all this, and a sufficient answer is, This is not evolution, but revolution. It necessitates the changing of human nature itself—a work of aeons, even if it were good to change it, which we cannot know. It is not practicable theoretically, it belongs to another and long succeeding sociological stratum. Our duty is with what is practicable now; with the next step possible in our day and generation. It is a criminal act to waste our energies in endeavoring to uproot, when all we can profitably or possibly accomplish is to bend the universal tree of humanity a little in the direction most favorable to the production of good fruit under existing circumstances. We might as well urge the destruction of the highest existing type of man because he failed to reach our ideal as to favor the destruction of Individualism, Private Property, the Law of Accumulation of Wealth, and the Law of Competition; for these are the highest results of human experience, the soil in which society so far has produced the best fruit. Unequally or unjustly perhaps, as the laws sometimes operate, and imperfect as they appear to the Idealist, they are, nevertheless, like the highest type of man, the best and most valuable of all that humanity has yet accomplished.

We start, then, with a condition of affairs under which the best interests of the race are promoted, but which inevitably gives wealth to the few. Thus far, accepting conditions as they exist, the situation can be surveyed and pronounced good. The question then arises,—and, if the foregoing be correct, it is the only question with which we have to deal— What is the proper mode of administering wealth after the laws upon which civilization is founded have thrown it into the hands of a few? And it is of this great question that I believe I offer the true solution. It will be understood that *fortunes* are here spoken of, not moderate sums saved by many years of effort, the returns from which are required for the comfortable maintenance and education of families. This is not *wealth*, but only *competence*, which it should be the aim of all to acquire.

There are but three modes in which surplus wealth can be disposed of. It can be left to the families of the descendants; or it can be bequeathed for public purposes; or, finally, it can be administered during their lives by its possessors. Under the first and second modes most of the wealth of the world that has reached the few has hitherto been applied. Let us in turn consider each of these modes. The first is the most injudicious. In monarchical countries, the estates and the greatest portion of the wealth are left to the first son, that the vanity of the parent may be gratified by the thought that his name and title are to descend to succeeding generations unimpaired. The condition of this class in Europe today teaches the futility of such hopes or ambitions. The successors have become impoverished through their follies or from the fall in the value of land. Even in Great Britain the strict law of entail has been found inadequate to maintain the status of an hereditary class. Its soil is rapidly passing into the hands of the stranger. Under republican institutions the division of property among the children is much fairer, but the question which forces itself upon thoughtful men in all lands is: Why should men leave great fortunes to their children? If this is done from affection, is it not misguided affection? Observation teaches that, generally speaking, it is not well for the children that they should be so burdened. Neither is it well for the state. Beyond providing for the wife and daughters moderate sources of income, and very moderate allowances indeed, if any, for the sons, men may well hesitate, for it is no longer questionable that great sums bequeathed oftener work more for the injury than for the good of the recipients. Wise men will soon conclude that, for the best interests of the members of their families and of the state, such bequests are an improper use of their means. . . .

As to the second mode, that of leaving wealth at death for public uses, it may be said that this is only a means for the disposal of wealth, provided a man is content to wait until he is dead before it becomes of much good in the world. Knowledge of the results of legacies bequeathed is not calculated to inspire the brightest hopes of much posthumous good being accomplished. The cases are not few in which the real object sought by the testator is not attained, nor are they few in which his real wishes are thwarted. In many cases the bequests are so used as to become only monuments of his folly. It is well to remember that it requires the exercise of not less ability than that which acquired the wealth to use it so as to be really beneficial to the community. Besides this, it may fairly be said that no man is to be extolled for doing what he cannot help doing, nor is he to be thanked by the community to which he leaves wealth at death. Men who leave vast sums in this way may fairly be thought men who would not have left it at all, had they been able to take it with them. The memories of such cannot be held in grateful remembrance, for there is no grace in their gifts. It is not to be wondered at that such bequests seem so generally to lack the blessing. . . .

There remains, then, only one mode of using great fortunes; but in this we have the true antidote for the temporary unequal distribution of wealth, the reconciliation of the rich and the poor—a reign of harmony—another ideal, differing, indeed, from that of the Communist in requiring only the further evolution of existing conditions, not the total overthrow of our civilization. It is founded upon the present most intense individualism, and the race is prepared to put it in practice by degrees whenever it pleases. Under its sway we shall have an ideal state, in which the surplus wealth of the few will become, in the best sense, the property of the many, because administered for the common good, and this wealth, passing through the hands of the few, can be made a much more potent force for the elevation of our race than if it had been distributed in small sums to the people themselves.

Even the poorest can be made to see this, and to agree that great sums gathered by some of their fellow citizens and spent for public purposes, from which the masses reap the principal benefit, are more valuable to them than if scattered among them through the course of many years in trifling amounts. . . .

Poor and restricted are our opportunities in this life; narrow our horizon; our best work most imperfect; but rich men should be thankful for one inestimable boon. They have it in their power during their lives to busy themselves in organizing benefactions from which the masses of their fellows will derive lasting advantage, and thus dignify their own lives. The highest life is probably to be reached, not by such imitation of the life of Christ as Count Tolstoi gives us, but, while animated by Christ's spirit, by recognizing the changed conditions of this age, and adopting modes of expressing this spirit suitable to the changed conditions under which we live; still laboring for the good of our fellows, which was the essence of his life and teaching, but laboring in a different manner.

This, then, is held to be the duty of the man of Wealth: First, to set an example of modest, unostentatious living, shunning display or extravagance; to provide moderately for the legitimate wants of those dependent upon him; and after doing so to consider all surplus revenues which come to him simply as trust funds, which he is called upon to administer, and strictly bound as a manner which, in his judgment, is best calculated to produce the most beneficial results for the community—the man of wealth thus becoming the mere agent and trustee for his poorer brethren, bringing to their service his superior wisdom, experience, and ability to administer, doing for them better than they would or could do for themselves.

We are met here with the difficulty of determining what are moderate sums to leave to members of the family; what is modest, unostentatious living; what is the test of extravagance. There must be different standards for different conditions. The answer is that it is as impossible to name exact amounts or actions as it is to define good manners, good taste, or the rules of propriety; but, nevertheless, these are verities, well known although undefinable. Public sentiment is quick to know and to feel what offends these. So in the case of wealth. The rule in regard to good taste in the dress of men or women applies here. Whatever makes one conspicuous offends the canon. If any family be chiefly known for display, for extravagance in home, table, equipage, for enormous sums ostentatiously spent in any form upon itself,—if these be its chief distinctions, we have no difficulty in estimating its nature or culture. So likewise in regard to the use or abuse of its surplus wealth, or to generous, freehanded cooperation in good public uses, or to unabated efforts to accumulate and hoard to the last, whether they administer or bequeath. The verdict rests with the best and most enlightened public sentiment. The community will surely judge, and its judgments will not often be wrong.

The best uses to which surplus wealth can be put have already been indicated. Those who would administer wisely must, indeed, be wise, for one of the serious obstacles to the improvement of our race is indiscriminate charity. It were better for mankind that the millions of the rich were thrown into the sea than so spent as to encourage the slothful, the drunken, the unworthy. Of every thousand dollars spent in so called charity today, it is probable that $950 is unwisely spent; so spent, indeed, as to produce the very evils which it proposes to mitigate or cure. A well-known writer of philosophic books admitted the other day that he had given a quarter of a dollar to a man who approached him as he was coming to visit the house of his friend. He knew nothing of the habits of this beggar; knew not the use that would be made of this money, although he had every reason to suspect that it would be spent improperly. This man professed to be a disciple of Herbert Spencer; yet the quarter-dollar given that night will probably work more injury than all the money which its thoughtless donor will be able to give in true charity will do good. He only gratified his own feelings, saved himself from annoyance,—and this was probably one of the most selfish and very worst actions of his life, for in all respects he is most worthy.

In bestowing charity, the main consideration should be to help those who will help themselves; to provide part of the means by which those who desire to improve may do so; to give those who desire to rise the aids by which they may rise; to assist, but rarely or never to do all. Neither the individual nor the race is improved by alms-giving. Those worthy of assistance, except in rare cases, seldom require assistance. The really valuable men of the race never do, except in cases of accident or sudden change. Every one has, of course, cases of individuals brought to his own knowledge where temporary assistance can do genuine good, and these he will not overlook. But the amount which can be wisely given by the individual for individuals is necessarily limited by his lack of knowledge of the circumstances connected with each. He is the only true reformer who is as careful and as anxious not to aid the unworthy as he is to aid the worthy, and, perhaps, even more so, for in alms-giving more injury is probably done by rewarding vice than by relieving virtue.

The rich man is thus almost restricted to following the examples of Peter Cooper, Enoch Pratt of Baltimore, Mr. Pratt of Brooklyn, Senator Stanford, and others, who know that the best means of benefiting the community is to place within its reach the ladders upon which the aspiring can rise—parks, and means of recreation, by which men are helped in body and mind; works of art, certain to give pleasure and improve the public taste, and public institutions of various kinds, which will improve the general condition of the people;—in this manner returning their surplus wealth to the mass of their fellows in the forms best calculated to do them lasting good. Thus is the problem of Rich and Poor to be solved. The laws of accumulation will be left free; the laws of distribution free. Individualism will continue, but the millionaire will be but a trustee for the poor; intrusted for a season with a great part of the increased wealth of the community, but administering it for the community far better than it could or would have done for itself. The best minds will thus have reached a stage in the development of the race in which it is clearly seen that there is no mode of disposing of surplus wealth creditable to thoughtful and earnest men into whose hands it flows save by using it year by year for the general good. This day already dawns. But a little while, and although, without incurring the pity of their fellows, men may die sharers in great business enterprises from which their capital cannot be or has not been withdrawn, and is left chiefly at death for public uses, yet the man who dies leaving behind him millions of available wealth, which was his to administer during life, will pass away "unwept, unhonored, and unsung," no matter to what uses he leaves the dross which he cannot take with him. Of such as these the public verdict will then be: "The man who dies thus rich dies disgraced."

Such, in my opinion, is the true Gospel concerning Wealth, obedience to which is destined some day to solve the problem of the Rich and the Poor, and to bring "Peace on earth, among men Good-Will."

The Relation of Wealth to Morals
William Lawrence

William Lawrence (1850-1941) was born into a family whose roots went back to the early Puritans. After graduation from Harvard in 1871, he received his theological degree from an Episcopalian school, where he later served as professor and dean. In 1893 he was named Episcopal Bishop of Massachusetts, a position he held until 1926. Lawrence was highly successful in raising money for his church and for Harvard, and often spoke out on the contemporary problem of wealth and morality. Denying any conflict necessarily existed between the two, he supported the Protestant ethic with its theory of the stewardship of wealth. The selection which follows, "The Relation of Wealth to Morals," *World's Week*, I (January, 1901), was first delivered as an address to the New York City Chamber of Commerce.

There is a certain distrust on the part of our people as to the effect of material prosperity on their morality. We shrink with some foreboding at the great increase of riches, and question whether in the long run material prosperity does not tend toward the disintegration of character.

History seems to support us in our distrust. Visions arise of their fall from splendor of Tyre and Sidon, Babylon, Rome, and Venice, and of great nations too. The question is stated whether England is not today, in the pride of her wealth and power, sowing the wind from which time she will reap the whirlwind.

Experience seems to add its support. Is it not from the ranks of the poor that the leaders of the people have always risen? Recall Abraham Lincoln and patriots of every generation.

The Bible has sustained the same note. Were ever stronger words of warning uttered against the deceitfulness of riches than those spoken by the peasant Jesus, who Himself had no place to lay His head? And the Church has through the centuries upheld poverty as one of the surest paths to Heaven: it has been a mark to the saint.

To be sure, in spite of history, experience, and the Bible, men have gone on their way making money and hailing with joy each age of material prosperity. The answer is: "This only proves the case; men are of the world, riches are deceitful, and the Bible is true; the world is given over to Mammon. In the increase of material wealth and the accumulation of riches the man who seeks the higher life has no part."

In the face of this comes the statement of the chief statistician of our census—from one, therefore, who speaks with authority: "The present census, when completed, will unquestionably show that the visible material wealth in this country now has a value of ninety billion dollars. This is an addition since 1890 of twenty-five billion dollars. This is a saving greater than all the people of the Western Continent had been able to make from the discovery of Columbus to the breaking out of the Civil War."

If our reasoning from history, experience, and the Bible is correct, we, a Christian people, have rubbed a sponge over the pages of the Bible and are in for orgies and a downfall to which the fall of Rome is a very tame incident.

May it not be well, however, to revise our inferences from history, experience and the Bible? History tells us that, while riches have been an item and an indirect cause of national decay, innumerable other conditions entered in. Therefore, while wealth has been a source of danger, it has not necessarily led to demoralization.

That leaders have sprung from the ranks of the poor is true and always will be true, so long as force of character exists in every class. But there are other conditions than a lack of wealth at the source of their uprising.

And as to the Bible:—while every word that can be quoted against the rich is as true as any other word, other words and deeds are as true; and the parables of our Lord on the stewardship of wealth, His association with the wealthy, strike another and complementary note. Both notes are essential to the harmony of His life and teachings. His thought was not of the conditions, rich or poor, but

of a higher life, the character rising out of the conditions—fortunately, for we are released from that subtle hypocrisy which has beset the Christian through the ages, bemoaning the deceitfulness of riches and, at the same time, working with all his might to earn a competence, and a fortune if he can.

Now we are in a position to affirm that neither history, experience, nor the Bible necessarily sustains the common distrust of the effect of material wealth on morality. Our path of study is made more clear. Two positive principles lead us on our path.

The first is that man, when he is strong, will conquer Nature, open up her resources, and harness them to his service. This is his play, his exercise, his divine mission.

"Man," says Emerson, "is born to be rich. He is thoroughly related, and is tempted out by his appetites and fancies to the conquest of this and that piece of Nature, until he finds his well being in the use of the planet, and of more planets than his own. Wealth requires, besides the crust of bread and roof, the freedom of the city, the freedom of the earth." "The strong race is strong on these terms."

Man draws to himself material wealth as surely, as naturally, and as necessarily as the oak tree draws the elements into itself from the earth.

The other principle is that, in the long run, it is only to the man of morality that wealth comes. We believe in the harmony of God's Universe. We know that it is only by working along His laws natural and spiritual that we can work with efficiency. Only by working along the lines of right thinking and right living can the secrets and wealth of Nature be revealed. We, like the Psalmist, occasionally see the wicked prosper, but only occasionally.

Put two men in adjoining fields, one man strong and normal, the other weak and listless. One picks up his spade, turns over the earth, and works till sunset. The other turns over a few clods, gets a drink from the spring, takes a nap, and loafs back to his work. In a few years one will be rich for his needs, and the other a pauper dependent on the first, and growling at his prosperity.

Put ten thousand immoral men to live and work in one fertile valley and ten thousand moral men to live and work in the next valley, and the question is soon answered as to who wins the material wealth. Godliness is in league with riches.

Now we return with an easier mind and clearer conscience to the problem of our twenty-five billion dollars in a decade.

My question is: Is the material prosperity of this Nation favorable or unfavorable to the morality of the people?

The first thought is, Who has prospered? Who has got the money?

I take it that the loudest answer would be, "The millionaires, the capitalists, and the incompetent but luxurious rich"; and, as we think of that twenty-five billion, our thoughts run over the yachts, the palaces, and the luxuries that flaunt themselves before the public. . . .

When, then, the question is asked, "Is the material prosperity of this nation favorable or unfavorable to the morality of the people?" I say with all emphasis, "In the long run, and by all means, favorable!"

In other words, to seek for and earn wealth is a sign of a natural, vigorous, and strong character. Wherever strong men are, there they will turn into the activities of life. In the ages of chivalry you will find them on the crusades or seeking the Golden Fleece; in college life you will find them high in rank, in the boat, or on the athletic field; in an industrial age you will find them eager, straining every nerve in the development of the great industries. The race is to the strong. The search for material wealth is therefore as natural and necessary to the man as is the pushing out of its roots for more moisture and food to the oak. This is man's play, his personality. You can no more suppress it than you can suppress the tide of the ocean. For one man who seeks money for its own sake there are ten who seek it for the satisfaction of the seeking, the power there is in it, and the use they can make of it. There is the exhilaration of feeling one's self grow in one's surroundings; the man reaches out, lays hold of this, that, and the other interest, scheme, and problem. He is building up a fortune? Yes, but his job is also that he is building up a stronger, abler, and more powerful man. There are two men that have none of this ambition: the gilded, listless youth and the ragged listless pauper to whom he tosses a dime; they are in the same class. . . .

One other dark shadow, and I am done. The persistent companion of riches—luxury and an ability to have what you want. That vice and license are rampant in certain quarters is clear; that vulgar wealth flaunts itself in the face of the people is beyond question; and that the people are rather amused at the spectacle must be confessed. The theatre syndicate will turn on to the boards whatever the people want; and the general tone of the plays speaks not well for the taste and morality of the people. The strain of temptation overwhelms a fraction of our youth. But one has no more right to test the result of prosperity by the small class of the lazy and luxurious than he has to test the result of poverty by the lazy tramp.

With all this said, the great mass of the people are self-restrained and simple. Material prosperity has come apace, and on the whole it uplifts. Responsibility sobers men and nations. We have learned how to win wealth: we are learning how to use and spend it. Every year marks a long step in advance in material prosperity, and character must march in step. Without wealth, character is liable to narrow and harden. Without character, wealth will destroy. Wealth is upon us, increasing wealth. The call of today is, then, for the uplift of character—the support of industry, education, art, and every means of culture; the encouragement of the higher life; and, above all, the deepening of the religious faith of the people; the rekindling of the spirit, that, clothed with her material forces, the great personality of this Nation may fulfill her divine destiny.

I have been clear, I trust, in my opinion that material prosperity is in the long run favorable to morality. Let me be as clear in the statement of that eternal truth, that neither a man's nor a nation's life consists in the abundance of things he possesseth.

In the investment of wealth in honest enterprise and business, lies our path of character. In the investment of wealth in all that goes towards the uplift of the people in education, art, and religion is another path of character. Above all, and first of all, stands the personal life. The immoral rich man is a traitor to himself, to his material as well as spiritual interests. Material prosperity is upon us; it is marching with us. Character must keep step, ay, character must lead. We want great riches; we want also great men.

Acres of Diamonds
Russell H. Conwell

Russell H. Conwell (1843-1925) was brought up the son of a poor farmer in the hills of western Massachusetts, where his father had known John Brown and Frederick Douglass. While attending school, Russell earned money by selling a biography of Brown. Following his service in the Civil War, Conwell invested in real estate, practiced law, and ran a large Bible class in Boston. He moved to Philadelphia where he used his fund-raising talent to erect a large Baptist temple and establish a night school that later became Temple University. Conwell insisted it was the duty of each person to make money and become rich, the key sentiment in his speech "Acres of Diamonds," which he delivered over 6000 times between 1868 and 1925. The following excerpt from the speech was taken from *Acres of Diamonds* (New York: Harper and Brothers, 1915), pp. 17-22.

Now then, I say again that the opportunity to get rich, to attain unto great wealth, is here in Philadelphia now, within the reach of almost every man and woman who hears me speak tonight, and I mean just what I say. I have not come to this platform even under these circumstances to recite something to you. I have come to tell you what in God's sight I believe to be the truth, and if the years of life have been of any value to me in the attainment of common sense, I know I am right; that the men and women sitting here, who found it difficult perhaps to buy a ticket to this lecture or gathering tonight, have within their reach "acres of diamonds," opportunities to get largely wealthy. There never was a place on earth more adapted than the city of Philadelphia today, and never in the history of the world did a poor man without capital have such an opportunity to get rich quickly and honestly as he has now in our city. I say it is the truth, and I want

you to accept it as such; for if you think I have come to simply recite something, then I would better not be here. I have no time to waste in any such talk, but to say the things I believe, and unless some of you get richer for what I am saying tonight my time is wasted.

I say that you ought to get rich, and it is your duty to get rich. How many of my pious brothers say to me, "Do you, a Christian minister, spend your time going up and down the country advising young people to get rich, to get money?" "Yes, of course I do." They say, "Isn't that awful! Why don't you preach the gospel instead of preaching about man's making money?" "Because to make money honestly is to preach the gospel." That is the reason. The men who get rich may be the most honest men you find in the community.

"Oh," but says some young man here tonight, "I have been told all my life that if a person has money he is very dishonest and dishonorable and mean and contemptible." My friend, that is the reason why you have none, because you have that idea of people. The foundation of your faith is altogether false. Let me say here clearly, and say it briefly though subject to discussion which I have not time for here, ninety-eight out of one hundred of the rich men of America are honest. That is why they are rich. That is why they are trusted with money. That is why they carry on great enterprises and find plenty of people to work with them. It is because they are honest men.

Says another young man, "I hear sometimes of men that get millions of dollars dishonestly." Yes, of course you do, and so do I. But they are so rare a thing in fact that the newspapers talk about them all the time as a matter of news until you get the idea that all the other rich men got rich dishonestly.

My friend, you take and drive—if you furnish the auto—out into the suburbs of Philadelphia, and introduce me to the people who own their homes around this great city, those beautiful homes with gardens and flowers, these magnificent homes so lovely in their art, and I will introduce you to the very best people in character as well as in enterprise in our city, and you know I will. A man is not really a true man until he owns his own home, and they that own their own homes are made more honorable and honest and pure, and true and economical and careful, by owning the home.

For a man to have money, even in large sums is not an inconsistent thing. We preach against covetousness, and you know we do, in the pulpit, and often times preach against it so long and use the terms about "filthy lucre" so extremely that Christians get the idea that when we stand in the pulpit we believe it is wicked for any man to have money until the collection basket goes around, and then we almost swear at the people because they don't give more money. Oh, the inconsistency of such doctrines as that!

Money is power, and you ought to be reasonably ambitious to have it. You ought because you can do more good with it than you could without it. Money printed your Bible, money builds your churches, money sends your missionaries, and money pays your preachers, and you would not have many of them, either, if you did not pay them. I am always willing that my church should raise my salary, because the church that pays the largest salary always raises it the easiest. You never knew an exception to it in your life. The man who gets the largest salary can do the most good with the power that is furnished to him. Of course he can if his spirit be right to use it for what it is given to him.

I say, then, you ought to have money. If you can honestly attain unto riches in Philadelphia, it is your Christian and godly duty to do so. It is an awful mistake of these pious people to think you must be awfully poor in order to be pious.

Some men say, "Don't you sympathize with the poor people?" Of course I do, or else I would not have been lecturing these years. I won't give in but what I sympathize with the poor, but the number of poor who are to be sympathized with is very small. To sympathize with a man whom God has punished for his sins, thus to help him when God would still continue a just punishment, is wrong, no doubt about it, and we do that more than we help those who are deserving. While we should sympathize with God's poor—that is, those who cannot help themselves—let us remember there is not a poor person in the United States who was not made poor by his own shortcomings, or by the shortcomings of some one else. It is all wrong to be poor, anyhow. Let us give in to that argument and pass that to one side.

A gentleman gets up back there, and says, "Don't you think there are some things in this world that are better than money?" Of course I do, but I am talking about money now. Of course there are some things higher than money. Oh yes, I know by the grave that has left me standing alone that there are higher and sweeter and purer than money. Well do I know there are some things higher

and grander than gold. Love is the grandest thing on God's earth, but fortunate the lover who has plenty of money. Money is power, money is force, money will do good as well as harm. In the hands of good men and women it could accomplish, and it has accomplished, good.

I hate to leave that behind me. I heard a man get up in a prayer meeting in our city and thank the Lord he was "one of God's poor." Well, I wonder what his wife thinks about that? She earns the money that comes into that house, and he smokes a part of that on the veranda. I don't want to see any more of the Lord's poor of that kind, and I don't believe the Lord does. And yet there are some people who think in order to be pious you must be awfully poor and awfully dirty. That does not follow at all. While we sympathize with the poor, let us not teach a doctrine like that.

11 The Social Gospel

And the King will answer and say to them, "Truly I say to you, to the extent that you did it to one of these brothers of Mine, even the least of them, you did it to Me."

—Matt. 25:40

Applied Christianity
Washington Gladden

Washington Gladden (1836-1918) was a major awakener of the American Protestant social conscience during the Gilded Age of the late nineteenth century. From the time he entered the Congregational ministry in 1860, he was identified as a theological liberal. His popular exposition of the New Theology was consistently linked with the social concern of the social gospel movement's liberal wing. In 1875 he began a seven-year ministry in the industrial city of Springfield, Massachusetts, where he gained first-hand knowledge of the problems of unemployed workers. During his ministry at the First Congregational Church of Columbus, Ohio from 1882 to 1914, he added thirty books to the six he had already written and became one of the nation's most influential clergymen. Though he never became a socialist, he was a severe critic of the free enterprise system who insisted from pen and pulpit that the churches must do more to bring America's economic life in line with the laws of God's kingdom. The following selection appears in Gladden's *Applied Christianity: Moral Aspects of Social Christianity* (Boston: Houghton Mifflin and Company, 1886), pp. 146-59, 162-69.

We often say that Christianity is the cure of the evils that threaten modern civilization, but the troublesome fact that rises up to confound us whenever we express this confidence is the fact that a large section of the population is wholly outside our churches, and apparently beyond the reach of their direct influence. It is true that Christian ideas and sentiments do, to a certain extent, pervade all our society; the social atmosphere contains more or less of its vital elements, and no man can breathe in this Christian land without unconsciously assimilating some of its truth. But the complete separation of large numbers of our people from the institutions of religion, their utter ignorance of us and of all that we are trying to do, is a discouraging fact. This was brought home to me a few years ago in a manner that ought to have humbled my conceit, whether it did or not. I had been working pretty busily for almost eight years in a city of New England where neighbors generally know one another, and where the church-going population is exceptionally large, and I had tried to bear my part in the social and political life of the city as well as in its religious life. One Sunday a friend of mine, unfamiliar with the city, was walking down the principal street looking for my church, and three of my fellow-citizens of whom he inquired, in succession, did not know where the church was, and did not appear to have ever heard of its pastor. I suspect we should all be somewhat surprised if we could know just how many people there are within hearing of our church bells who do not know the name of the churches or of their ministers, to whose thought all our interests are foreign, to whose ear our familiar speech is an unknown tongue. Many others there are who know something of us, but do not love us; who listen with indifference, if not with resentment, when our church bells ring; who regard our assemblies with suspicious criticism; who are not so accessible to our influence as those who know less about us.

I do not mean to be understood as affirming that the majority of our population is thus wholly outside of all church relations. This class of entire neglecters is, as yet, a minority in most of our cities, but it is a minority large enough to cause us anxiety and to furnish us one of our hardest problems. Certain it is that Christianity can never cure the social ills under which we are suffering while so large a class remains practically untouched by its healing influences.

Our perplexity increases when we discover that this neglect is greatest in that class to be specially interested, to which it has always made its most gracious promises and its most successful appeals, with which its Founder himself was identified while He was on the earth—the wage-workers and the poor. The strongest of the evidences of Christianity has always been that one to which our Lord himself pointed the disciples of John: "The Gospel is preaching to the poor." It must be confessed that this proof of Christ's divine mission is losing its cogency.

I do not think that church neglect is increasing, as a rule, in other classes of the population. There are exceptional cities in which this neglect pervades all orders to an alarming degree, and seems to be steadily growing. But, generally, in our cities and large towns, I am inclined to think that the proportion of the people who attend the church or the Sunday school—who are present in the house of God during some part of the Lord's day—is as large as ever it was. The merchants, the clerks, the professional people, the teachers, are not deserting the churches. Of course there are multitudes of these persons who do not come to church now, and such multitudes have always been with us; but neglect does not *increase* among them, and it does increase among the wage-workers. The *proportion* of wage-workers in our churches is diminishing.

Proof of this proportion is not easily furnished, and I would much rather those who listen to me would search out the facts for themselves, than take my word for them. I suppose that there are localities in which the statements just made would not hold good, but a pretty careful study convinces me that they do hold good of the country at large, and especially of the cities. My analysis of the census makes it probable to me that the mechanics, the shop hands, and the common laborers—the wage-workers employed in manual labor of one kind or another, with their families, constitute fully one-fourth of the population. Is it true that one-fourth of the membership of our city churches belongs to this class? That is a question that every pastor can easily answer for himself, so far as his own church is concerned. It is true that in our Roman Catholic churches the proportion of wage laborers will be found to be much larger than one-fourth; the average in our Protestant churches should, therefore, be somewhat less than one-fourth. It would be well for every pastor to satisfy himself what the proportion is in his congregation. Of course the reckoning must be made by families, rather than by individuals. In my own congregation, which worships in a very plain church, the seats of which are free, in a neighborhood easily accessible to the working classes, and which has been known always as an extremely democratic congregation, I find only about one-tenth of the families on my list belonging to this class. The proportion would be slightly increased if I added the families which are represented in our Sunday-school, but which send no adults to any of our services. This is the result of repeated special efforts made in the interest of the working classes, with several courses of lectures on Sunday evenings for their benefit. Goodly numbers of them have attended these lectures, and there is, I think, a kindly feeling among them toward our church—certainly toward its pastor; but the number of those who identify themselves with us is still very small.

It is true that there are missions in all our cities into which larger numbers of these people are drawn; all these must be taken into account in our estimates, for although the arrangement whereby the rich are separated from the poor in their worship is not the ideal of Christianity, and although it may be a question whether in the long run church neglect may not be caused rather than cured by this arrangement; yet the question we are now considering respects the actual church attendance of the working classes—it is the question whether the proportion of wage-workers in our churches and missions is as large as it is in our population.

To get at the workingmen's ideas respecting this question, whether the people of their class are drawing away from the churches, and, if so, why, I sent out circulars, a few months ago, to workingmen connected with the various manufacturing industries of my own city, and obtained from them a large number of replies. From establishments employing in the aggregate between three and four thousand men, I had letters, and out of these, as nearly as I can estimate, from the figures given me, not more than one-third attend church; and of those who do go, a good share are Roman Catholics.

How is it with the other extreme of society? In this same city I asked one of the best informed citizens to make me out a list of fifty of the leaders of business. He did not know my reason for wishing such a list, but after it was put into my hands, I found that fifty-five percent of these men were communicants in the churches, and that seventy-seven percent of them were regular attendants upon the churches. A large proportion of the capitalists are more or less closely identified, and the number tends to decrease rather than to increase.

This statement is sometimes disputed, but I am quite sure that it cannot be successfully controverted. Some of those who have expressed a contrary opinion have counted clerks, bookkeepers, teachers, and office-boys into the "working class," but the question we are considering has nothing to do with these. We are talking now about the manual wage-workers—the mechanics, the operatives, and the day laborers; as to what may be the degree of neglect among those other classes, I am not prepared to express an opinion.

If the tendency of the class with which we are now dealing is what I have represented it to be, the fact is one of grave significance. If the churches are losing their hold on these working people, not only are they exhibiting a most alarming sign of their own degeneracy, but they are permitting the growth of elements and forces which will prove fatal to the peace, and even to the existence, of society. There is no other cement that can hold society together but that genuine goodwill which is the heart of Christianity. The weakening of this bond is an ominous sign. I do not think that it is the part of wisdom to ignore it. If it is true, we cannot too speedily discover it, nor too frankly confess it, nor too earnestly seek to know what it means.

What is the cause of this tendency? Why is it that the working people are slowly and sullenly drawing apart from the churches?

Many reasons are given. First, and most conclusive to the minds of some philosophers, is the comprehensive fact of total depravity. The working people stay away from church because their hearts are set against God and divine things; because they prefer to spend the day in idleness and pleasuring. Undoubtedly the working people have their full share of this universal moral disability; but I am not prepared to admit that they have any more than their share. Total depravity will account for just as much church neglect among working people as it will account for among traders, and lawyers, and teachers, and no more; and what we are now considering is the exceptional degree of church neglect existing among working people. The cause assigned will not account for this unless we assume that their depravity is considerably more than total.

Another explanation finds the reason of this fact in the infidelity prevalent among the working classes. It then becomes necessary to show that infidelity is more prevalent in these classes than in the mercantile and professional classes. I am not sure that this can be shown. Admit, for the sake of the argument, that there is more skepticism among wage-workers than among the other classes of society. The next question is, how came this to be so? What has made skeptics of these workingmen? Infidelity is not what Dr. Emmons said Romanism was, "an ultimate fact." It needs to be explained, quite as much as church neglect needs to be explained. Perhaps the same cause that drove these people out of the churches robbed them also of their faith in the doctrines on which the churches are founded. Perhaps when we have learned the reason of their church neglect we shall know the reason of their doubt.

When we ask the working people themselves to tell us why they are not in the churches, they give us various responses. I have a large bundle of letters at home in which this question is answered in many different ways. Some of these reasons are manifestly pretexts, destitute of serious meaning. One says that it costs too much to support the churches; but this objection was made respecting a church which it costs no man a cent to attend; where he can contribute as much or as little as he chooses, and the amount of his contribution will be known to nobody. Another says that some ministers preach politics; but he is perfectly aware, of course, that some ministers do not. Another urges that workingmen need the day for rest; but he can hardly be ignorant of the fact that the Sabbath rest is not prevented, but most effectually promoted by the quiet and refreshing service of the sanctuary. All these are pleas that the advocates do not expect us to take very seriously.

The real reasons for the absence of the working people from church, as they reveal themselves in this correspondence of mine, resolve themselves into two: first, their inability to dress well enough to appear in a place as stylish and fashionable as the average church; secondly, their sense of the injustice that workingmen, as a class, are receiving at the hands of capitalist employers, as a class. These two reasons are often combined. It is because the workingman is not receiving a fair compensation for his labor, that he cannot dress his wife and children well enough to go to church. The plain or shabby raiment is the badge of his poverty, the evidence of the wrong that he is suffering.

One reason [writes one of my correspondents] for not attending the larger churches, which have wealthy congregations and good ministers, is that they are composed of the class who hire men to work for them, and, of course, dress themselves and their families better than the mere wage-worker can afford to do. When we see our employers going to church in broadcloth, and silk, and satin, and furs, and laces, and ribbons, it is natural for the man with a faded and patched coat, and the woman with a calico dress, to feel rather uncomfortable in the midst of such finery.

One reason of their absence [writes another] is their inability to clothe themselves in a manner to make a respectable appearance in church, owing to the starvation-wages paid to them.

You want to know what the workingmen think about capitalists? [writes another] We think [he answers compendiously] that they are thieves and robbers.

Of course [writes another] the manufacturers can and should dress better than the laborer; when we see them so full of religion on Sunday, and but then grinding the faces of the poor on the other six days, we are apt to think they are insincere. They say to us, "We are not making as much as we would like; we will have to reduce the cost of our goods by cutting down your wages a little." We say, "Hard work gives us a good appetite, and we can't set a substantial table." They say, "Corn is cheap; your table ought not cost too much." This creates an ill-feeling between capital and labor. When the capitalist prays for us one day in the week, and preys on us the other six, it can't be expected that we will have much respect for his Christianity.

This letter fairly expresses the sentiment that runs through a good share of my correspondence. The assumption of most of the letters is that the churches are chiefly attended and controlled by the capitalist and the employing classes; they make it evident that there is but little sympathy between these classes and the laboring class; and they show that the laborers have no desire to attend the churches in which their employers worship. The social barrier between them is high and strong on week days; they are not inclined to lower it on Sundays. Beyond a doubt, a great many conversations of the same nature as that reported by the workingman above do take place between masters and men; and when, after all this talk about reduced wages, and consequent corn cake and calico for the workman's family, the workman sees his employer's family faring sumptuously, and walking or riding abroad in the most gorgeous array, he is not, naturally, in the proper mood to sing the same hymns and pray the same prayers.

Nothing is more certain than that the wage-workers of this country feel that they are falling behind in the race for life. They know that the nation's wealth is increasing with almost miraculous rapidity, the figures of the census tell them so, and the fact thrusts itself upon their senses on every side. They know, moreover, if they have memories reaching back twenty or thirty years, that their condition is not greatly improved; that the *real* wages of labor are but little increased; and that, relatively to the rest of the community, they are worse off than they were thirty years ago. The annual expenditure for living purposes of the average employer has enormously increased, the annual expenditure of the average mechanic or operative has not greatly increased.

The workman feels that this tendency is due to the pitiless action of natural forces which the employing classes do not try to restrain. If he does reason much about it, he has a pretty strong notion that the fates are against him, and that his employer is on the side of fate. He knows that money, when it is massed in great corporations or companies, or heaped up in accumulations, is power. . . .

It is evident that the wage-workers, as a class, are discontented. They feel that they are not getting their fair share of the gains of advancing civilization.

It is evident that they are becoming more and more widely separated from their employers in the social scale.

It is evident that the old relations of friendliness between the two classes are giving place to alienation and enmity.

It is evident that the working people have the impression that the churches are mainly under the control of the capitalists and of those in sympathy with them.

If all these things are so, the reasons why the working people are inclined to withdraw from the churches ought also to be plain.

The fact of a great and growing discontent among the working classes, the fact of the increasing separation and alienation between wage-workers and their employers, are facts that cannot be disputed by any intelligent person. It may be doubted whether existing circumstances are bearing as severely upon the laborers as he imagines; it may be that he is better off than he thinks he is. But the question with which we are now concerned is: What does he think about it? He may be wrong in cherishing such unfriendly and resentful feelings toward his employer; but does he cherish them? He may be in error in thinking that the capitalist classes exercise a preponderating influence in the churches; but does he think so? If his state of mind is what it is assumed to be in this discussion, you have reason for church neglect which is widespread and deep-seated; you have a disorder to cure which is constitutional and obstinate, and which will never be removed by the sprinkling of rose-water; you have a problem on your hands which calls for clear thinking and heroic endeavor.

The "masses" of our cities that we are trying to reach are composed, to a large extent, of these wage-workers, and we shall never reach them over this barrier. The sooner the churches recognize this fact and adjust their theories and their methods to it, the sooner they will begin to see daylight shine through this dark problem of church neglect. So long as we ignore this fundamental difficulty, all our efforts to allure these neglecters will be in vain. A few of them will come in now and then in response to our urgent invitations; some of them, less thoughtful, or more hopeful, or more long-suffering than the rest, will continue to worship with us, finding in the promise of the life to come some help to bear hardships of the life that now is; but the great multitude will turn upon us suspiciously or resentfully when they hear our invitations, saying: We want none of your free seats, we can do without your fine music and your pious common-places, we do not greatly care for your handshaking in the house of God and the perfunctory calls of your visitors at our houses. All we ask is justice. We want a chance to earn a decent living. We want a fair share of the wealth that our labor is helping to produce. We do not want to be left far behind when our neighbors, the employers, the traders, the professional people, are pushing on to plenty and prosperity. In the midst of all this overflowing bounty, we want something more than meager subsistence. We are not quite sure whether you people of the churches want us to have it or not. Many of you, as we are bitterly aware, act as though you did not greatly care what became of us; and we hear from many of you hard and heartless comments on every effort we make to fight the fates that are bearing us down. It looks to us as though your sympathies were chiefly given to the people who are getting rich at our expense. Until our minds are clearer on this score, we shall never be drawn to your churches, charm you never so wisely.

What are you going to do with people who talk in this way? That is the one tremendous question which the Church of God is called to answer today.

Suppose you say that these people are all wrong in these theories, and all astray in their censure. Suppose you insist that they are getting their full share of the gains of this advancing civilization, or, if they are failing to do so, that it is wholly their own fault. Then it is your business to convince them of this by patient and thorough discussion. You cannot remove their misconceptions by denouncing them, or contemptuously ignoring them. You cannot disabuse them by abusing them. If they are wholly in error with respect to this matter, their error is most deplorable and hurtful to them, and to society at large; and the Church has no more urgent duty than that of convincing them that they are wrong.

Suppose that they are all wrong in their impression that the sympathies of the churches are on the side of the classes with which they are in conflict. The impression is there, and no headway can be made in bringing them into the churches until it is somehow eradicated.

"The only cure of all this trouble," some one will confidently answer, "is the gospel. Preach the gospel faithfully, and it will make an end of all this strife." This answer assumes that the fault all lies with the people now in the churches. What effect can the faithful preaching of the gospel have upon those who do not and will not hear it? If the gospel thus preached reaches these neglecting multitudes, it can only be through those who now listen to it. And the very trouble we are considering is that those who now frequent the churches find it difficult, and almost impossible, to put themselves into friendly relations with the neglecting multitudes.

What is meant by those who use this language is simply this: That the strife between labor and capital arises from the natural depravity of the human heart; and that, if men were soundly converted, all these grounds of contention would be removed. Unfortunately, this reasoning overlooks some important facts. The gospel, considered simply as an evangelistic or converting agency, will never put an end to this trouble. There are plenty of people in our churches today, who give every evidence of having been soundly converted, but who are conducting themselves continually in such a manner as to cause this trouble, instead of curing it. When a man is converted, he has a purpose to do right; and if you choose to go a little farther and say that he has the disposition to do right, I will not stop to dispute you. But he may have very crude ideas as to what right is; his heart may be regenerated, but his head may still be sadly muddled. And there are thousands of people in all our churches who mean to do right by their working people, but those ideas have been so perverted by a false political economy that they are continually doing them grievous wrong. If a man has been taught the wage-fund theory, or if he has got into his head the idea that *laissez faire* is the chief duty of man, the gospel, in the ordinary acceptance of that term, will not correct the defects in his conduct towards his work people. He may believe that he is a sinner, that he cannot save himself, that he must be saved from his sins by faith in Christ; and he may humbly confess his conscious faults, and trust in Christ for forgiveness and salvation. But his habit of taking the law of supply and demand as his sole guide in dealing with his working people is not a conscious fault. He has been diligently taught that labor is simply a commodity; that what Carlyle calls the "cash-nexus" is the only bond between himself and his employees. As Toynbee puts it, Political Economy has steadily said to him, whenever he has thought of governing himself, in his relations with his work people, by Christian principles, "You are doing a very foolish thing. You might as well try to make iron swim as to alter the rate of wages by your individual will. The rate of wages, like the succession of night and day, is independent of the will of either employer or employed. Neither workmen nor employers can change the rate determined by competition at any particular time." Fortified by this philosophy, the converted employer feels that any attempt to give his men a larger share of his gains would be superfluous, if not mischievous; that the fates will have it all their own way in spite of him; that all he can do is to buy his labor in the cheapest market, and sell his wares in the dearest. In other words, he has been taught, and he believes, that the industrial world is a world in which the Christian laws of conduct have no sway; in which sympathy is fallacious, and goodwill foolishness. What can preaching the gospel, in the ordinary sense of the word, do for such a man? His purpose is right, his heart is right, but his theories are all wrong. Some people say that it makes no difference what man believes if his heart is right. It makes a tremendous difference!

The gospel, then, as the simple evangel, will not cure this evil. But Christianity will cure it. Christianity is something more than a gospel. Christianity is a law, as well as a gospel. And the Christian law, faithfully preached, as the foundation of the gospel, will put an end to all this trouble. We sometimes hear it said that the pulpit of the present day is derelict, because there is not enough preaching of the law. It is true. What the Church needs is a great deal more enforcement of law—not necessarily more threatening of penalty, but more preaching of law—of the law of Christ, in its application to the relations of men in their everyday life. By the law is the knowledge of sin. Many of the Christian people in our churches have not been convicted of their sins, because the law has not been laid down to them. . . .

Cardinal Gibbons Defends the Knights of Labor
James Cardinal Gibbons

James Gibbons (1834-1921) was the Catholic archbishop of Baltimore when he was named a cardinal in 1886. At that time the leadership and Catholic community were in the midst of a controversy which split them over the question of the desired extent of American Catholic accommodation to the American culture. In his devotion to American ideals that led him to sympathize with the Americanist party in the controversy, Gibbons presented the Vatican with a document he signed but probably did not write. It argued that the Knights of Labor, two-thirds of whose members were Roman Catholic, should not be condemned as a secret society in the United States, as had been done in the Canadian Province of Quebec in 1884. This statement presented by Gibbons was successful in convincing the Vatican not to oppose the Knights in America.

To His Eminence Cardinal Simeoni, Prefect of the Sacred Congregation of the Propaganda:

Your Eminence:

In submitting to the Holy See the conclusions which after several months of attentive observation and reflection, seem to me to sum up the truth concerning the association of the Knights of Labor, I feel profoundly convinced of the vast importance of the consequences attaching to this question, which forms but a link in the great chain of the social problems of our day, and especially of our country. . . .

1. In the first place, in the constitution, laws and official declarations of the Knights of Labor, there can clearly be found assertions and rules [though there may be found . . . things—*peuvent bien*

se trouver des assertions ou des règles] which we would not approve; but we have not found in them those elements so clearly pointed out by the Holy See, which places them among condemned associations. . . .

2. That there exists among us, as in the other countries of the world, grave and threatening social evils, public injustices, which call for strong resistance and legal remedy, is a fact which no one dares to deny, and the truth of which has been already acknowledged by the Congress and the President of the United States. Without entering into the sad details of these wrongs,—which does not seem necessary here,—it may suffice to mention only that monopolies on the part of both individuals and of corporations, have already called forth not only the complaints of our working classes

but also the opposition of our public men and legislators; that the efforts of these monopolists, not always without success, to control legislation to their own profit, cause serious apprehension among the disinterested friends of liberty; that the heartless avarice which, through greed of gain, pitilessly grinds not only the men, but particularly the women and children in various employments, make it clear to all who love humanity and justice that it is not only the right of the laboring classes to protect themselves, but the duty of the whole people to aid them in finding a remedy against the dangers with which both civilization and the social order are menaced by avarice, oppression and corruption.

It would be vain to deny either the existence of the evils, the right of legitimate resistance, or the necessity of a remedy. At most doubt might be raised about the legitimacy of the form of resistance and the remedy employed by the Knights of Labor. This then ought to be the next point of our examination.

3. It can hardly be doubted that for the attainment of any public end, association—the organization of all interested persons—is the most efficacious means, a means altogether natural and just. This is so evident, and besides so conformable to the genius of our country, of our essentially popular social conditions, that it is unnecessary to insist upon it. It is almost the only means to invite public attention, to give force to the most legitimate resistance, to add weight to the most just demands. . . .

4. Let us now consider the objections made against this sort of organization.

(a) It is objected that in these organizations Catholics are mixed with Protestants, to the peril of their faith.

Naturally, yes, they are mixed with Protestants in the workers' associations, precisely as they are at their work; for in a mixed people like ours, the separation of religions in social affairs is not possible. But to suppose that the faith of our Catholics suffer thereby is not to know the Catholic workers of America who are not like the workingmen of so many European countries—misguided and perverted children, looking on their Mother the Church as a hostile stepmother—but they are intelligent, well instructed and devoted children ready to give their blood, as they continually give their means (although small and hard-earned) [hard-earned—*chétifs et péniblement gagnés*] for her support and protection. And in fact it is not in the present case that Catholics are mixed with Protestants, but rather that Protestants are admitted to the advantages of an association, two-thirds of whose members and the principal officers [many of whose members and officers—*des duex tiers des membres et les officiers principaux*] are Catholics; and in a country like ours their exclusion would be simply impossible.

(b) But it is said, could there not be substituted for such an organization confraternities which would unite the workingmen under the direction of the priests and the direct influence of religion? I answer frankly that I do not believe that either possible or necessary in our country. I sincerely admire the efforts of this sort which are made in countries where the workers are led astray by the enemies of religion; but thanks be to God, that is not our condition. We find that in our country the presence and explicit influence of the clergy would not be advisable where our citizens, without distinction of religious belief, come together in regard to their industrial interests alone. Without going so far, we have abundant means for making our working people faithful Catholics, and simple good sense advises us not to go to extremes.

(c) Again, it is objected that the liberty of such an organization exposes Catholics to the evil influences of the most dangerous associates, even of atheists, communists and anarchists. That is true; but it is one of the trials of faith which our brave American Catholics are accustomed to meet almost daily, and which they know how to disregard with good sense and firmness. The press of our country tells us the president of the Knights of Labor has related to us, how these violent and aggressive elements have endeavored to seize authority in their councils, or to inject their poison into the principles of the association; but they also verify with what determination these evil spirits [machinators— *mauvais esprits*] have been repulsed and defeated. The presence among our citizens of this destructive element, which has come for the most part from certain nations of Europe, is assuredly for us an occasion of lively regrets and careful precautions; it is an inevitable fact, however, but one which the union between the Church and her children in our country renders comparatively free from danger. In truth, the only grave danger would come from an alienation between the Church and her children, which nothing would more certainly occasion than imprudent condemnations.

(d) An especially weighty charge is drawn from the outbursts of violence, even to bloodshed, which have characterized [accompanied— *charactérizé*] several of the strikes inaugurated by labor organizations. Concerning this, three things are to be remarked: first, strikes are not an invention of the Knights of Labor, but a means almost everywhere and always resorted to by employees in our land and elsewhere to protest against what they consider unjust and to demand their right; secondly in such a struggle of the poor and indignant multitudes against hard and obstinate monopoly, anger and violence, [outbursts of anger— *colère et le violence*] are often as inevitable as they are regrettable; thirdly, the laws and chief authorities of the

Knights of Labor, far from encouraging violence or the occasions of it, exercise a powerful influence to hinder it, and to keep strikes within the limits of good order and legitimate action. A careful examination of the acts of violence which have marked the struggle between capital and labor during the past year, leaves us convinced that it would be unjust to attribute them to the association of the Knights of Labor. This was but one of several associations of workers that took part in the strikes, and their chief officers, according to disinterested witnesses, used every possible effort to appease the anger of the crowds and to prevent the excesses which, in my judgement, could not justly be attributed to them. Doubtless among the Knights of Labor as among thousands of other workingmen, there are violent, or even wicked and criminal men, who have committed inexcusable deeds of violence, and have urged their associates to do the same; but to attribute this to the organization, it seems to me, would be as unreasonable as to attribute to the Church the follies and crimes for her children against which she protests. I repeat that in such a struggle of the great masses of the people against the mail-clad power, which, as it is acknowledged, often refuses them the simple rights of humanity and justice, it is vain to expect that every error and every act of violence can be avoided; and to dream that this struggle can be prevented, or that we can deter the multitudes from organizing, which is their only practical means [hope—*moyen pratique*] of success, would be to ignore the nature and forces of human society in times like ours. The part of Christian prudence evidently is to try to hold the hearts of the multitude by the bonds of love, in order to control their actions by the principles of faith, justice and charity, to acknowledge frankly the truth and justice in their cause, in order to deter them from what would be false and criminal, and thus to turn into a legitimate, peaceable and beneficent contest what could easily become for the masses of our people a volcanic abyss, like that which society fears and the Church deplores in Europe.

Upon this point I insist strongly, because from an intimate acquaintance with the social conditions of our country I am profoundly convinced that here we are touching upon a subject which not only concerns the rights of the working classes, who ought to be especially dear to the Church which our Divine Lord sent to evangelize the poor, but with which are bound up the fundamental interests of the Church and of human society for the future. This is a point which I desire, in a few additional words to develop more clearly.

5. Whoever meditates upon the ways in which divine Providence is guiding contemporary history cannot fail to remark how important is the part which the

power of the people takes therein at present and must take in the future. We behold, with profound sadness, the efforts of the prince of darkness to make this power dangerous to the social weal by withdrawing the masses of the people from the influence of religion, and impelling them towards the ruinous paths of license and anarchy. Until now our country presents a picture of altogether different [most consolingly different—*tout différent*] character—that of popular power regulated by love of good order, by respect for religion, by obedience to the authority of the laws, not a democracy of license and violence, but that true democracy which aims at the general prosperity through the means of sound principles and good social order.

In order to preserve so desirable a state of things it is absolutely necessary that religion should continue to hold the affections, and thus rule the conduct of the multitudes. As Cardinal Manning has so well written, "In the future era the Church has no longer to deal with princes and parliaments, but with the masses, with the people. Whether we will or no this is our work; we need a new spirit, a new direction of our life and activity." To lose influence over the people would be to lose the future altogether; and it is by the heart, far more than by the understanding, that we must hold and guide this immense power, so mighty either for good or for evil. Among all the glorious titles of the Church which her history has merited for her, there is not one which at present gives her so great influence as that of *Friend of the People*. Assuredly, in our

democratic country, it is this title which wins for the Catholic Church not only the enthusiastic devotedness of the millions of her children, but also the respect and admiration of all our citizens, whatever be their religious belief. It is the power of precisely this title which renders persecution almost an impossibility, and which draws toward our holy Church the great heart of the American people.

And since it is acknowledged by all that the great questions of the future are not those of war, of commerce or finance, but the social questions, the questions which concern the improvement of the condition of the great masses of the people, and especially of the working people, it is evidently of supreme importance that the Church should always be found on the side of humanity, of justice toward the multitudes who compose the body of the human family. . . .

6. Now let us consider for a moment the consequences which would inevitably follow from a contrary course, from a lack of sympathy for the working class, from a suspicion of their aims, from a hasty condemnation of their methods.

(a) First, there is the evident danger of the Church's losing in popular estimation her right to be considered the friend of the people. The logic of men's hearts goes swiftly to its conclusions, and this conclusion would be a pernicious one for the people and for the Church. To lose the heart of the people would be a misfortune for which the friendship of the few rich and powerful would be no compensation.

(b) There is a great danger of rendering hostile to the Church the political power of our country, which openly takes sides with the millions who are demanding justice and the improvement of their condition. The accusation of being, "*un-American*," that is to say, alien to our national spirit, is the most powerful weapon which the enemies of the Church know how to employ against her. It was this cry which aroused the Know-Nothing persecution thirty years ago, and the same would be quickly used again if the opportunity offered itself. . . .

(c) A third danger, and the one which touches our hearts the most, is the risk of losing the love of the children of the Church, and of pushing them into an attitude of resistance against their Mother. The whole world presents no more beautiful spectacle than that of their filial devotion and obedience. . . .

7. But besides the danger which would result from such a condemnation and the impossibility of having it respected and observed [putting it into effect—*de la faire respecter et observer*] one should note that the form of this organization is so little permanent, as the press indicates nearly every day, that in the estimation of practical men in our country, it cannot last very many years. . . .

8. In all this discussion I have not at all spoken of Canada, nor of the condemnation concerning the Knights of Labor in Canada. For we would consider it an impertinence to involve ourselves in the ecclesiastical affairs of another country which has a hierarchy of its own, and with whose needs and social conditions we do not pretend to be acquainted. We believe, however, that the circumstances of a people almost entirely Catholic, as in lower Canada, must be very different from those of a mixed population like ours. . . .

With complete confidence, I leave the case to the wisdom and prudence of your Eminence and the Holy See.

Rome, February 20, 1887.

J. Cardinal Gibbons,
Archbishop of Baltimore.

In His Steps
Charles M. Sheldon

Charles M. Sheldon (1857-1946), minister of the Central Congregational Church in Topeka, Kansas, was perhaps best known as an author of over fifty books and hundreds of articles, along with many poems, hymns, and plays. As a timeless pastor and reformer, he was a strong supporter of the social gospel movement and its principal aim of establishing the kingdom of God on earth here and now. He strove to improve living and working conditions, and helped campaign for religious reform, world peace, and prohibition. In his most famous work, *In His Steps* (1896), Sheldon mused what it would be like if the people of any small town would consistently ask, "What would Jesus do?" Appropriate responses would move America toward a new era of social millennialism.

The sermon was interesting. It was full of striking sentences. They would have commanded attention printed. Spoken with the passion of a dramatic utterance that has the good taste never to offend with a suspicion of ranting or declamation, they were very effective. If the Rev. Henry Maxwell that morning felt satisfied with the conditions of his pastorate, the First Church also had a similar feeling as it congratulated itself on the presence in the pulpit of this scholarly, refined, somewhat striking face and figure, preaching with such animation and freedom from all vulgar, noisy, or disagreeable mannerism.

Suddenly into the midst of this perfect accord and concord between preacher and audience, there came a very remarkable interruption. It would be difficult to indicate the extent of the shock which this interruption measured. It was so unexpected, so entirely contrary to any thought of any person present that offered no room for argument, or, for the time being, of resistance.

The sermon had come to a close. Mr. Maxwell had just turned the half of the big Bible over upon his manuscript and was about to sit down, as the quartette prepared to rise to sing the closing selection,

"All for Jesus, All for Jesus,
All my being's ransomed powers."

when the entire congregation was startled by the sound of a man's voice. It came from the rear of the church, from one of the seats under the gallery. The next moment the figure of a man came out of the shadow there and walked down the middle aisle.

Before the startled congregation barely realized what was going on, the man had reached the open space in front of the pulpit and had turned about, facing the people.

"I have been wondering since I came in here"—they were the words he used under the gallery, and he repeated them—"if it would be just the thing to say a word at the close of this service. I'm not drunk and I'm not crazy, and I'm perfectly harmless; but if I die, as there is every likelihood I shall in a few days, I want the satisfaction of thinking that I said my say in a place like this, and before this sort of a crowd."

Mr. Maxwell had not taken his seat, and he now remained standing, leaning on his pulpit, looking down at the stranger. It was the man who had come to his house the Friday before—the same dusty, worn, shabby-looking young man. He held his faded hat in his two hands. It seemed to be a favorite gesture. He had not been shaved, and his hair was rough and tangled. It was doubtful if anyone like this had ever confronted the First Church within the sanctuary. It was tolerably familiar with this sort of humanity out on the street around the railroad shops, wandering up and down the avenue; but it had never dreamed of such an incident as this so near.

There was nothing offensive in the man's manner or tone. He was not excited, and he spoke in a low but distinct voice. Mr. Maxwell was conscious, even as he stood there smitten into dumb astonishment at the event, that somehow the man's action reminded him of a person he had once seen walking and talking in his sleep.

No one in the house made any motion to stop the stranger or in any way interrupt him. Perhaps the first shock of his sudden appearance deepened into genuine perplexity concerning what was best to do. However that may be, he went on as if he had no thought of interruption, and no thought of the unusual element which he had introduced into the decorum of the First Church service. And all the while he was speaking the minister leaned over the pulpit, his face growing more white and sad every moment. But he made no movement to stop him, and the people sat smitten into breathless silence. One other face, that of Rachel Winslow, from the choir, stared white and intent down at the shabby figure with the faded hat. Her face was striking at any time. Under the pressure of the present unheard-of incident, it was as personally distinct as if it had been framed in fire.

"I'm not an ordinary tramp, though I don't know of any teaching of Jesus that makes one kind of a tramp less worth saving than another. Do you?" He put the question as naturally as if the whole congregation had been a small Bible class. He paused just a moment, and coughed painfully. Then he went on. "I lost my job ten months ago. I am a printer by trade. The new linotype machines are beautiful specimens of inventions, but I know six men who have killed themselves inside of the year just on account of those machines. Of course, I don't blame the newspapers for getting the machines. Meanwhile, what can a man do? I know I never learned but the one trade, and that's all I can do. I've tramped all over the country trying to find something. There are a good many others like me. I'm not complaining, am I? Just stating facts. But I was wondering, as I sat there under the gallery, if what you call following Jesus is the same thing as what he taught. What did he mean when he said, 'Follow me?' The minister said,"—here the man turned about and looked up at the pulpit—"that it was necessary for the disciple of Jesus to follow his steps, and he said the steps were obedience, faith, love, and imitation. But I did not hear him tell you just what he meant that to mean, especially the last step. What do you Christians mean by following the steps of Jesus? I've tramped through this city for three days trying to find a job, and in all that time I've not had a word of sympathy or comfort except from your minister here, who said he was sorry for me and hoped I would find a job somewhere. I suppose it is because you get so imposed on the professional tramp that you have lost your interest in the other sort. I'm not blaming anybody, am I? Just stating facts. Of course, I understand you can't go out of your way to hunt jobs for people like me. I'm not asking you to, but what I feel puzzled about is, what is meant by following Jesus? What do you mean when you sing, 'I'll go with him, with him all the way?' Do you mean that you are suffering and denying yourselves and trying to save lost, suffering humanity just as I understand Jesus did? What do you mean by it? I see the ragged edge of things a good deal. I understand there are more than five hundred men in this city in my case. Most of them have families. My wife died four months ago. I'm glad she is out of trouble. My little girl is staying with a printer's family until I find a job. Somehow I get puzzled when I see so many Christians living in luxury and singing, 'Jesus, I my cross have taken, all to leave and follow thee,' and remember how my wife died in a tenement in New York City gasping for air, and asking God to take the little girl, too. Of course I don't expect you people can prevent everyone from dying of starvation, lack of proper

nourishment, and tenement air, but what does following Jesus mean? I understand that Christian people own a good many of the tenements. A member of a church was the owner of the one where my wife died, and I have wondered if following Jesus all the way was true in his case. I heard some people singing at a church prayer meeting the other night,

'All for Jesus, all for Jesus;
All my being's ransomed powers;
All my thoughts and all my doings,
All my days and all my hours;'

and I kept wondering as I sat on the steps outside just what they meant by it. It seems to me there's an awful lot of trouble in the world that somehow wouldn't exist if all the people who sing such songs went and lived them out. I suppose I don't understand. But what would Jesus do? Is that what you mean by following his steps? It seems to me sometimes as if the people in the big churches had good clothes and nice houses to live in, and money to spend for luxuries, and could go away on summer vacations and all that, while the people outside the churches, thousands of them, I mean, die in tenements and walk the streets for jobs, and never have a piano or a picture in the house, and grow up in misery and drunkenness and sin." The man gave a queer lurch over in the direction of the communion table and laid one grimy hand on it. His hat fell upon the carpet at his feet. A stir went through the congregation. Dr. West half rose from his pew, but as yet the silence was unbroken by any voice or movement worth mentioning in the audience. The man passed his other hand across his eyes, and then, without any warning, fell heavily forward on his face, full length, up the aisle.

Henry Maxwell spoke, "We will consider the service closed." He was down the pulpit stairs and kneeling by the prostrate form before anyone else. The audience instantly rose and the aisles were crowded. Dr. West pronounced the man alive. He had fainted away. "Some heart trouble," the doctor also muttered as he helped carry him out to the pastor's study.

Henry Maxwell and a group of his church members remained some time in the study. The man lay on the couch there and breathed heavily. When the question of what to do with him came up, the minister insisted upon taking the man to his house. He lived near by and had an extra room. Rachel Winslow said, "Mother has no company at present. I am sure we would be glad to give him a place with us." She looked strangely agitated. No one noticed it particularly. They were all excited over the strange event, the strangest that First Church people could remember. But the minister insisted on taking charge of the man, and, when a carriage came, the unconscious but living form was carried to his house, and with the entrance of that humanity into the minister's spare room a new chapter in Henry Maxwell's life began, and yet no one, himself least of all, dreamed of the remarkable change it was destined to make in all his after definition of Christian discipleship.

The event created a great sensation in the First Church parish. People talked of nothing else for a week. It was the general impression that the man had wandered into the church in a condition of mental disturbance caused by his troubles, and that all the time he was talking he was in a strange delirium of fever and really ignorant of his surroundings. That was the most charitable construction to put upon his action; it was the general agreement also that there was a singular absence of anything bitter or complaining in what the man had said. He had throughout spoken in a mild apologetic tone, almost as if he were one of the congregation seeking for light on a very difficult subject.

The third day after his removal to the minister's house there was a marked change in his condition. The doctor spoke of it, but offered no hope. Saturday morning he still lingered, although he had rapidly failed as the week drew near its close. Sunday morning just before the clock struck one, he rallied and asked if his child had come. The minister had sent for her at once as soon as he had been able to secure her address from some letter found in the man's pocket. He had been conscious and able to talk coherently only a few moments since his attack. "The child is coming. She will be here," Mr. Maxwell said as he sat there, his face showing marks of the strain of the week's vigil. For he had insisted on sitting up nearly every night.

"I shall never see her in this world," the man whispered. Then he uttered with great difficulty the words, "You have been good to me. Somehow I feel as if it was what Jesus would do." After a few moments he turned his head slightly, and before Mr. Maxwell could realize the fact, the doctor said, quietly, "He's gone."

The Sunday morning that dawned on the city of Raymond was exactly like the Sunday of a week before. Mr. Maxwell entered his pulpit to face one of the largest congregations that had ever crowded the First Church. He was haggard and looked as if he had just risen from a long illness. His wife was at home with the little girl, who had come on the morning train an hour after her father had died. He lay in that spare room, his troubles over, and the minister could see the face as he opened the Bible and arranged his different notices on the side of the desk as he had been in the habit of doing for ten years.

The service that morning contained a new element. No one could remember when Henry Maxwell had preached in the morning without notes. As a matter of fact he had done so occasionally when he first entered the ministry, but for a long time he had carefully written every word of his morning sermon, and nearly always his evening discourse as well. It cannot be said that his sermon this morning was striking or impressive. He talked with considerable hesitation. It was evident that some great idea struggled in his thought for utterance, but it was not expressed in the theme he had chosen for his preaching. It was near the close of his sermon that he began to gather a certain strength that had been painfully lacking at the beginning. He closed the Bible and, stepping out at the side of the desk, faced his people, and began to talk to them about the remarkable scene of the week before.

"Our brother," somehow the words sounded a little strange coming from his lips, "passed away this morning. I have not yet had time to learn all his history. He had one sister liv-ing in Chicago. I have written her and have not received an answer. His little girl is with us and will remain for the time."

He paused and looked over the house. He thought he had never seen so many earnest faces during his entire pastorate. He was not able yet to tell his people his experiences, the crisis through which he was even now moving. But something of his feeling passed from him to them, and it did not seem to him that he was acting under a careless impulse at all to go on and break to them, this morning, something of the message he bore in his heart. So he went on.

"The appearance and words of this stranger in the church last Sunday made a very powerful impression on me. I am not able to conceal from you or myself the fact that what he said, followed as it has been by his death in my house, has compelled me to ask as I never asked before, 'What does following Jesus mean?' I am not in a position yet to utter any condemnation of this people, or, to a certain extent, of myself, either in our Christlike relations to this man or the number he represents in the world. But all that does not prevent me from feeling that much that the man said was so vitally true that we must face it in an attempt to answer it or else stand condemned as Christian disciples. A good deal that was said here last Sunday was in the nature of a challenge to Christianity as it is seen and felt in our churches. I have felt this with increasing emphasis every day since. And I do not know that any time is more appropriate than the present for me to propose a plan or a purpose which has been forming in my mind as a satisfactory reply to much that was said here last Sunday."

Again Henry Maxwell paused and looked in to the faces of his people. There were some strong, earnest men and women in the First Church. He could see Edward Norman, Editor of the Raymond "Daily News." He had been a member of First Church for ten years. No man was more honored in the community. There was Alexander Powers, Superintendent of the great railroad shops in Raymond, a typical railroad man, one who had been born into the business. There sat Donald Marsh, President of Lincoln College, situated in the suburbs of Raymond. There was Milton Wright, one of the great merchants of Raymond, having in his employ at least one hundred men in various shops. There was Dr. West, who, although still comparatively young, was quoted as authority in special surgical cases. There was young Jasper Chase, the author, who had written one successful book, and was said to be at work on a new novel. There was Miss Virginia Page, the heiress, who, through the recent death of her father, had inherited a million, at least, and was gifted with unusual attractions of person and intellect. And not least of all, Rachel Winslow, from her seat in the choir glowed with her peculiar beauty of light this morning because she was so intensely interested in the whole scene.

There was some reason, perhaps, in view of such material in the First Church, for Henry Maxwell's feeling of satisfaction whenever he considered his parish as he had the previous Sunday. There was a large number of strong individual characters who claimed membership there. But as he noted their faces this morning he was simply wondering how many of them would respond to the strange proposition he was about to make.

He continued slowly, taking time to choose his words carefully and giving the people an impression they had never felt before, even when he was at his best, with his most dramatic delivery.

"What I am going to propose now is something which ought not to appear unusual or at all impossible of execution. Yet I am aware that it will be so regarded by a large number, perhaps of the members of the church. But in order that we may have a thorough understanding of what we are considering, I will put my proposition very plainly, perhaps bluntly. I want volunteers from the First Church who will pledge themselves earnestly and honestly for an entire year not to do anything without first asking the question, 'What would Jesus do?' And after asking that question, each one will follow Jesus as exactly as he knows how, no matter what the results may be. I will of course, include myself in this company of volunteers, and shall take for granted that my church here will not be surprised at my future conduct as based upon this standard of action, and will not oppose whatever is done if they think Christ would do it. Have I made my meaning clear? At the close of the service I want all those members who are willing to join such a company to remain, and we will talk over the details of the plan. Our motto will be, 'What would Jesus do?' Our aim will be to act just as he would if he were in our places, regardless of immediate results. In other words, we propose to follow Jesus' steps as closely and as literally as we believe he taught his disciples to do. And those who volunteer to do this will pledge themselves for an entire year, beginning with today, so to act."

Henry Maxwell paused again and looked out over his people. It is not easy to describe the sensation that such a simple proposition, apparently, made. Men glanced at one another in astonishment. It was not like Henry Maxwell to define Christian discipleship in this way. There was evident confusion of thought over his proposition. It was understood well enough, but there was apparently a great difference of opinion as to the application of Jesus' teaching and example.

He calmly closed the service with a brief prayer. The organist began his postlude immediately after the benediction and the people began to go out. There was a great deal of conversation. Animated groups stood all over the church, discussing the minister's proposition. It was evidently provoking great discussion. After several minutes he asked all who expected to remain to pass into the lecture room which joined the large room, on the side. He was himself detained at the front of the church talking with several persons there, and when he finally turned around the church was empty. He walked over to the lecture room entrance and went in. He was almost startled to see the people who were there. He had not made up his mind about any of his members, but he hardly expected that so many were ready to enter into such a literal testing of their Christian discipleship as now awaited them. There were perhaps fifty present. Among them Rachel Winslow and Virginia Page, Mr. Norman, President Marsh, Alexander Powers, the Railroad Superintendent; Milton Wright, Dr. West, and Jasper Chase.

He closed the door of the lecture room and went and stood before the little group. His face was pale and his lips trembled with emotion. It was to him a genuine crisis in his own life and that of his parish. No man can tell until he is moved by the Divine Spirit what he may do, or how he may change the current of a lifetime of fixed habits of thought and speech and action. Henry Maxwell did not, as we have said, yet know himself all that he was passing through, but he was conscious of a great upheaval in his definition of Christian discipleship, and he was moved with a depth of feeling he could not measure, as he looked into the faces of these men and women on this occasion.

It seemed to him that the most fitting word to be spoken first was that of prayer. He asked them all to pray with him. And almost with the first syllable he uttered there was a distinct presence of the Spirit felt by them all. As the prayer went on, this presence grew in power. They all felt it. The room was filled with it as plainly as if it had been visible. When the prayer closed there was a silence that lasted several moments. All the heads were bowed. Henry Maxwell's face was wet with tears. If an audible voice from heaven had sanctioned their pledge to follow the Master's steps, not one person present could have felt more certain of the divine blessing. And so the most serious movement ever started in the First Church of Raymond was begun.

"We all understand," said he, speaking very quietly, "what we have undertaken to do. We pledge ourselves to do everything in our daily lives after asking the question, 'What would Jesus do?' regardless of what may be the result to us. Some time I shall be able to tell you what a marvelous change has come over my life within a week's time. I cannot now. But the experience I have been through since last Sunday has left me so dissatisfied with my previous definition of discipleship that I have been compelled to take this action. I did not dare begin it alone. I know that I am being led by the hand of divine love in all this. The same divine impulse must have led you also. Do we understand fully what we have undertaken?"

"I want to ask a question," said Rachel Winslow. Everyone turned toward her. Her face glowed with a beauty that no physical loveliness could ever create. "I am a little in doubt as to the source of our knowledge concerning what Jesus would do. Who is to decide for me just what he would do in my case? It is a different age. There are many perplexing questions in our civilization that are not mentioned in the teaching of Jesus. How am I going to tell what he would do?"

"There is no way that I know of," replied the pastor, "except as we study Jesus through the medium of the Holy Spirit. You remember what Christ said, speaking to his disciples about the Holy Spirit: 'Howbeit, when He, the Spirit of Truth is come. He shall guide you into all the truth; for He shall not speak from Himself; but what things soever He shall hear, these shall He speak: and He shall declare unto you the things that are to come. He shall glorify me: for He shall take of mine and shall declare it unto you. All things whatsoever the Father hath are mine: therefore said I that He taketh of mine and shall declare it unto you.'

"There is no other test that I know of. We shall all have to decide what Jesus would do after going to that source of knowledge." "What if others say of us when we do certain things, that Jesus would not do so?"

asked the superintendent of railroads. "We cannot prevent that. But we must be absolutely honest with ourselves. The standard of Christian action cannot vary in most of our acts." "And yet what one church member thinks Jesus would do, another refuses to accept as his possible course of action. What is to render our conduct uniformly Christlike? Will it be possible to reach the same conclusions always in all cases?" asked President Marsh. Mr. Maxwell was silent some time. Then he answered: "No; I don't know that we can expect that. But when it comes to a genuine, honest, enlightened following of Jesus' steps, I cannot believe there will be any confusion either in our own minds or in the judgment of others. We must be free from fanaticism on one hand and too much caution on the other. If Jesus' example is the example for the world, it certainly must be feasible to follow it. But we need to remember this great fact. After we asked the Spirit to tell us what Jesus would do and have received an answer to it, we are to act regardless of the results to ourselves. Is that understood?"

All the faces in the room were raised toward the minister in solemn assent. There was no misunderstanding the proposition. Henry Maxwell's face quivered again as he noted the President of the Endeavor Society, with several members, seated back of the older men and women.

They remained a little longer talking over details and asking questions, and agreed to report to one another every week at a regular meeting the result of their experiences in following Jesus in this way. Henry Maxwell prayed again. And again, as before, the Spirit made Himself manifest. Every head remained bowed a long time. They went away finally in silence. There was a feeling that prevented speech. The pastor shook hands with them all as they went out. Then he went into his own study room back of the pulpit and kneeled. He remained there alone nearly half an hour. When he went home, he went into the room where the dead body lay. As he looked at the face, he cried in his heart again for strength and wisdom. But not even yet did he realize that a movement had begun which would lead to the most remarkable series of events that the city of Raymond had ever known.

CHAPTER 11—THE SOCIAL GOSPEL

For each of the three documents in this chapter, describe in the space provided the interaction of religion with another socio-cultural, economic, political, or diplomatic factor. Use the questions to prompt your description.

Applied Christianity, **Washington Gladden**

How does Gladden account for the lack of church attendance on the
part of wage-workers living in cities? On what grounds does he argue that
the preaching of the gospel itself is not sufficient to meet the needs of workers living in the cities? What does Gladden suggest as the solution for the
problems of the urban workers?

_____

_____

_____

_____

_____

_____

_____

_____

_____

_____

Cardinal Gibbons Defends the Knights of Labor, **James Cardinal Gibbons**

How does this document answer specific criticisms of the Knights? What
injustices done to labor needed correction? How is this document a "social
gospel" statement of American Catholicism?

_____

_____

_____

_____

_____

_____

_____

_____

_____

_____

In His Steps, Charles M. Sheldon

How did the people of the First Church of Raymond respond to the Rev. Henry Maxwell's challenge to do what Jesus would do? What are the implications of this excerpt for the social gospel?

_____

_____

_____

_____

_____

_____

_____

_____

_____

12 Theology

Therefore, just as through one man sin entered into the world, and death through sin, and so death spread to all men because all sinned.

—Rom. 5:12

The New Theology
Theodore T. Munger

Theodore T. Munger (1830-1910) was graduated from Yale in 1851 and from Yale Divinity School in 1855. From 1856 to 1875 he pastored several New England Congregational churches before going to San Jose, California where he stayed long enough to establish a church in 1876. From that time until 1885 he pastored in North Adams, Massachusetts, at which church he authored *The Freedom of Faith*. This was a pioneer work in developing the New Theology, a theology which resulted in a fundamental reorientation of American Protestantism. Munger merged the latest ideas of science, evolution, and historical criticism with his theistic, though undogmatic, faith, thereby resulting in a theology for the social gospel which implied that Christian duty meant the application of Christianity to society itself. The following selection from *The Freedom of Faith* (Boston: Houghton Mifflin and Co., 1883), is Munger's attempt to define the basic elements of the New Theology.

In attempting to give some expression of the New Theology, I wish to state with the utmost emphasis that I do not speak for any party, but only describe things as I see them. And especially would I disclaim any *exca-thedra* tone that may seem to issue from any form of words. I speak from the standpoint of the sharpest and even most isolated individuality,—for myself alone.

I will first refer to certain negative features, indicating what it is *not*; and then more fully to its positive character.

1. It does not propose to do without a theology.

   It seeks no such transformation of method or form that it can no longer claim

221

the name of a science. It does not re-solve belief into sentiment, nor ethereal-ize it into mysticism, nor lower it into mere altruism; yet it does not deny an element of sentiment, it acknowledges an element of mysticism, and it insists on a firm basis in ethics. It is the deter-mined foe of agnosticism, yet it recog-nizes a limitation of human knowledge. While it insists that theology is a sci-ence, and that therefore its parts should be coordinate and mutually supporting, and an induction from all the facts known to it, it realizes that it deals with eternal realities that cannot be wholly compassed, and also with mysteries and contradictions of a war involved in mys-tery and beset by contradictory forces. If it finds itself driven into impenetrable mystery, as it inevitably must, it prefers to take counsel of the higher sentiments and better hopes of our nature, rather than project into it the framework of a formal logic, and insist on its conclu-sion. It does not abjure logic, but it re-fuses to be held by what is often deemed logic. While it believes in a harmony of doctrines, it regards with suspicion what have been known as systems of theolo-gy, on the ground that it rejects the methods by which they are constructed. It will not shape a doctrine in order that it may fit another which has been shaped in the same fashion,—a merely mechanical interplay, and seeking a me-chanical harmony. Instead, it regards theology as an induction from the reve-lations of God—in the Bible, in history, in the nation, in the family, in the mate-rial creation, and in the whole length and breadth of human life. It will have, therefore, all the definiteness and har-mony it can find in these revelations un-der a process still enacting, and not as under a finality. . . .

2. The New Theology does not part with the historic faith of the Church, but rath-er seeks to put itself in its line while rec-ognizing a process of development. It does not propose to commit "retrospec-tive suicide" at every fresh stage of ad-vance. It holds to progress by slow and cosmic growth rather than the later the-ologies, and finds in the early Greek theology conceptions more harmonious with itself than those in the theology shaped by Augustine.

3. It does not reject the specific doctrines of the church of the past. It holds to the Trinity, though indifferent to the use of the word, but not to a formal and psy-chologically impossible Trinity; to di-vine sovereignty, but it does not make it the cornerstone of its system, preferring for that place the divine righteousness, i.e., a moral rather than a dynamic basis; to the Incarnation, not as a mere physi-cal event, for that has entered into many religions, but as the entrance into the world through a person of a moulding and redeeming force in humanity,—the central and broadest fact of theology; to the Atonement as a divine act and pro-cess of ethical and practical import— not as a mystery of the distant heavens and isolated from the struggle of the world, but a comprehensible force in the actual redemption of the world from its evil; to the Resurrection as covering the whole essential nature of man; to Judg-ment as involved in the development of a moral nature; to the eternal awards of

conduct considered as laws and principles of character, but not necessarily set in time-relations; to human sinfulness under a conception of moral freedom; to Justification by faith in the sense of a faith that, by its law, induces an actual righteousness—a simple, rational process realized in human experience; to Regeneration and Sanctification by the Spirit as most imperative operations based on the utmost need, and on the actual presence and power of the Spirit in the life of humanity. It does not explain away from these doctrines their substance, nor minimize them, nor aim to do else than present them as revealed in the Scriptures and as developed in history and in the life of the church and of the world.

4. It is not iconoclastic in its temper; it is not pervaded by a spirit of denial, but us constructive—taking away nothing without supplying its place; it does not, indeed, find so much occasion to take away and replace as to uncover and bring to light. Believing that revelation is not so much *from* God as *of* God, its logical attitude is that of seeing and interpreting.

5. It is not disposed to find a field and organization outside of existing churches, conscious that it is building on the Eternal Foundation which alone has given strength to the church in every age. It claims only that liberty whereunto all are called in the church of Christ. It asserts that the real ground of membership in the church is fidelity to the faith, and that this ground is not forfeited because it refuses to assent to human and formal conditions that the church has taken on, and which are not of the substance of the faith. Emphasizing as it does the headship of Christ in the visible as well as invisible church, it would retain its place in the church on the basis of its loyalty to Christ and as its all-sufficient warrant, paying small heed to a narrow, ecclesiastical logic that now confounds, and now distinguishes between the bounds of the visible body and the breadth and freedoms of Christ's church.

I pass now to the positive features of the New Theology.

1. It claims for itself a somewhat larger and broader use of reason than has been accorded to theology. . . .

    There are indeed limits to reason, and it has in it an element of faith, but so far as it goes, it goes surely and firmly; it is not a rotten foundation, it is not a broken reed, it is not false light. It may be so sure that it can justly protest in the face of Heaven, "Shall not the Judge of all the earth do right?" It will be humble and docile and trustful, but these qualities are not abrogations of itself. It does not claim for itself the ability to measure the whole breadth and reach of truth; it does not say, I will not believe what I cannot understand, for it knows full well that human reason is not commensurate with eternal truth. . . .

2. The New Theology seeks to interpret the Scriptures in what may be called a more natural way, and in opposition to a

hard, unsympathetic, and unimaginative way.

Its strongest denial and its widest divergence from the Old Theology lie here. It holds profoundly to inspiration, but it also holds that the Scriptures were written by living men, whose life entered into their writings; it finds the color and temper of the writer's mind in his work; it finds also the temper and habit of the age; it penetrates the forms of Oriental speech; it seeks to read out of the mind and conception and custom of the writer instead of reading present conceptions into his words. In brief, it reads the Scriptures as literature, yet with no derogation from their inspiration. It refuses to regard the writers as automatic organs of the Spirit, —"moved," indeed, but not carried outside of themselves nor separated from their own ways and conceptions. It is thus that it regards the Bible as a *living* book; it is warm and vital with the life of a divine humanity, and thus it speaks to humanity. . . .

3. The New Theology seeks to replace an excessive individuality by a truer view of the solidarity of the race.

It does not deny a real individuality, it does not predicate an absolute solidarity, but simply removes the emphasis from one to the other. It holds that every man must live a life of his own, build himself up into a full personality, and give an account of himself to God: but it also recognizes the blurred truth that man's life lies in its relations; that it is a derived and shared life; that it is carried on and perfected under laws of heredity and of the family and the nation; that while he is "himself alone" he is also a son, a parent, a citizen, and an inseparable part of the human race; that in origin and character and destiny he cannot be regarded as standing in a sharp and utter individuality. It differs from the Old Theology in a more thorough and consistent application of this distinction. That holds to an absolute solidarity in evil, relieved by a doctrine of election of individuals; this holds to a solidarity running throughout the whole life of humanity in the world,—not an absolute solidarity, but one modified by freedom. . . .

Still, it does not submerge the individual in the common life, nor free him from personal ill desert, nor take from him the crown of personal achievement and victory. It simply strives to recognize the duality of truth, and hold it well poised. It turns our attention to the corporate life of man here in the world,— an individual life, indeed, but springing from common roots, fed by a common life, watched over by one Father, inspired by one Spirit, and growing to one end; no man, no generation, being "made perfect" by itself. Hence its ethical emphasis; hence its recognition of the nation, and of the family, and of social and commercial life, as fields of the manifestation of God and of the operation of the Spirit; hence its readiness to ally itself with all movements for bettering the condition of mankind, —holding that human society itself is to be redeemed, and that the world itself, in its corporate capacity, is being reconciled to God; hence also an apparently secular tone, which is, however, but a widening of the field of the divine and spiritual.

4. This theology recognizes a new relation to natural science; but only in the respect that it ignores the long apparent antagonism between the kingdom of faith and of natural law,—an antagonism that cannot, from the nature of things, have a bias in reality. But while it looks on the external world as a revelation of God and values the truth it may reveal; while even it recognizes in it analogies to the spiritual world and a typical similarity of method, it does not merge itself in natural science. It is not yet ready, and it shows no signs that it ever will be ready, to gather up its beliefs, and go over into the camp of natural science, and sit down under the manipulations of a doctrine of evolution, with its one category of matter and one invariable force. It is not ready to commit itself to a finite system, a merely phenomenal section of the universe and of time, with no *whence*, or *whither*, or *why*,—a system that simply supplies man with a certain kind of knowledge, but solves no problem that weighs on his heart, answers no question that he much cares to ask, and throws not one glimmer of additional light on his origin, his nature, or his destiny. It accepts gratefully the knowledge it discloses of the material universe, its laws and its processes; it admits that science has anticipated theology in formulating the method of creation known as evolution, that its has corrected modern theology by suggesting a closer and more vital relation between God and creation, and so has helped it throw off a mechanical

theory and regain its forgotten theory of the divine immanence in creation. . . .

5. The New Theology offers a contrast to the Old in claiming for itself a wider study of man.

It chooses for its field the actual life of men in the world in all their varying conditions, rather than as masses in a few ideal conditions. It finds its methods in the every-day processes of humanity, rather than in a formal logic. It deals with human life as do the poets and dramatists: it views humanity by a direct light, looks straight at it, and into it, and across its whole breadth. A recognition of human nature and life,—this is a first principle with the New Theology. . . .

6. The New Theology recognizes the necessity of a restatement of belief in Eschatology, or the doctrine of Last Things. . . .

But the New Theology does not plant its entire conception of the subject upon the word. It seeks rather to enlighten itself by the general light of the entire revelation of God; and thus it finds itself driven to such conclusions as these: namely, that every human being will have the fullest opportunity for attaining to the end of his creation as a child of God; that every human being will receive from the Spirit of God all the influence impelling to salvation that his nature can endure and retain its moral integrity; that no human being will be given over to perish while there is a possibility of his salvation. These are the very truisms of the faith, its trend, its drift, its logic, its spirit, and its letter, when the letter is interpreted under the spirit; and they are equally the demand of the human reason. . . .

Such are some of the features of this fresh movement in the realm of theology, for it can scarcely be called more than a movement, an advance to meet the unfolding revelation of God. It is not an organization, it is little aggressive, it does not herald itself with any Lo here or Lo there, it does not crowd itself upon the thought of the age, it is not keyed to such methods. It has no word of contempt for those who linger in ways it has ceased to walk in; it has no sympathy with those who have forsaken the one way. It does not reduce the proportions of evil nor dim the glory of righteousness; it does not chill the enthusiasm of faith, nor hold it back from its mightiest effort of sacrifice. It seeks no conquest represented in outward form, but is content to add its thought to the growing thought of the world, and if it speaks, content to speak to those who have ears to hear. It makes no haste, it seeks no revolution, but simply holds itself open and receptive under the breathing of the Spirit that has come, and is ever coming, into the world; passive, yet quick to respond to the heavenly visions that do not cease to break upon the darkened eyes of humanity.

Present Day Theology
Washington Gladden

Washington Gladden (1836-1918) was a giant among the social gospelers of the late nineteenth century, as well as an early formulator of the New Theology which supported it. The following excerpt appears in his *Present Day Theology* (Cleveland: McClelland and Co., 1913), pp. 69-81, *passim*.

———————

What, now, is the nature of sin?

It is well to dispose at once of some of the traditional theories, which have played a great part in the history of Christian thought.

The theology on which most of us older folks were brought up divided sin into two categories—original and actual sin. Actual sin was the conscious and intentional transgressions of the moral law, the evil deeds or the culpable omissions of which we in our own persons and by our choices are guilty. This is the kind of sin of which we have been talking. Concerning this the new theology, as I understand it, raises no question. It is a phenomenon too sadly familiar to be disputed.

But the other kind of sin—what the theologians call original sin—the new theology does not believe in. The old theology held that on account of the sin of Adam all the descendants of Adam were made sinners. It was not only that we inherited from our first ancestor weakened or impaired moral natures, tendencies to evil. That might well have been true. The doctrine was that we had inherited his guilt; that God held us blameworthy on account of his sin and pun-

ishable because of it. Adam, as the theory figured it, was the federal head of the race. God had a covenant with him, that if he was obedient all his descendants should be virtuous and blessed; while if he disobeyed and as the old catechism says, we "all have sinned in him and fell with him in his first transgression,"—or as the New England pioneer more tersely put it:

"In Adam's fall
    We sinned all."

In consequence of this sin of our first parent we all come into the world "under the wrath and curse" of God, "and (are) so made liable to all the miseries of this life and the pains of hell forever." Thus, for nothing that we had done, or consented to, the old theology told us that God held us all deserving of eternal punishment in hell.

The doctrine of election came in here, however, and assured us that God, out of his mere good pleasure, has chosen some of these doomed and lost ones upon whom he would bestow his grace; and the sins of these were remitted through the expiation made by Christ upon the cross. Among infants who died in infancy, before they were capable of actual transgression some were elect and some non-elect; the elect infants were saved by the blood of Christ; the non-elect infants were consigned to eternal misery on account of original sin,—their implication in the sin of Adam. . . .

It is amazing that a notion, so horribly unethical, should linger in the minds of human beings in the twentieth century. It is strange that any one who has known anything about the God and Father of our Lord Jesus Christ should deem it possible that he could count all the children of Adam guilty of Adam's sin, and worthy of eternal death because of something that happened thousands of years before they were born.

But is it not true, you ask, that we suffer the consequences of sin of our ancestors? Yes, we are so linked together that the evil that parents do entails upon their children weakness and disability and suffering; but sin is not entailed; sin is not inherited. The children are not to blame for what their parents did, nor are they to blame for being in this weak and disabled condition; they are not to blame for anything which they inherit; every just man pities them for that evil inheritance; how much more does our heavenly Father regard them with compassion, and seek to rescue them from their infirmities! If they come into the world with blunted sensibilities, and abnormal cravings, and tendencies to evil, he takes all that into consideration, in judging their conduct. You and I would do that, and if we, being evil, can make such allowances, how much more will our heavenly Father deal mercifully with children!

So then, the new theology puts aside, as essentially pagan, the old doctrine of original sin by which most of the old theology was shaped. Sin cannot be inherited. God is just. Do I call this the new theology? It is not really so very new. Listen to the prophet Ezekiel:

> "The soul that sinneth, it shall die; the son shall not bear the iniquity of the father, neither shall the father bear the iniquity of the son; the righteousness of the wicked shall be upon him."

How the framers of that old dogma managed to interpret this eighteenth chapter of Ezekiel I have never been able to understand. There is no such thing as inherited sin. Sin, as old Dr. Emmons insisted, consists in sinnings. All sin is actual sin. And now what is the nature of actual sin?

It is sometimes supposed to be simple animalism—the predominance of the bodily appetites. But the bodily appetites are not necessarily sinful. Under normal control they are elements of wholesome life. It is true that the progress of man is from animalism to spirituality, and that many of his worst temptations are due to the imperfect subjugation of the lower nature to the higher, yet as one says, "the sin does not dwell in the fact that man still retains a nature akin to that of the animals below him, but in this, that the nature that is akin to God yields to the nature that is common to man and beasts." Yet it still remains true that the worst sins of man have nothing to do with the flesh; the perversion of the higher nature is deadlier than the indulgence of the lower.

We still may say that sin is simply abnormal action. It is the violation by the soul, of its own law of life. Whatever tends to the perfection of my soul of my manhood in its physical, intellectual and moral elements, is right; whatever interferes with that tendency and prevents me from realizing my manhood is wrong.

Does some one say that sin is an offense against God? Well, that is true. But what Matthew Arnold says is also profoundly true, that the stream of tendency by which all things strive to fulfill the law of their being is only another name for God. Any action of my will which hinders me from fulfilling the law of my being is therefore a sin against God. God is working in me, to perfect my manhood. Whatever I do to obstruct that working, to impair manhood is a sin against him.

But we have not yet reached the heart of the matter. And here we will let Professor Clarke help us once more:

> "Sin may be viewed with reference to its motive and inner moral quality; we observe the evil, whether in act or in character and estimate it in the light of the principles from which it springs. Thus sin is *the placing of self-will and selfishness above the claims of love and duty*" . . .

If this is the essential nature of sin,—if it is essentially a kind of self-love which makes us indifferent to the welfare of others,—it is rather absurd to deny its existence or its prevalence. The new theology, at any rate, is not disposed to ignore it. It is a stubborn fact of portentous dimensions. We do not need to go back to Adam, or to resort to any theories of imputation; the evidence confronts us whenever we open our eyes.

To prove that a man is a sinner is not necessary, then, to show that he is a murderer or a liar or a thief or a counterfeiter or a forger or a burglar; he may even be a man who never drinks nor smokes nor dances nor plays cards nor goes to the theater; the only question is whether he is chargeable with putting selfishness or self-will above love and duty. That sin is enough to shut any man out of heaven. There cannot be any heaven where that spirit is. That spirit brings hell wherever it goes, in this world and every other world.

If this is the nature of sin, what is the penalty of sin? The old theology made this penalty to consist of suffering inflicted upon the sinner by a judicial process in the future life. Hell was a place of eternal punishment, provided by the divine justice, to which were consigned after death and the judgment all unforgiven sinners. Of the meaning of heaven and hell I shall speak in the next lecture. The penalty of sin will also be more fully considered at that time. It is sufficient to say that the new theology regards those conceptions of judicial punishment as based on analogies which convey much less than the whole truth, and teaches that the reality of punishment is something much closer to our experience and more verifiable than those old theories made it.

The penalty of sin, as the new theology teaches, consists in the natural consequences of sin. Sin is selfishness; what, then are the natural consequences of selfishness? If a man freely indulges this disposition to place his own interest and pleasure above the claims of love and duty what will be the natural effect upon the character of that man? You do not need to go to the creeds or to the Bible or to the theologians to find out; just read the newspapers and the novels, and keep your eyes open to what is going on about you. The new theology doesn't refer you to authorities on this subject—it goes straight to human life for its facts.

In the first place the man who indulges this selfish disposition will find it strengthening its hold upon him; that is a law of mind, and it works itself out in his experience. The habit of preferring his own happiness to other peoples' grows on him; he has less and less compunction about prospering at the expense of other people; he has less and less compassion for those less fortunate; he is more and more inclined to say that those whom he pushes from his path in his progress are themselves to blame for their misfortunes; he becomes more and more self-centered and intolerant and unsocial. This is the natural penalty of selfishness.

Other sins grow out of this by a logical necessity. The man who makes his own interest supreme is apt to think that those who interfere with his interests have no right to the truth, and deception or falsehood is the natural consequences. When he begins to lie it is easy to keep on; every lie he tells is a seed from which other lies spring and multiply, thirty, sixty, an hundred fold. His love of the truth is weakened and gradually disappears.

Perhaps the animal propensities in him clamor for indulgence, and as it is always the self to which they minister; they easily get their own way. These indulgences, also,

grow into habits which strengthen as time goes on; the man comes more and more under the domain of his fleshly nature; his finer sensibilities are dulled; his imagination is filled with pictures of sensual delights; he loses his relish for cleanliness and manliness and purity; he becomes false and foul in thought and life.

It is needless to protract this analysis. These are facts which every one of you can verify in your daily observation. These are the natural penalties of sin, as they are working themselves out in the characters of men before your eyes every day. Perhaps some of you have even clearer evidence of them within your own consciousness, in your own experiences. The penalty of sin is sin. Whatever a man soweth that shall he also reap. If you sow selfishness you will reap selfishness. If you sow falsehood you will reap falsehood. If you sow to the flesh you will reap corruption. These are natural consequences. They are immediate. They are inevitable. They are cumulative.

There are also social consequences, of vast importance, on which I cannot dwell. Such a life affects others lives continually; it entails suffering and loss upon the victims of its selfishness; it communicates contagion; it kindles resentments and antagonisms; it tends to produce enmity and strife and malevolence. What kind of a society would it be in which every man freely indulged his selfish tendencies, and permitted them to produce their natural fruits in his character?

It is generally assumed that pain and suffering of some kind is the penalty of sin. It often does bring suffering as its consequence, but that is not always true, and it is by no means the worst consequence of sin. The wages of sin is always death, not always suffering, for spiritual death is often a painless process. It may be accompanied by numbness,—by insensibility. Deterioration, degradation, is the penalty of sin. He that sows to the flesh reaps not always suffering, but always corruption.

There is, indeed, one natural consequence of sin, of which most of us have some knowledge. That is remorse, the ranking memory of wrong committed, which is now, perhaps, remediless; the bitter scourgings of conscience for faithlessness or disloyalty or cruelty or neglect for which it is now beyond our power to atone.

Such then is sin, and such is the penalty of sin. . . .

A Theology for the Social Gospel
Walter Rauschenbusch

Walter Rauschenbusch (1861-1918) was raised in Rochester, New York, where he gained both his university and seminary educations. He was ordained a Baptist minister and served as a pastor of a New York City church for eleven years, during which time he saw firsthand the hardships of the industrial depression that began in 1893. His extensive reading in socialist and reform literature led him to renovate orthodox theology. In the process he became the foremost American philosopher of the social gospel, advocating a form of revisionist socialism whereby a new society could be created with the application of the concept of the Kingdom of God to the social organism. Though he held out hope for a better world to come, he did not believe the Kingdom could be fully realized on earth. The selection which follows is from his most important work, *A Theology for the Social Gospel* (New York: Macmillan, 1917), pp. 23-26, 131-37.

In these introductory chapters my aim is to win the benevolent and serious attention of conservative readers for the discussions that are to follow. I have thus far tried to show that the spread of the social gospel will inevitably react on theology, and that this influence is likely to be constructive and salutary. Let us add the important fact that the social gospel imports into theology nothing that is new or alien.

Frequent attempts have been made in the history of our religion to blend alien elements with it. The early Gnostics and medieval Albigenses, for instance, tried to combine historical Christianity with dualistic conceptions of the universe and strict asceticism. Modern Mormonism, Theosophy, and Christian Science represent syncretistic formation, minglings of genuine Christianity with new and alien elements.

The belief in the universal reign of law, the doctrine of evolution, the control of nature by man, and the value of education and liberty as independent goods,—these are among the most influential convictions of modern life and have deeply modified our religious thought. But they are novel elements of theology. They are not alien, but certainly they held no such controlling position in the theology of the past as they do with us. We may discover prophetic forecasts of them in the Bible, but we have to look for them.

On the other hand the idea of the redemption of the social organism is nothing alien. It is simply a proper part of the Christian faith in redemption from sin and evil. As soon as the desire for salvation becomes strong and intelligent enough to look beyond the personal sins of the individual, and to discern how our personality in its intake and output is connected with the social groups to which we belong, the problem of social redemption is before us and we can never again forget it. It lies like a larger concentric circle around a smaller one. It is related to our intimate personal salvation like astronomy to physics. Only spiritual and intellectual immaturity have kept us from seeing it clearly before. The social gospel is not an alien element in theology.

Neither is it novel. The social gospel is, in fact, the oldest gospel of all. It is "built on the foundation of the apostles and prophets." Its substance is the Hebrew faith which Jesus himself held. If the prophets ever talked about the "plan of redemption," they meant the social redemption of the gospel, the Kingdom of God was its central word, and the ethical teaching of both, which was their practical commentary and definition of the Kingdom idea, looked toward a higher social order in which new ethical standards would become practicable. To the first generation of disciples the hope of the Lord's return meant the hope of a Christian social order on earth under the personal rule of Jesus Christ, and they would have been amazed if they had learned that his hope was to be motioned out of theology and other ideas substituted.

The social gospel is nothing alien or novel. When it comes to a question of pedigree and birth-right, it may well turn on the dogmas on which the Catholic and Protestant theologies are based and inquire for their birth certificate. They are neither dominant in the New Testament nor clearly defined in it. The more our historical investigations are laying bare the roots of Catholic dogma, the more

we see them running back into alien Greek thought, and not into the substance of Christ's message nor into the Hebrew faith. We shall not get away again from the central proposition of Harnack's History of Dogma, that the development of Catholic dogma was the process of the Hellenization of Christianity; in other words, that alien influences streamed into the religion of Jesus Christ and created a theology which he never taught nor intended. What would Jesus have said to the symbol of Chalcedon or the Athanasian Creed if they had been read to him?

The doctrine of the Kingdom of God was left undeveloped by individualistic theology and finally mislaid by it almost completely, because it did not support nor fit in with that scheme of doctrine. In the older handbooks of theology it is scarcely mentioned, except in the chapters on eschatology; in none of them does it dominate the table of contents. What a spectacle, that the original teaching of our Lord has become an incongruous element in so-called evangelical theology, like a stranger with whom the other doctrines would not associate, and who was finally ejected because he had no wedding garment! In the same way the distinctive ethics of Jesus, which is part and parcel of his Kingdom doctrine, was long the hidden treasure of suppressed democratic sects. Now, as soon as the social gospel began once more to be preached in our own time, the doctrine of the Kingdom was immediately loved and proclaimed afresh, and the ethical principles of Jesus are once more taught without reservation as the only alternative for the greedy ethics of capitalism and militarism. These antipathies and affinities are a strong proof that the social gospel is neither alien nor novel, but is a revival of the earliest doctrines of Christianity, of its radical ethical spirit, and of its revolutionary consciousness. . . .

If theology is to offer an adequate doctrinal basis for the social gospel, it must not only make room for the doctrine of the Kingdom of God, but give it a central place and revise all other doctrines so that they will articulate organically with it.

This doctrine is itself the social gospel. Without it, the idea of redeeming the social order will be but an annex to the orthodox conception of the scheme of salvation. It will live like a negro servant family in a detached cabin back of the white man's house in the South. If this doctrine gets the place which has always been legitimate right, the practical proclamation and application of social morality will have a firm footing.

To those whose minds live in the social gospel, the Kingdom of God is a dear truth, the marrow of the gospel, just as the incarnation was to Athanasius, justification by faith alone to Luther and the sovereignty of God to Jonathan Edwards. It was just as dear to Jesus. He too lived in it, and from it looked out on the world and the work he had to do.

Jesus always spoke of the Kingdom of God. Only two of his reported sayings contain the word "Church," and both passages are of questioned authenticity. It is safe to say that he never thought of founding the kind of institution which afterward claimed to be acting for him.

Yet immediately after his death, groups of disciples joined and consolidated by inward necessity. Each local group knew that it was part of a divinely founded fellowship mysteriously spreading through humanity, and awaiting the return of the Lord and the establishing of his Kingdom. This universal Church was loved with the same religious faith and reverence with which Jesus had loved the Kingdom of God. It was the partial and earthly realization of the divine Society, and at the Parousia the Church and The Kingdom would merge.

But the Kingdom was merely a hope, the Church a present reality. The chief interest and affection flowed toward the Church. Soon, through a combination of causes, the name and idea of "the kingdom" began to be displaced by the name and idea of "the church" in the preaching, literature, and theological thought of the Church. Augustine completed this process in his *De Civitate Dei*. The Kingdom of God which has, throughout human history, opposed the Kingdom of Sin, is today embodied in the Church. The millennium began when the Church was founded. This practically substituted the actual, not the ideal Church for the Kingdom of God. The beloved ideal of Jesus became a vague phrase which kept intruding from the New Testament. Like Cinderella in the kitchen, it saw the other great dogmas furbished up for the ball, but no prince of theology restored it to its rightful place. The reformation, too, brought no renascence of the doctrine of the Kingdom; it had only eschatological value, or was defined in blurred phrases borrowed from the Church. The present revival of the Kingdom idea is due to the combined influence of the historical study of the Bible and of the social gospel.

When the doctrine of the Kingdom of God shriveled to an undeveloped and pathetic remnant in Christian thought, this loss was bound to have far-reaching consequences. We are told that the loss of a single tooth from the arch of the mouth in childhood may spoil the symmetrical development of the skull and produce malformations affecting the mind and character. The atrophy of that idea which had occupied the chief place in the mind of Jesus, necessarily affected the humanity, and the structure of theology. I shall briefly enumerate some of the consequences affecting theology. This list, however, is by no means complete.

1. Theology lost its contact with the synoptic thought of Jesus. Its problems were not at all the same which had occupied his mind. It lost his point of view and became to some extent incapable of understanding him. His ideas had to be rediscovered in our time. . . .

2. The distinctive ethical principles of Jesus were the direct outgrowth of his conception of the Kingdom of God. When the latter disappeared from theology, the former disappeared from ethics. Only persons having the substance of the Kingdom ideal in their minds, seem to be able to get relish out of the ethics of Jesus. Only those church bodies which have been in opposition to organized society have looked for abetter city with its foundation in heaven, have taken the Sermon on the Mount seriously.

3. The Church is primarily a fellowship for worship; the Kingdom is a fellowship of righteousness. When the latter was neglected in theology, the ethical force of Christianity was weakened; when the former was emphasized in theology, the importance of worship was exaggerated. The prophets and Jesus had cried down sacrifices and ceremonial performances, and cried up righteousness, mercy, solidarity. . . .

4. When the Kingdom ceased to be the dominating religious reality, the Church moved up into the position of the supreme good. To promote the power of the Church and its control over all rival political forces was equivalent to promoting the supreme ends of Christianity. This increased the arrogance of churchmen and took the moral check off their policies. For the Kingdom of God can never be promoted by lies, draft, crime or war, but the wealth and power of the Church have often been promoted by these means. The medieval ideal of the supremacy of the Church over the State was the logical consequences of making the church the highest good with no superior ethical standard by which to test it. . . .

5. The Kingdom ideal is the test and corrective of the influence of the Church. When the Kingdom ideal disappeared, the conscience of the Church was muffled. It became possible for the missionary expansion of Christianity to halt for centuries without creating any sense of shortcoming. It became possible for the most unjust social conditions to fasten themselves on Christian nations without awakening any consciousness that the purpose of Christ was being defied and beaten back. . . .

6. The Kingdom ideal contains the revolutionary force of Christianity. When this ideal faded out of the systematic thought of the Church, it became a conservative social influence and increased the weight of the other stationary forces in society. If the kingdom of God had remained part of the theological and Christian consciousness, the Church could not, down to our times have been salaried by autocratic class governments to keep the democratic and economic impulses of the people under check.

7. Reversely, the movements for democracy and social justice were left without a religious backing for lack of the Kingdom idea. The Kingdom of God as the fellowship of righteousness, would be advanced by the abolition of industrial slavery and the disappearance of slums of civilization; the Church would only indirectly gain through such social changes. Even today many Christians cannot see any religious importance in social justice and fraternity because it does not increase the number of conversions nor fill the churches. . . .

8. Secular life is belittled as compare with church life. Services rendered to the Church get higher religious rating than services rendered to the community. Thus the religious value is taken out of the activities of the common man and the prophetic services to society. Wherever the Kingdom of God is a living reality in Christian thought, any advance of social righteousness is seen as a part of redemption and arouses inward joy and the triumphant sense of salvation. When the Church absorbs interest a subtle asceticism creeps back into our theology and the world looks different.

9. When the doctrine of the Kingdom of God is lacking in theology, the salvation of the individual is seen in its relation to the Church and to the future life, but not in its relation to the task of saving the social order. Theology had left this important point in a condition so hazy and muddled that it has taken us almost a generation to see that the salvation of the individual and the redemption of the social order are closely related, and how.

10. Finally, theology has been deprived of the inspiration of great ideas contained in the idea of the Kingdom and in labor for it. The Kingdom of God breeds prophets; the Church breeds priests and theologians. The Church runs to tradition and dogma; the Kingdom of God rejoices in forecasts and boundless horizons. The men who have contributed the most fruitful impulses to Christian thought have been men of prophetic vision, and their theology has been most concerned with past history, with present social problems and with the future of human society.

13 Religion and International Relations

. . . The voice of one crying in the wilderness, "make ready the way of the Lord, make his paths straight!"

—Matt. 3:3

Our Country
Josiah Strong

Josiah Strong (1847-1916) was raised in an orthodox Protestant home, but became an admirer of the New Theology during the late nineteenth century. As a central figure in the social gospel movement, he believed the movement was the solution to not only America's domestic perils, which he discussed in great detail in his writings, but also to the outstanding problems of the world. In 1885, while serving as minister of the Central Congregational Church in Cincinnati, he expounded his ideas in one of the most influential books of the nineteenth century, *Our Country: Its Possible Future and Its Present Crisis.* In it Strong combined the social gospel with Anglo-Saxonism, the social Darwinian principle of the "survival of the fittest," and the doctrine of God's providence—a combination which posited the argument that Anglo-Saxons were destined to transmit their superior civilization to inferior races abroad. This was dynamite in the pulpits of churchmen who used it in support of America's openly expansionist policies in the late nineteenth century. The following excerpt was taken from *Our Country*, rev. ed. (New York: Baker and Taylor Co., 1891), pp. 200-18, *passim.*

The Anglo-Saxon and the World's Future

Every race which has deeply impressed itself on the human family has been representative of some great idea—one or more—which has given direction to the nation's life and form to its civilization. Among the Egyptians this seminal idea was life, among the Persians it was light, among the Hebrews it was purity, among the Greeks it was beauty, among the Romans it was law. The Anglo-Saxon is the representative of two great ideas, which are closely related. One of them is that of civil liberty. Nearly all of the civil liberty of the world is enjoyed by Anglo-Saxons: the English, the British colonists, and the people of the United States. To some, like the Swiss, it is permitted by the sufferance of their neighbors; others, like the French, have experimented with it; but, in modern times, the peoples whose love of liberty has won it, and whose genius for self-government has preserved it, have been Anglo-Saxons. The noblest races have always been lovers of liberty. The love ran strong in early German blood, and has profoundly influenced the institutions of all the branches of the great German family; but it was left for the Anglo-Saxon branch fully to recognize the right of the individual to himself, and formally to declare it the foundation stone of government.

The other great idea of which the Anglo-Saxon is the exponent is that of a pure *spiritual* Christianity. It was no accident that the great reformation of the sixteenth century originated among a Teutonic, rather than a Latin people. It as the fire of liberty burning in the Saxon heart that flamed up against the absolutism of the Pope. Speaking roughly, the peoples of Europe which are Celtic are Roman Catholic, and those which are Teutonic are Protestant; and where the Teutonic race was purest, there Protestantism spread with the greatest rapidity. But, with beautiful expectations, Protestantism on the continent has degenerated into mere formalism. By confirmation at a certain age, the state churches are filled with members who generally know nothing of a personal spiritual experience. In obedience to a military order, a regiment of German soldiers files into church and partakes of the sacrament, just as

it would shoulder arms to obey any other word of command. It is said that, in Berlin and Leipsic, only a little over one percent of the Protestant population are found in church. Protestantism on the continent seems to be about as poor in spiritual life and power as Romanism. That means that most of the spiritual Christianity in the world is found among Anglo-Saxons and their converts; for this is the great missionary race. If we take all of the German missionary societies together, we find that, in the number of workers and amount of contributions, they do not equal the smallest of the three great English missionary societies. The year that the Congregationalists in the United States gave one dollar and thirty-seven cents per caput to foreign missions, the members of the great German State Church gave only three quarters of a cent per caput to the same cause. Evidently it is chiefly to the English and American peoples that we must look for the evangelization of the world.

It is not necessary to argue to those for whom I write that the two great needs of mankind, that all men may be lifted up into the light of the highest Christian civilization, are, first a pure, spiritual Christianity, and second, civil liberty. Without controversy, these are the forces which, in the past, have contributed most to the elevation of the human race, and they must continue to be, in the future, the most efficient ministers to its progress. It follows, then, that the Anglo-Saxon, as the great representative of these two ideas, the depository of these two greatest blessings, sustains peculiar relations to the world's future, is divinely commissioned to be, in a peculiar sense, his brother's keeper. Add to this the fact of his rapidly increasing strength in modern times, and we have well nigh a demonstration of his destiny. . . .

And it is possible that, by the close of the next century, the Anglo-Saxons will outnumber all the other civilized races of the world. Does it not look as if God were not only preparing in our Anglo-Saxon civilization the die with which to stamp the peoples of the earth, but as if he were also massing behind that die the mighty power with which to press it? My confidence that this race is eventually to give its civilization to mankind is not based on mere numbers—China forbid! I look forward to what the world has never yet seen united in the some race; viz., the greatest numbers, *and* the highest civilization.

There can be no reasonable doubt that North America is to the great home of the Anglo-Saxon, the principal of his power, the center of his life and influence. . . .

America is to have the great preponderance of numbers and of wealth, and by the logic of events will follow the scepter of controlling influence. This will be but the consummation of a movement as old as a civilization—a result to which men have looked forward for centuries. . . .

Mr. Darwin is not only disposed to see, in the superior vigor of our people, an illustration of his favorite theory of natural selection, but even intimates that the world's history thus far has been simply preparatory for our future, and tributary to it. He says: "There is apparently much truth in the belief that the wonderful progress of the United States, as well as the character of the people, are the results of natural selection; for the more energetic, restless, and courageous men from all parts of Europe have emigrated during the last ten or twelve generations to that great country, and have there succeeded best. Looking at the distant future, I do not think that the Rev. Mr. Zincke takes an exaggerated view when he says: 'All other series of events—as that which resulted in the Empire of Rome—only appear to have purpose and value when viewed in connection with, or rather as subsidiary to, the great stream of Anglo-Saxon emigration to the West!'"

There is abundant reason to believe that the Anglo-Saxon race is to be, is, indeed, already becoming, more effective here than in the mother country. The marked superiority of this race is due in large measure, to its highly mixed origin. . . .

It seems to me that God, with infinite wisdom and skill, is training the Anglo-Saxon race for an hour sure to come in the world's future. Heretofore there has always been in the history of the world a comparatively unoccupied land westward, into which the crowded countries of the East have poured their surplus populations. But the widening waves of migration, which millenniums ago rolled east and west from the valley of the Euphrates, meet today on our Pacific coast. There are no more new worlds. The unoccupied arable lands of the earth are limited, and will soon be taken. The time is coming when the pressure of population on the means of subsistence will be felt here as it is now felt in Europe and Asia. Then will the world enter upon a new stage of its history—*the final competition of races, for which the Anglo-Saxon is being schooled.* Long before the thousand millions are here, the mighty *centrifugal* tendency, inherited in this stock and strengthened in the United States, will assert itself. Then this race of unequaled energy, with all the majesty of numbers and the might of wealth behind it—the representative, let us hope, of the largest liberty, the purest Christianity, the highest civilization—having developed peculiarly aggressive traits calculated to impress its institutions upon mankind, will spread itself over the earth. If I read not amiss, this powerful race will move down upon Mexico, down upon Central and South America, out upon the islands of the sea, over upon Africa and beyond. And can any one doubt that the result of this competition of races will be the "survival of the fittest?" "Any people," says Dr. Bushnell, "that is physiologically advanced in culture, though it be only in a degree beyond another which is mingled with it on strictly equal terms, is sure to live down and finally live out its inferiority. Nothing can save the inferior race but a ready and pliant assimilation. Whether the feebler and more abject races are going to be regenerated and raised up, is already very much of a question. What if it should be God's plan to people the world with better and finer material?"

"Certain it is, whatever expectations we may indulge, that there is a tremendous overbearing surge of power in the Christian nations, which, if the others are not speedily raised to some vastly higher capacity, will inevitably submerge and bury them forever. These great populations of Christendom— what are they doing, but throwing out their colonies on every side, and populating themselves, if I may so speak, into the possession of all countries and climes?" To this result no war of extermination is needful;

the contest is not one of arms, but of vitality and of civilization. "At the present day," say Mr. Darwin, "civilized nations are everywhere supplanting barbarous nations, excepting where the climate opposes a deadly barrier; and they succeed mainly, though not exclusively, through their arts, which are the products of the intellect." Thus the Finns were supplanted by the Aryan races in Europe and Asia, the Tartars by the Russians, and thus the aborigines of North America, Australia, and New Zealand are now disappearing before the all-conquering Anglo-Saxons. It seems as if these inferior tribes were only precursors of a superior race, voices in the wilderness crying: "Prepare ye the way of the Lord!"

Some of the stronger races, doubtless, may be able to preserve their integrity; but, in order to compete with the Anglo-Saxons, they will probably be forced to adopt his methods and instruments, his civilization and his religion. Significant movements are now in progress among them. While the Christian religion was never more vital, or its hold upon the Anglo-Saxon mind stronger, there is taking place among the nations a widespread intellectual revolt against traditional beliefs. "In every corner of the world," says Mr. Froude, "there is the same phenomenon of the decay of established religions. . . . Among the Mohammedans, Jews, Buddhists, Brahmins, traditionary creeds are losing their hold. An intellectual revolution is sweeping over the world, breaking down established opinions, dissolving foundations on which historical faiths have been built up." The contact of Christian with heathen nations is awakening the latter to new life. Old superstitions are loosening their grasp. The dead crust of fossil faiths is being shattered by the movements of life underneath. In Catholic countries, Catholicism is losing its influence over educated minds, and in some cases the masses have already lost all faith in it. Thus, while on this continent God is training the Anglo-Saxon race for its mission, a complemental work has been in progress in the great world beyond. God has two hands. Not only is he preparing in our civilization the die with which to stamp the nations, but, by what Southey called the "timing of Providence," he is preparing mankind to receive the impress.

Is there room for reasonable doubt that this race, unless devitalized by alcohol and tobacco, is destined to dispossess many weaker races, assimilate others, and mold the remainder, until, in a very true and important sense, it has Anglo-Saxonized mankind? Already "the English language, saturated with Christian ideas, gathering up into itself the best thought of all the ages, is the great agent of Christian civilization throughout the world; at this moment affecting the destinies and molding the character of half the human race." Jacob Grimm, the German philologist, said of this language: "It seems chosen, like its people, to rule in future times in a still greater degree in all the corners of the earth." He predicted, indeed, that the language of Shakespeare would eventually become the language of mankind. Is not Tennyson's noble prophecy to find its fulfillment in Anglo-Saxondom's extending its dominion and influence—

"Till the war-drum throb no longer, and the battle-flags are furl'd, In the Parliament of man, the Federation of the world."

In my mind, there is no doubt that the Anglo-Saxon is to exercise the commanding influence in the world's future; but the exact nature of that influence is, as yet, undetermined. How far his civilization will be materialistic and atheistic, and how long it will take thoroughly to Christianize and sweeten it, how rapidly he will hasten the coming of the kingdom wherein dwelleth righteousness, or how many ages he may retard it, is still uncertain; but *is now being swiftly determined*. Let us weld together in a chain the various links of our logic which we have endeavored to forge. Is it manifest that the Anglo-Saxon holds in his hands the destinies of mankind for ages to come? Is it evident that the United States is to be the home of this race, the principal seat of his power, the great center of his influence? Is it true that the great West is to dominate the nation's future? Has it been shown that this generation is to determine the character, and hence the destiny of the West? Then may God open the eyes of this generation! When Napoleon drew up his troops before the Mamelukes, under the shadow of the Pyramids, pointing to the latter, he said to his soldiers: "Remember that from yonder heights forty centuries look down on you." Men of this generation, from the pyramid top of opportunity on which God has set us, *we look down on forty centuries*! We stretch our hand into the future with power to mold the destinies of unborn millions.

"We are living, we are dwelling,
In a grand and awful time,
In an age on ages telling—
To be living is sublime!"

Notwithstanding the great perils which threaten it, I cannot think our civilization

244 ◆ Energizing America

will perish; but I believe it is fully in the hands of the Christians of the United States, during the next ten or fifteen years, to hasten or retard the coming of Christ's kingdom in the world by hundreds, and perhaps thousands, of years. We of this generation and nation occupy the Gibraltar of the ages which commands the world's future.

The March of the Flag
Albert J. Beveridge

Albert J. Beveridge (1862-1927) served as United States senator from Indiana from 1899 to 1911. As one of the leading imperialist senators at the turn of the century, he declared himself for "America first! Not only America first, but America only!" He was a pronounced nationalist who was suspicious of foreign countries, and therefore it was natural that he should support American expansion abroad during his term in office. The selection below appears in Thomas B. Reed, ed., *Modern Eloquence*, Vol. 2 (Philadelphia: John D. Morris and Co., 1903), pp. 224-43, *passim*.

It is a noble land that God has given us; a land that can feed and clothe the world; a land whose coast lines would inclose half the countries of Europe; a land set like a sentinel between the two imperial oceans of the globe; a greater England and a nobler destiny. It is a mighty people that He has planted on this soil; a people sprung from the most masterful blood of history; a people perpetually revitalized by the virile working folk of all the earth; a people imperial by virtue of their power, by right of their institutions, by authority of their heaven-directed purposes, the propagandists and not the misers of liberty. It is a glorious history our God has bestowed upon His chosen people; a history whose keynote was struck by the Liberty Bell; a history heroic with faith in our mission and our future; a history of statesmen, who flung the boundaries of the Republic out into unexplored lands and savage wildernesses; a history of soldiers, who carried the flag across blazing deserts and through the ranks of hostile mountains, even to the gates of sunset; a history of a multiplying people, who overran a continent in half a century; a history divinely logical, in the process of whose tremendous reasoning we find ourselves today.

Therefore, in this campaign the question is larger than a party question. It is an American question. It is a world question. Shall the American people continue their restless march toward the commercial supremacy of the world? Shall free institutions broaden their blessed reign as the children of liberty wax in strength until the empire of our principles is established over the hearts of all mankind? Have we no mission to perform—no duty to discharge to our fellow man? Has the Almighty endowed us with gifts beyond our deserts, and marked us as the people of His peculiar favor, merely to rot in our own selfishness, as men and nations must who take cowardice for their companion and self for their deity as China has, as India has, as Egypt has? Shall we be as the man who had one talent and hid it, or as he who had ten talents and used them until they grew to riches? And shall we reap the reward that waits on the discharge of our high duty as the sovereign power on earth; shall we occupy new markets for what our farmers raise, new markets for what our factories make, new markets for what our merchants sell, aye, and please God, new markets for what our ships will carry? Shall we avail ourselves to new sources of supply of what we do not raise or make, so that what are luxuries today shall be necessities tomorrow? Shall we conduct the mightiest commerce of history with the best money known to man or shall we use the pauper money of Mexico, China, and the Chicago platform? Shall we be worthy of our mighty past of progress, brushing aside, as we have always done, the spider webs of technicality, and march ever onward upon the highway of development, to the doing of real deeds, the achievement of real things, and the winning of real victories?

In a sentence, shall the American people endorse at the polls the American administration of William McKinley, which, under the guidance of Divine Providence, has started the Republic on its noblest career of prosperity, duty and glory, or shall the American people rebuke that administration, reverse the wheels of history, halt the career of the flag . . .?

William McKinley is continuing the policy that Jefferson began, Monroe continued, Seward advanced, Grant promoted, Harrison championed. Hawaii is ours; Puerto Rico is to be ours; at the prayer of its people Cuba will finally be ours; in the islands of the East, even to the gates of Asia, coaling stations are to be ours; at the very least the flag of a liberal government is to float over the Philippines, and it will be the stars and stripes of glory. And the burning question of this campaign is whether the American people will accept the gifts of events; whether they will rise, as lifts their soaring destiny; whether they will proceed along the lines of national development surveyed by the statesmen of our past, or whether, for the first time, the American people doubt their mission, question their fate, prove apostate to the spirit of their race, and halt the ceaseless march of free institutions?

The opposition tells us that we ought not to govern a people without their consent. I answer, the rule of liberty that all just government derives its authority from the consent of the governed, applies only to those who are capable of self-government. We govern the Indians without their consent; we govern our Territories without their consent; we govern our children without their consent. I answer, would not the natives of the Philippines prefer the just, humane, civilizing government of this Republic to the savage, bloody rule of pillage and extortion from which we have rescued them? Do not the blazing fires of joy and the ringing bells of gladness in Puerto Rico prove the welcome of our flag? And regardless of this formula of words made only for enlightened, self-governing peoples, do we owe no duty to the world? Shall we turn these peoples back to the reeking hands from which we have taken them? Shall we save them from those nations, to give them to a self rule of tragedy? It would be like giving a razor to a babe telling it to shave itself. It would be like giving a typewriter to an Esquimau and telling him to publish one of the great dailies of the world. . . .

Today, we are making more than we can use. Therefore, we must find new markets for our produce, new occupation for our capital, new work for our labor. And so, while we did not need the territory taken during the past century at the time it was acquired, we do need what we have taken in 1898, and we need it now. Think of the thousands of Americans who will pour into Hawaii and Puerto Rico when the Republic's laws cover those islands with justice and safety. Think of the tens of thousands of Americans who will invade the Philippines when a liberal government shall establish order and equity there. Think of the hundreds of thousands of Americans who will build a soap and water, common school civilization of energy and industry in Cuba, when a government of law replaces the double reign of anarchy and tyranny. . . .

The resources of the Philippines have hardly been touched by the finger tips of modern methods. And they produce what we cannot, and they consume what we produce—the very predestination of reciprocity. And William McKinley intends that their trade shall be ours. It means an opportunity for the rich man to do something with his money, besides hoarding it or lending it. It means occupation for every workingman in the country at wages which the development of new resources, the launching of new enterprises, the monopoly of new markets always brings . . . Why mumble the meaningless phrases of a tale that is told when the golden future is before us, the world calls us, its wealth awaits us and God's command is on us? . . .

Fellow-Americans, we are God's chosen people. Yonder at Bunker Hill and Yorktown His providence was above us. At New Orleans and on ensanguined seas His hand sustained us. Abraham Lincoln was His minister, and His altar of freedom the boys in blue set up on a hundred battlefields. His power directed Dewey in the east, and He delivered the Spanish fleet into our hands on Liberty's natal day as He delivered the elder Armada into the hands of our English sires two centuries ago. His great purposes are revealed in the progress of the flag, which surpasses the intentions of Congresses and Cabinets, and leads us, like a holier pillar of cloud by day and pillar of fire by night, into situations unforeseen by finite wisdom and duties unexpected by the unprophetic heart of selfishness. The American people cannot use a dishonest medium of exchange; it is ours to set the world its example of right and honor. We cannot fly from our world duties; it is ours to execute the purposes of a fate that has driven us to be greater than our small intentions. We cannot retreat from any soil where Providence has unfurled our banner; it is ours to save that soil for liberty and civilization. For liberty and civilization and God's promises fulfilled, the flag must henceforth be the symbol and the sign of all mankind.

America's Mission
William Jennings Bryan

Williams Jennings Bryan (1860-1925), who was twice elected to Congress (1890 and 1892), was a three-time Democratic presidential nominee, as well as secretary of state in the Wilson administration. Among the major issues of his second bid for the presidency was the imperialistic policy of the Republican administration of William McKinley. Though Bryan had volunteered for military service in Cuba during the Spanish-American War, he spoke against American expansionism in the 1900 presidential campaign. No doubt his position on the issue contributed to his defeat in the election, as some voters doubted his sincerity, while many others had been thoroughly convinced by the expansionists that they opposed Bryan without questioning his sincerity. The following excerpt, which was part of a 1900 campaign speech, was taken from his *Speeches, Newspaper Articles, and Interviews* (Chicago: Bently and Co., 1900), pp. 20-24.

When the advocates of imperialism find it impossible to reconcile a colonial policy with the principles of our government or with the cannons of morality when they are unable to defend it upon the ground of religious duty or pecuniary profit, they fall back in helpless despair upon the assertion that it is destiny. "Suppose it does violate the constitution," they say; "suppose it does break all the commandments; suppose it does entail upon the nation an incalculable expenditure of blood and money; it is destiny and we must submit."

The people have not voted for imperialism; no national convention has declared for it; no Congress has passed upon it. To whom then, has the future been revealed? Whence this voice of authority? We can all prophesy, but our prophecies are merely guesses, colored by our hopes and our surroundings.

Man's opinion of what is to be is half wish and half environment. Avarice paints destiny with a dollar mark before it, militarism equips it with a sword.

He is the best prophet who, recognizing the omnipotence of truth, comprehends most clearly the great forces which are working out the progress, not of one party, not of one nation, but of the human race.

History is replete with predictions which once wore the hue of destiny, but which failed of fulfillment because those who uttered them saw too small an arc of the circle of events. When Pharaoh pursued the fleeing Israelites to the edge of the Red Sea he was confident that their bondage would be renewed and that they would again make bricks without straw, but destiny was not revealed until Moses and his followers reached the farther shore dry shod and the waves rolled over the horses and chariots of the Egyptians. When Belshazzar, on the last night of his reign, led his thousand lords into the Babylonian banquet hall and sat down to a table glittering with vessels of silver and gold he felt sure of his kingdom for many years to come, but destiny was not revealed until the hand wrote upon the wall those awe-inspiring words, "Mene, Mene, Tekel Upharsin." When Abderrahman swept northward with his conquering hosts his imagination saw the Cresent triumphant throughout the world, but destiny was not revealed until Charles Martel raised the cross above the battlefield of Tours and saved Europe from the sword of Mohammedanism. When Napoleon emerged victorious from Marengo, from Ulm and from Austerlitz he thought himself the child of destiny, but destiny was not revealed until Blucher's forces joined the army of Wellington and the vanquished Corsican began his melancholy march toward St. Helena. When the red-coats of George the Third routed the New Englanders at Lexington and Bunker Hill there arose before the British sovereign visions of wealth by foreign made laws, but destiny was not revealed until the surrender of Cornwallis completed the work begun at Independence Hall and ushered into existence a government deriving its just powers from the consent of the governed.

We have reached another crisis. The ancient doctrine of imperialism, banished from our land more than a century ago, has recrossed the Atlantic and challenged democracy to mortal combat upon American soil.

Whether the Spanish war shall be known in history as a war for property or as a war of conquest; whether the principles of self-government shall be strengthened or abandoned; whether this nation shall remain a homogenous republic or become a heterogeneous empire—these questions must be answered by the American people—when they speak, and not until then will, destiny be revealed.

Destiny is not a matter of chance, it is a matter of choice; it is not a thing to be waited for, it is a thing to be achieved.

No one can see the end from the beginning, but every one can make his course an honorable one from beginning to end, by adhering to the right under all circumstances. Whether a man steals much or little may depend upon his opportunities, but whether he steals at all depends upon his own volition.

So with our nation. If we embark upon a career of conquest no one can tell how many islands we may be able to seize, or how many races we may be able to subjugate; neither can any one estimate the cost, immediate and remote, to the nation's character, but whether we shall enter upon such a career is a question which the people have a right to decide for themselves.

Unexpected events may retard or advance the nation's growth but the nation's purpose determines its destiny.

What is the nation's purpose?

The main purpose of the founders of our government was to secure for themselves and for posterity the blessings of liberty, and that purpose has been faithfully followed up to this time. Our statesmen have opposed each other upon economic questions, but they have agreed in defending self-government as the controlling national idea. They have quarreled among themselves over tariff and finance, but they have been united in their opposition to an entangling alliance with any European power.

Under this policy our nation has grown in numbers and in strength. Under this policy its beneficent influence has encircled the globe. Under this policy the taxpayers have been spared the burden and the menace of a large military establishment and the young men have taught the arts of peace rather than the science of war. On each returning Fourth of July our people have met to celebrate the signing of the Declaration of Independence; their hearts have renewed their vows to free institutions and their voices have praised the forefathers whose wisdom and courage and patriotism made it possible for each succeeding generation to repeat the words, "My country, 'tis of thee, Sweet land of liberty, Of thee I sing."

This sentiment was well-nigh universal until a year ago. It was to this sentiment that the Cuban insurgents appealed; it was this sentiment that impelled our people to enter into the war with Spain. Have the people so changed within a few short months that they are now willing to apologize for the War of the Revolution and force upon the Filipinos the same system of government against which the colonists protested with fire and sword?

The hour of temptation has come, but temptations do not destroy, they merely test the strength of individuals and nations; they are stumbling blocks or stepping stones; they lead to infamy or fame, according to the use made of them.

Benedict Arnold and Ethan Allen served together in the Continental army and both were offered British gold. Arnold yielded to the temptation and made his name a synonym for treason; Allen resisted and lives in the affections of his countrymen.

Our nation is tempted to depart from its "standard of morality" and adopt a policy of "criminal aggression." But will it yield?

If I mistake not the sentiment of the American people they will spurn the bride of imperialism, and, by resisting temptation, win such a victory as has not been won since the battle of Yorktown. Let it be written of the United States: Behold a republic that took up arms to aid a neighboring people, struggling to be free; a republic that, in the progress of the war, helped distant races whose wrongs were not in contemplation when hostilities began; a republic that, when peace was restored, turned a deaf ear to the clamorous voice of greed and to those borne down by the weight of a foreign yoke, spoke the welcome words, Stand up; be free—let this be the record made on history's page and the silent example of this republic, true to its principles in the hour of trial, will do more to extend the area of self-government and civilization than could be done by all the wars of conquest that we could wage in a generation.

The forcible annexation of the Philippine islands is not necessarily to make the United States a world power. For over ten decades our nation has been a world power. During its brief existence it has exerted upon the human race an influence more potent for good than all the other nations of the earth combined, and it has exerted upon the human race that influence without the use of sword or Gatling gun. Mexico and the republics of Central and South America testify to the design influence of our institutions, while Europe and Asia give evidence of the working of the leaven of self-government. In the growth of democracy we observe the triumphant march of an idea—an idea that would be weighted down rather than aided by the armor and weapons preferred by imperialism.

Much has been said of late about Anglo-Saxon civilization. Far be it for me to detract from the service rendered to the world by the sturdy race whose language we speak. The union of the Angle and the Saxon formed a new and valuable type, but the process of race evolution was not completed when the Angle and the Saxon met. A still later type appeared which is superior to any which has existed heretofore; and with this new type will come a higher civilization than any which has preceded it. Great has been the Greek, the Latin, the Slav, the Celt, the Teuton and the Anglo-Saxon, but greater than any of these is the American, in whom are blended the virtues of them all. Civil and religious liberty, universal education and the right to participate, directly or through representatives chosen by himself, in all the affairs of government— these give to the American citizen an opportunity and an inspiration which can be found nowhere else.

Standing upon the vantage ground already gained the American people can aspire to a grander destiny than has opened before any other race.

Anglo-Saxon civilization has taught the individual to protect his own rights, American civilization will teach him to respect the rights of others.

Anglo-Saxon civilization has taught the individual to take care to himself, American civilization proclaiming the equality of all before the law, will teach him that his own highest good requires the observance of the commandment: "Thou shalt love thy neighbor as thyself."

Anglo-Saxon civilization has carried its flag to every clime and defended it with forts and garrisons. American civilization will imprint its flag upon the hearts of all who long for freedom.

To American civilization, all hail!

Part IV Evaluating America Since 1920

Changes brought about in America due to industrialization, urbanization, and the spread of technology, along with crucial events on the world scene in the twentieth century—the World Wars, the Great Depression, the struggles of the League of Nations and United Nations—have forced Americans to evaluate often the state of the nation since 1920. The search for national meaning has led some to repudiate supernaturalistic religion, only to return to lives of faith. In the course of the search, uncertainty has characterized the people's evaluation of the individual and collective conscience.

The armistice which brought World War I to an end did not remove this distant conflict from the minds of Americans who engaged in a conscious attempt to "return to normalcy." Idealism and reform were dismissed, while materialism nurtured by laissez-faire was welcomed enthusiastically. Calvin Coolidge's declaration that "the business of America is business" captured the spirit of the age not only for the captains of industry, but also for many in the religious community who fashioned their churches in accord with the latest business practices and values. Some, like pentecostal Aimee Semple McPherson, reacted to the growing emphasis on materialism in modern America. Bruce Barton's redesigned image of Jesus illustrated the impact of business upon religion. The evaluation of America was sparked, too, by intellectual currents inherited from the late nineteenth century. One of these currents, Darwin's theory of evolution, produced a showdown at Dayton, Tennessee, when fundamentalists challenged the teaching of the theory in the public schools.

The growth of religious liberalism, fostered in the 1920s by the good times of economic prosperity, survived into the early 1930s, as noted by the Humanist Manifesto I. But it was soon challenged, as Edwin Lewis was only one of the new breed of neo-orthodox religionists whose evaluation of liberalism resulted in a new synthesis of biblical ideals and forces in the modern world. Some religious figures like Gerald L. K. Smith, Gerald Winrod, and Charles Coughlin were in the vanguard of protestors who proclaimed the hopelessness of American capitalism and democracy, and called for solutions ranging from the far left, such as communism, to the extreme right, which included fascism.

World War I had left a bad taste in the mouths of Americans, and a new course had to be charted for the future. During the twenties and most of the thirties, the church lent its collective voice to the nationalist pursuit of peace-at-all-costs. Ray Abrams traced the steps of the church as it moved from neutrality in the late thirties to belligerency in the early forties.

255

Upon the conclusion of World War II the United States entered the era of the Cold War. Among the problems Americans addressed were the threats of mass destruction represented by atomic weaponry, and the expansion of communism. The Federal Council of Churches and evangelist Billy Graham discuss the tensions of these issues.

The turbulent decade of the 1960s saw American religionists enter into the mix of controversies both at home and abroad. From his Birmingham jail cell, Martin Luther King, Jr., made a strong case for Christian participation in the civil rights movement. Charles C. West helped lay the groundwork for dialogue among Christians concerning their response to the war in Vietnam. Sociologist Ronald Enroth examines the development of the religious counterculture as the sixties moved into the seventies.

The writings of Charles Colson, Stephen Carter, and Ronald Reagan reflect America's search for national stability since the mid-1970s, and demonstrate the interaction of religion with American society. That the religious community has not only affected the shaping of society, but also has been shaped by that society is illustrated by their writings which address the condition of America during the past two decades. This is the same reciprocal relationship experienced by the colonists in the seventeenth century.

14 America and Religion in the Uncertain Twenties

Why is it that you were looking for Me? Did you not know that I had to be in My Father's house?

—Luke 2:49

This is That
Aimee Semple McPherson

Aimee Semple McPherson (1890-1944) was a Pentecostal evangelist and founder of the International Church of the Foursquare Gospel. In 1915 she began a decade-long ministry of itinerant evangelism during which time she crisscrossed the nation eight times, conducting revival crusades in large cities from Philadelphia to St. Louis to Denver. In 1923 she opened the Angelus Temple, a 5,000-seat church in Los Angeles. She dedicated it as the Church of the Foursquare Gospel, centered on "the fourfold ministry of the Lord Jesus Christ" as Savior, Healer, Baptizer, and Coming King. She preached "a baptism with the Holy Spirit evidenced by tongues speech as well as healing."

"We cannot but speak those things which we have seen and heard," (Acts 4:20) said the Apostle Peter when called before Annas, the High Priest.

"None of these things move me, neither count I my life dear unto myself, so that I might finish my course with joy, and the ministry, which I have received of the Lord Jesus, to testify the Gospel of the Grace of God," (Acts 20:24) declared the Apostle Paul when standing before the elders at Ephesus.

There are tears in my eyes and a holy awe in my heart, as I look back over the past fifteen

---

The following excerpt is from her *This Is That: Personal Experiences, Sermons and Writings* (1923), and is used with the permission of the International Church of the Foursquare Gospel.

257

years of ministry and consider the loving kindness and the tender mercies of the Lord Jesus Christ unto this, his unworthy hand-maiden.

Hallelujah! Glory, glory to His name! To think that He ever could have loved me and have called me from a life of carelessness and frivolity unto His own dear service! To think that He could have permitted me to be a cup-bearer for the King! A worm within His dear Hand, with which He might thrash a mountain! An empty pitcher with which He might water His lilies! A yielded channel through whom He might pour streams of blessing upon a thirsty desert! A poor, but a willing mouthpiece through whom the story of the Saviour's Love might be preached unto hundreds of thousands in Canada, Ireland, England, China, Australia, and the United States of America! To think that He ever could have permitted me to lead tens of thousands of penitent sinners to the Fountain of Blood opened in the House of David for sin and uncleanness.

Hallelujah! All of the glory, the honor and the praise belongeth unto Him both now and forever!

The very memory of His goodness, His patience, and His dealings set my heart to singing and my lips to shouting the glory of His matchless Name!

The recounting of His mercies, His leadings and His gentle ministrations flood my soul with unutterable joy and sweep me out into the midst of a sea of infinite love, all a-wonder that He could have cared for one so unworthy as I and have called me to Himself!

"I stand all amazed in the presence
    Of Jesus, the Nazarene;
And wonder how He could love me,
    A sinner condemned unclean;
Oh, how marvelous! oh, how wonderful!
    And my song shall ever be
Oh, how marvelous! oh, how wonderful,
    Is my Saviour's love for me!"

When, several years ago, I took in hand to set forth in order a declaration of those things which the Lord had done for me, the task was undertaken under the most unfavorable circumstances. I was at that time traveling from city to city, and from state to state, writing the story page by page, often in the midnight hours when a revival service was closed and the crowds had gone to their homes, and were fast asleep.

As I thought of His great goodness to me and lived the meetings over again, I would write a while and cry a while; and write a while and smile a while. I pray this testimony may be as great a blessing to those who read as to the one who wrote.

Remember, as you peruse these pages, that the Lord is no respecter of persons. That what He did for one so unworthy as I, he waits to do for all! . . .

Personal Testimony

My Mother

"The word of the Lord came unto me, saying,
Before I formed thee . . . I knew thee; and before thou camest forth . . . I sanctified thee and I ordained thee a prophet unto the nations. Then said I, Ah! Lord God! behold, I cannot speak; for I am a child. But the Lord said unto me, Say not, I am a child;

for thou shalt go to all that I shall send thee, and whatsoever I command thee thou shalt speak. Benot afraid of their faces; for I am with thee to deliver thee. Then the Lord put forth His hand, and touched my mouth, and said unto me, Behold, I have put My Words in thy mouth." Jer. 1:(4-9).

When I was a girl seventeen years of age, the Lord spoke these words plainly into my startled ears, as I was alone in my bedroom praying one day. It was a solemn time when He ordained me there to preach the Gospel. At first it seemed too astounding and impossible to be true that the Lord would ever call such a simple, unworthy little country girl as I to go out and preach the Gospel but the call and ordination were so real that, although later set apart and ordained by the saints of God, the memory of my little bedroom, flooded with the glory of God as He spoke those words, has always been to me my real ordination.

It is because the words, "Before I formed thee I knew thee, and before thou camest forth I sanctified thee," are so true in my life that I must begin my testimony by taking you back some twenty years before I was born. Our lives are like a great loom, weaving many threads together, and the first threads of my life are inseparably woven about my dear Mother: it is with her, therefore, that the story of my life really begins.

Returning from school at the age of twelve, she read excitedly of a strange "Army who were announced to bombard the town and take prisoners for the King. Prevailing upon her mother to risk the danger, they stood in a downpour of rain, awaiting the advent of the army. Presently the word was passed—

"Here they come!"

But where were they? Could this be all? Three strangers, cloaked in quiet blue, stepped forth into the square, and knelt in silent prayer.

The humility, seriousness and sweetness of it swept over her heart. She realized the tender drawing of the Holy Spirit, and before a word had been spoken she knew that these were God's people and her people. As they sang—

"We are bound for the land of the pure and the holy,
    The home of the happy, the kingdom of love.
Ye wanderers from God, in the broad road of folly,
    O! say—will you go to the Eden above?"

Her heart, melting in love and adoration, answered — "I will go."

Her mother had talked much of the mighty power of God manifested in the early Methodist church, and here in the [Salvation] Army she found it again, and it was nothing uncommon to see men and women slain as in the church of John Wesley's day. Her heart was filled with a desire to win other souls for Jesus; the love of Christ constrained her to His glad service, and the all-absorbing purpose of her soul was to prepare in obedience to the divine call.

Soon came the illness and death of her mother, who had talked to her solemnly of the time soon coming when the little girl should be left alone in the world, telling her that she would commend her to the tender care of God and the Captain's wife, who had been her spiritual mother. She did not waver for an instant in answering the call to the ranks of the Army and after quickly packing her simple belongings, my mother left all, friends and home, and native land, to follow Jesus.

The period of service which followed her arrival at the Army quarters in the distant town, brought blessed help and inspiration. The godly life of her leaders, and the prayers of the Captain, who frequently spent whole nights on his face before God in intercession for precious souls, the hours spent in visiting the sick and sinful—the trudging five miles to assist in "Outpost" duties, the "War Cry" selling, and meetings, all helped comprise the routine of life.

But again fell the shadows—this time an illness which necessitated an extended change of scene and work; this meant a painful goodby to her comrades, and a visit to a country farm.

Then it was, while weak in body, depressed in spirit, and mourning over the loss of a mother's sympathetic hand, that she married, hoping to be able to continue her work for God, but amidst the strenuous and unaccustomed duties of heavy farm work, she was compelled to acknowledge that she was caught in the devil's net, and helpless as far as active service was concerned, and must largely devote herself to the manifold cares of life and home.

Even so environed, she stood true to her Lord, setting up a family altar, and helping with meetings in the homes of the neighborhood, often driving or walking the six miles to the nearest corps, and counted it the one bright hour of her day, even when weary and worn with heavy toil and care. Yet, realizing ever that she had failed the Lord, who had redeemed and set her apart for His glorious purpose, life grew more and more dreary; her spirit grieved sore, with no ray of hope to rectify herself toward God, and the souls she had been called to win.

Ah! Many who read this experience will know how to enter into her feelings, for alas, many grow faint and falter by the wayside, or seek to find an easier pathway, only to discover themselves outside the paths of obedience and blessing.

My Mother's pathway, in these days, was hedged about with difficulties. Shorn of her usefulness, fettered by circumstances, she truly did grind in the prison house; but, strange as it may seem, during all the time that her body was fettered, her soul was turning Heavenward. Each hour the longing became more intense to go on with the work for which God had ordained her, and for which purpose she had left home and friends and separated herself unto the Lord. Finally it absorbed her every thought in waking, and became her one dream in repose—*she must* make good her belated pledge. She must "come back" to the glorious calling of the Cross.

Hope's One Ray

One day, after reading over and over the story of Hannah, she went to her room, and closing the door, kneeled by her bed, and prayed unto the Lord, and vowed a vow, saying—

"Oh, Lord, You called me to preach the Gospel, but somehow I have failed You and cannot go, but if You will only hear my prayer, as You heard Hannah's prayer of old, and give me a little baby girl, I will give her unreservedly into your service, that she may preach the word I should have preached, fill the place I should have filled, and live the life I should have lived in Thy service. O Lord, hear and answer me; give me the witness that Thou hast heard me, O Lord, for Thine own Name's sake. Amen."

Turning to the window, she swept back the curtains and gazed wistfully up at the dark clouds shrouding the face of the sky and shutting out the sunshine beyond.

Suddenly there came a rift in the clouds, and a ray of sunlight illumined yonder hilltop, moved quickly down the slope of the hill, reached the valley, the orchard, the house itself, and fell full upon the white, anxious face with its tear-reddened eyes, framed in the window, lighting it with divine radiance, hope and courage, and swept on into the room, flooding it with golden glory.

To the longing little heart of my Mother, as she kneeled at the window, it seemed that surely here was the divine witness from above—the sealing of her vow unto God.

Again she read and reread the story of Hannah, and the child she had dedicated unto the Lord. She sat on, gazing far away—dreaming of the future years. Over the distant hills the sun was fast sinking, transforming the sombre sky into a glorious mirage of hope, flaming with crimson, purple and gold.

O Hope! dazzling, radiant Hope!—What a change thou bringest to the hopeless; brightening the darkened paths, and cheering the lonely way.

Calling into the Vineyard, and Marriage

> "Come, my beloved, and let us go forth into the field; let us lodge in the villages." S. of S. 7:11.

The chain of events related in the foregoing chapters brings us right up to the place where God spoke to His poor little handmaiden, whose heart was rejoicing in the new-found Savior—the time when He called me to preach The Word, and ordained me in my room as related in the beginning of chapter one. (If you have forgotten, turn back and refresh your memory).

An intense, heaven-sent longing to be a soul winner for Jesus was born of the Spirit within my soul. He had done so much for me; He had plucked my feet out of the mire and the clay. Oh, to be able to win other souls, shining jewels to lay at His precious feet! Oh, to be able to tell of the Redeemer's love to perishing humanity! God spoke within the depths of my being and told me that "Before

I called thee, I knew thee; before thou cam-est forth I sanctified thee; and I ordained thee."

"Why, you are but a child; no one would lis-ten or have confidence in you," whispered the Enemy. "What do you know about preaching, anyway?" nodded Self and Common-sense. "Here are preachers, a country full of them, learned, college-bred, who have read books and digested theologi-cal studies for years. It is preposterous for you even to think of going out as a worker."

"But, *not many wise men after the flesh, not many mighty, not many noble, are called: but God hath chosen the foolish things of the world to confound the wise; and God hath chosen the weak things of the world to con-found the things that are mighty,*" argued the Word. "Has He not declared that with a worm He shall thrash a mountain—that when we are weak, then we are strong—and that a little child shall lead them? Has He not said that upon the servants and upon the handmaidens He would pour out His Spirit in the last days, and that they should prophe-sy? Did He not say that after the Spirit had come *'come out of your innermost being'* (not out of your head, intellect or knowl-edge) *'should flow rivers of living water'?* You know the rivers are flowing. Just open your mouth wide and He will fill it."

"Yes, but remember in addition to your youth and lack of mental equipment," cried Human Affection, "there is your Mother to be considered. You are an only child, her only comfort and object of affection in this world. Surely you would not consider leav-ing her out here in the country all alone, af-ter all that she has done for you?"

"Here you have love and home and comfort, all you can wish for. If you went forth as a worker you would have to leave all these," added Love of Comfort.

"If any man love Father or Mother more than Me, he is not worthy of Me," said the tender voice of Jesus. "No man hath given up houses or lands for My sake and the gos-pel's, but he shall receive a hundred-fold now in this time, and in the world to come eternal life. If you would come after Me you must take up your cross daily, denying your-self, and follow Me."

"But, Lord, these Pentecostal people have no earthly board behind them, no salary," cried Prudence and Forethought. "What about shoes and clothes, and necessary ex-penses?"

"Take no thought for what you shall eat or for what you shall drink or what you shall put on, for the Lord knoweth you have need of these things," calmly interrupted implicit Faith.

"Oh, yes, Lord, by Your grace I will take up my cross, 'twill be a joy," sang Consecra-tion. "I will trust You and follow You, come what may. My all is on the altar, have Your dear way with me, whether 'tis 'go' or whether 'tis 'stay' let Your perfect will be wrought out in my life. I feel my own weak-ness and insufficiency—know not what the future holds—am but a child, but

'I can hear my Savior calling,
Take your cross and follow, follow Me.'

"Oh, here I am, Lord, send me. Such a bur-den for souls is mine that I would be willing to crawl upon my hands and knees from the Atlantic to the Pacific just to say to one poor, lost soul—

'Dear sinner, Jesus loves you.'"

"You must go with me, Jesus, you must help my infirmities and speak for me, for behold I can not speak, I am a child."

But the Lord said unto me, *"Say not, I am a child, for thou shalt go to all that I shall send thee, whatsoever I command thee thou shalt speak. Be not afraid of their faces, for I am with thee to deliver thee, saith the Lord. Then the Lord put forth His hand, and touched my mouth, and said unto me, Behold, I have put my words in thy mouth."*

The battle over, the conflict ended, the consecration made, come what might, no matter who should doubt the transaction that took place in that sacred hour, I had been ordained, not of man but of God.

Day by day the call grew louder, rang more clearly in my ears. Sitting at the piano I would sing, hour after hour, from the fullness of my heart.

"I'll go where you want me to go, dear Lord,
Over mountain or plain or sea;
I'll say what you want me to say, dear Lord,
I'll be what you want me to be."

Tears would roll down my face; my body was there, but my Spirit was far away out in the harvest fields working for Jesus.

So enwrapt was I in the call of the Master that I was often but dimly conscious of my Mother's leaving her work each time I be-

gan to play, no matter what part of the house she was in, and coming to the parlor door, leaning against it and wiping the big tears from her eyes on the corner of her apron. God was speaking to her Mother heart, taking her back to the day of her prayer for the little girl, reminding her of the dedication service when she had promised to let her go where He would send, even to the ends of the earth. She realized that the great divine call had come to her daughter, and that the time for her supreme sacrifice was near. She remembered the words of Hannah:

> *"Oh, my lord, I am the woman that stood by thee here, praying unto the Lord. For this child I prayed; and the Lord hath given me my petition which I asked of Him: therefore also have I lent him to the Lord; as long as he liveth he shall be lent to the Lord, and she worshipped the Lord there."*

Just how it was all to come about, little did we know. The meetings were a feast to our souls. Workers came freely to our country home, and when the Evangelist, Robert Semple, that blessed man of God who, because of his Christ-like bearing, moved as a prince among men, passed on to another town, he continued to encourage and instruct me in the Lord by many long letters, all of which were filled with scriptures and food from God's storehouse.

Never has it been my privilege to read such letters as those that came from the inspired pen of this saintly man of prayer. He walked and lived and breathed in the atmosphere of heaven. To know him was to love and respect him.

Then came the time of his return visit to our town and the memorable night when I had volunteered to nurse the two little children of the sister in whose home I had received my baptism. The little ones had been stricken down with typhoid fever, and the mother was fatigued with long care and watching.

Late in the evening, as I was tending the little ones and setting things to rights in the room, the door opened and in walked Robert Semple, offering his services and prayers. After he had prayed, the children fell into a quiet sleep, and we sat down side by side to read the Bible by the light of the shaded lamp. Robert talked earnestly of the Savior and His love, of the work, of the great fields of golden grain, white already unto the harvest, of the need for laborers in these closing hours of the dispensation, of the soon coming of Jesus and the many souls yet to be saved, of what a life of faith meant—the sacrifice, the joy, the reward—then, reaching over he took my hand in his and, telling me of his love, asked me to become his wife and enter the work as a helpmate by his side.

This is the first time I have ever attempted to lift the veil even a little from that sacred, hallowed hour, when we kneeled side by side, hand in hand, and he reverently prayed God to look down and solemnize our engagement and send us forth as true laborers, in obedience to His call, to rescue poor perishing souls from eternal destruction.

While on my knees, with closed eyes and throbbing heart—(Why, this was the very room in which I had received my baptism!) the room seemed filled with angels who lined either side of the golden, sunlit path of life that stretched away into the vista of coming days of glorious love and joyful service to our Lord and King.

Here was the visible answer to the call.

Here was the loving human God had sent to unlatch the gate of opportunity and guide my steps into that shining path and start me well upon the way—that way that has led through sunshine and shadow, tears and smiles, joys and sorrow, life and death, mountain-top and valley.

Little did I know that night, as I contemplated the shining way that led on and on to the Father's throne, how soon the strong, dear arm that was now about me as we prayed, and led me to into the work, would be removed; that after two years of married life I should be left alone, yet not alone.

The impenetrable mist with which God mercifully veils the future remained unrent, yet, had I known of the little mound of fresh-digged earth that should mark the grave of this dear heart in Happy Valley, Hong Kong, China, I should not have hesitated in that softly whispered "yes," with which I met his question; nor would I have shrunk one instant from the call to stand by his side. I deemed it one of the greatest privileges and honors I had ever known.

Oh, Jesus! Jesus! how wonderfully He had planned it all for poor, unworthy me! How he had sought and called and chosen me! Is it any wonder my heart sang with rapturous love and praise for such a Redeemer?

The straight-forward, manly way in which Robert went to my Mother for her consent, coupled with the dealings of the Lord in her heart on the subject, made her willing to part with her daughter, though she declared, mother-like, that it took the sunshine and the laughter and the music from the farm and from the home.

I am not going to try to describe the little wedding which took place under the flower-decked arch on the lawn the following August, nor the long tables spread beneath the apple trees for the wedding supper, nor the Mother-face that tried to keep brave and smiling as the little white wedding-dress was laid aside and the navy-clad bride entered the carriage that was soon hidden by a cloud of dust as it sped away to catch the train for Stratford—the mission field of which my husband was in charge.

> "Were the whole realm of nature mine,
> That were an offering far too small;
> Love so amazing, so divine,
> Demands my love, my life, my all."

The Man Nobody Knows
Bruce Barton

Bruce Barton (1886-1967), the son of a preacher, and a partner in the high-powered advertising company of Batten, Barton, Durstine, and Osborn, did much during the 1920s to make religion relevant to modern America. Written in a vein compatible with Russell Conwell's "Acres of Diamonds," Barton's first book, *The Man Nobody Knows*, was the fourth best-selling work of nonfiction in 1925 and the top seller in 1926. It redesigned the image of Christ from a meek and lowly man into a man of strength and drive who knew how to gain success through the use of love and charisma. The following is taken from *The Man Nobody Knows* (New York: Grosset and Dunlap, 1925).

The little boy's body sat bolt upright in the rough wooden chair, but his mind was very busy.

This was his weekly hour of revolt.

The kindly lady who could never seem to find her glasses would have been terribly shocked if she had known what was going on inside the little boy's mind.

"You must love Jesus," she said every Sunday, "and God."

The little boy did not say anything. He was afraid to say anything; he was almost afraid that something would happen to him because of the things he thought.

Love God! Who was always picking on people for having a good time and sending little boys to hell because they couldn't do better in a world which he had made so hard! Why didn't God take on some one his own size?

Love Jesus! The little boy looked up at the picture which was on the Sunday-school wall. It showed a pale young man with flabby forearms and a sad expression. The young man had red whiskers.

Then the little boy looked across to the other wall. There was Daniel, good old Daniel, standing off the lions. The little boy liked Daniel. He liked David, too, with the trusty sling that landed a stone square on the forehead of Goliath. And Moses, with his rod and his big brass snake. They were winners—those three. He wondered if David

---

could whip Jeffries. Samson could! Say, that would have been a fight!

But Jesus! Jesus was the "lamb of God." The little boy did know what that meant, but it sounded like Mary's little lamb. Something for girls—sissified. Jesus was also "meek and lowly," a "man of sorrows and acquainted with grief." He went around for three years telling people not to do things.

Sunday was Jesus' day; it was wrong to feel comfortable or laugh on Sunday.

The little boy was glad when the superintendent thumped the bell and announced: "We will now sing the closing." One more bad hour was over. For one more week the little boy had got rid of Jesus.

Years went by and the boy grew up and became a business man.

He began to wonder about Jesus.

He said to himself: "Only strong magnetic men inspire great enthusiasm and build great organizations. Yet Jesus built the greatest organization of all. It is extraordinary."

The more sermons the man heard and the more books he read the more mystified he became.

One day he decided to wipe his mind clean of books and sermons.

He said, "I will read what the men who knew Jesus personally said about him. I will read about him as though he were a new historical character, about whom I had never heard anything at all."

The man was amazed.

A physical weakling! Where did they get that idea? Jesus pushed a plane and swung an adze; he was a successful carpenter. He slept outdoors and spent his days walking around his favorite lake. His muscles were so strong that when he drove the money-changers out, nobody dared to oppose him!

A kill-joy! He was the most popular dinner guest in Jerusalem! The criticism which proper people made was that he spent too much time with republicans and sinners (very good fellows, on the whole, the man thought) and enjoyed society too much. They called him a "wine bibber and a gluttonous man."

A failure! He picked up men from the bottom ranks of business and forged them into an organization that conquered the world.

When the man had finished his reading he exclaimed, "This is a man nobody knows."

"Some day," said he, "some one will write a book about Jesus. Every business man will read it and send it to his partners and his salesmen. For it will tell the story of the founder of modern business."

So the man waited for some one to write the book, but no one did. Instead, more books were published about the "lamb of God" who was weak and unhappy and glad to die.

The man became impatient. One day he said, "I believe I will try to write that book, myself."

And he did. . . .

His Method

Many leaders have dared to lay out ambitious programs, but this is the most daring of all:

"Go ye into all the world," Jesus said, "and preach the gospel *to the whole creation*."

Consider the sublime audacity of that command. To carry Roman civilization across the then known world had cost millions of lives and billions in treasure. To create any sort of reception for a new idea or product today involves a vast machinery of propaganda and expense. His organization was a tiny group of uneducated men, one of whom had already abandoned the cause as hopeless, deserting to the enemy. He had come proclaiming a Kingdom and was to end upon a cross; yet he dared to talk of conquering all creation. What was the source of his faith in that handful of followers? By what methods had he trained them? What had they learned from him of the secrets of influencing men?

We speak of the law of "supply and demand," but the words have got turned around. With anything which is not a basic necessity the supply always precedes the demand. Elias Howe invented the sewing machine, but it nearly rusted away before American women could be persuaded to use it. With their sewing finished so quickly what would they ever do with their spare

time? Howe had vision, and had made his vision come true; but he could not sell! So his biographer paints a tragic picture—the man who had done more than any other in his generation to lighten the labor of women is forced to attend the funeral of the woman he loved in a borrowed suit of clothes! . . .

Surely no one will consider us lacking in reverence if we say that every one of the principles of "modern salesmanship" on which businessmen so much pride themselves, are brilliantly exemplified in Jesus' talk and work. The first of these and perhaps the most important is the necessity for "putting yourself in step with your prospect." A great sales manager used to illustrate it in this way:

> "When you want to get aboard a street car which is already in motion, you don't run at it from right angles and try to make the platform in one wild leap," he would say. "If you do, you are likely to find yourself on the floor. No. You run along beside the car, increasing your pace until you are moving just as rapidly as it is moving and in the same direction. Then you step aboard easily, without danger or jolt.

> "The minds of busy men are in motion," he would continue. "They are engaged with something very different from the thought you have to present. You can't jump directly at them and expect to make an effective landing. You must put yourself in the other man's place; try to imagine what he is thinking; let your first remark be in line with his thoughts; follow it by another with which you know he will easily agree. Thus,

gradually, your two minds reach a point where they can join without conflict. You encourage him to say 'yes' and 'yes' and 'that's right' and 'I've noticed that myself,' until he says the final 'yes' which is your favorable decision."

Jesus taught all this without ever teaching it. Every one of his conversations, every contact between his mind and others, is worthy of the attentive study of any sales manager. Passing along the shores of a lake one day, he saw two of the men whom he wanted as disciples. *Their* minds were in motion; their hands were busy with their nets; their conversation was about conditions in the fishing trade, and the prospects of a good market for the day's catch. To have broken in on such thinking with the offer of employment as preachers of a new religion would have been to confuse them and invite a certain rebuff. What was Jesus' approach?

"Come with me," he said, "and I will make you fishers of men."

Fishers . . . that was a word they could understand . . . fishers of men . . . that was a new idea . . . what was he driving at . . . fishers of men . . . it sounded interesting . . . well, what is it, anyway?

He sat on a hillside overlooking a fertile country. Many of the crowd who gathered around him were farmers, with their wives and sons and daughters. He wanted their interest and attention; it was important to make them understand, at the very outset, that what he had to say was nothing vague or theoretical but of direct and immediate application to their daily lives.

"A sower went forth to sow," he began, "and when he sowed some seeds fell by the wayside and the fowls came and devoured them up. . . ." Were they interested . . . *were* they? Every man of them had gone through that experience . . . the thievish crows . . . many a good day's work *they* had spoiled . . . So this Teacher knew something about the troubles that farmers had to put up with, did he? Fair enough . . . let's hear what he has to say. . . .

I propose in this chapter to speak of the advertisements of Jesus which have survived for twenty centuries and are still the most potent influence in the world.

Let us begin by asking why he was so successful in mastering public attention and why, in contrast, his churches are less so? The answer is twofold. In the first place he recognized the basic principle that all good advertising is news. He was never trite or commonplace; he had no routine. If there had been newspapers in those days, no city editor could have said, "No need to visit him to-day; he will be doing just what he did last Sunday." Reporters would have followed him every single hour, for it was impossible to predict what he would say or do; every action and word were news.

The activity begins at sunrise. Jesus was an early riser; he knew that the simplest way to live *more* than an average life is to add an hour to the fresh end of the day. At sunrise, therefore, we discover a little boat pushing out from the shore of the lake. It makes its steady way across and deposits Jesus and his disciples in Capernaum, his favorite city. He proceeds at once to the house of a friend, but not without being discovered. The report spreads instantly that he is in town, and before he can finish breakfast a crowd has collected outside the gate—a poor palsied chap among them.

The day's work is at hand.

Having slept soundly in the open air he meets the call with quiet nerves. The smile that carried confidence into even the most hopeless heart spreads over his features; he stoops down toward the sufferer.

"Be of good cheer, my son," he cries, "your sins are all forgiven."

Sins forgiven! Indeed! The respectable members of the audience draw back with sharp disapproval. "What a blasphemous phrase," they exclaim. "Who authorized him to exercise the functions of God? What right has he to decide whose sins shall be forgiven?"

Jesus sensed rather than heard their protest. He never courted controversy but he never dodged it; and much of his fame arose out of the reports of his verbal victories. Men have been elected to office—even such high office as the Presidency—by being so good-natured that they never made an enemy. But the leaders who are remembered are those who had plenty of critics and dealt with them vigorously.

"What's the objection?" he exclaimed, turning on the dissenters. "Why do you stand there and criticize? Is it easier to say, 'Thy sins be forgiven thee,' or to say, 'Arise, take up thy bed and walk?' The results are the same." Bending over the sick man again he

said: "Arise, take up thy bed and go unto thine house."

The man stirred and was amazed to find that his muscles responded. Slowly, doubtingly he struggled to his feet, and with one great shout of happiness started off, surrounded by his jubilant friends. The critics had received their answer, but they refused to give up. For an hour or more they persisted in angry argument, until the meeting ended in a tumult.

Can you imagine the next day's issue of the *Capernaum News*, if there had been one?

PALSIED MAN HEALED
JESUS OF NAZARETH CLAIMS RIGHT
TO FORGIVE SINS
PROMINENT SCRIBES OBJECT
"BLASPHEMOUS," SAYS LEADING CITIZEN.
"BUT ANYWAY I CAN WALK,"
HEALED MAN RETORTS.

Front page story number one and the day is still young.

One of those who had been attracted by the excitement was a tax collector named Matthew. Being a man of business he could not stay through the argument, but slipped away early and was hard at work when Jesus passed by a few minutes before noon.

"Matthew, I want you," said Jesus.

That was all. No argument; no offer of inducements; no promise of rewards. Merely "I want you"; and the prosperous tax collector closed his office, made a feast for the brilliant young teacher and forthwith announced himself a disciple. . . .

He was advertised by his service, not by his sermons; this is the second noteworthy fact. Nowhere in the Gospels do you find it announced that:

Jesus of Nazareth Will Denounce
The Scribes and Pharisees in the
Central Synagogue
To-night at Eight O'Clock
Special Music

His preaching was almost incidental. On only one occasion did he deliver a long discourse, and that probably interrupted often by questions and debates. He did not come to establish a theology but to lead a life. Living more healthfully than any of his contemporaries he spread health wherever he went. Thinking more daringly, more divinely, he expressed himself in thoughts of surpassing beauty, as naturally as a plant bursts into bloom. His sermons, if they may be called sermons, were chiefly explanatory of his service. He healed a lame man, gave sight to a blind man, fed the hungry, cheered the poor; and by these works he was advertised much more than by his words. . . .

These are Jesus' works, done in Jesus' name. If he were to live again, in these modern days, he would find a way to make them known—to be advertised by his service, not merely by his sermons. One thing is certain: he would not neglect the market-place. . . .

The present day market-place is the newspaper and the magazine. Printed columns are the modern thoroughfares; published advertisements are the cross-roads where the sellers and the buyers meet. Any issue of a national magazine is a world's fair, a bazaar filled with the products of the world's work.

Clothes and clocks and candle-sticks; soup and soap and cigarettes; lingerie and limousines—the best of all of them are there, proclaimed by their makers in persuasive tones. That every other voice should be raised in such great market-places, and the voice of Jesus of Nazareth be still—this is a vital omission which he would find a way to correct. He would be a national advertiser today, I am sure, as he was the great advertiser of his own day. . . .

The Founder of Modern Business

When Jesus was twelve years old his father and mother took him to the Feast at Jerusalem.

It was the big national vacation; even peasant families saved their pennies and looked forward to it through the year. Towns like Nazareth were emptied of their inhabitants except for the few old folks who were left behind to look after the very young ones. Crowds of cheerful pilgrims filled the highways, laughing their way across the hills and under the stars at night.

In such a mass of folk it was not surprising that a boy of twelve should be lost. When Mary and Joseph missed him on the homeward trip, they took it calmly and began a search among the relatives.

The inquiry produced no result. Some remembered having seen him in the Temple, but no one had seen him since. Mary grew frightened: Where could he be? Back there in the city alone? Wandering hungry and tired through the friendless streets? Carried away by other travelers into a distant country? She pictured a hundred calamities. Nervously she and Joseph hurried back over the hot roads, through the suburbs, up through the narrow city streets, up to the courts of the Temple itself.

And there he was.

Not lost; not a bit worried. Apparently unconscious that the Feast was over, he sat in the midst of a group of old men, who were tossing questions at him and applauding the shrewd common sense of his replies. Involuntarily his parents halted—they were simple folk, uneasy among strangers and disheveled by their haste. But after all they *were* his parents, and a very human feeling of irritation quickly overcame their diffidence. Mary stepped forward and grasped his arm.

"Son, why hast thou thus dealt with us?" she demanded. "Behold thy father and I have sought thee sorrowing."

I wonder what answer she expected to receive. Did she ever know exactly what he was going to say: did any one in Nazareth quite understand this keen, eager lad, who had such curious moments of abstraction and was forever breaking out with remarks that seemed so far beyond his years?

He spoke to her now with deference, as always, but in words that did not dispel but rather added to her uncertainty.

"How is it that ye sought me?" he asked. "Wist ye not that I must be about my father's *business*? . .

What interests us most in this one recorded incident of his boyhood is the fact that for the first time he defined the purpose of his career. He did not say, "Wist ye not that I must get ready to meet the arguments of men like these?" The language was quite different, and well worth remembering. "Wist ye not that I must be about my father's *business*?" he said. He thought of his life as *business*. What did he mean by business? To what extent are the principles by which he conducted his business applicable to ours? And if he were among us again, in our highly competitive world, would his business philosophy work?

On one occasion, you recall, he stated his recipe for success. It was on the afternoon when James and John came to ask him what promotion they might expect. They were two of the most energetic of the lot called "Sons of Thunder," by the rest, being noisy and always in the midst of some sort of a storm. They had joined the ranks because they liked him, but with no very definite idea of what it was all about; and now they wanted to know where the enterprise was heading, and just what there would be in it for them.

"Master," they said, "we want to ask what plans you have in mind for us. You're going to need big men around you when you establish your kingdom; our ambition is to sit on either side of you, one on your right and the other on your left."

Who can object to that attitude? If a man fails to look after himself, certainly no one will look after him. If you want a big place, go ask for it. That's the way to get ahead.

Jesus answered with a sentence which sounds poetically absurd.

"Whosoever will be great among you, shall be your minister," he said, "and whosoever of you will be the chiefest, shall be the servant of all."

A fine piece of rhetoric, now isn't it? Be a good servant and you will be great; be the best possible servant and you will occupy the highest possible place. Nice idealistic talk but utterly impractical; nothing to take seriously in a common sense world. That is just what men thought for some hundreds of years; and then, quite suddenly, Business woke up to a great discovery. You will hear that discovery proclaimed in every sales convention as something distinctly modern and up to date. It is emblazoned in the advertising pages of every magazine. . . .

The World's Most Famous Court Trial:
Tennessee Evolution Case

More commonly known as the "monkey trial" the Scopes trial in 1925 was a test case that involved the public school teaching of evolution. When first-year high school teacher John Scopes was indicted for teaching evolution in violation of Tennessee's Butler Act, the case gained national publicity when the famous trial lawyer Clarence Darrow and the American Civil Liberties Union represented Scopes. Across the court aisle providing special counsel to the prosecution was William Jennings Bryan, who was making his last public appearance before his death which came a few days after the completion of the trial. The court found Scopes guilty of the charges, but the State Supreme Court of Tennessee rejected its findings on a technicality. The following transcript excerpt is found in *The World's Most Famous Court Trial: Tennessee Evolution Case* (Cincinnati: National Book Company, 1925).

Q. You have given considerable study to the Bible, haven't you, Mr. Bryan?

A. Yes, sir, I have tried to.

Q. Well, we all know you have, we are not going to dispute that at all. But you have written and published articles almost weekly, and sometimes made interpretations of various things.

A. I would not say interpretations, Mr. Darrow, but comments on the lesson.

Q. If you comment to any extent these comments have been interpretations.

A. I presume that my discussion might be to some extent interpretations, but they have not been primarily intended as interpretations.

Q. But you have studied that question, of course?

A. Of what?

Q. Interpretation of the Bible.

A. On this particular question?

Q. Yes, sir.

A. Yes, sir.

Q. Then you have made a general study of it.

A. Yes, I have. I have studied the Bible for about fifty years, or sometime more than that, but, of course, I have studied it more as I have become older than when I was but a boy.

Q. Do you claim that everything in the Bible should be literally interpreted?

A. I believe everything in the Bible should be accepted as it is given there; some of the Bible is given illustratively. For instance: "Ye are the salt of the earth." I would not insist that man was actually salt, or that he had flesh of salt, but it is used in the sense of salt as saving God's people. . . .

THE WITNESS. These gentlemen have not had much chance—they did not come here to try this case. They came here to try revealed religion. I am here to defend it, and they can ask me any question they please.

THE COURT. All right.

(*Applause from the court yard.*)

MR. DARROW. Great applause from the bleachers.

THE WITNESS. From those whom you call "yokels."

MR. DARROW. I have never called them yokels.

THE WITNESS. That is the ignorance of Tennessee, the bigotry.

MR. DARROW. You mean who are applauding you?

THE WITNESS. Those are the people whom you insult.

MR. DARROW. You insult every man of science and learning in the world because he does not believe in your fool religion.

THE COURT. I will not stand for that.

MR. DARROW. For what he is doing?

THE COURT. I am talking to both of you.

GEN. STEWART. This has gone beyond the pale of a lawsuit, your honor. I have a public duty to perform, under my oath and I ask the court to stop it. Mr. Darrow is making an effort to insult the gentleman on the witness stand, and I ask that it be stopped, for it has gone beyond the pale of a lawsuit. . . .

Q. But when you read that Jonah swallowed the whale—or that the whale swallowed Jonah—how do you literally interpret that?

A. When I read that a big fish swallowed Jonah—it does not say whale.

Q. Doesn't it? Are you sure?

A. That is my recollection of it. A big fish, and I believe it, and I believe in a God who can make a whale and can make a man and make both to do what He pleases.

Q. Mr. Bryan, doesn't the New Testament say whale?

A. I am not sure. My impression is that it says fish; but it does not make so much difference; I merely called your attention to where it says fish—it does not say whale.

Q. But in the New Testament it says whale, doesn't it?

A. That may be true; I cannot remember in my own mind what I read about it.

Q. Now, you say, the big fish swallowed Jonah, and he there remained how long—three days—and then he spewed him upon the land. You believe that the big fish was made to swallow Jonah?

A. I am not prepared to say that; the Bible merely says it was done.

Q. You don't know whether it was the ordinary run of fish, or made for that purpose?

A. You may guess; you evolutionists guess.

Q. But when we do guess, we have a sense to guess right.

A. But do not do it often.

Q. You are not prepared to say whether that fish was made especially to swallow a man or not?

A. The Bible doesn't say, So I am not prepared to say.

Q. You don't know whether that was fixed up especially for the purpose.

A. No, the Bible doesn't say.

Q. But do you believe He made them—that He made such a fish and that it was big enough to swallow Jonah?

A. Yes, sir. Let me add: One miracle is just as easy to believe as another.

Q. It is for me.

A. It is for me.

Q. Just as hard?

A. It is hard to believe for you, but easy for me. A miracle is a thing performed beyond what man can perform. When you get within the realm of miracles; and it is just as easy to believe the miracle of Jonah as any other miracle in the Bible.

Q. Perfectly easy to believe that Jonah swallowed the whale?

A. If the Bible said so; the Bible doesn't make as extreme statements as evolutionists do.

MR. DARROW. That may be a question, Mr. Bryan, about some of those you have known?

A. The only thing is, you have a definition of fact that includes imagination.

Q. And you have a definition that excludes everything but imagination, everything but imagination?

GEN. STEWART. I object to that as argumentative.

THE WITNESS. You . . .

MR. DARROW. The Witness must not argue with me, either.

Q. Do you consider the story of Jonah and the whale a miracle?

A. I think it is . . .

Q. What do you think?

A. I do not think about things I don't think about.

Q. Do you think about things you do think about?

A. Well, sometimes.

(*Laughter in the courtyard.*)

THE POLICEMAN. Let us have order. . . .

Q. Do you think the earth was made in six days?

A. Not six days of twenty-four days.

Q. Doesn't it say so?

GEN. STEWART. I want to interpose another objection. What is the purpose of this examination?

MR. BRYAN. The purpose is to cast ridicule on everybody who believes in the Bible, and I am perfectly willing that the world shall know that these gentlemen have no other purpose than ridiculing every Christian who believes in the Bible.

MR. DARROW. We have the purpose of preventing bigots and ignoramuses from controlling the education of the United States and you know it, and that is all.

MR. BRYAN. I am glad to bring out that statement. I want the world to know that this evidence is not for the view Mr. Darrow and his associates have filed affidavits here stating, the purposes of which I understand it, is to show that the Bible story is not true.

MR. MALONE. Mr. Bryan seems anxious to get some evidence in the record that would tend to show that those affidavits are not true.

MR. BRYAN. I am not trying to get anything into the record. I am simply trying to protect the word of God against the greatest atheist or agnostic in the United States. (*Prolonged applause.*) I want the papers to know I am not afraid to get on the stand in front of him and let him do his worst. I want the world to know. (*Prolonged applause.*)

MR. DARROW. I wish I could get a picture of these clackers.

GEN. STEWART. I am not afraid of Mr. Bryan being perfectly able to take care of himself, but this examination cannot be a legal examination and it cannot be worth a thing in the world, and, your honor, I respectfully except to it, and call on your honor, in the name of all that is legal, to stop this examination and stop it here.

MR. HAYS. I rather sympathize with the general, but Mr. Bryan is produced as a witness because he is a student of the Bible and he presumably understands what the Bible means. He is one of the foremost students in the United States, and we hope to show Mr. Bryan, who is a student of the Bible, what the Bible really means in connection with evolution. Mr. Bryan has already stated that the world is not merely 6,000 years old and that is very helpful to us, and where your evidence is coming from, this Bible which goes to the jury, is that the world started in 4004 B.C.

MR. BRYAN. You think the Bible says that?

MR. HAYS. The one you have taken in evidence says that.

MR. BRYAN. I don't concede that it does.

MR. HAYS. You know that chronology is made up by adding together the ages of the people in the Bible, counting their ages; and now then, let us show the next stage from a Bible student, that these things are not to be taken literally, but each man is entitled to his own interpretation.

GEN. STEWART. The court makes the interpretation.

MR. HAYS. But the court is entitled to information on what is the interpretation of an expert Bible student.

GEN. STEWART. This is resulting in a harangue and nothing else.

MR. DARROW. I didn't do any of the haranguing; Mr. Bryan has been doing that.

GEN. STEWART. You know absolutely you have done it.

MR. DARROW. Oh, all right.

MR. MALONE. Mr. Bryan doesn't need any support.

GEN. STEWART. Certainly he doesn't need any support, but I am doing what I conceive my duty to be, and I don't need any advice, if you please, sir. (*Applause.*)

THE COURT. That would be irrelevant testimony if it was going to the jury. Of course, it is excluded from the jury on the point it is not competent testimony, on the same ground as the affidaviting.

MR. HICKS. Your honor, let me say a word right there. It is in the discretion of the court how long you will allow them to question witnesses for the purpose of taking testimony to the supreme court. Now, we as taxpayers of this county, feel that this has gone beyond reason.

THE COURT. Well, now, that taxpayers' concern doesn't appeal to me so much, when it is only fifteen or twenty minutes time.

MR. DARROW. I would have been through in a half-hour if Mr. Bryan had answered my questions.

GEN. STEWART. They want to put in affidavits as what other witnesses would swear, why not let them put in affidavits as to what Mr. Bryan would swear?

MR. BRYAN. God forbid.

MR. MALONE. I will just make this suggestion. . . .

GEN. STEWART. It is not worth anything to them, if your honor please, even for the record in the supreme court.

MR. HAYS. Is not it worth anything to us if Mr. Bryan will accept the story of creation in detail, and if Mr. Bryan, as a Bible student states you cannot take the Bible necessarily as literally true?

GEN. STEWART. The Bible speaks for itself.

MR. HAYS. You mean to say the Bible itself tells whether these are parables? Does it?

GEN. STEWART. We have left all annals of procedure behind. This is an harangue between Col. Darrow and his witness. He makes so many statements that he is forced to defend himself.

MR. DARROW. I do not do that.

GEN. STEWART. I except to that as not pertinent to this lawsuit.

THE COURT. Of course, it is not pertinent, or it would be before the jury.

GEN. STEWART. It is not worth anything before a jury.

THE COURT. Are you about through, Mr. Darrow?

MR. DARROW. I want to ask a few more questions about the creation.

THE COURT. I know. We are going to adjourn when Mr. Bryan comes off the stand for the day. Be very brief, Mr. Darrow. Of course, I believe I will make myself clearer. Of course, it is incompetent testimony before the jury. The only reason I am allowing this to go in at all is that they may have it in the appellate courts, as showing what the affidavit would be.

MR. BRYAN. The reason I am answering is not for the benefit of the superior court. It is to keep these gentlemen from saying I was afraid to meet them and let them question me, and I want the Christian world to know that any atheist, agnostic, unbeliever, can question me any time as to my belief in God, and I will answer him.

MR. DARROW. I want to take an exception to this conduct of this witness. He may be very popular down here in the hills. I do not need his explanation for his answer.

THE COURT. Yes.

MR. BRYAN. If I had not, I would not have answered the question.

MR. HAYS. May I be heard? I do not want your honor to think we are asking questions of Mr. Bryan with the expectation that the higher court will not say that those questions are proper testimony. The reason I state that is this, your law speaks for the Bible. Your law does not say the literal interpretation of the Bible. If Mr. Bryan, who is a student of the Bible, will state that everything in the Bible need not be interpreted literally, that each man must judge for himself; if he will state that, of course, then your honor would charge the jury. We are not bound by a literal interpretation of the Bible. If I have made my argument clear enough for the attorney-general to understand, I will retire.

GEN. STEWART. I will admit you have frequently been difficult of comprehension, and I think you are as much to blame as I am.

MR. HAYS. I know I am. . . .

Q. Mr. Bryan, do you believe that the first woman was Eve?

A. Yes.

Q. Do you believe she was literally made out of Adam's rib?

A. I do.

Q. Did you ever discover where Cain got his wife?

A. No sir; I leave the agnostics to hunt for her.

Q. You have never found out?

A. I have never tried to find.

Q. You have never tried to find?

A. No.

Q. The Bible says he got one, doesn't it? Were there other people on the earth at that time?

A. I cannot say.

Q. You cannot say. Did that ever enter your consideration?

A. Never bothered me.

Q. There are not others recorded, but Cain got a wife.

A. That is what the Bible says.

Q. Where she came from you do not know. All right. Does the statement, "The morning and the evening were the first day," and "The morning and the evening were the second day," mean anything to you?

A. I do not think it necessarily means a twenty-four-hour day.

Q. You do not?

A. No.

Q. What do you consider it to be?

A. I have not attempted to explain it. If you will take the second chapter—let me have the book. (*Examining Bible.*) The fourth verse of the second chapter says: "These are the generation of the heavens and of the earth, when they were created in the day that the Lord God made the earth and the heavens," the word "day" there in the very next chapter is used to describe a period. I do not see that there is any necessity for constructing the words, "the evening and the morning," as meaning necessarily a twenty-four day, "in the day when the Lord made the heaven and the earth."

Q. Then, when the Bible said, for instance, "and God called the firmament heaven. And the evening and the morning were the second day," that does not necessarily mean twenty-four hours?

A. I do not think it necessarily does.

Q. Do you think it does or does not?

A. I know a great many think so.

Q. What do you think?

A. I do not think it does.

Q. You think those were not literal days?

A. I do not think they were twenty-four-hour days?

Q. What do you think about it?

A. That is my opinion—I do not know that my opinion is better on that subject than those who think it does.

Q. You do not think that?

A. No. But I think it would be just as easy for the kind of God we believe in to make the earth in six days as in six years or in 6,000,000 years or in 600,000,000 years. I do not think it important whether we believe one or the other.

Q. Do you think those were literal days?

A. My impression is they were periods, but I would not attempt to argue as against anybody who wanted to believe in literal days.

Q. Have you any idea of the length of the periods?

A. No; I don't.

Q. Do you think the sun was made on the fourth day?

A. Yes.

Q. And they had evening and morning without the sun?

A. I am simply saying it is a period.

Q. They had evening and morning for four periods without the sun, do you think?

A. I believe in creation as there told, and if I am not able to explain it I will accept it. Then you can explain it to suit yourself.

Q. Mr. Bryan, what I want to know is, do you believe the sun was made on the fourth day?

A. I believe just as it says there. . . .

15 Religion in the Age of Depression

. . . My house shall be called a house of prayer; but you are making it a robbers' den.

—Matt. 21:13

Humanist Manifesto I

A climax of humanist trends that had long been developing came in 1933 with the issuing of a Humanist Manifesto signed by fourteen Unitarian and Universalist ministers, a rabbi, eleven professors, and numerous independent writers and thinkers. Among the signees were educator John Dewey and historian Harry Elmer Barnes. They confessed to a belief in a new religion called Humanism, which they expected would soon be acknowledged "as the logical faith of those whose modern point of view forces them to abandon the inevitable supernaturalism of the theistic position." It was not atheistic, said one signee, but a movement which "simply ignores the existence of God." Though it went largely unnoticed by the American population at large, it did reflect "a creed of official anti-God religion" in the minds of some onlookers.

Preface

Humanism is a philosophical, religious, and moral point of view as old as human civilization itself. It has its roots in classical China, Greece, and Rome; it is expressed in the Renaissance and the Enlightenment, in the scientific revolution, and in the twentieth century.

Each age seeks to define what its distinctive values are, what it seeks to cherish and enhance. Each age has to contend with alienating and restrictive forces that seek to denigrate the individual, undermine humane values, and suppress social justice.

In the twentieth century, humanist awareness has developed at a rapid pace; yet it has

From Paul Kurtz (ed.), *Humanist Manifestos I and II* (Buffalo, N.Y.: Prometheus Books). Copyright © 1973 by Prometheus Books. Reprinted by permission of the publisher.

to overcome powerful antihumanist forces that seek to destroy it.

In 1933 a group of thirty-four liberal humanists in the United States defined and enunciated the philosophical and religious principles that seemed to them fundamental. They drafted Humanist Manifesto I, which for its time was a radical document. It was concerned with expressing a general religious and philosophical outlook that rejected orthodox and dogmatic positions and provided meaning and direction, unity and purpose to human life. It was committed to reason, science, and democracy. . . .

The time has come for widespread recognition of the radical changes in religious beliefs throughout the modern world. The time is past for mere revision of traditional attitudes. Science and economic change have disrupted the old beliefs. Religions the world over are under the necessity of coming to terms with new conditions created by a vastly increased knowledge and experience. In every field of human activity, the vital movement is now in the direction of a candid and explicit humanism. In order that religious humanism may be better understood we, the undersigned, desire to make certain affirmations which we believe the facts of our contemporary life demonstrate.

There is great danger of a final, and we believe fatal, identification of the word *religion* with doctrines and methods which have lost their significance and which are powerless to solve the problem of human living in the Twentieth Century. Religions have always been means for realizing the highest values of life. Their end has been accomplished through the interpretation of the total environing situation (theology or world view), the sense of values resulting therefrom (goal or ideal), and the technique (cult) established for realizing the satisfactory life. A change in any of these factors results in alteration of the outward forms of religion. This fact explains the changefulness of religions through the centuries. But through all changes religion itself remains constant in its quest for abiding values, an inseparable feature of human life.

Today's man's larger understanding of the universe, his scientific achievements, and his deeper appreciation of brotherhood, have created a situation which requires a new statement of the means and purposes of religion. Such a vital, fearless, and frank religion capable of furnishing adequate social goals and personal satisfactions may appear to many people as a complete break with the past. While this age does owe a vast debt to traditional religions, it is none the less obvious that any religion that can hope to be a synthesizing and dynamic force for today must be shaped for the needs of this age. To establish such a religion is a major necessity of the present. It is a responsibility which rests upon this generation. We therefore affirm the following:

First: Religious humanists regard the universe as self-existing and not created.

Second: Humanism believes that man is a part of nature and that he has emerged as the result of a continuous process.

Third: Holding an organic view of life, humanists find that the traditional dualism of mind and body must be rejected.

Fourth: Humanism recognizes that man's religious culture and civilization, as clearly depicted by anthropology and history, are the product of a gradual development due to his interaction with his natural environment and with his social heritage. The individual born into a particular culture is largely molded to that culture.

Fifth: Humanism asserts that the nature of the universe depicted by modern science makes unacceptable any supernatural or cosmic guarantees of human values. Obviously humanism does not deny the possibility of realities as yet undiscovered, but it does insist that the way to determine the existence and value of any and all realities is by means of intelligent inquiry and by the assessment of their relation to human needs. Religion must formulate its hopes and plans in the light of the scientific spirit and method.

Sixth: We are convinced that the time has passed for theism, deism, modernism, and the several varieties of "new thought."

Seventh: Religion consists of those actions, purposes, and experiences which are humanly significant. Nothing human is alien to the religious. It includes labor, art, science, philosophy, love, friendship, recreation—all that is in its degree expressive of intelligently satisfying human living. The distinction between the sacred and the secular can no longer be maintained.

Eighth: Religious humanism considers the complete realization of human personality to be the end of man's life and seeks its development and fulfillment in the here and now. This is the explanation of the humanist's social passion.

Ninth: In place of the old attitudes involved in worship and prayer the humanist finds his religious emotions expressed in a heightened sense of personal life and in a cooperative effort to promote social well-being.

Tenth: It follows that there will be no uniquely religious emotions and attitudes of the kind hitherto associated with belief in the supernatural.

Eleventh: Man will learn to face the crises of life in terms of his knowledge of their naturalness and probability. Reasonable and manly attitudes will be fostered by education and supported by custom. We assume that humanism will take the path of social and mental hygiene and discourage sentimental and unreal hopes and wishful thinking.

Twelfth: Believing that religion must work increasingly for joy in living, religious humanists aim to foster the creative in man and to encourage achievements that add to the satisfactions of life.

Thirteenth: Religious humanism maintains that all associations and institutions exist for the fulfillment of human life. The intelligent evaluation, transformation, control, and direction of such associations and institutions with a view to the enhancement of human life is the purpose and program of humanism. Certainly religious institutions, their ritualistic forms, ecclesiastical methods, and communal activities must be reconstituted as rapidly as experience allows, in order to function effectively in the modern world.

Fourteenth: The humanists are firmly convinced that existing acquisitive and profit-motivated society has shown itself to be inadequate and that a radical change in methods, controls, and motives must be instituted. A socialized and cooperative economic order must be established to the end that the equitable distribution of the means of life be possible.

The goal of humanism is a free and universal society in which people voluntarily and intelligently cooperate for the common good. Humanists demand a shared life in a shared world.

Fifteenth and last: We assert that humanism will: (a) affirm life rather than deny it; (b) seek to elicit the possibilities of life, not flee from it; and (c) endeavor to establish the conditions of a satisfactory life for all, not merely for the few. By this positive *morale* and intention humanism will be guided, and from this perspective and alignment the techniques and efforts of humanism will flow.

So stands the theses of religious humanism. Though we consider the religious forms and ideas of our fathers no longer adequate, the quest for the good life is still the central task for mankind. Man is at last becoming aware that he alone is responsible for the realization of the world of his dreams, that he has within himself the power for its achievement. He must set intelligence and will to the task.

[concluded with names of 34 signers]

A Christian Manifesto
Edwin Lewis

Edwin Lewis (1881-1959) was born in England and educated in Canada, Scotland, and the United States. From 1918 to 1951 he was professor of systematic theology and philosophy of religion at Drew Theological Seminary in Madison, New Jersey. Upon his retirement from Drew, he taught for a time at Temple University in Philadelphia. In the late 1920s while he was editing the *Abingdon Bible Commentary*, Lewis changed his own understanding of the Christian faith. He moved from modern liberalism to neo-orthodoxy, and in the process acknowledged the extensive influence of Karl Barth. In his best known book, *A Christian Manifesto*, he describes his rejection of his former liberalism and criticizes the church, especially his own Methodist Episcopal Church, for abandoning the heart of the gospel and becoming too involved in the world. Like other spokesmen of neo-orthodoxy, however, he did not reject the social gospel or modern science.

Forward

In the fall number, 1933, of *Religion in Life*, I published an article entitled "The Fatal Apostasy of the Modern Church." The article attracted a good deal of attention, if I may judge by the correspondence arising from it. Most of the letters I received expressed gratitude for the position I took in the article. A considerable number, however, were definitely hostile (the word is not too strong). I was told that I had evidently "gone Barthian," that I had "sold out to the Fundamentalists," that I had "abandoned my own cause," that clearly I had "passed my creative period and was becoming senile and conservative," and so on. I was remind-ed of certain books I had written, and of the theological position which those books were generally supposed to represent, and I was asked if I desired to be regarded as a man who had "slipped back into orthodoxy." Nobody enjoys criticism of this kind, especially when it comes, as much of it did, from loyal friends whose affection one would wish to keep. But some things cannot but be as they are, and some steps are taken not of choice but of necessity. Consistency is always a consideration, but consistency may come too high. The intellectual record is far less important than the moral record, and it may be that the first must be marred to keep the second intact.

Many who read the article referred to above urged me to elaborate it into a book. I was loath to do so, partly because I was conscious of the ferment in my own mind, and partly because I realized how sharply the implications of the article cut across much of the accepted thinking of the time. The hesitation, however, had the curious result of clarifying my own mind at the very points where I had been most uncertain, and when that had taken place, the natural shrinking from what I know is inevitable criticism largely disappeared, and I wrote the book. Because the book is intended primarily as "A Christian Manifesto," I have tried to keep it free from the usual paraphernalia of mere scholarship. In the first half of the book, however, it seemed impossible to avoid some discussion of certain rather technical questions raised by modern criticism. I have tried to keep the discussion of them as simple as possible.

Just as I was finishing the book, one day, after a class in which I had been saying some of the things here written, a student came to me and said, "Professor, I think that something has happened lately deep down inside of you." I did not deny it. The real question is as to the *meaning* of what "happened."

Chapter IX: The Great Tribulation

Our age prides itself on being pragmatic. It burns its incense at the shrine of the great god "Results." It has surrendered to the guidance of the efficiency expert, and the basic principle of the efficiency expert seems to be that nothing is justifiable which cannot show a definite, tangible, measurable result. Action for the joy of the action, emotion for the sake of the emotion, belief for the satisfaction it yields, life as an end in itself—in many quarters these are all tabooed. Apparently, the only reason for your existence is that you might "bring things to pass." You must count that day wasted on which you have not "done things," and the "things" to be "done" are such as can be put down in black and white, entered in a ledger, where they may be seen by the eyes of all. The measuring rod could well enough be chosen for the symbol of the age in which we live: perhaps it will be done for us by some future historian. State policies, educational practice, economic readjustments, social schemes of all sorts, are to be judged exclusively by how well they conform to a neatly turned pragmatic yardstick. The whole of life is to be regimented. The individual is to be as "totalitarianized" as the state. The goose step is to be universalized—and the race will then be a flock of geese! Somebody is to say "Go!" and we are all to move in a prearranged way to a prearranged position, having reached which we are again to move when the same somebody is once more moved to say "Go!" Spontaneity is to be abolished. Individuality is to be penalized. Qualities just as these interfere with the precision of the social machine. A straight line is the shortest distance between two points, and the most efficient man is the man who can travel that shortest distance in the least time. It matters not that he is so intent on reaching his goal that he has never a moment on the way for beautiful sights and melodious sounds. Even our homes, we are told, are to be built on the straight-line principle, architecturally and every other way. Slough off the superfluous! Do away with unnecessary movements! It never seems to occur to the reformers that since the time and energy that are "saved" by their devices are only saved so that still other "things" may be "done," more bridge may be played, more radio buttons may be turned, the alleged "gains" may prove in the end to be of very doubtful advantage. A man does today in two hours what called yesterday for four hours—and we name that "progress." It may be that or it may not. What does he do with the two hours he has "saved?" If he uses them for "increased productivity" of what nobody wants or can buy, or if he adds them to his "leisure" which he does not know how to use, of what advantage is the saving? It is infinitely more important that a man should be enabled to find joy of his work than it is that he should ever be seeking to lessen the amount of it. It is infinitely more important that ways should be devised whereby the conditions under which work is done should be agreeable than it is that ways should be devised in the name of "efficiency" for getting out of a man every last bit of productivity of which he is capable. In a word, it is indefinitely more important that life should be judged by the satisfactions that accompany it and that these satisfactions be of the kind that are lasting, than it is that life should be judged by its "measurable output"—measurable because of the value it has in the exchange markets of the world.

Under the leadership of "practical" men, this utilitarian and efficiency philosophy has laid hold upon the modern church. Anyone who knows what has been going on in American Protestantism during the last twenty years or so knows that too many of its leaders have conceived the church as exclusively an "organization" to be "run" according to the most approved "business methods." I am far from suggesting that the conducting of the affairs of the church does not call for common sense. Where property and funds and social obligations of various sorts are involved, it goes without saying that there should be the most scrupulous care in their use and administration! Carelessness is none the less blamable because it is connected with the corporate aspects of religion: If anything, it is the more blamable. Nevertheless, when it is supposed—as it has been—that the cultivation and propagation of religious faith calls for the same methods that are employed by "men of the world" as they seek their ends, then religion is given an almost fatal blow. If there is one thing more than another that religion needs to do in our time, it is to bear witness to another side of life and that form of reality which is present to men at almost every moment of their secular pursuits. Yet what have we seen happening but the attempt of religion to "talk the language of the street?" Without question, religion should make every possible effort to win the hearing of men, but when "a religious talk" (an impossible phrase!) is couched in the same language as "a sales talk," it is only natural that the audience should suppose that the speaker is trying to "sell something." Indeed, of all the abominations that have entered the vocabulary of modern religious propaganda, incomparably the worst is the expression that "the church is in the business of selling religion." Religion—at least, Christianity—ought to be the one thing in all the world which should be kept free from the suggestion of the market place: which, by the way, is very far from saying that religion is to be kept out of business. Only, you do not necessarily get religion into business simply by teaching religion to talk business jargon. Do you "sell" the music of the spheres, or "buy" the beauties of "rosy-fingered dawn?" It is true that you may need to be taught how to appreciate these great free gifts of God to his creatures, but to "buy" them or to "sell" them—no! The church is confronted with a task incredibly great in bringing the appeal of religion to bear upon an age such as ours; but if the church thinks that because the age is "business-minded" and "pragmatic," the message of religion must be couched in business terms and its appeal be based on pragmatic considerations, and that the success of the church is to be judged by an auditing committee, then the church is surely sounding its own death-knell.

I would not presume to be critical of the church in general as respects matters such as these, but I may perhaps be conceded the right to speak frankly of the particular church to which I belong. Concerning that church at least, I am sure I am not wrong when I say that we have too generally abandoned the passion which was once our glory and which had no great difficulty in finding appropriate avenues of expression: we have abandoned the passion for carefully worked out programs which had "efficiency" written all over them, but which have been strangely futile in keeping the fires burning on the altars of the church and in bringing the gospel to bear in an overwhelming way

on the life of the world. I have what I believe is a justly grounded pride in the history and achievements of Methodism, the church in which I was cradled and to which I have given my life. It has written a great chapter in the story of Christian conquest. It has done a work for Jesus Christ second to none done by any other branch of Protestantism. In the Old World and in the New, and in the lands beyond the seas, it has borne a valiant and successful testimony of the power of the Evangel in the transformation of human lives and in the creation of social institutions which seek the good of men. It can be only a question of time before the Methodist Church as such must cease to exist as a separate entity and be gathered up into a reunited Protestantism—dare one say even a reunited Christendom? But its contribution when that day comes will be of value in proportion to its continued loyalty to the spirit and the faith and the purpose in which it has its origin. And what we have seen in recent years all along the line has been a weakening of that loyalty because we have fallen victim to the lure of grandiose schemes whose counterparts in the secular world are the hundred story skyscraper, the vast corporation whose energies head up at the cash register, the advertising "drive" aimed to reach "the last man" by whatever means may be. Anyone who knows the life of our church for the last twenty years or so knows that under the goading of the "experts" we have adopted scheme after scheme, participated in drive after drive, set ourselves even the impossible task of making America "dry" by legislation, and the total result of the prodigious efforts—what is it? That there is some gain in the total need not to be denied, but there has certainly been much more of loss. We have created in the minds of many a totally false conception of nature and the function of the Christian Church. We have laid financial and property burdens on the backs of our people that either altogether discourage them or demand so much of their time and energy that little is left for active and aggressive and constructive Christian work. We have built churches that we can neither pay for nor adequately man. We have thrown out a missionary line so long that it lacks depth and striking power, and so detached from sacrificial support at home that its chief occupation in recent years has been conducting strategic retreats. We have incurred the distrust, even the antagonism, of great numbers of people in America because we have suffered the machinery of the church to be operated for the ends which, while moral in themselves, were foolishly made contingent on political action. It is questionable whether even yet we have learned our lesson, for if it was an error to commit the church to legislative Prohibition, it is equally an error to commit it to legislative Socialism. "A bigger and better Church" had been our slogan, but let those who know the truth tell, if they dare, what we meant by "bigger" and what we meant by "better." We borrowed our criteria of evaluation from the world about us—a world gone mad in its worship of mere size, a world that had set itself to create bigger ships, bigger aeroplanes, bigger locomotives, bigger buildings, bigger universities, bigger corporations, bigger banks, bigger everything—except men! It will be well if the monstrous Frankenstein does not yet turn and rend us. And we were guilty of the incredible folly of supposing that "Christ's church was of this world," to be judged by the world's standards, to be modeled on the world's ways, to walk in the world's procession, and to keep step to the crashing discord of its brazen shawms. The result could not be but what it has been. We have seen the bursting of the inflated bubble into which a mad world poured its lungs. The huge thing was mostly air—and the church may be grateful if it has escaped going so completely flat as the world it sought to imitate.

You will say that this is nothing but rhetorical pessimism. Nevertheless look about you. In a time like this, the church which ought to be as a lion rampant is as a lion supine—supine because an enemy has it by the throat. The enemy is naturalism, or if you prefer the more recent term, secularism, which is but a new name for an ancient foe. Not once nor twice in the long history of the church has that enemy threatened it, but it is to be questioned if ever before the threat was so menacing, the peril so deadly. What makes the peril so deadly is the fact that the supineness of the church today comes rather of a weakening from within than because of an overpowering force from without. The church can never be overthrown save as it abandons its own natural defense, which is the faith once received. Let it keep that, and the gates of hell cannot prevail against it. Let it surrender that, and it puts itself in competition with a secular spirit before which it is as impotent as a newborn babe before a pack of wolves. Are there not signs that to a very considerable extent the church has made that surrender? There has been a chiseling of the ancient faith: Wherefore the defenses of the church are weakening, and wild beasts beginning to trample over the erstwhile pleasant vineyard of the Lord.

Why the surrender? Because as a church we listened too readily to those who assured us that unless we spoke a new language the world would not heed our message. We were told that we had come into a new age—a fact which nobody would want to deny. We were told that therefore we must cut our garment according to the cloth, which turns out to have been only another way of saying that before we delivered our message we were to be sure that our message had the approval of the censors. To their everlasting honor be it said that there were those among us as there have always been, who would not so easily be deprived their convictions. They were willing to be counted as refuse that so they might gain Christ and proclaim Him and His gospel to others. Not of these do I speak now, save to express the hope that their tribe may increase. I am speaking, rather, of that vast body in the church who followed the lead of those who saw in the church nothing whatever but a social institution, whose test of its worth was a purely external test, and who would eliminate from its faith, and therefore from its message, everything that savored of "other-worldliness." I am not questioning their *motive*. I am quite sure that they "meant all right." Nevertheless, they were blind, and we were as blind who followed them. They wanted the church to be a great and glorious reality in the nation's life—and who of us would not? They saw visions and they dreamed dreams—and may the vision never pass nor the dreams vanish! But what they saw could never come by the means which they advocated.

Five Years of the New Deal
Charles Coughlin

Charles Coughlin (1891-1979), better known as the "radio priest," rose to fame during the 1930s. The Great Depression spawned many fiery preachers who played upon the emotions of the American populace, but none was more revered by his followers and loathed by his opponents than Father Coughlin. As the poverty and unrest of the depression beset America in 1930, Coughlin used the radio broadcasts from his parish in Royal Oak, Michigan, the Shrine of the Little Flower, to spread his political opinions. In 1932 he climbed on the Roosevelt bandwagon, but by 1934 he had moved away from the New Deal and spoke in favor of isolationism and anti-unionism. Due to the controversies which surrounded his broadcasts, in 1936 CBS dropped his program, but Coughlin continued the broadcasts on his own network of stations. That same year he formed his own Union Party and was rebuked by his Catholic Church superiors for attacking labor and the New Deal, as well as for his friendly references to Hitler and Mussolini.[*]

Motivated by a spirit of helpfulness and construction, I am impelled to offer you an explanation of my attitude towards the New Deal both prior to November, 1936 and following that date.

For more than ten years I was acutely conscious of the failure on the part of the government to act for the common welfare of the people. I was aware that politics in America had so degenerated that Congress became the protector and abettor of the social crimes committed by capitalism in the name of law and good government. The party leaders of both Democrats and Republi-

cans, to my mind, were nothing more than supine servants of the financial classes. Plutocracy, the wolf which devoured the substance of the laboring and agricultural classes, reigned supreme in the sheep's clothing of democracy.

Thus, as early as 1928 I was happy to cast my lot with those whom capitalism and so-called democracy were exploiting in the name of sound economics and of sound government.

By 1932 I became a public sponsor of the New Deal because it pledged to drive the

---

The selection is from his *Sixteen Radio Lectures*, 1938 Series (Royal Oak, Mich.: Rev. Chas. E. Coughlin, 1938), pp. 79-88. Used by permission of the Shrine of the Little Flower.

money changers and their servants from the temple. Like millions of Americans, I was convinced that the greedy individualism of capitalism had run its course; that living annual wages would be substituted for insufficient hourly wages; that the gospel of plenty would supplant the gospel of scarcity; and that the private control of money and, through it, of government, of prosperity and of human lives, would cease forthwith.

By 1934 I began to suffer the pangs of disillusionment. I suspected that the policy of the New Dealers was unsound when I discovered that the commercial gold of the United States had been confiscated for the private use of the privately owned Federal Reserve Banking System and was not nationalized for the common use of the American public. Gradually this suspicion gave way to moral certainty when the new Banking Act of 1935 made it plain to every informed person that this government had no intention of destroying the monopoly of money; that it still persisted in permitting a small group of citizens to issue and control, on a scarcity level, 95 percent of the life-blood of our nation—its money—and thereby curtail the productivity of factories and farms and the purchasing power of our people.

Planned want in the midst of plenty, although not advertised, was still the order of the day.

It is true that the hungry were fed, that the naked were clothed and the homeless sheltered. It is true that certain public works were undertaken to alleviate unemployment, but it was still true that these things were accomplished through manufactured credit borrowed by our Government from privately owned banks to whom the very recipients of the crust of bread and the rag of clothing were obligated, through the process of taxation, to restore wealth-money for the debt-money which had been borrowed.

The fundamental economic error which had characterized the administration of Hoover, of Coolidge and their predecessors in office, was accepted by the New Deal. Accidentally the New Deal differed from the Old Deal. Substantially, one was the left wing and the other the right wing of the same bird of prey.

If similar causes produced similar effects, it was a foregone conclusion that a similar depression was just around the corner for America.

Deliberately, therefore, in 1936 I chose to stand in the unpopular side at a moment when the majority of my fellow citizens still believed that the policies of the New Deal were remedial.

Although the laboring class and many of the agricultural class were not conscious of the deception practiced upon them, nevertheless, my conscience would not permit me to sustain them in their error lest, at a later and inevitable date, when this bad tree would produce only the bad fruit of another depression, I should be blamed as being partly responsible for the disaster about to follow.

Permit me, therefore, to present to you official facts and figures to sustain the statement that the New Deal is still wedded to a policy of wealth concentration and scarcity.

Surrounding us are 14-million able-bodied citizens unemployed through no fault of their own. The vast majority of them are under forty years of age.

Never before was Government relief so necessary as at the moment. Local governments at Detroit, Philadelphia, Buffalo, Minneapolis, Cleveland, Seattle and elsewhere are endeavoring to feed and clothe their starving populations after all their funds have been exhausted.

"We planned it that way and don't let anybody tell you to the contrary," are the unfortunate words of our Chief Executive, who was responsible for spending 10-billion dollars on relief that failed to relieve, and for piling up a national debt of 38-billion dollars.

Confronted with this crisis, Mr. Morgenthau, the Secretary of the Treasury, in an official statement recently said:

> This situation is most acute. I consider it a very serious emergency. For the unemployed it could not be worse.

> Whether we have reached the bottom of this downturn or not, I do not know and I do not think anybody else knows.

These are bitter words for the millions who, a few years ago, thought they did not know; humiliating words for those who, with pontifical certitude, maintained that the back of the depression had been broken.

In his statement, the Secretary of the Treasury inadvertently admitted the point long since maintained that this Administration does not know where it is going and has sustained the argument that the more bankers' credit money the nation borrows, the darker is the prospect for all its citizens.

What has resulted from the insane taxation which this kind of borrowing necessitated? Last year the sum of 375-million dollars was collected as the undistributed corporation surplus tax.

Stocks and bonds depreciated 30-billion dollars in 1937.

A shrinkage of 7-billion dollars in the surplus funds of business concerns is recorded on the books of our nation since 1933—7 billion dollars less with which to operate factories, hire laborers and pay wages.

Only an untutored child could applaud such a tax policy, thinking that such huge levies against industry pointed towards the redistribution of wealth. Every thoughtful person knows the present tax policy in concentrating wealth in the hands of Federal Reserve bankers for whom labor and industry and agriculture and commerce are all working.

And many analytical minds go a step beyond this thought to a more pertinent conclusion. They are conscious that this is the beginning of state socialism; for after the Federal Reserve Banks and the bondholders will have gained ownership or control over the action, then it will be possible for a government, that confessedly admits it does not know how far this thing is going, to seize the Federal Reserve Banks and gain control of the wealth of the state.

"How could this Administration have done otherwise?" questions the innocent critic.

The answer is brief. By constitutional authority Congress has the right to coin and issue and regulate the value of money. Against the billions of dollars of idle gold buried in the vaults of Kentucky, Congress could have issued its own credit, tax-free; Congress could have issued an adequate amount of currency to raise the price levels to a proper standard.

This appears to be recognized by every informed person except the officials at Washington.

Even the *Wall Street Journal*, on February 16, 1938 states:

> The essential thing involved in the issue of more currency is that it increases the supply of price-measured money. . . .

> The sole function of bank credit is the making of exchanges . . . the volume of substantial bank credit does not act upon prices at all.

Thus, even the bankers' economists indirectly inveigh against this Administration for keeping a scarcity of money in circulation with its consequent scarcity of production, scarcity of employment and scarcity of bread and butter, or clothing and shelter in the midst of plenty.

Time after time you have heard spokesmen for this administration decry the poverty which surrounds us and castigate the economic royalists who are exploiting our people. For five years the airways have been thundering with denunciations of the princes of privilege. But after years of this wordy war, after the smoke of the sham battle has cleared away, behold, the princes of privilege are more secure in their privileges following five years of the New Deal than they were before it.

Here is the official picture of "before and after," painted by New Deal Government statisticians: In 1929, 93 percent of our people received incomes under $5,000. This represented 60 percent of the total wealth produced in that year. Seven percent of our population obtained 40 percent of the national income and they represented people receiving more than $5,000 a year.

That was back in 1929. Those official figures certainly gave us something to complain about relative to the uneconomic distribution of wealth—93 percent of our population with 60 percent of its wealth, representing incomes under $5,000 a year; and 7 percent of our population with 40 percent of the income, representing persons with incomes over $5,000 a year. But what are the latest available figures after five years of New Deal activity and rhetoric?

From the Federal Reserve Bulletin we find that 96.7 percent of all deposits, according to number and not according to amount, in member banks of the Federal Reserve, were $2,500 or less. In other words, 33-million depositors—96.7 percent of all depositors—were in the $2,500 or less, with deposits amounting in their total to 5-billion 800-million dollars or 22 percent of the total deposits of the nation.

Keep that figure clearly in mind: 96.7 percent of our population hold only 22 percent of the total deposits.

The same chart shows that 49,000 depositors own 12-billion 800-million dollars or 42.8 percent of all deposits; that a little more than one-tenth of one percent of our depositors had in the banks more than twice as much as 96.7 percent of all the depositors. And almost 90-million people have no deposits at all in the Federal Reserve Banks and their affiliates.

There is a picture for you. Under the New Deal wealth has become more concentrated and poverty more widespread than they were under the Old Deal.

To bear out this statement with another proof, I invite you to read Volume One, page 32 of Senate Document No. 415 of the Sixty-Fourth Congress in its first session.

In that year, 1916, the United States Commission on Industrial Relations, in its final report and testimony says:

> The ownership of wealth in the United States has become concentrated to a degree which is difficult to grasp.

> The rich 2 percent of the people own 60 percent of the wealth; the middle class, 33 percent of the people, own 35 percent of the wealth; the poor, 65 percent of the people, own 5 percent of the wealth.

Contrast the condition of wealth concentration and mass poverty with 1937. In 1937, 35 percent of our people owned scarcely any wealth. Sixty-four percent of our people owned outright only 10 percent of our wealth. One and seven-tenths percent of our people owned and controlled 90 percent of the wealth.

Ladies and gentlemen, let us be honest even though we are critical. Whose chief responsibility is this chaotic condition of affairs? We maintain that the party system of government, broadly speaking, and the Congress of the United States, specifically speaking, must share the major portion of blame for these outrageous conditions.

Congress is the law-making body. It has failed to pass equitable laws, and in doing so it has not only left Congressmen open to attack but it has called into question the advisability of continuing with a Congress of the United States.

In no sense am I even intimating a return to the Old Deal with its abject disregard of human rights even though I cannot support the present policies of the New Deal which have produced the record which I have exposed to you.

It is the New Deal record, it is not mine.

In no sense am I suggesting the adoption either of state socialism which is identified with Communism or of parliamentary socialism which, under the guise of democracy, sizes industry, enslaves labor, regiments agriculture and protects the private coinage and regulation of money for the international bankers.

I am appealing for a restoration of American democracy divorced from partyism and pledged to the service of all people independent of party, of race and of creed. I am appealing to all classes, rich and poor alike, to sacrifice, if necessary, the ephemeral value of debt bonds in order to save our institutions and our people from being converted to the fallacies of Fascism or Communism through the inefficiency of a Congress that could, if it would, issue sufficient money to enable wealth to be produced and consumed with a living annual wage for all who are willing to work and able to work.

Failing to do this, our present Congressmen are betraying the traditions of our fathers, the spirit of our people and the usefulness of representative government.

It is impossible to continue with the dole system forever; 10-billion dollars spent over a period of five years left us worse off than we were. Its record has taught that lesson to everyone.

And, above all, it is doubly absurd to continue with the scarcity program under the pretext that there was over-production when, as a matter of fact, there is sinful, malicious under-consumption.

Do you doubt that statement? Permit me to prove it with official figures submitted by the very Government which advocates the policy of destruction, and bear with me while I cite New Deal statistics to prove that the chief beneficiaries of agricultural doles were the so-called princes of privilege.

Mr. Wallace, the Secretary of Agriculture, recently was asked to disclose the names of the beneficiaries of agriculture doles. He was reluctant to do so. Finally, Congress compelled him to submit only those names of persons who had received more than $10,000 of agricultural dole.

Thus, we find that 21 big rice growers in Louisiana, Arkansas, Texas and California received over $800,000 of these farm benefits—nearly $40,000 each.

Seventy-four corporations and other concerns in Louisiana received an average of $50,000 each to not produce sugar. One sugar producer received $256,000 not to raise sugar.

In the island of Puerto Rico one sugar monopoly received nearly $1,000,000 to let its lands lie fallow, and 28 other concerns received an average of $33,000 each not to produce sugar.

Three big cotton concerns in Arkansas and two in Mississippi received nearly $500,000 not to grow cotton. The State penitentiary of Mississippi was paid $43,200 not to grow cotton as if cotton growing was the business of the State penitentiary. One corporation in California was paid $157,020 and another one in New Jersey was paid $45,000 not to raise hogs.

Twenty-seven beet-sugar producers in California and Colorado were paid approximately $540,000 not to produce sugar beets.

The Delta Pine and Land Company was paid more then $60,000 and the Arizona Citrus Land Company received $47,000 under the Soil Conservation Act. The Equitable Life

Assurance Company was paid $80,000 of these farm benefits.

Oh, yes, the New Deal was of great assistance to the farmers of the nation in view of these official figures which I have read to you—Official figures which prove that the New Deal has been wedded to big business and to the money changers.

As far back as 1934 and 1936 I was intimating these things to the American people who could not lend credence to them because they were so fantastic.

Nevertheless, since we are in the mood of give statistics and official figures, kindly consider these facts which are now uncontradictable because this Government has been forced through its own officials to publish them.

While the Government was busied in plowing under cotton and paying monopolists and private farmers not to produce sugar and hogs and wheat and corn, what was happening in America?

It is now officially disclosed that last year we imported 1-billion 600-million dollars worth of agricultural products and substitutes valuated as such in foreign money and priced at 3-billion 200-million dollars in American money.

Specifically, during 1937 we imported 494,945 head of cattle; approximately 16,500,000 head of live hogs, 250,000 live chickens and turkeys; 191,906,000 pounds of meat and meat products; 11,110,000 pounds of butter; 181,000,000 pounds of wool; 201,000,000 pounds of cottonseed oil

used as substitute for butter and lard; 319,000 pounds of coconut oil used for the butter substitute; 360,000 pounds of palm oil used in the manufacture of soap instead of the fats of cattle, sheep, and hogs of this country; 119,000,000 pounds of soybeans and soybean oil; and last, but not least, 364,668,945 pounds of fish.

Last year we imported more than 312-million pounds of raw hides, more than $102-million worth of grain represented by 86-million bushels of corn; 206-thousand bushels of rye; 17-million bushels of wheat and 371-million pounds of malt barley and $2-million worth of flour and flour products.

All this was going on when we were taught that there was over-production.

Oh, yes! Billions of dollars for destruction at home forced upon us the expenditure of billions of dollars to import from abroad.

We took 40,000,000 acres of productive land out of cultivation; we regimented agriculture. It would have required millions of farmers and their families to cultivate these 40,000,000 acres and produce the farm products that were brought into this country from the West Indies, South America, India, China, Japan and other countries, and produced by underpaid labor. It would have required every acre of these 40,000,000 to produce these foreign farm products. This policy of destruction and curtailment put our own people out of work and on relief and gave the jobs to the foreigners and the poorly paid workers of all parts of the world.

Just the day before yesterday, the fifth anniversary of the New Deal, Mr. Morgenthau described the new crop-control law as a step towards more purchasing power. More purchasing power for the peon labor in China and in the West Indies and for the food monopolists, and less work and more taxes for the American laborer and farmer—so one could explain in view of the facts I have just disclosed.

My friends, be not mistaken in that I think that the sole panacea rests only with instructing Congress to coin and regulate the value of money for the welfare of all the nation. Nevertheless, the New Deal and this Congress are doomed to failure and disgrace unless they take this action.

It is regrettable that the scientists of rugged individualism cling to the error that the financial world is flat. It is not too late for the New Deal to become a new Columbus and prove that the world can enjoy a well-rounded prosperity by recognizing that work makes wealth, and by abandoning the notion that destruction makes prosperity.

Ladies and gentlemen, behind every lasting reform are the social principles of Jesus Christ.

The pagan practices current in the world today must give place to Christian practices.

Pagan usury must bow before the Christian concept of finance. Pagan destruction must give way to Christian production.

16 Religion During Hot and Cold Wars

Then they will hammer their swords into plowshares and their spears into pruning hooks; nation will not lift up sword against nation, and never again will they train for war.

—Micah 4:3

The Churches and the Clergy in World War II
Ray Abrams

Ray Abrams, who lived in Lansdowne, Pennsylvania, had been a student of the interaction between the clergy and warfare for over a half century. In 1933 he authored *Preachers Present Arms* which extensively documented the extent to which the clergy embraced American participation in World War I. In the article below he traced the steps by which the pacifism and neutrality of the clergy in the 1930s yielded to belligerency with the coming of a "holy war," World War II.

When the armies of Hitler started their triumphal march into Poland on September 1, 1939, Americans, after they had partially recovered from their initial shock, gave immediate attention to trying to keep the United States out of the European conflict.

There was a widespread belief that the Neutrality Acts passed between 1935 and 1937 would help keep this country out of another European or world war. The President on September 5, 1939 issued a proclamation of neutrality, and by a second proclamation made necessary by the Neutrality—in which an embargo was placed on the shipment of war material to belligerents—travel of Americans on belligerent ships in the war zones was banned.

Excerpt from "The Churches and the Clergy in World War II," *The Annals of the American Academy of Political and Social Science* 256 (March 1948): 110-19, and is reproduced here with the permission of the author and *The Annals*.

From Neutrality to Belligerency

As the war progressed in Europe it seemed evident to many Americans that a defense of the Western Hemisphere was necessary. Canada and Latin America were virtually unprotected. We could not permit the invasion and conquest of these areas. In 1941 the United States occupied Greenland and Iceland, the two governments involved having given consent. In September 1940 Great Britain received fifty "overage" destroyers from the United States and in return granted us the right to lease naval and air bases in Newfoundland, Bermuda, Bahamas, Jamaica, St. Lucia, Trinidad, Antigua, and British Guiana. By the end of 1941 the construction of these bases had proceeded rapidly.

In the meanwhile the conviction was growing in this country that Great Britain was our "first line of defense." "The British Navy alone stands between us and Hitler"—that was the phrase one heard.

Congress was called into session soon after war started, and the Neutrality Act of 1937 was revised so that the Allies might obtain arms and munitions from this country. Belligerents could purchase arms and munitions here, but on a "cash and carry" basis. By January 1941 the famous Lend-Lease Acts were introduced. After two months of heated debate the President's proposals were passed with certain amendments.

It would seem that most Americans had never really been neutral, and it was not long before the majority came to believe that the "Allied cause" was our cause. The Neutrality Acts were weakened and we were virtually in the war as a partner to the Allies except in terms of armed conflict. Dunkerque, the fall of France, and the threatened invasion of England began to frighten large sections of the population when they contemplated the consequences in the event of the fall of Great Britain. Rational and influential citizens were predicting that Hitler would be over here in three weeks.

During 1940 a total of $17.692 billion was appropriated for national defense. A two-ocean navy was in the making. Furthermore the Selective Training and Service Act of 1940 brought in compulsory military training in peacetime. We began to mobilize all our resources for war.

Our four-year attempt to check Japanese expansion in the Pacific had been a failure. The sudden and unexpected attack of the Japanese on Pearl Harbor, December 7, 1941, gave them an initial success in the "shooting war." But this "treachery" united the people of this country as probably nothing else could have done. On Monday, December 8 the Senate voted to declare war against Japan 82 votes to zero, and in the House of Representatives the vote was 388 to 1. (Only Jeanette Rankin voted "no.")

On December 10 Germany and Italy declared war against the United States, and the next day Congress, without a dissenting vote, passed resolutions to the effect that a state of war with these countries existed.

President Roosevelt in his war message of December 8 said: "No matter how long it may take us to overcome this premeditated invasion, the American people in their *righteous* [italics mine] might, will win through to absolute victory."

Position of the Churches, 1940-41

Keeping in mind this brief resume of some of the major trends in this country between the time that war broke out in Europe and the Pearl Harbor attack, what were the churches and the forces of organized religion doing with respect to the war in those twenty-seven months prior to December 7, 1941?

A survey of the religious periodicals and literature, of many sermons preached in that period and of material based on interviews with religious leaders indicates that the churches and the clergy were hopelessly divided in their attitudes toward the war in Europe. Moreover, there was a great deal of confusion over the causes of the war, the role that the United States should play, and what the churches should or should not do. Like the historians, the economists, the political scientists, and the political leaders of the time, the men of the cloth were to be found in many diverse camps. The editors of *Fortune* in January 1940 complained in an article on the "The Failure of the Church":

> We are asked to turn to the church for our enlightenment, but when we do so we find that the voice of the church is not inspired. The voice of the church, we find, is the echo of our own voices. And the result of this experience, already manifest, is disillusionment.

They even said that "so far as the record goes, the American people would do as well by their souls to follow the advice of the industrial leaders [with reference to the war] as to follow the advice of the spiritual leaders." . . .

The Religious Press

In this pre-Pearl Harbor period, of all the influential Protestant weeklies the *Christian Century* seems to have been among the most outspoken of the noninterventionist journals. The aims of President Roosevelt's administration were denounced in practically every issue. Dr. Charles Clayton Morrison, the editor, opposed any revision of the Neutrality Acts, the "destroyer deal," Lend-Lease, Selective Service, and so forth. By January 1941 Dr. Morrison was talking about "the President's war" and maintaining that "the President has gone on the assumption that Great Britain is fighting America's war." In October of the same year he wrote:

> . . . the obsession of our statesman with the weird illusion that this is in any true sense America's war must be broken. America's only genuine and rational responsibility in this war is to mediate for peace—not the peace of a mere armistice, but the peace of justice.

As late as the first week of December 1941, in the last editorial before the fatal Sunday, December 7, Dr. Morrison wrote, "Every national interest and every moral obligation to civilization dictates that this country shall keep out of the insanity of war which is in no sense America's war." He declared, "The romanticists are the interventionists. In general they pride themselves on taking a realistic view, and charge that noninterventionists are star-gazing romantics. . . ."

Other equally honest, sincere, and conscientious Christians were convinced that the *Christian Century* and those who supported its position were naive romanticists and misguided Christians.

Perhaps somewhat to counteract the influence of the *Christian Century*, a new religious periodical started up under the name of *Christianity and Crisis* with Reinhold Niebuhr, a professor in Union Theological Seminary, as the chief editor. Here was expounded the interventionist position and the "Aid to Britain" program. Niebuhr frankly stated that the Neutrality Act was "one of the most immoral laws that were ever spread upon the Federal statute book." "The essence of immorality," wrote he, "is the evasion or denial of moral responsibility." According to him, "misguided idealism" was "evoked in its support" at the time of passage.

That the clergy were divided in their appraisal of the merits of the war and the part that the United States should play is further evidenced by innumerable group resolutions and recommendations of one type and another.

Before our entrance into the struggle of the nations for survival, the Fellowship of Reconciliation announced that over two thousand clergy from every state in the Union had signed a statement of "unalterable opposition to America's present threatened belligerency" and pledged themselves never to use their ministry to "bless, sanction or support war." Early in February 1941, 648 churchmen signed a statement calling for "peace without victory now." Many eminent ministers were on this list.

The files of the religious periodicals are filled with articles and letters on both sides of the fence. Clergymen had a perfect field day in writing letters and engaging in endless discussion over finespun theological questions about religion and war.

For ten weeks beginning in early December 1940, the Christian Century ran a series on "If America Enters the War What Shall I Do?" Prominent clergy took opposite sides in the debate.

Preparedness Propaganda

Gradually, however, the social forces which were to bring America into World War II became stronger and more dynamic. Events proved much stronger than philosophical reasoning. The isolationist groups, the "American First" and "Keep America Out of the War" committees, were being offset by those who gathered around the banners of "Aid to Britain," "Defend America by Aiding the Allies," and similar organizations. Leading churchmen took an active part in several of these important propaganda groups.

In the early days of 1940 a manifesto was issued by a rather large number of influential clergymen for an "enlistment of our moral and material resources in support of the Allied nations." They believed, in general, that if "the American people are determined to take effective action toward the establishment of peace, one and only one course opens to them—the enlistment of their full national resources in assistance to Great Britain." During the next year similar and stronger statements and resolutions appeared with signatures from the clergy from practically all over the country and from the leading denominations.

In World War I, during the "preparedness era," the Episcopalians and the clergy with British and Canadian ancestry were the most conspicuous among the religious groups in arousing sympathy for Britain and promoting preparedness propaganda. To a certain extent this was true in World War II (though more research is needed on this point to determine how widespread the phenomenon was). Of the Episcopalians, Bishop William T. Manning was probably the most outspoken and seemed to be much in the limelight of publicity. He had been active before 1917 in World War I on behalf of the mother country. In World War II he followed the identical pattern. In the summer of 1941 at the convention of his diocese the Bishop announced:

> Speaking as an American, as a Christian, and as a bishop of the Christian church, I say that it is our duty as a Nation to take full part in this struggle, to give our whole strength and power to bring this world calamity and world terror to an end, and to do this now while Great Britain still stands.

This statement, it should be said, aroused considerable discussion within Episcopalian ranks. Sixty-four Episcopalians issued a pronouncement in the New York *Times* which seems to have been directed at their Bishop, repudiating the notion that the conflict across the Atlantic Ocean was a "holy war."

Adjustment to War

Up to December 7, 1941, then, the forces of organized religion were divided into several camps ranging all the way from the absolute pacifists to the interventionists who wanted us to declare war at once. Each, however, appealed to the same authorities—the Bible and Jesus of Nazareth—to support his position.

The complete surprise of the Japanese attack on Pearl Harbor settled, for the time being at least, many of the finespun theological and philosophical arguments that had been going on for over two years. War was no longer a possibility. It was a reality.

Correspondence with nearly all the editors of the leading Protestant and Catholic religious periodicals reveals that they accepted the war as fact and did not attempt to hinder the all-out war effort. Most of these journals seem to have supported our Government, and some quite actively. A few stood idly by and watched the process of events.

In the case of *Unity*, a comparatively small but influential liberal religious periodical, a novel situation arose. Dr. John Haynes Holmes, who was the editor (and continued to be up to 1946), was in opposition to the war. The managing editor, Dr. Curtis W. Reese, supported the war. So each of these gentlemen wrote signed editorials and each approved articles for publication. For the most part, both the editor and the managing editor were in agreement on the matter of conscientious objectors.

It will be observed that several types of adjustments or readjustments were possible for the Christian groups. Confronted with a shooting war, religious institutions are called upon to shift, for the time being, patterns of thought in a manner that is not characteristic of any of our other institutions.

One example of this is furnished in an editorial in the *Living Church* (Episcopalian), December 17, 1941: "May we seek always, not that God may be on our side, but that we may be on His side, so that the victory may in the end be His." . . .

The Holy War

One example of this is with respect to the use of the phrase "holy war." In 1917-18 the struggle had frequently been referred to as "the most holy war of all the ages." However, with the events that had intervened between the two wars, the phrase had fallen into thorough disrepute.

Karl Barth, the distinguished Swiss theologian, had shocked a great many of the faithful when, addressing the Christians of Great Britain, he declared war "is a righteous war which God commands us to wage ardently."

The Archbishop of York, Dr. William Temple, solved the theological dilemma by stating: "We are fighting for Christian civilization. I cannot use the phrase `holy war,' for war in its own nature is always an expression of the sin of man. But without hesitation I speak of this as, for us, a righteous war."

The theologians' frame of reference is very important. Hence among the theologians (and in one sense every clergyman *must* be a theologian) it is important to know what God thinks about the war. Once having discovered the "mind of God" on this subject, the major premise can be stated. The rest of the syllogism, or line of logic, is comparatively easy, particularly for a master dialectician. This helps immensely to reassure religious folks that God is still on his throne and is greatly concerned with the triumph of righteousness.

Wartime Trends

After the United States entered the war as an active belligerent the following major trends seem to be significant as far as the churches are concerned.

When compared with 1917-18, the population in World War II took the conflict and the horrors of war more in its stride. Twenty-four years before, there had been a great deal of hysteria. This time, while there was plenty of denunciation of the "Japs" and of Hitler *et al.*, far less real excitement prevailed. One heard and saw less of the wild-eyed patriot. The clergy in their utterances reflected the same differences. A few bellicose warmongers, yes, but they were not outstanding, certainly. In general, the clergy were calm about the struggle, and, in fact, in their sermons seem to have paid relatively less attention to the current problems of the war than one might have supposed. The generalization is based on data gathered from all over the United States. The war was a grim necessity— something to be gotten over as soon as possible.

Again, a greater toleration of diverse opinions was demonstrated. The Jehovah's Witnesses fared badly, it is true. Yet, the record of civil liberties appears better this time than for the previous war. The churches regarded the pacifist or near-pacifist clergymen with more urbanity than in 1917-18. No one knows how many preachers were pacifist, but they undoubtedly numbered several thousands. A few of them were exceedingly prominent.

The conscientious objectors were more highly regarded than in World War I, when they were damned or spurned by the clergy in general. The pacifist movement of the twenties and the thirties carried right on through the war with remarkable strength. On this point Dr. F. Ernest Johnson comments: "The number of objectors has been extremely small in view of the strength of the pacifist movement, but they constitute a symbol of religious freedom, and the churches in general seem so to regard them."

Approximately 12,000 conscientious objectors served in the Civilian Public Service and in the alternate service to war. About 6,500 spent an average of thirty months in prison for their violation of the Selective Training and Service Act of 1940. They came from 240 religious denominations and sects. The Mennonite group numbered 4,665; the Church of the Brethren, 1,353; the Society of Friends, 951; the Methodist, 673; the Jehovah's Witnesses, 409, and the remainder was distributed through various denominations and small sects.

The furnishing of chaplains to the armed forces was one of the outstanding contributions of the religious bodies. The Army and the Navy recognized the importance of chaplains in maintaining the morale of the men in the service.

Since this paper is primarily concerned with attitudes rather than activities of the churches and clergy during the war period, no attempt will be made to appraise the many ways in which the religious people contributed their support to the war effort. . . .

A Dilemma

It was a Christian soldier of three hundred years ago, Miles Standish, who is credited with saying:

> War is a terrible trade;
> But in the cause that is righteous
> Sweet is the smell of powder. . . .

Cromwell and many other stalwarts of bygone days would have agreed with the soldier of Plymouth. It is doubtful, however, whether today many followers of Jesus of Nazareth really relish war or enjoy the sweet smell of powder even in a righteous cause.

Thus times have changed but how much? As has been observed, when groups of Christians believe that their country is fighting for its life, the attempt by force of arms to preserve its institutions becomes at least a "righteous" cause. Prayers for victory are heard over the land. The soldier dead are buried with the blessing of the Almighty. Yet between wars many of these same groups of believers in the Prince of Peace have declared that for them war is a colossal sin.

Here, then, is one of the great dilemmas of the Christian church. In time of peace, war is against God. In time of war, except for the absolute pacifists, there comes the intellectual and emotional necessity of making the war acceptable in terms of some kind of moral objective. Though war is recognized as a tragedy, fighting to preserve a Christian civilization against the "paganism" of the Axis is essentially waging war to defeat the enemies of Christ. When it became apparent that World War II was a fight to the finish, not many of even the pacifists could honestly say that it made no difference to them which side won.

Why is there often this hesitation on the part of those who believe in a sovereign God to ask him to bless their cause? Why are all manner of circumlocutions resorted to in the use of words and phrases (that in the end mean practically the same thing) to avoid labeling our cause as righteous or just? To answer that the pacifist movement has had a sobering effect upon the thought of the churches is only a step in the direction of the answer. Whatever cultural factors have been involved, the final answer must be sought in the understanding of the basic human motivations.

There is clear evidence that some of the institutional patterns that have developed to resolve the conflict within Christendom have a schizophrenic quality. An analysis of the theological arguments over war would seem to indicate that frequently the emotions and the intellect are split off from each other. Furthermore, many of the rationalizations that are used to cover up the real underlying motives are symptomatic of the unresolved conflicts and emotional turmoil within individuals themselves. For example, repressed hostility, frustrations, feelings of guilt, sadistic and masochistic tendencies, the fear of death, attachments to love objects on an infantile level, and dozens of other psychological and psychoanalytic phenomena may often lie behind attitudes toward war. The conflict over the relationship of the church to the god Mars may often be a projection of these more personal and emotional difficulties. Moreover, not infrequently debates regarding the nature of war from the Christian point of view were carried on as if in a vacuum, with little reference to reality. That fact also is diagnostic.

There is nothing new in the above statements. They are emphasized again because frequently men become so engrossed with the more dramatic aspects of the death struggle of civilizations that these primary considerations are forgotten.

How much longer the forces of organized religion will continue to serve the gods of nationalism is perhaps a moot question. At least it is evident that many drastic changes will have to be made in man's social institutions before he can enjoy the warless world envisioned by Isaiah: " . . . and they shall beat their swords into plowshares, and their spears into pruning hooks; nation shall not lift up sword against nation, neither shall they learn war any more."

The Christian Conscience and Weapons of Mass Destruction
Federal Council of Churches

The perplexity of Christians with modern war prior to World War II intensified following the calculated use of the atomic bomb on Hiroshima and Nagasaki in August 1945. The warfare of the atomic age caused representatives of many religious traditions to look upon this new use of atomic energy as a demonstration of human sinfulness. Even some of the physicists who devised the bomb noted that they "had come to know sin" in a new way. Early in 1950 the Federal Council of Churches (known later that year as the National Council of Churches) appointed a Special Commission to study the moral problems involved in the controversial issues raised by the threat of atomic destruction. The first section of the Commission's report, *The Christian Conscience and Weapons of Mass Destruction*, most of which appears below, includes the debate between pacifist and nonpacifist Christians. It is reprinted with the permission of the National Council of Churches.

What are the decisions open to us?

The clearest and least ambiguous alternative is that urged upon us by our most uncompromising pacifist fellow-Christians. They believe that the refusal of all kinds of military service and an unqualified witness against war and for peace is for them the will of God. They would summon all Christian people and all Churches to unite with them in this witness. For them the infinitely heightened destructiveness and the morally catastrophic character of modern war confirm their conviction that followers of Christ can make no compromise with so great an evil. They find themselves called to follow the way of love and reconciliation at whatever cost and to accept the historical consequences of a repudiation of armaments and of war. For those who make this radical decision need for debate as to the choice of weapons is ruled out by a repudiation of all weapons.

Pacifist and non-pacifist Christians can probably agree that, as men are, responsible political leaders could not take the pacifist position and continue to hold positions of effective political leadership. But that fact does not relieve those of us who are Christians from making our own decisions in the sight of God and urging what we believe to be right Christian decisions on those who govern as our representatives.

The large majority of professing Christians are not pacifists. But Christian non-pacifists share with their pacifist brethren abhorrence of war and with them see in it a sign of man's Godlessness. They agree that in all human conflicts the most righteous side is never so righteous as it thinks it is. They acknowledge that whatever good may ever come out of war, incalculable evil always comes out of it, too. We believe that God calls some men to take the way of non-violence as a special and high vocation in order to give a clearer witness to the way of love than those can give who accept responsibility for the coercions in civil society. We rejoice that God has called some of our brethren in the universal Christian fellowship to bear this witness and are humbled by the faithfulness of many in bearing it. Without minimizing the moral heroism it can require, we are even envious of the greater inner simplicity of that non-violent way.

But most of us find ourselves called to follow a course which is less simple and which appears to us more responsible because more directly relevant to the hard realities of our situation. And we believe it is the way in which most Christians must go.

There can be no justice for men and no responsible freedom without law and order. When men confront one another with their contending egotisms, without moral or spiritual bonds, they take the law into their own hands and work what is at best a very crude justice. They reach beyond that only when they have achieved some substantial moral community and a sovereign law rooted in moral community. This we have reached, however imperfectly, where we find ordered society. Even then the law which gives any just order must be sustained by power, and, when necessary, by coercive power.

The world we live in, the world of states and of great masses of men struggling towards nationhood, is without strong uniting moral or spiritual bonds. It possesses no

overruling law and in the United Nations an institution which marks only the beginnings of common order. In large measure our world is a "frontier" of self-regarding, mutually distrustful human masses. God's will for justice and for mercy broods over this disorder in which we find ourselves. We Christians believe that we are called to be the servants of His justice and His mercy. But can we be just to men if we do not struggle to maintain for them and for ourselves some order of justice in which good faith and freedom and truth can find a dwelling place? And can we extend the beginnings of this order in the United Nations, if we do not undergird it with effective power?

So most Christians, faced with the lawlessness of our world of nations, see no way of serving the righteousness of God in the presence of brutal and irresponsible violence save by taking responsible collective action against aggression within the framework of the United Nations. That we must do in fear and trembling, as those who know how our own self-interest blinds us. We must take upon ourselves the dreadful responsibilities of conflict, if we are to accept even the imperfect justice and freedom which others have painfully won and for which others fight and die even now. In the last resort we are in conscience bound to turn to force in defense of justice even though we know that the destruction of human life is evil. There are times when this can be the lesser of two evils, forced upon us by our common human failure to achieve a better relationship.

The deep disorder within men and among men, which Christian faith calls sin, leads to both brutal dominion and conflict. Today, two great dangers threaten mankind, the danger that totalitarian tyranny may be extended over the world and the danger of global war. Many of us believe that the policies most likely to avoid both dangers inevitably carry the risk of war.

Does this mean that for those who take this position the love of God and the judgments of God and the commandments of God cease to have meaning? We know that Christ died for our enemies as well as for us. We know that we are bidden to pray for our enemies as for ourselves. We know that we stand with them in need of forgiveness. We know that our failure to find another way of dealing with our deep differences and conflicts of interest and distrust of one another is a judgment of us and our forefathers as well as on them. But this does not extricate us from the hard realities of our situation.

We cannot lightly assume that a victory for our own nation, or a victory for the United Nations, is in itself a victory for God and his righteousness. Even in war we cannot rejoice that more of the enemy are killed than of our own people. Even in victory we can rejoice only if, from the sacrifices of so much life, some little gain is made for order and freedom, and renewed opportunity is found for mercy and reconciliation.

Concepts of Total War

Christians who have decided that in the last resort they may be compelled to accept the terrible responsibilities of warfare are now confronted with these questions: Does that mean warfare without any limits? Does that mean warfare with any weapons which man's ingenuity can provide?

War has developed rapidly in the direction of "total war" in two meanings, which it is important to distinguish.

In the first meaning total war refers to the fact that in a conflict between highly industrialized nations all human and material resources are mobilized for war purposes. The traditional distinction between combatants and non-combatants is far less clear. Only small children and the helpless sick and aged stand outside the war effort. It is practically impossible to distinguish between guilty and innocent. Certainly men who are drafted into uniform may be among the least guilty. Total war, in this sense of the involvement of the whole nation in it, cannot be avoided if we have a major war at all.

Total war, in the second sense, means war in which all moral restraints are thrown aside and all the purposes of the community are fully controlled by sheer military expediency. We must recognize that the greater the threat to national existence the greater will be the temptation to subordinate everything, all civil rights, the liberty of conscience, all moral judgments regarding the means to be used, and all consideration of postwar international relations, to the single aim of military victory.

Christians and Christian Churches, if they admit that occasions can arise when the use of military force by a nation or a group of nations may be less evil than surrender to some malignant power, cannot deny that total war in the first sense may be inescapable.

But Christians and Christian Churches can never consent to total war in the second sense. The only possible justification for war is that it offers a possibility of achieving a moral result, however imperfect, to prevent an overwhelming moral evil and to offer a new opportunity for men to live in freedom and decency and in just and merciful relationships. . . .

The Weapons of Mass Destruction

What then of the weapons we shall or shall not be prepared to use?

Can we find some absolute line we can draw? Can we say that Christians can approve of using swords and spears, but not guns; conventional bombs or jellied fire, but not atomic bombs; uranium bombs, but not hydrogen bombs? Can we say that Christians must pledge themselves or seek to pledge their nations not to stock this or that weapon, even though the enemy stocks them; or not to use some weapons, even though the enemy uses them?

We find no "clean" methods of fighting, but some methods are dirtier than others. Some cause more pain and maiming without commensurate military decisiveness. Some are more indiscriminate.

We have no more—nor any less—right to kill with a rifle or a bazooka than with an A-bomb or an H-bomb. In the sight of Him, "to whom all hearts are open," the inner quality of an act is to be distinguished from its consequences. There may be more hatred and less penitence in the heart of a man who kills one enemy with a rifle, or in the heart of a frenzied super-patriot in his armchair, than in the heart of an airman who devastates a city with a bomb. Sin in its inward meaning cannot be measured by the number of people who are affected. But a reckoning of consequences is also a part of a Christian's decision. It is more dreadful to kill a thousand men than one man, even if both are done in the service of justice and order. We cannot, therefore, be released from the responsibility for doing no more hurt than must be.

Here a distinction can be drawn between precision weapons, which can be directed with reasonable control at primary military objectives, and weapons of mass destruction. But we are compelled to recognize that the increasing distance from which bombs or projectiles are released and the speed of planes and guided missiles are likely to offset all gains in precision. If, as we have felt bound to acknowledge, certain key industrial targets are inescapably involved in modern war, we find no moral distinction between destroying them by tons of T.N.T. or by fire as compared with an atomic bomb, save as greater precision is possible in one as compared with others. But this recognition that we cannot isolate the atomic bomb or even the projected H-bombs as belonging to an absolutely different moral category must not blind us to the terrible dimensions of the moral problem they present.

With a single atomic bomb, destruction is produced that is as great as that from a large fleet of airplanes dropping conventional explosives. If the H-bomb is made, it will be destructive on a still more horrible scale. If such weapons are used generally upon centers of population, we may doubt whether enough will remain to rebuild decent human society.

But the abandonment of atomic weapons would not eliminate mass destruction. Conventional or new weapons may produce comparable destruction. The real moral line between what may be done and what may not be done by the Christian lies not in the realm of the distinction between weapons but in the realm of the motives for using and the consequences of using all kinds of weapons. Some measures corrupt the users, and destroy the humanity of the victims. Some may further the victory but impair the peace. There are certainly things which Christians should not do to save self, or family, or nation, or free civilization. There seems to us, however, no certain way to draw this moral line in advance, apart from all the actual circumstances. What may or may not be done under God can be known only in relation to the whole, concrete situation by those responsibly involved in it. We can find no moral security, or moral hiding place, in legalistic definitions. The terrible burden of decision is the Christian man's responsibility, standing where he does before God.

Nevertheless, real distinctions can be made to illumine and help the conscience in its trouble. The destruction of life clearly incidental to the destruction of decisive military objectives, for example, is radically different from mass destruction which is aimed primarily at the lives of civilians, their morale, or the sources of their livelihood. In the event of war, Christian conscience guides us to restraint from destruction not essential to our total objectives, to a continual weighing of the human values that may be won against those lost in the fighting, and to the avoidance of needless human suffering.

Unhappily we see little hope at this time of a trustworthy international agreement that would effectively prevent the manufacture or use of weapons of mass destruction by any nation. This should not deter us from the search for such an agreement, perhaps as a part of a general disarmament program, and for a restoration of mutual confidence that would make an agreement possible and effective.

As long as the existing situation holds, for the United States to abandon its atomic weapons, or to give the impression that they would not be used, would leave the non-communist world with totally inadequate defense. For Christians to advocate such a policy would be for them to share responsibility for the worldwide tyranny that might result. We believe that American military strength, which must include atomic weapons as long as any other nation may possess them, is an essential factor in the possibility of preventing both world war and tyranny. If atomic weapons or other weapons of parallel destructiveness are used against us or our friends in Europe or Asia, we believe that it could be justifiable for our government to use them with all possible restraint to prevent the triumph of an aggressor. We come to this conclusion with troubled spirits but any other conclusion would leave our own people and the people of other nations open to continuing devastating attack and to probable defeat. Even if as individuals we would choose rather to be destroyed than to destroy in such measure, we do not believe it would be right for us to urge policies on our government which would expose others to such a fate.

Having taken the position that no absolute line can be drawn we are especially concerned to emphasize checks on every step towards the increased destructiveness of war.

To engage in reckless and uncontrolled violence against the people of any other nation is to reduce the possibilities of peace and justice and freedom after the war's end and even to destroy the foundation of ordered society. Military judgment must not yield to the vengefulness that too often possesses civilians in wartime; nor must the national government yield to the military its own responsibility for the immediate and the post-war consequences of the conduct of the war.

We have recognized that indiscriminate mass destruction may be caused by atomic bombs or by a fleet of armored tanks or by a ruthless army laying waste cities and countryside. We have found no moral distinction between these instruments of warfare, apart from the ends they serve and the consequences of their use. We would, however, call attention to the fact that the first use of atomic weapons in another war, even if limited to sharply defined military targets, would open the way for their use in retaliation. Because of the very power of these weapons, it would be difficult to prevent their use from extending to military targets that would involve also the destruction of non-combatants on a massive scale. If the United States should use atomic weapons, it would expose its allies to similar attack. The nation that uses atomic weapons first, therefore, bears a special burden of responsibility for the almost inevitable development of extensive mass destruction with all its desolation and horror.

Even more fundamental, the dreadful prospect of devastation that must result from any major war illuminates with special clarity the immorality of those in any country who initiate an aggression against which the only effective means of defense may be the resort to atomic weapons, and which may thus be expected to lead to an atomic war. If general war comes it will probably be a war for survival, not only for the survival of a free civilization, but for the physical survival of peoples. In such a war the temptation will be tremendous to forget all other considerations and to use every available means of destruction. If this happens, physical survival may be bought at the price of the nation's soul, of the moral values which make the civilization worth saving.

America's Hour of Decision
Billy Graham

Billy Graham (1918-   ) is probably the best known international evangelist and the most influential evangelical of the twentieth century. His evangelistic campaign in Los Angeles (1949) brought him to national attention. The following year he founded the Billy Graham Evangelistic Association and went on the air with "The Hour of Decision" program. His sermons were often punctuated with allusions to the threat of communism, as is noted in the sermon from *America's Hour of Decision* (1950) reprinted below.

MILLIONS IN the western world are asking themselves on this closing day of the old year the question, what does the new one hold for me? What lies just ahead? Whither are we bound? How soon will the terminal be reached? Are we facing peace or war? Prosperity or adversity? What is to be the next act in the great human drama?

Such are the questions that are forcing themselves upon us at this hour. Men know not which way to turn. Nations are perplexed. Uncertainty characterizes the attitude of every statesman and diplomat in the world capitols. The future is concealed in obscurity. Everyone seems to agree that a terrible catastrophe lies just ahead. But what? And from which direction will it come? Selfishness seems to have gripped the entire human race. The worst that is in man is now manifesting itself. A spirit of greed and lust for power dominates human hearts. We wonder if the abyss has not already been opened to release its myriad demons for the ruin of man both nationally and individually. Thousands, anxious and perplexed at the beginning of 1951 are asking the question, what next?

As we stand on the threshold of a new year, it might be well if we review the fateful year, 1950. As we look in retrospect today, we are convinced that the year 1950 will go down in history as one of the most momentous in the history of the world—A year when our nation began its fight for survival; when American prestige abroad has sunk to the lowest ebb in the history of our Republic; when former friends and allies are deserting us or questioning our leadership and our nation stands almost alone and isolated this moment faced by the most powerful and ruthless enemy the nation has ever known. Even the bleak, cold days at Valley Forge or the darkest days of the Civil War, or that black December Sunday in 1941 were not as forboding as the present hour is for the future of our nation. A year when a diplomat, committing suicide in Washington, left a note saying, "It is more than I can bear." Statesmen making one statement one day and completely reversing themselves the next day. A year when communism unmasked itself, shouted its defiance to the world and boldly began the march to world conquest. Communism, the avowed enemy of everything Americans stand for—our schools, our social order, our God, our Bible, our churches, our homes.

Millions of Americans are awakening to the realization that for the first time in American history our soil may be invaded, our cities bombed, our nation becoming a bloody battlefield. Nineteen fifty was a year in which war in the far East has already caused nearly 35,000 American casualties, and billions of dollars and yet our government still hesitates to call it war. As historians write the history of 1950, they will read with shocked amazement that Americans considered Korea a police action and sent thousands of American boys to face overwhelming odds while our nation at home continued business as usual. A year in which finally a national emergency has been declared at home; when belts are beginning to tighten and a lower standard of living is in prospect. Ah, yes, the American people refused to give of their substance for world evangelization and the work of the gospel of Jesus Christ. Now, it's to be taken from them for guns, bullets and bombs — a national emergency that will probably extend for another generation. A year in which more money was spent on luxuries and entertainment than ever before. More drunkenness, more suicides, more immorality, more

lawlessness, more divorces than ever before in the history of our nation. When magazines and newspapers told the story of immorality and crime, subversive activities that threaten to destroy the moral fibre of America faster than the pressure of communism on the outside. A year in which moral deterioration began to worry even national leaders.

Nineteen fifty has been a year in which the church has been amazingly asleep in her golden hour of opportunity; lethargy and spiritual stupor almost unbelievable in Christendom's hour of greatest crisis. Not since the battle of Tours in 732 when Charles Martel with his motley army threw back the Mohammedan horde and saved Europe from Mohammedanism, has Christianity faced such an onslaught that threatens to completely wipe out all semblance of the Christian church from the earth; the church, busy with its bickerings, backbitings, name callings, division and strifes—the church busy with oiling its tremendous organizational machinery. As a Methodist bishop told me a few day ago, we are like firemen trying to put out a fire and instead of putting the water on the fire, we are standing with fire hoses arguing about who should put more water on the fire when no water is coming out of the hose at all. Some firemen are standing near the blaze arguing about what color hats we should wear into the fight.

Dr. Harold Ockenga, pastor of the great Park Street Church in Boston, was preaching in Poland a few years ago. After the service a fine-faced intelligent Polish man approached him in private to learn the content of the Christian message. He was thinking of his country and its future. He summed up the situation thus: communism bids for Poland. Christianity also challenges Poland. Whichever makes its message a flame of fire will win. In the face of such a remark our hearts fail. For Christianity seemingly has lost her flame. The early church was so boiling hot, so fervent in spirit that she boiled over into the whole Roman Empire and the then known world within a few years. Amy Carmichael says, "The soldier who simmers but does not boil is no soldier; he is a sham. Of all the futile figures on the battlefield, he is the most futile." Christianity may be losing her day in America because she refuses to boil. The fires of the reformation have all but flickered out, leaving a great religious desolation of tombs and ashes and dead men's bones in many places.

Yet with all this dark and hopeless picture of the year 1950, there have been encouraging signs that lead us to believe that millions of Americans are beginning to turn to God. There have been millions on their knees beseeching God to spare our nation the coming judgment. During the past year revivals have broken out on college and university campuses almost unprecedented in the history of education in this country. Great cities have been swept by citywide campaigns and literally thousands have been ushered into the Kingdom of God. Many of our national leaders have called us to revival. Great denominations are beginning to awaken. There are stirrings here and there that we have not seen in over a generation.

Is the Church Awakening?

Perhaps the church is beginning to awaken. In our own campaigns during the past year we have seen nearly seventy-five thousand souls coming to a saving knowledge of Jesus Christ and we have had the privilege of preaching to well over two million people face to face beside the other millions, by the miracle of radio. During the past year we have knelt a thousand times with hundreds of people who had everything—money, power, popularity—I have heard them cry, "Oh God, my life is such a mess, such a futile failure. The harder I try the deeper I go into sin. It is like quicksand trying to smother me. Isn't there any power to deliver me from the ache of my sinful heart?" That desire has been voiced in a hundred phrases. But all have uttered the same heart cry to God for His power and deliverance. I could tell you of a movie star in Hollywood, or the congressman in Washington, or the state senator from Georgia, or the all-American basketball star from Washington. I could tell you about the multi-millionaire in New England, the brilliant Harvard and Yale students who have made their way down the long aisles saying "yes" to Jesus Christ.

Thousands have tried to forget the realism of life in hectic pleasure, drown it in liquor, cauterize it with pseudoscience, vaporize it with poetry, explain it away with philosophy — but it still lingers as a haunting problem in every heart. Sin is the root of our troubles and difficulties and during the past year thousands have turned from sin to Christ: from darkness to light, and found victory, conquest and faith. All this leads us to believe that faith is not yet dead on this earth.

But 1950 is history. It can never be relived. The mistakes, failures and sins are on the record books to await the day of judgment and reckoning when every man shall give an account before Almighty God. What lies ahead? Tonight at midnight, the new year will come fearfully into the world, almost afraid of its own shadow. Danger lurks behind every corner. Tragedy stares it straight in the face. The thunder of the four horses of the Apocalypse can be heard drawing ever closer for the American people: the red horse of war; the black horse of famine; the pale horse of death and hell which followed him. As we stand at this fateful hour on the brink of the unknown, I suggest three possibilities.

Three Alternatives

First—further disintegration and war. Everything that is happening to China and Europe could happen here. Governments perilously weakened by war, inflation, economic chaos, lowered moral standards of its people, internal corruption undermined by a steady barrage of propaganda within and without—that is exactly how communism came to China. Fantastic for America you say. So was communism fantastic to thinking Chinese ten years ago. They said it is not compatible with the Chinese mind nor their way of life. Yet it was in the wake of economic collapse and diplomatic betrayal, in spite of the fact that probably eighty percent of the people did not want it. America, the bulwark of free nations prosperous enough to support a vast, worldwide foreign missions program requiring millions of dollars each year: wipe out her economy, crumble this last bulwark of freedom, turn her populace into panic-stricken, bankrupt, desperate beings thinking with their stomachs and primitive instincts—is a matter of tremen-

dous concern to thinking people at this moment.

There is sure to be a strong, rising, dictatorial leadership, promising a way out during the months ahead. Moral, economic and spiritual collapse in America would bring about anarchy. It would leave a political vacuum for communism to move in and take over. I do not fear the landing of communist troops on our shores this year. I do not even fear the bombing of our cities this year. But I am tremendously concerned about the mad plunge that America is taking at this moment morally and spiritually. On this Sunday, New Years Eve, millions of Americans will be jamming cocktail bars. Places of amusement will be filled. Drunkenness, immorality will be a stench in the nostrils of God tonight that may well hasten the day of reckoning and judgment upon our people. We are told that there are over eleven hundred social sounding organizations that are communist and communist operated in this country. They control the minds of a great segment of our people, the infiltration of the left wing though both pink and red into the intellectual strata of America. Educational, religious culture is almost beyond repair— so many of our leaders feel.

The inflationary spiral in which we find ourselves is costing us ten times as much to fight Russia as it cost us to fight Germany and Japan. The vultures are now encircling our debt-ridden inflationary economy with its fifteen-year record of deficit finance and with its staggering national debt to close in for the kill. All of this, I say, ladies and gentlemen, suggests that in 1951 we could see the beginning of anarchy in this country.

The second alternative I suggest to the American people at this moment is a spiritual awakening, and an old-fashioned revival of faith in the Blood-sprinkled way of Calvary. Revivals are not out of date. Not while trouble and sin flood the world. Not while salvation is yet offered at the Cross. Not while Christians are spiritually indifferent. We limit God when we do not believe, when we do not pray, when we do not expect and we do not cash in on the promises of God. There are said to be three thousand prayer promises in the Word. Promises which may be used as signed and guaranteed checks. The Bible says, "Ye have not because ye ask not."

How our hearts are stirred with longing as we read of the great revivals of yesterday—the Puritan revival was born when God's power touched England's great uncrowned king, valiant Oliver Cromwell, spirit-filled Baxter and zealous Tindell. All England was stirred. God's power touched the heart of John Livingston who in 1625 knelt and felt the Holy Fire at Glasgow College. For five years his heart burned to preach. The Fire of God touched Jonathan Edwards in this great New England country who in spite of his weak voice and defective sight was so filled with a burning passion for souls that men listened spellbound and sometimes leaped to their feet to grip the church pillars lest they should fall into eternal judgment. The Power of God touched the lives of John Wesley, George Whitfield, Francis Asbury, David Brainerd, William Carey and scores of others down through the years who have burned in their hearts with the spirit of real revival.

Of every revival it can be said, "this is an indication of the power of God." Where is the soul anguish of yesteryear, the wounded conscience, the sleepless nights, the heart cries and groanings of deep conviction? The sobbing and weeping of the lost? Christians of America, I beg of you that we fall upon our faces before Almighty God pleading and crying for a spiritual awakening that may well save the day and win the battle for our nation. The story of Evan Roberts, when all Wales was set afire with God's Power, makes us hungry to see such a revival again. In five weeks twenty thousand believed on Christ and joined the churches—infidels, drunkards, thieves and gamblers and many were rescued from the depths of sin and were claimed for God. Confessions of sin were lifted to high heaven. May we see today what Roberts saw in 1904?

The great stories coming from the life of Charles G. Finney astound ordinary believers today and nourish faith in our hearts. When Finney began preaching he found the American churches divided into two opposing factions. The nerve of gospel ministry was cut and dull apathy prevailed. Finney preached the Word of God and God answered with power when over one hundred thousand were converted and joined the churches in one winter alone as revival fires spread in every direction.

I have reminded you that the hour is dark. What better time to light the fires of a revival? Somehow I feel in 1951 we are going to see a flame sweep across America. From the Appalachians into the great prairie states through the Rockies to the West coast and our generation will taste the thrilling sweetness of a real revival that we have not known.

II Chronicles 7:14 gives the remedy for any nation which is sin-sick: "If my people which are called by my name shall humble themselves and pray and seek my face and turn from their wicked ways, then will I hear from heaven and will forgive their sin and will heal their land."

America, I challenge you at this hour to a spiritual revival. More than bullets, guns, bombs—this could be America's protection and by the sign of the cross we could conquer as Constantine did of old.

The Glorious Third Alternative

The third alternative that I suggest to the American people is the glorious, blessed hope of the second coming of Jesus Christ. Maranatha—it is a long cry between Enoch and John, the Genesis Patriarch with prophetic trumpet peals forth. Enoch cried, "Behold the Lord cometh with ten thousand of His Saints." John in estactic rapture cries, "Behold He cometh with clouds and every eye shall see Him." Watch the early Christians—listen as they meet and as they part. Their password is Maranatha—it means "the Lord cometh." Someone says, "but he has come." That is true. Here Scripture and history agree. Prophets spoke glowingly and psalmists sang rapturously of that advent. And when He came, angelic hosts chanted His praises. A brilliant star proclaimed his presence and men hastened from tending sheep watching stars to worship at His feet that first Christmas morning. Christ's last promise was, "surely I come quickly." His

coming, according to the Scriptures, is as certain as the dawn. It is as sure as seedtime and harvest, cold and heat, summer and winter and day and night. It is as positive as God sits upon His Throne.

One uncertainty governs the event. It is the time element. We cannot say when it will take place. To attempt to set a date would overstep the Divine boundary. That would be lawlessness. Let us never forget Christ's words: "But of that day and that hour knoweth no man, no not the angels which are in Heaven, neither the Son but the Father." He told His disciples, "It is not for you to know the times nor the seasons which the Father hath put in His own power." Much harm has been done and positive dishonor brought upon our Lord and this precious truth of His return by date fixers. But that does not do away with the glorious hope and anticipation of the church of Christ at this hour that 1951 could and may be the year of His coming. "Ye men of Galilee why stand ye gazing up into Heaven, this same Jesus which is taken up from you into Heaven shall so come in like manner as ye have seen Him go into Heaven." Read the words of Paul: "For the Lord himself shall descend from Heaven with a shout, with the voice of the Archangel and with the trump of God and the dead in Christ shall rise first. Then we which are alive and remain shall be caught up together with them in the clouds to meet the Lord in the air and so shall we ever be with the Lord. Wherefore comfort one another with these words."

I do not know when Christ is coming back. I do not know all the answers to prophetic Scriptures. But of this one thing I am certain as I read the Word of God: that Jesus Christ is planning to come back, that God has set a date at which His Son is to come and set up a worldwide reign. It may be this year or it may be a thousand years from now. But hope burns eternal within the breast of every Christian that our Lord is soon coming. For the American people at this hour, again I say I offer you three alternatives: First, further disintegration and war; second, spiritual awakening and revival that could stay the judgment hand of God; third, the second coming of Jesus Christ which is the hope of the Christian but means judgment for the sinner.

17 Religious Responses to the Turbulent Sixties

Namely, that God was in Christ reconciling the world to Himself, not counting their trespasses against them, and He has committed to us the word of reconciliation.

—2 Cor. 5:19

Letter from Birmingham City Jail
Martin Luther King, Jr.

Martin Luther King, Jr. (1929-1968) was an African-American Baptist minister and civil rights leader. In 1955 while pastoring a Montgomery, Alabama, church, he led the Montgomery bus boycott. During this first major campaign of the civil rights movement, King formulated his philosophy and strategy of nonviolent protest to produce social change. In 1963 he was jailed, along with 2,400 other antisegregationists, for participating in civil rights demonstrations in Birmingham, Alabama. While he was serving his sentence, eight prominent white "liberal" Alabama clergymen published an open letter that criticized King for his civil rights activities. His response to them in the letter printed below soon became the focal point of the national discussion of the theory of civil disobedience.

———

My dear Fellow Clergymen,

While confined here in the Birmingham city jail, I came across your recent statement calling our present activities "unwise and untimely." Seldom, if ever, do I pause to answer criticism of my work and ideas. If I sought to answer all of the criticisms that cross my desk, my secretaries would be engaged in little else in the course of the day, and I would have no time for constructive work. But since I feel that you are men of genuine good will and your criticisms are sincerely set forth, I would like to answer your statement in what I hope will be patient and reasonable terms.

I think I should give the reason for my being in Birmingham, since you have been influenced by the argument of "outsiders coming in." I have the honor of serving as president of the Southern Christian Leadership Conference, an organization operating in every southern state, with headquarters in Atlanta, Georgia. We have some eighty-five affiliate organizations all across the South—one being the Alabama Christian Movement for Human Rights. Whenever necessary and possible we share staff, educational and financial resources with our affiliates. Several months ago our local affiliate here in Birmingham invited us to be on call to engage in a nonviolent direct-action program if such were deemed necessary. We readily consented and when the hour came we lived up to our promises. So I am here, along with several members of my staff, because we were invited here. I am here because I have basic organizational ties here.

Beyond this, I am in Birmingham because injustice is here. Just as the eighth century prophets left their little villages and carried their "thus saith the Lord" far beyond the boundaries of their hometowns; and just as the Apostle Paul left his little village of Tarsus and carried the gospel of Jesus Christ to practically every hamlet and city of the Graeco-Roman world, I too am compelled to carry the gospel of freedom beyond my particular hometown. Like Paul, I must constantly respond to the Macedonian call for aid.

Moreover, I am cognizant of the inter-relatedness of all communities and states. I cannot sit idly by in Atlanta and not be concerned about what happens in Birmingham. Injustice anywhere is a threat to justice everywhere. We are caught in an inescapable network of mutuality, tied in a single garment of destiny. Whatever affects one directly affects all indirectly. Never again can we afford to live with narrow, provincial "outside agitator" idea. Anyone who lives in the United States can never be considered an outsider anywhere in this country.

You deplore the demonstrations that are presently taking place in Birmingham. But I am sorry that your statement did not express a similar concern for the conditions that brought the demonstrations into being. I am sure that each of you would want to go beyond the superficial social analyst who looks merely at effects, and does not grapple with underlying causes. I would not hesitate to say that it is unfortunate that so-called demonstrations are taking place in Birmingham at this time, but I would say in more emphatic terms that it is even more unfortunate that the white power structure of this city left the Negro community with no other alternative.

In any nonviolent campaign there are four basic steps: (1) collection of the facts to determine whether injustices are alive, (2) negotiation, (3) self-purification, and (4) direct action. We have gone through all of these steps in Birmingham. There can be no gainsaying of the fact that racial injustice engulfs this community.

Birmingham is probably the most thoroughly segregated city in the United States. Its ugly record of police brutality is known in every section of this country. Its injust treatment of Negroes in the courts is a notorious reality. There have been more unsolved bombings of Negro homes and churches in Birmingham than any city in this nation. These are the hard, brutal and unbelievable facts. On the basis of these conditions Negro leaders sought to negotiate with the city fathers. But the political leaders consistently refused to engage in good faith negotiation.

Then came the opportunity last September to talk with some of the leaders of the economic community. In these negotiating sessions certain promises were made by the merchants—such as the promise to remove the humiliating racial signs from the stores. On the basis of these promises Rev. Shuttlesworth and the leaders of the Alabama Christian Movement for Human Rights agreed to call a moratorium on any type of demonstrations. As the weeks and months unfolded we realized that we were the victims of a broken promise. The signs remained. Like so many experiences of the past we were confronted with blasted hope, and the dark shadow of a deep disappointment settled upon us. So we had no alternative except that of preparing for direct action, whereby we would present our very bodies as a means of laying our case before the conscience of the local and national community. We were not unmindful of the difficulties involved. So we decided to go through a process of self-purification. We started having workshops on nonviolence and repeatedly asked ourselves the questions, "Are you able to accept blows without retaliating?" "Are you able to endure the ordeals of jail?" We decided to set our direct-action program around the Easter season, realizing that with the exception of Christmas, this was the largest shopping period of the year. Knowing that a strong economic withdrawal program would be the by-product of direct action, we felt that this was the best time to bring pressure on the merchants for the needed changes. Then it occurred to us that the March election was ahead and so we speedily decided to postpone action until after election day. When we discovered that Mr. Connor was in the run-off, we decided again to postpone action so that the demonstrations could not be used to cloud the issues. At this time we agreed to begin our nonviolent witness the day after the run-off.

This reveals that we did not move irresponsibly into direct action. We too wanted to see Mr. Connor defeated; so we went through postponement after postponement to aid in this community need. After this we felt that direct action could be delayed no longer.

You may well ask, "Why direct action? Why sit-ins, marches, etc.? Isn't negotiation a better path?" You are exactly right in your call for negotiation. Indeed, this is the purpose of direct action. Nonviolent direct action seeks to create such a crisis and establish such creative tension that a community that has constantly refused to negotiate is forced to confront the issue. It seeks so to dramatize the issue that it can no longer be ignored. I just referred to the creation of tension as a part of the work of the nonviolent resister. This may sound rather shocking. But I must confess that I am not afraid of the word tension. I have earnestly worked and preached against violent tension, but there is a type of constructive nonviolent tension that is necessary for growth. Just as Socrates felt that it was necessary to create a tension in the mind so that individuals could rise from the bondage of myths and half-truths to the unfettered realm of creative analysis and objective appraisal, we must see the need of having nonviolent gadflies to create the kind of tension in society that will help men to rise from the dark depths of prejudice and racism to the majestic heights of understanding and brotherhood. So the purpose of the direct action is to create a situation so crisis-packed that it will inevitably open the door to negotiation. We, therefore, concur with you in your call for negotiation. Too long has our beloved Southland been bogged down in the tragic attempt to live in monologue rather than dialogue.

One of the basic points in your statement is that our acts are untimely. Some have asked, "Why didn't you give the new administration time to act?" The only answer that I can give to this inquiry is that the new administration must be prodded about as much as the outgoing one before it acts. We will be sadly mistaken if we feel that the election of Mr. Boutwell will bring the millennium to Birmingham. While Mr. Boutwell is much more articulate and gentle than Mr. Connor, they are both segregationists, dedicated to the task of maintaining the status quo. The hope I see in Mr. Boutwell is that he will be reasonable enough to see the futility of massive resistance to desegregation. But he will not see this without pressure from the devotees of civil rights. My friends, I must say to you that we have not made a single gain in civil rights without determined legal and nonviolent pressure. History is the long and tragic story of the fact that privileged groups seldom give up their privileges voluntarily. Individuals may see the moral light and voluntarily give up their unjust posture; but as

Reinhold Niebuhr has reminded us, groups are more immoral than individuals.

We know through painful experience that freedom is never voluntarily given by the oppressor; it must be demanded by the oppressed. Frankly, I have never yet engaged in a direct action movement that was "well-timed," according to the timetable of those who have not suffered unduly from the disease of segregation. For years now I have heard the words "Wait!" It rings in the ear of every Negro with a piercing familiarity. This "Wait" has almost always meant "Never." It has been a tranquilizing thalidomide, relieving the emotional stress for a moment, only to give birth to an ill-formed infant of frustration. We must come to see with the distinguished jurist of yesterday that "justice too long delayed is justice denied." We have waited for more than 340 years for our constitutional and God-given rights. The nations of Asia and Africa are moving with jetlike speed toward the goal of political independence, and we still creep at horse and buggy pace toward the gaining of a cup of coffee at a lunch counter. I guess it is easy for those who have never felt the stinging darts of segregation to say, "Wait." But when you have seen vicious mobs lynch your mothers and fathers at will and drown your sisters and brothers at whim; when you have seen hate-filled policemen curse, kick, brutalize and even kill your black brothers and sisters with impunity; when you see the vast majority of your twenty million Negro brothers smothering in an airtight cage of poverty in the midst of an affluent society; when you suddenly find your tongue twisted and your speech stammering as you seek to explain to your six-year-old daughter why she can't go to the public amusement park that has just been advertised on television, and see tears welling up in her little eyes when she is told that Funtown is closed to colored children, and see the depressing clouds of inferiority begin to form in her little mental sky, and see her begin to distort her little personality by unconsciously developing a bitterness toward white people; when you have to concoct an answer for a five-year-old son asking in agonizing pathos: "Daddy, why do white people treat colored people so mean?"; when you take a cross-country drive and find it necessary to sleep night after night in the uncomfortable corners of your automobile because no motel will accept you; when you are humiliated day in and day out by nagging signs reading "white" and "colored"; when your first name becomes "nigger" and your middle name becomes "boy" (however old you are) and your last name becomes "John," and when your wife and mother are never given the respected title "Mrs."; when you are harried by day and haunted by night by the fact that you are a Negro, living constantly at tiptoe stance never quite knowing what to expect next, and plagued with inner fears and outer resentments; when you are forever fighting a degenerating sense of "nobodiness"; then you will understand why we find it difficult to wait. There comes a time when the cup of endurance runs over, and men are no longer willing to be plunged into an abyss of injustice where they experience the blackness of corroding despair. I hope, sirs, you can understand our legitimate and unavoidable impatience.

You express a great deal of anxiety over our willingness to break laws. This is certainly a legitimate concern. Since we so diligently urge people to obey the Supreme Court's decision of 1954 outlawing segregation in the public schools, it is rather strange and paradoxical to find us consciously breaking laws. One may well ask, "How can you advocate breaking some laws and obeying others?" The answer is found in the fact that there are two types of laws: there are *just* and there are *unjust* laws. I would agree with Saint Augustine that "An unjust law is no law at all."

Now what is the difference between the two? How does one determine when a law is just or unjust? A just law is a manmade code that squares with the moral law or the law of God. An unjust law is a code that is out of harmony with the moral law. To put it in the terms of Saint Thomas Aquinas, an unjust law is a human law that is not rooted in eternal and natural law. Any law that uplifts human personality is just. Any law that degrades human personality is unjust. All segregation statutes are unjust because segregation distorts the soul and damages the personality. It gives the segregator a false sense of superiority, and the segregated a false sense of inferiority. To use the words of Martin Buber, the great Jewish philosopher, segregation substitutes an "I-it" relationship for the "I-thou" relationship, and ends up relegating persons to the status of things. So segregation is not only politically, economically and sociologically unsound, but it is morally wrong and sinful. Paul Tillich has said that sin is separation. Isn't segregation an existential expression of man's tragic separation, an expression of his awful estrangement, his terrible sinfulness? So I can urge men to disobey segregation ordinances because they are morally wrong.

Let us turn to a more concrete example of just and unjust laws. An unjust law is a code that a majority inflicts on a minority that is not binding on itself. This is difference made legal. On the other hand a just law is a code that a majority compels a minority to follow that it is willing to follow itself. This is sameness made legal.

Let me give another explanation. An unjust law is a code inflicted upon a minority which that minority had no part in enacting or creating because they did not have the un-hampered right to vote. Who can say that the legislature of Alabama which set up the segregation laws was democratically elected? Throughout the state of Alabama all types of conniving methods are used to prevent Negroes from becoming registered voters and there are some counties without a single Negro registered to vote despite the fact that the Negro constitutes a majority of the population. Can any law set up in such a state be considered democratically structured?

These are just a few examples of unjust and just laws. There are some instances when a law is just on its face and unjust in its application. For instance, I was arrested Friday on a charge of parading without a permit. Now there is nothing wrong with an ordinance which requires a permit for a parade, but when the ordinance is used to preserve segregation and to deny citizens the First Amendment privilege of peaceful assembly and peaceful protest, then it becomes unjust.

I hope you can see the distinction I am trying to point out. In no sense do I advocate evading or defying the law as the rabid segregationist would do. This would lead to anarchy. One who breaks an unjust law must do it *openly, lovingly* (not hatefully as the white mothers did in New Orleans when they were seen on television screaming, "nigger, nigger, nigger"), and with a willingness to accept the penalty. I submit that an individual who breaks a law that conscience tells him is unjust, and willingly accepts the penalty by staying in jail to arouse the conscience of the community over its injustice, is in reality expressing the very highest respect for law.

Of course, there is nothing new about this kind of civil disobedience. It was seen sublimely in the refusal of Shadrach, Meshach and Abednego to obey the laws of Nebuchadnezzar because a higher moral law was involved. It was practiced superbly by the early Christians who were willing to face hungry lions and the excruciating pain of chopping blocks, before submitting to certain unjust laws of the Roman Empire. To a degree academic freedom is reality today because Socrates practiced civil disobedience.

We can never forget that everything Hitler did in Germany was "legal" and everything the Hungarian freedom fighters did in Hungary was "illegal." It was "illegal" to aid and comfort a Jew in Hitler's Germany. But I am sure that if I had lived in Germany during that time I would have aided and comforted my Jewish brothers even though it was illegal. If I lived in a Communist country today where certain principles dear to the Christian faith are suppressed, I believe I would openly advocate disobeying these anti-religious laws. I must make two honest confessions to you, my Christian and Jewish brothers. First, I must confess that over the last few years I have been gravely disappointed with the white moderate. I have almost reached the regrettable conclusion that the Negro's great stumbling block in the stride toward freedom is not the White Citizen's Councilor or the Ku Klux Klanner, but the white moderate who is more devoted to "order" than to justice; who prefers a negative peace which is the absence of tension to a positive peace which is the presence of justice; who constantly says, "I agree with you in the goal you seek, but I can't agree with your methods of direct action"; who paternalistically feels that he can set the timetable for another man's freedom; who lives by the myth of time and who constantly advised the Negro to wait until a "more convenient season." Shallow understanding from people of ill will. Lukewarm acceptance is much more bewildering than outright rejection.

I had hoped that the white moderate would understand that law and order exist for the purpose of establishing justice, and that when they fail to do this they become dangerously structured dams that block the flow of social progress. I had hoped that the white moderate would understand the present tension of the South is merely a necessary phase of the transition from an obnoxious negative peace, where the Negro passively accepted his unjust plight, to a substance-filled positive peace, where all men will respect the dignity and worth of human personality. Actually, we who engage in nonviolent direct action are not the creators of tension. We merely bring to the surface the hidden tension that is already alive. We bring it out in the open where it can be seen and dealt with. Like a boil that can never be cured as long as it is covered up but must be opened with all its pus-flowing ugliness to the natural medicines of air and light, injustice must likewise be exposed, with all of the tension its exposing creates, to the light of human conscience and the air of national opinion before it can be cured.

In your statement you asserted that our actions, even though peaceful, must be condemned because they precipitate violence. But can this assertion be logically made? Isn't this like condemning the robbed man because his possession of money precipitated the evil act of robbery? Isn't this like condemning Socrates because his unswerving commitment to truth and his philosophical delvings precipitated the misguided popular mind to make him drink the hemlock? Isn't this like condemning Jesus because His unique God-consciousness and never-ceasing devotion to his will precipitated the evil act of crucifixion? We must come to see, as federal courts have consistently affirmed, that it is immoral to urge an individual to withdraw his efforts to gain his basic constitutional rights because the quest precipitates violence. Society must protect the robbed and punish the robber.

I had also hoped that the white moderate would reject the myth of time. I received a letter this morning from a white brother in Texas which said: "All Christians know that the colored people will receive equal rights eventually, but it is possible that you are in too great of a religious hurry. It has taken Christianity almost two thousand years to accomplish what it has. The teachings of Christ take time to come to earth." All that is said here grows out of a tragic misconception of time. It is the strangely irrational notion that there is something in the very flow of time that will inevitably cure all ills. Actually time is neutral. It can be used either destructively or constructively. I am coming to feel that the people of ill will have used time much more effectively than the people of good will. We will have to repent in the generation not merely for the vitriolic words and actions of the bad people, but for the appalling silence of the good people. We must come to see that human progress never rolls in on wheels of inevitability. It comes through the tireless efforts and persistent work of men willing to be coworkers with God, and without this hard work time itself becomes an ally of the forces of social stagnation. We must use time creatively, and forever realize that the time is always ripe to do right. Now is the time to make real the promise of democracy, and transform our pending national elegy into a creative psalm of brotherhood. Now is the time to lift our national policy from the quicksand of racial injustice to the solid rock of human dignity.

You spoke of our activity in Birmingham as extreme. At first I was rather disappointed that fellow clergymen would see my non-violent efforts as those of the extremist. I started thinking about the fact that I stand in the middle of two opposing forces in the Negro community. One is a force of complacency made up of Negroes who, as a result of long years of oppression, have been so completely drained of self-respect and a sense of "somebodiness" that they have adjusted to segregation, and, of a few Negroes in the middle class who, because of a degree of academic and economic security, and because at points they profit by segregation, have unconsciously become insensitive to

the problems of the masses. The other force is one of bitterness and hatred, and comes perilously close to advocating violence. It is expressed in the various black nationalist groups that are springing up over the nation, the largest and best known being Elijah Muhammad's Muslim movement. This movement is nourished by the contemporary frustrations over the continued existence of racial discrimination. It is made up of people who have lost faith in America, who have absolutely repudiated Christianity, and who have concluded that the white man is an incurable "devil." I have tried to stand between these two forces, saying that we need not follow the "do-nothingism" of the complacent or the hatred and despair of the black nationalist. There is the more excellent way of love and nonviolent protest. I'm grateful to God that, through the Negro church, the dimension of nonviolence entered our struggle. If this philosophy had not emerged, I am convinced that by now many streets of the South would be flowing with floods of blood. And I am further convinced that if our white brothers dismiss us as "rabble-rousers" and "outside agitators" those of us who are working through the channels of nonviolent direct action and refuse to support our nonviolent efforts, millions of Negroes, out of frustration and despair, will seek solace and security in black nationalist ideologies, a development that will lead inevitably to frightening racial nightmare.

Oppressed people cannot remain oppressed forever. The urge for freedom will eventually come. This is what happened to the American Negro. Something within has reminded him of his birthright of freedom; something without has reminded him that he can gain it. Consciously and unconsciously, he has been swept in by what the Germans call the *Zeitgeist*, and with his black brothers of Africa, and his brown and yellow brothers of Asia, South America and the Caribbean, he is moving with a sense of cosmic urgency toward the promised land of racial justice. Recognizing this vital urge that has engulfed the Negro community, one should readily understand public demonstrations. The Negro has many pentup resentments and latent frustrations. He has to get them out. So let him march sometime; let him have his prayer pilgrimages to the city hall; understand why he must have sit-ins and freedom rides. If his repressed emotions do not come out in these non-violent ways, they will come out in ominous expressions of violence. This is not a threat; it is a fact of history. So I have not said to my people "get rid of your discontent." But I have tried to say that this normal and healthy discontent can be channelized through the creative outlet of nonviolent direct action. Now this approach is being dismissed as extremist. I must admit that I was initially disappointed in being so categorized.

But as I continued to think about the matter I gradually gained a bit of satisfaction from being considered an extremist. Was not Jesus an extremist in love—"Love your enemies, bless them that curse you, pray for them that despitefully use you." Was not Amos an extremist for justice—"Let justice roll down like waters and righteousness like a mighty stream." Was not Paul an extremist for the gospel of Jesus Christ—"I bear in my body the marks of the Lord Jesus." Was not Martin Luther an extremist—"Here I stand; I can do none other so help me God." Was not John Bunyan an extremist—"I will stay in jail to the end of my days before I make a butchery of my conscience." Was not Abraham Lincoln an extremist—"This nation cannot survive half slave and half free." Was not Thomas Jefferson an extremist—"We hold these truths to be self-evident, that all men are created equal." So the question is not whether we will be extremist but what kind of extremist will we be. Will we be extremists for hate or will we be extremists for love? Will we be extremists for the preservation of injustice—or will we be extremists for the cause of justice? In that dramatic scene on Calvary's hill, three men were crucified. We must not forget that all three were crucified for the same crime—the crime of extremism. Two were extremists for immorality and thusly fell below their environment. The other, Jesus Christ, was an extremist for love, truth and goodness, and thereby rose above his environment. So, after all, maybe the South, the nation and the world are in dire need of creative extremists.

I had hoped that the white moderate would see this. Maybe I was too optimistic. Maybe I expected too much. I guess I should have realized that few members of a race that has oppressed another race can understand or appreciate the deep groans and passionate yearnings of those that have been oppressed and still fewer have the vision to see that injustice must be rooted out by strong, persistent and determined action. I am thankful, however, that some of our white brothers have grasped the meaning of this social revolution and committed themselves to it. They are still all too small in quantity, but they are big in quality. Some like Ralph McGill, Lillian Smith, Harry Golden and James Dabbs have written about our struggle in eloquent, prophetic and understanding terms. Others have marched with us down nameless streets of the South. They have languished in filthy roach-infested jails, suffering the abuse and brutality of angry policeman who see them as "dirty nigger-lovers." They, unlike so many of their moderate brothers and sisters, have recognized the urgency of the moment and sensed the need for powerful "action" antidotes to combat the disease of segregation.

Let me rush on to mention my other disappointments. I have been so greatly disappointed with the white church and its leadership. Of course, there are some notable exceptions. I am not unmindful of the fact that each of you has taken some significant stands on this issue. I commend you, Rev. Stallings, for your Christian stance on this past Sunday, in welcoming Negroes to your worship service on a non-segregated basis. I commend the Catholic leaders of this state for integrating Springhill College several years ago.

But despite these notable exceptions I must honestly reiterate that I have been disappointed with the church. I do not say that as one of the negative critics who can always find something wrong with the church. I say it as a minister of the gospel, who loves the church; who was nurtured in its bosom; who has been sustained by its spiritual blessings and who will remain true to it as long as the cord of life shall lengthen.

I had the strange feeling when I was suddenly catapulted into the leadership of the bus protest in Montgomery several years ago that we would have the support of the white church. I felt that the white ministers, priests and rabbis of the South would be some of our strongest allies. Instead, some have been outright opponents, refusing to understand the freedom movement and misrepresenting its leaders; all too many others have been more cautious than courageous and have remained silent behind the anesthetizing security of the stained-glass windows.

In spite of my shattered dreams of the past, I came to Birmingham with the hope that the white religious leadership of this community would see the justice of our cause, and with deep moral concern, serve as the channel through which our just grievances would get to the power structure. I had hoped that each of you would understand. But again I have been disappointed. I have heard numerous religious leaders of the South call upon their worshippers to comply with a desegregation decision because it is the *law*, but I have longed to hear white ministers say, "Follow this decree because integration is morally *right* and the Negro is your brother." In the midst of blatant injustices inflicted upon the Negro, I have watched white churches stand on the sideline and merely mouth pious irrelevancies and sanctimonious trivialities. In the midst of a mighty struggle to rid our nation of racial economic injustice, I have heard so many ministers say, "Those are social issues with which the gospel has no real concern," and I have watched so many churches commit themselves to a completely otherworldly religion which made a strange distinction between body and soul, the sacred and the secular.

So here we are moving toward the exit of the twentieth century with a religious community largely adjusted to the status quo, standing as a taillight behind other community agencies rather than a headlight leading men to higher levels of justice.

I have traveled the length and breadth of Alabama, Mississippi and all the other southern states. On sweltering summer days and crisp autumn mornings I have looked at her beautiful churches with their lofty spires pointing heavenward. I have beheld the impressive outlay of her massive religious education buildings. Over and over again I have found myself asking: "What kind of people worship here? Who is their God? Where were their voices when the lips of Governor Barnett dripped with words of interposition and nullification? Where were they when Governor Wallace gave the clarion call for defiance and hatred? Where were their voices of support when tired, bruised and weary Negro men and women decided to rise from the dark dungeons of complacency to the bright hills of creative protest?"

Yes, these questions are still in my mind. In deep disappointment, I have wept over the laxity of the church. But be assured that my tears have been tears of love. There can be no deep disappointment where there is not deep love. Yes, I love the church; I love her sacred walls. How could I do otherwise? I am in the rather unique position of being the son, the grandson and the great-grandson of preachers. Yes, I see the church as the body of Christ. But, oh! How we have blemished and scarred that body through social neglect and fear of being nonconformists.

There was a time when the church was very powerful. It was during that period when the early Christians rejoiced when they were deemed worthy to suffer for what they believed. In those days the church was not merely a thermometer that recorded the ideas and principles of popular opinion; it was a thermostat that transformed the mores of society. Wherever the early Christians entered a town the power structure got disturbed and immediately sought to convict them for being "disturbers of the peace" and "outside agitators." But they went on with the conviction that they were "a colony of heaven," and had to obey God rather than man. They were small in number but big in commitment. They were too God-intoxicated to be "astronomically intimidated." They brought an end to such ancient evils as infanticide and gladiatorial contest.

Things are different now. The contemporary church is often a weak, ineffectual voice with an uncertain sound. It is so often the arch-supporter of the status quo. Far from being disturbed by the presence of the church, the power structure of the average community is consoled by the church's silent and often vocal sanction of things as they are.

But the judgment of God is upon the church as never before. If the church of today does not recapture the sacrificial spirit of the early church, it will lose its authentic ring, forfeit the loyalty of millions, and be dismissed as an irrelevant social club with no meaning for the twentieth century. I am meeting young people every day whose disappointment with the church has risen to outright disgust.

Maybe again, I have been too optimistic. Is organized religion too inextricably bound to the status quo to save our nation and the world? Maybe I must turn my faith to the inner spiritual church, the church within the church, as the true *ecclesia* and the hope of the world. But again I am thankful to God that some noble souls from the ranks of organized religion have broken loose from the paralyzing chains of conformity and joined us as active partners in the struggle for freedom. They have left their secure congregations and walked the streets of Albany, Georgia, with us. They have gone through the highways of the South on tortuous rides for freedom. Yes, they have gone to jail with us. Some have been kicked out of their churches, and lost support of their bishops and fellow ministers. But they have gone with faith that right defeated is stronger than evil triumphant. These men have been the leaven in the lump of the race. Their witness has been the spiritual salt that has preserved the true meaning of the gospel in these troubled times. They have carved a tunnel of hope through the dark mountain of disappointment.

I hope the church as a whole will meet the challenge of this decisive hour. But even if the church does not come to the aid of justice, I have no despair about the future. I have no fear about the outcome of our struggle in Birmingham, even if our motives are presently misunderstood. We will reach the goal of freedom in Birmingham and all over the nation, because the goal of America is freedom. Abused and scorned though we may be, our destiny is tied up with the destiny of America. Before the Pilgrims landed at Plymouth we were here. Before the pen of Jefferson etched across the pages of history the majestic words of the Declaration of Independence, we were here. For more than two centuries our foreparents labored in this country without wages; they made cotton king; and they built the homes of their masters in the midst of brutal injustice and shameful humiliation—and yet out of a bottomless vitality they continued to thrive and

develop. If the inexpressible cruelties of slavery could not stop us, the opposition we now face will surely fail. We will win our freedom because the sacred heritage of our nation and the eternal will of God are embodied in our echoing demands.

I must close now. But before closing I am impelled to mention one other point in your statement that troubled me profoundly. You warmly commended the Birmingham police force for keeping "order" and "preventing violence." I don't believe you would have so warmly commended the police force if you had seen its angry violent dogs literally biting six unarmed, nonviolent Negroes. I don't believe you would so quickly commend the policemen if you would observe their ugly and inhuman treatment of Negroes here in the city jail; if you would watch them push and curse old Negro women and young Negro girls; if you would see them slap and kick old Negro men and young boys; if you will observe them, as they did on two occasions, refuse to give us food because we wanted to sing our grace together. I'm sorry that I can't join you in your praise for the police department.

It is true that they have been rather disciplined in their public handling of the demonstrators. In this sense they have been rather publicly "nonviolent." But for what purpose? To preserve the evil system of segregation. Over the last few years I have consistently preached that nonviolence demands that the means we use must be as pure as the ends we seek. So I have tried to make it clear that it is wrong to use immoral means to attain moral ends. But now I must affirm that it is just as wrong, or even more so, to use moral means to preserve immoral ends. Maybe Mr. Connor and his policemen have been rather publicly nonviolent, as Chief Pritchett was in Albany, Georgia, but they have used the moral means of nonviolence to maintain the immoral end of flagrant racial injustice. T.S. Eliot has said that there is no greater treason than to do the right deed for the wrong reason.

I wish you had commended the Negro sit-inners and demonstrators of Birmingham for their sublime courage, their willingness to suffer and their amazing discipline in the midst of the most inhuman provocation. One day the South will recognize its real heroes. They will be the James Merediths, courageously and with a majestic sense of purpose facing jeering and hostile mobs and the agonizing loneliness that characterizes the life of the pioneer. They will be old, oppressed, battered Negro women, symbolized in a seventy-two-year-old woman of Montgomery, Alabama, who rose up with a sense of dignity and with her people decided not to ride the segregated buses, and responded to one who inquired about her tiredness with ungrammatical profundity: "My feet is tired, but my soul is rested." They will be the young high school and college students, young ministers of the gospel and a host of their elders courageously and nonviolently sitting-in at lunch counters and willingly going to jail for conscience's sake. One day the South will know that when these disinherited children of God sat down at lunch counters they were in reality standing up for the best in the American dream and the most sacred values in our Judeo-Christian heritage, and thusly, carrying our whole nation back to those great wells of democracy which were dug deep by the Founding Fa-

thers in the formulation of the Constitution and the Declaration of Independence.

Never before have I written a letter this long (or should I say a book?). I'm afraid that it is much too long to take your precious time. I can assure you that it would have been much shorter if I had been writing from a comfortable desk, but what else is there to do when you are alone for days in the dull monotony of a narrow jail cell other than write long letters, think strange thoughts, and pray long prayers?

If I have said anything in this letter that is an overstatement of the truth and is indicative of an unreasonable impatience, I beg you to forgive me. If I have said anything in this letter that is an understatement of the truth and is indicative of my having a patience that makes me patient with anything less than brotherhood, I beg God to forgive me.

I hope this letter finds you strong in the faith. I also hope that circumstances will soon make it possible for me to meet each of you, not as an integrationist or a civil rights leader, but as a fellow clergyman and a Christian brother. Let us all hope that the dark clouds of racial prejudice will soon pass away and the deep fog of misunderstanding will be lifted from our fear-drenched communities and in some not too distant tomorrow the radiant stars of love and brotherhood will shine over our great nation with all of their scintillating beauty.

Yours for the cause of Peace
and Brotherhood,
Martin Luther King, Jr.

The Christian and Vietnam
Charles C. West

"There is no moral issue more urgently confronting our Church and nation than the war in Vietnam. The hour is late; the church dare not remain silent." These words were adopted by The United Presbyterian Church in the United States of America in its general assembly in 1967. The assembly directed a special committee to prepare "a serious study of (1) the issues and dangers in the Vietnam situation, and (2) the responsibility of the Church to bear witness to the gospel in the formation of national policy."

Let me start with three observations on which I think all sides agree. *First*, the present struggle in Vietnam represents a pro-found conflict of moral responsibility. It is this which makes peace by negotiation so difficult. If the issues were defined in terms of the interests of opposing powers alone, the disproportion of the means now being used to any conceivable rational end would long since have led to compromise. The fact is, however, that all sides in the conflict are driven by a profound sense of obligation to purposes in which they believe, and which transcend their interests. For Ho Chi Minh and the Communist leadership in Vietnam the war is part of the struggle of exploited peoples all over the world to overthrow their imperialist and capitalist enemies in order to build a socialist society. For a great majority of non-Communists in the Eastern world, and a large number in the West, it represents the struggle of a nationalist movement with democratic tendencies to establish control by the people of Vietnam over their own country. For those in the United States and in the West who support the American effort uncritically the issue is containment of an international Communist conspiracy which would clamp a totalitarian system on one country after another unless its methods of terrorism and guerrilla warfare are stopped once and for all. For the many who are seeking a negotiated compromise the moral issue is peace itself, out of which may grow the healing forces of reconciliation and social reconstruction.

From these various moral imperatives come differing analyses of what is actually happening. Each of these analyses is far too much a creature of the moral ideal which it supports. The ambiguous realities of Vietnam are remade in the image of a world as the various partners to the dispute wish it

---

Included in its study *Vietnam—The Christian—The Gospel—The Church* (1967) was an article by Charles C. West, Professor of Applied Christianity at Princeton Theological Seminary, which is used here with permission of the General Assembly of the United Presbyterian Church in the United States of America.

could be. Here lies the basic problem for Christian understanding. Whence come the resources to understand the human conflict in that country in a way which reflects in some degree God's effort to overrule our bias and pass judgment on our actions?

Second, although it is expected that nations, political groups, economic powers and others will reflect the bias and the interest of their backgrounds and even that they will claim universal moral validity for their own power and program, it is the task of the Church to think and speak in the light of the way the God whom we know in Jesus Christ judges and transforms the biased perspectives of its members through the ecumenical community. Christians are not allowed a good conscience about their moral principles or their political analyses when these proceed from the perspective of one nation or one side of a conflict. They are bound by their faith to seek the wisdom of the Church Universal as the Word of God speaks to all its parts. This will lead the Church into conflict with the interest and security of many social and political groups to which its members belong. This is a risk which it must take. Its obligation is to speak to this world not of its victory or security but of the things that belong to its peace.

Third, for Christians the central focus of responsible analysis must be directly on the human beings involved in the struggle. Broad terms such as freedom, democracy, communism, revolution and liberation must be resolved into descriptions of the human relations they imply before we will know what value to give them. As authority and standard we have the living relation of Jesus Christ to other persons in all the variety of

its creative promise. It is from this relation that we understand justice and judgment, reconciliation and peace. For the Christian world is a complex of ongoing human relations in which the qualities of faithfulness, justice and love mean more than any structural society we seek to establish or maintain. The Church can therefore not help but be inherently skeptical of programs which inflict great human suffering today to realize an ideal tomorrow. It should on the other hand be especially sensitive to the ways in which relations of mutual trust and respect may be built up between nations and peoples in their day to day decisions.

Taking these three factors into consideration we face a moral dilemma in Vietnam which it would be well to state in all its force.

On the one side we are engaged in combat alongside many Vietnamese whose security depends on us, with a revolutionary movement basically under the control of the People's Revolutionary Party of Vietnam, a Communist organization under the direct control and command of North Vietnam. Although there are other elements in the National Liberation Front, none of them has a serious influence. The record of the People's Revolutionary Party parent body, the North Vietnamese Lao Dong under the leadership of Ho Chi Minh, is not one to inspire hope for justice or freedom should effective resistance to its power break down. Its ideology is rigidly Communist in the Chinese style. Every nationalist organization the Vietnamese Communists have joined they have subverted. They have consistently betrayed, terrorized and assassinated non-Communist leaders of the nationalist movement who would not accept their leadership and tactics. Their purges of the population from 1951 to 1956 did to death many thousands and imprisoned or enslaved many more under the pretext of eliminating exploiters, traitors and opponents to land reform. The rich and the reactionary were only a small portion of these. Their tactics of assassination and torture in the present war have been aimed at removing precisely the courageous and responsible leaders from the areas they wish to control.

There is no evidence that this line of action would change were the National Liberation Front to come to power in South Vietnam today. It is determined by the basic concepts of class war, of revolution through guerrilla tactics, and of control by a centralized Communist party—all of which are rooted in Communist dogma itself. One does not have to make a case for Chinese or Russian control over the strategy and tactics of Vietnamese Communism. The dogma itself as expounded by native Vietnamese leaders accounts for this inhumanity sufficiently, and explains also the solidarity which these leaders feel with China and the Soviet Union.

It is to save millions of innocent people in South Vietnam from the power of this movement that we are fighting there. There is little evidence that the National Liberation Front is a popular movement among those who know enough about it to make an intelligent choice. Almost no influential non-Communist leaders have lent their support to it. Vietnamese society is a bewildering complex of ethnic, religious and cultural groups which find it hard to unite around any common concept of the nation or loyalty to it. A long period of growing together accompanied inevitably by struggles for power, shifts of government and compromises of interest is inevitable in such a situation. This process is being subverted, however, by a terrorist movement, supported by its ideological comrades outside the country, which is using internal tensions and conflict for its own ends.

One might make the case that the United States nevertheless need not attempt to rescue the people of Vietnam from this fate if no internal forces arise to give responsible focus to the struggle. Given the character of Communist dogma and its tactics of revolution, however, the question of the safety of neighboring countries arises. Laos is already divided, and should South Vietnam fall the United States and its allies would face the same choices there. Thailand is also vulnerable, first through the Vietnamese, Laotians and Chinese who live on its soil and form a substantial proportion of its population. The struggle in Malaya would probably flare up again. There is of course no inevitability to Communist triumph through its tactics of guerrilla warfare. The situation in each of these countries is somewhat different. But a guerrilla war is far easier to prevent than to control once it has started. Even where it may not succeed in controlling a country it can destroy it from within. Given the fact that the United States has the power to absorb the energies of this destructive force in South Vietnam, what is its responsibility to the neighbors of that country who still enjoy a degree of peace and the hope of development? What suffering would we bring upon peoples in other countries around Vietnam by a unilateral withdrawal?

These are the hard moral facts which underlie our active engagement in the Vietnamese conflict. They do not depend on raising the spectre of an international Communist conspiracy directed from Peking or Moscow. The powerful political problem of containing Communist China is not the first issue here. Nor need we pretend that the government of South Vietnam is a democratic or even a military success. Enough that American power in this area provides the balance which protects the lives and a few of the liberties of hundreds of thousands of people in Vietnam itself and makes it possible for other nations in Southeast Asia to retain some control over their own destinies. This is one side of the dilemma. But there is another.

American efforts to suppress guerrilla warfare in Vietnam can hardly be called successful. Instead they have led us into actions which have inflicted suffering on vast numbers of Vietnamese comparable to that which we seek to overcome. Terror has been used by both sides in the war, though perhaps less discriminately and to less effect by our soldiers and the army of South Vietnam. Our answer to Vietcong infiltration has been the removal of whole villages and the bombing of other villages which did not move. The price of victory seems to be the destruction of any economy which the Vietcong had only taxed and controlled. The bombing of North Vietnam has only engaged that part of the country more actively in the conflict. Though the rising tide of Vietcong control has been arrested by massive American intervention during the last two years, the tide has not been turned. There are few areas peaceful enough that the construction of a non-Communist justice and freedom may begin. The government of South Vietnam

has been neither strong enough nor popular enough, assuming that it had the desire, to institute serious social reform. In short, our intervention in South Vietnam has increased the suffering of its people while their hopes for a free and peaceful future are continually postponed. It is about our responsibility for this suffering which we inflict that the Church must speak most seriously to the nation.

All of this is intensified by the tendency of our government to impose its own ideology on the Vietnamese situation. The result has been to obscure unpleasant facts, and to cut off dialogue with other peoples, including those of Vietnam itself, about our moral responsibility. Our leaders have continually overstressed the ideological conflict between Communism and the so-called free world. Thereby they have ignored the element of nationalist ambition that also drives the National Liberation Front and its North Vietnamese mentors. They forget that Ho Chi Minh has been for years the most powerful symbol of Vietnamese unity despite his Communism, and that the alliance he leads is the only all-Vietnamese political force not based on some ethnic, religious or regional interest. Our government has tended to overmilitarize the conflict, forgetting the subtle influences at work in the villages where the Vietcong, along with Saigon government influence and the presence of Americans, are accepted as one of the facts of life in the bargaining struggle for survival. Finally, our government has overestimated the capacity of foreign intervention to accomplish good. Increasing American strength has led to greater Vietnamese dependence which festers in anti-Americanism. We understand too little the religious and ethnic conflicts, the values and desires of the people of Vietnam caught in the midst of civil war. Our very foreignness and our power make this difficult. Our overconfidence in our own plans and programs make it impossible.

Are we then deceiving ourselves? Are we polarizing good and evil in our own way which does not correspond to the complex realities in Vietnam? To whom are we listening in order to discover that truth which lies outside the circle of our own ideology and is not intimidated by our power?

Thus the dilemma besets us. The more realistically we analyze the false pictures which our self-justifying desires beget, the harder it is to see any way forward which God does not judge. The more deeply we feel our human involvement with minds sensitized by Christ, the less bearable our actions become. Quite bluntly, if we are to find a tolerably human way out of this dilemma, if we are to speak of hope realistically, the basis for it must be given us from outside the human conflict. Self-manufactured hopes are illusions and self-justified actions are the most profoundly inhuman.

It is in this context that the Christian faith speaks of hope for the human situation. "God was in Christ, reconciling the world to himself, not counting their trespasses against them; and entrusting to us the message of reconciliation" (II Cor. 5:19). This is the first movement of history. It is the context of political and social understanding and action. It does not depend upon some other analysis, but rather informs all analysis. Because we know by faith that the future belongs to the God whose character and

purpose are revealed in Jesus Christ, we are called on to find signs of his grace overruling and guiding the conflicting plans and hopes of human societies today. "The root of Jesse shall come, he who rises to rule the nations. In him shall the nations hope" (Rom. 15:12). It is the creative task of Christians then to offer political authorities, in our own nation and others, a hope for the future which is not based on their strength or analyses, but in the relationship with God which has been given to all of us. Hope is a matter of trusting the future of this relation. This has a number of consequences for our attitude and action in Vietnam.

First, because our hope does not depend on our analyses we can afford to see facts as they are. We need no longer argue if we support our government in Vietnam that a free and democratic society is just around the corner, or if we oppose it that a Vietcong victory will bring peace and social justice. We gain from our faith the power to be profoundly skeptical of these hopes which are mere justifications for a particular line of policy. In most cases actions bespeak quite a different way of reckoning with the forces of reality than words express. The Chinese Communists speak belligerently of an international class conflict carried on by guerrilla warfare encircling the great urban centers of the world. Their actions, however, are cautious and restrained, and their commitment to the Vietnamese war is remarkably limited. The South Vietnamese National Liberation Front speaks mildly of democracy. Its actions, however, betray the classic pattern of Maoist tactics for the conquest of power. On our side the desire for negotiated peace is constantly belied by our ever-increasing commitment of troops and our bombing of the North. It is a gift of God's grace to our faith that we should be able to see ourselves as we look to those who oppose us, and our opponents as they look to God, and not to themselves. From this insight new and more realistic policies might flow.

Second, a proper understanding of the way God works ought to make us profoundly aware of the relative and biased nature of our own morality. Public order and justice in any form in this world are possible only as God's grace overrules the private and group ambitions of men, and forces them into responsible relations with one another. The sphere of international relations is no exception. A wise nation, therefore, will not make an absolute of its own cause, for it too is under judgment. It is honesty before God to recognize that the perspectives of our nation or our group are relative to our interests, and that our ideals and principles also reflect the bias of our experiences and desires. The peace which Christ makes on this earth judges and transforms every people's idea of what is just and good. Christians therefore will commend to their government realism in evaluating both friend and foe, and a responsible relation to both. To idealize our allies and demonize our enemies is to forget who it is through whom we are related to both. Because we know ourselves as an ambitious, sinful nation, able to get along with other peoples only because there is grace and forgiveness in the world, we ought also to recognize other nations as peoples like ourselves, who pursue their interests as they see them and live by the same grace we do. "While we were yet enemies, we were reconciled to God by the death of his Son" (Rom. 5:10). We therefore have a responsibility to our enemy, not to define

the conflict as the final reality between us, but to seek for ways of reconciliation which may transcend and transform the biased righteousness each of us claims to uphold. Because the future belongs to Christ, no human conflict is quite as absolute as we imagine it to be. Compromise, therefore, and peace without victory, can be channels of grace and hope.

Third, there is implied in this Christian realism a quality of human relations which reflects the quality of God's relation with man, reflected in the word faithfulness. "The Lord is faithful in all his words and gracious in all his deeds" writes the Psalmist (Ps. 145:13), and illustrates it by his upholding the weak, giving food in due season, executing justice, and saving those who call on him. Faithfulness is a relation of constancy, sincerity, and openness to the needs of the neighbor. It is an attitude which upholds a relation even when the other party breaks it off, as God remains faithful to his covenant with man in spite of man's disobedience. Faithfulness is a quality which discerns and reckons with hope and truth in a responsible relation to God, to nature, and to other men. Because the faithful man is conscious of the limit and correction of God, he is prepared to listen to, and learn from, and give himself to other men. The same should be true of a nation. Faithfulness means consistency of character in the give and take of human relations, not absoluteness of principle. It bears witness not to our own goodness but to the God we serve, that is, to the governing reality in this world with which we reckon. It is this quality for which other nations look when they are determining their relations with us. It is this quality in the long run, as shown by nations to each other, which will determine the peace of the world. For our nation this has definite consequences.

a. As a strong nation we are responsible for demonstrating our subjection to the will of God by subjecting our military and political power to the judgment and correction of other nations. Unilateral action on our part which cannot be checked by others whose interests are involved, raises suspicion and fear among friends as well as enemies. It destroys responsible cooperation and creates a relation in which other peoples react to our power itself, rather than to our reasons and our hopes. This is a serious consequence of our position in Vietnam.

b. As a strong and wealthy nation we are called to demonstrate our stewardship of God's gifts by the way we share them with peoples less fortunately placed. It is God's faithfulness and not our virtue that has made us rich. This very wealth and our natural acceptance of it, however, has placed a barrier between poor peoples and ourselves. The judgment of God falls with special severity upon the strong and the rich. One reason is that a small act of selfishness and insensitivity by those who have so much can be so widespread in its consequences. The task posed for our faithfulness is to help our neighbors find their independence over against us as they seek to achieve justice and prosperity for themselves. Once again, international control of the instruments of economic development and justice is required. We who are wealthy need to learn neither to keep our wealth to ourselves not to use it to dominate others. The problem of the responsible use of wealth is the creative renunciation of power over wealth.

c. We are also required to be faithful to our enemies. As a very minimum this means respecting the written and unwritten rules of warfare, and the tacit agreements which limit our conflict. It means further, however, active seeking for a new relation with our enemy, and a new understanding of him which might be the basis of peace between us. We are commanded by Jesus, himself, to love our enemies and to pray for them, and by Paul to feed and clothe them. The latter means respecting his basic right to live. The former means understanding him from within, from the point of view of his own true interests and best ideals. It means being aware of the way in which God is transforming his society as well as ours, so that the future may not repeat the past. We have done far too little of this in Vietnam and with relation to China. We have not yet created the spiritual tools of perception which would make peace a possibility.

Fourth, all of this leads to a final truth which is hardest for us to accept. We know from the New Testament that there are powers in this world that seek to rebel against God and yet in spite of themselves do his will. Nuclear armaments, predominance in sea and air, and a stable wealthy economy all are such powers as these. By means of them the United States is the strongest power in the world. Yet all of them are incapable of accomplishing anything except destruction, save as servants of the reconciling power of the servant of all men, Jesus Christ. This is the paradox of our position in Vietnam. We cannot impose a healthy democracy in South Vietnam; we can only win the respect and friendship of the people there by the quality of our concern for them and our understanding of their desires and points of view. We cannot conquer the Communist ideology by force of arms. We cannot even dismiss it by force of argument. We can only show Communists in various places in the world that we also are concerned for the welfare of our neighbors and that we respect the freedom of those neighbors a little more successfully than they. The power to redeem social chaos and to build justice and peace is the power of renunciation and service, "Behold my servant whom I uphold; my chosen in whom my soul delights; he will not cry nor lift up his voice or make it heard in the street; a bruised reed he will not break and a dimly burning wick he will not quench; he will faithfully bring forth justice" (Isa. 42:1-3). Military power in Vietnam or elsewhere can only be a blessing therefore if it is used in full consciousness of its provisional, limited character. It is the disproportion of power to service which is so disquieting there today.

A corollary follows from this. The power of the strongest nation on earth to accomplish anything for peace and freedom is severely limited. With all our force we cannot control the events of the world nor even the course of history in Vietnam. There is suffering we cannot prevent and there are injustices we cannot set right. The way of the servant of God goes through suffering to the establishment of justice. The way of Christ's reconciliation is the way of the cross.

For the Church this means that Christians belong on both sides of every battle line and especially in those areas where their enemies are in power. For a nation like ours it means risks and perhaps sacrifices of our prestige, our capital, and even our security. It means entrusting our diplomats and our citizens to hostile lands. It means subjecting our power to international control and seeking patterns of relations where there are no dominant and dominated partners. There are examples for this in the modern world. Britain has never been so creatively related to India as during the past twenty years since independence. France has never been so popular in Africa as today when her last colony has gone. Our own relations to Indonesia are an example of what is possible. In all of these there has been suffering and loss. In many of them injustice has been done which the dominant power might have sought to prevent. But all of them are informed by a quality of renunciation, of faithfulness between equals, and of modesty in moral claims which characterize a society judged and redeemed by Jesus Christ. They suggest a quality which we should be seeking in Vietnam today.

The Jesus People
Ronald M. Enroth

Ronald M. Enroth (1938-   ) is professor of sociology at Westmont College in Santa Barbara, California. He has written extensively on contemporary social issues which have faced the church over the past twenty-five years. The rise of the counter-culture during the 1960s had a profound effect on the institutionalized church which was a target of the antiestablishment sentiment of that turbulent decade. In *The Jesus People: Old-Time Religion in the Age of Aquarius* co-authored by Enroth, Edward E. Ericson, and C. Breckinridge Peters, one facet of the religious counterculture is examined, with special attention given to the reasons for its rise and its significance for the 1960s.

The Jesus People as a Social Movement: A Great Awakening or a Gentle Stir?

Any social movement—religious, political, economic—must be understood in the context of its social and cultural setting. To comprehend fully how the movement arises and develops and where it ends up, we must first describe the "spirit of the age" within which it functions. In his book, *Modern Social Movements*, William Bruce Cameron notes: "The purposes of a social movement cannot be evaluated, nor the actions of members understood, unless we clearly perceive the background of the society against which they play their part. Social movements . . . are made of the stuff that is at hand" (p. 21).

The "stuff" of the sixties and seventies has been delineated, categorized, and analyzed by sociologists, journalists, philosophers, psychologists, and assorted other "people-watchers." One of the more provocative endeavors at this is Rollo May's *Love and Will*. Another is *The Making of a Counter Culture* by Theodore Roszak. We shall draw on the works of these and other commentators on the American scene in order to place the Jesus Movement in a context appropriate for analysis.

We live in an impersonal, computerized, assembly-line, shopping-center society where all the old anchorages have been lost or weakened and where alienation has become the common malaise.

Thomas Cottle, in his perceptive volume, *Time's Children*, speaks of "our televised and instant replay society" where few secrets are allowed and "we become frustrated when we cannot discover the exact frame on which is recorded a President's death" (pp. 86-87). It is a society in which young people especially have been subjected to a tremendous over-stimulation—by the various media, by the myriad of confusing alternatives of vocation, religion, and morals, and by the mechanisms of an economic system that provides unparalleled affluence and seemingly endless stream of material goods for consumption.

At the same time that modern technological man has felt that he has the tools to control the universe and material possessions to make life worthwhile, he has experienced a spiritual emptiness and personal disorganization perhaps unequaled in human history. Our technical sophistication has not brought any culmination of human happiness, as Barbara Hargrove explains in her book *Reformation of the Holy*.

> There is a growing awareness in modern society that the basic assumptions of technical progress and scientific knowledge may be leading, not to Utopia, but to a loss of humanity if not total destruction. Not only is this so, but that awareness is compounded by the feeling that the technological machine cannot be stopped, that we are caught in an ever-descending spiral of our own making from which there is no escape (p. 281).

The introductory chapter of May's *Love and Will* is entitled "Our Schizoid World." "Schizoid" means "out of touch; avoiding close relationships; the inability to feel" (p. 16). He sees this schizoid orientation as a general condition of our culture and the people who comprise our society. He describes our world as one

> where numbers inexorably take over as our means of identification, like flowing lava threatening to suffocate and fossilize all breathing life in its path . . . where "normality" is defined as keeping your cool; where sex is so available that the only way to preserve any inner center is to learn to have intercourse without committing yourself . . . (p. 32).

Young people experience this schizoid world more directly than their elders, according to May, because "they have not had time to build up the defenses which dull the senses of their elders" (p. 32). Without the old values and symbols that served as a touchstone of orientation for past generations, today's generation is increasingly forced inward, pushed toward apathy, toward a state of affectlessness. This results in a society characterized by estrangement, indifference, anomie, and depersonalization. Ultimately, asserts May, such a process eventuates in violence. "When inward life dries up, when feeling decreases and apathy increases, when one cannot affect or even genuinely touch another person, violence flares up as a daimonic necessity for contact, a mad drive forcing touch in the most direct way possible" (pp. 30-31). The contemporary age has been characterized as one of "new freedom" and a new morality. Our highly vaunted permissiveness in the area of male-female relations has revealed the fact that "sex for many people has become more meaningless as it is more available . . ."

(May, p. 14). May continues: "What we did not see in our shortsighted liberalism in sex was that throwing the individual into an unbounded and empty sea of free choice does not in itself give freedom, but is more apt to increase inner conflicts" (p. 42).

If this is the age of liberated man and anonymous man, it is certainly the age of technocratic man. "Technocracy's Children" are the offspring of a social and economic system, writes Theodore Roszak, "which is so organized that it is inextricably beholden to expertise" (*The Making of a Counter Culture*, p. 19). They have come of age in a society of experts and scientism where efficiency and successful management are the order of the day. They have learned that performance counts, and the pressures to compete and succeed are often overwhelming. "One must be good in school, good at home, good at sports, good at pot and good in bed" (Cottle, p. 87).

It was in this complex social and cultural milieu that the Jesus Movement emerged. The 1960s saw armies of young people attempting to get "involved" with society's ills, trying to effect changes in the system. Barbara Hargrove relates the sequence of events that led to what she calls the "apocalyptic mood" of the present:

> Failure of civil rights and poverty programs, and of anti-war activity increased the feeling that the present system could not be changed or redirected. By the mid-sixties the quest had begun to turn inward. The disastrous political campaign of 1968, with its assassinations, its hope, and its riots, added to the disenchantment with political solutions. The widespread politicization of the campuses after the Cambodia-Kent State-Jackson State debacle in 1970 has apparently ended in the spread of disillusion and alienation from political processes (p. 282).

The decade of the sixties was a period of radical cultural disjuncture in America. It was a decade of transition, which gave birth to the counter-culture and witnessed the emergence of the hippie as a new social type. The hippie subculture represented a protest against the sterile technocratic society of the middle-class establishment. "What makes the youthful disaffiliation of our time a cultural phenomenon, rather than merely a political movement, is the fact that it strikes beyond ideology to the level of consciousness, seeking to transform our deepest sense of the self, the other, the environment" (Roszak, p. 49). Roszak describes the contemporary youth culture as being obsessed with feeling and passion as opposed to intellect and reason. There is a searching after visionary experience and an unprecedented penchant for occult and magical phenomena (pp. 124-25). Perhaps most significant of all is the counterculture's preoccupation with drugs, particularly the hallucinogenic drugs. In their frantic search for new experience and meaning, the flower children of the sixties sought to modify their consciousness through psychedelics and to connect with a new form of reality through pharmacological linkages. Hargrove observes that the so-called "mind-expanding" drugs represent "symbols of membership in a new society with different cultural values" and have been used "as a means of establishing new patterns of perception upon which that society could be based" (p. 283).

With the demise of the Haight-Asbury scene in San Francisco came the realization that "personal salvation and the social revolution [cannot] be packed in a capsule" (Roszak, p. 177).

As the use of drugs (especially the so-called "hard" drugs like heroin) leveled off and even declined, interest in mystical and Eastern religions increased. As Hargrove notes:

> More and more the young are rejecting the drug-induced experience as part of the unnatural "plastic" world they seek to escape, and they turn instead to the consciousness-manipulation of Eastern religions. The greater apparent willingness of Eastern religions to treat man as a part of nature rather than as its master has much appeal in a time of awareness of Western environmental bungling (p. 283).

While some hip youth looked to Eastern mysticism, American Indian religious lore, or meditation for some kind of transcendental experience, others discovered Jesus—not in the institutional church, for organized religion held little appeal, but in the simple message of the gospel and the teachings of Christ. It is significant that these experience-oriented members of the counterculture found meaning not only in conversion and the dramatic transformation that it entails, but also in those practices of primitive Christianity that had been all but forgotten by the historical Christian churches—healing, tongues, and other gifts of the Holy Spirit. In addition to meeting very real and deeply felt spiritual needs, the charismatic gifts experienced by many Jesus People may be thought of as ways to resolve more gen-

eral inner conflicts. The teeny-boppers and flower children of the technocratic society are, more often than not, the victims of multiple inner conflicts. These tensions arise from several sources: from relations with parents and other authority figures in the establishment, from the demands for performance and achievement that haunt young people at every turn, from the desperate search for identity and the means to cope with the problems of our society.

The notion that charismatic phenomena fulfill a need in the lives of individuals who are experiencing conflict is discussed convincingly by Marvin Mayers in the September 1971 *Journal of the American Scientific Affiliation*. Although Mayers primarily is concerned with the attraction that charismatic groups have for some members of traditional churches, his explanation is also valid for new converts from the hip subculture:

> The established church seems to be traditional in its ways, impersonal in its approach to outsiders and even towards its own members. It appears to be like a machine that is interested more in keeping moving and keeping its gears oiled than in developing spiritual insight and experience in the lives of its members. Especially young people want to be thought of not as a part of a machine, but as unique persons. They thus become disgruntled with the church and its practices. At this point they seek out more personal organizations, leaders who relate to them more individually and personally, who treat them as valid persons, and who communicate personalness to them. Too often, in the impersonal established church the individual feels unwanted,

rejected, alienated. Holy Spirit movements reverse this process. The key is involvement, participation, the bringing of the individual into the total experience (p. 92).

This no doubt explains why an increasing number of young people attend a church like Calvary Chapel (chapter four) on weeknights and perhaps Sunday nights while attending the church of their parents on Sunday morning—and why some traditional church people seek out small charismatic prayer and fellowship groups while retaining ties to the home church.

Mayers does not suggest that the individual who resolves his conflicts through encounter with charismatic groups is necessarily emotionally disturbed. He recognizes, however, that "there are varying stages of conflict that may or may not result in emotional disturbance. But more, these people are ready for a new experience; one that promises them vitality, involvement, and participation. They are ready to flee from some bad experience or some bad situation" (p. 92).

Many of the converts in the Jesus Movement are indeed fleeing from bad experiences and deteriorating life situations. Large numbers of them were heavy drug users. They had withdrawn from society. Their encounter with Jesus Christ made them once again participating members of the human race. Frequently, but not always, they were encouraged to get jobs, return to school, and make amends with parents and the law. The Jesus Movement provided the opportunity to restore some sort of order, stability, and meaning to their lives. It put them in touch with the supernatural and made involvement in the form of witnessing a new and vital dimension to their lives.

The teen-aged runaway is one of the sad by-products of our schizoid culture. This social phenomenon represents, as Roszak points out, much more a flight *from* than a flight *toward*. "Certainly for a youngster of seventeen, clearing out of the comfortable bosom of the middle-class family to become a beggar is a formidable gesture of dissent. One makes light of it at the expense of ignoring a significant measure of our social health" (p. 34). The tragic dimensions of this youthful exodus can only be fully understood when one talks in person to the parties involved, as we did in the course of research for this book. Thomas Cottle eloquently discusses the failure of the parental generation in his volume, *Time's Children*:

> No one as yet has studied the notes written by parents to their runaway children in New York's East Village or San Francisco's Haight Asbury district. . . .These pitiful missives document so well the lack of generational space and the confession of failure in parenthood and adulthood. They could almost be the letters of children who, wishing to come home, promise never again to misbehave. . . . The "Come back home —all is forgiven" notes stand as a testament to what must be seen by the young as a crumbling structure or a tragic reversal of intentionally and interpersonal competence (p. 89).

Whatever their reason for leaving home, hundreds of teenagers have been converted to Christ at places like Bethel Tabernacle in Redondo Beach, California, and have been reunited with their parents. Older teenagers and young adults have found a strong sense of family in Christian communes and with groups like the Children of God. "Their rigid discipline and strong fellowship provide a solid base for anomic young people who have found no place for themselves in the technological culture of the society" (Hargrove, p. 284).

The need for fellowship and close interaction felt by the Jesus People reflects the quest for community that characterizes the youth culture in general. Hargrove relates this quest to a more general search for religious meaning on the part of young people today.

> Young people are especially affected by the loss of strong kinship and community support, particularly since social patterns relegate them to a category somewhat separate from the rest of society. They attempt to overcome feelings of isolation by banding together in groups which can offer personal and social support. ... One reaction to this is withdrawal into intimate groups in which effort is made to reveal and support the identities of members. Much of this kind of activity falls within broad definitions of religion, and often it is specifically labeled religious. . . .

A social movement can be defined as a large-scale, widespread, informal effort by a fairly large number of people to modify or in some way influence the existing social order. Social movements usually rise spontaneously and assume various forms. Some comprise an indefinite, shifting, unstruc-

tured membership, with the members rarely if ever meeting face to face. Other movements are more highly organized, tightly knit, intimate groups who collectively promote some program of change. The Jesus Movement is an unorganized social movement in the sense that it is composed of widely scattered subgroups that, although sharing common interests and certain basic concerns, are not united under a single leadership structure or a clearly articulated set of goals and objectives. The various subgroups are, however, internally often highly structured and influenced by very strong leaders. While they sometimes acknowledge a vague linkage with a larger movement that is not well defined—to them at least—these groups are often fiercely independent and ethnocentric. If we keep this kind of grassroots diversity clearly in focus, it is valuable to consider the Jesus People as constituting a social movement.

Members of social movements are usually highly committed to "the cause." This commitment may become so fervent that, in effect, the person relinquishes an autonomous individual existence. The following comments by Eric Hoffer are directly applicable to a group like the Children of God:

> An individual existence, even when purposeful, seems to him futile and sinful. To live without an ardent dedication is to be adrift and abandoned. He sees in tolerance a sign of weakness, frivolity, and ignorance. He hungers for the deep assurance which comes with total surrender—with the wholehearted clinging to a creed and a cause. . . . He is even ready to join in a holy crusade against his former holy cause, but it

must be a genuine crusade—uncompromising, intolerant, proclaiming the one and only truth (*The True Believer*, p. 82).

Virtually every act of membership, Toch reminds us, "involves a sacrifice of privacy and autonomy, at least in the sense that the member must accomplish some of his objectives as part of a group, rather than as an individual" (p. 133). Some students of mass movements feel that this sacrifice, in and of itself, appeals to certain kinds of people. "Although there unquestionably are *some* persons in *some* social movements whose main concern is to lose themselves in a collective enterprise, most members view their group commitments—including their sacrifices of individuality—as necessary attributes of their brand of life, rather than as ends in themselves" (p. 133).

Compared to their "unsaved" counterparts in the youth culture, most Jesus Freaks lead sober, disciplined lives. They readily submit to the restrictive rules and regimented existence of the many Christian houses and communes. For many outsiders the word *commune* conjures up images of unbridled freedom and permissiveness. As we have seen, this is not true in the Jesus communes. The converts recognize their need for structure and a new sense of order in their lives. Their reaction is against what Will Herberg calls "the moral laxity and putrid permissiveness that have gone so far in corrupting American middle-class, especially suburban middle-class, society" (*New Guard*, Nov. 1971, p. 15). For Herberg the Jesus People represent a movement seeking "to exorcise the demons and heal the putridities of [the] counterculture, and reintegrate it

into the continuing American consensus" (p. 16).

The Jesus People come from a society characterized not only by permissiveness, but one saturated with boredom. The children of technocracy are restless, dissatisfied, and bored. And as Hoffer has stated, "There is perhaps no more reliable indicator of a society's ripeness for a mass movement than the prevalence of unrelieved boredom" (p. 53). In the Jesus groups the old boredom has been replaced by a new and purposeful activism—the frantic round of witnessing excursions, the invigorating devotional exercises of speaking in tongues, group singing, and quoting memorized Scripture passages, and the satisfaction of intimate sharing.

A tightly knit group can easily lead to a tightly closed mind. We have referred again and again in the preceding chapters to the dogmatism of many Jesus groups. Social psychologists have devoted considerable attention to the phenomenon of "closed-mindedness" in their research of social movements. The implications for the Jesus Movements of Hans Toch's observations are obvious:

> The social movement that presents its inductee with authoritatively reinforced beliefs responsive to his problems unwittingly initiates a chain of events which may culminate in the confined, self-contained world of the veteran member. . . . As the believer becomes more intensely dedicated to the repair and buttressing of his current constructs, these come to assume greater personal significance for him. Moreover, supporting

efforts tend to systematize beliefs. As a result, it becomes of greater import that the new data conform and extreme pains are soon taken to this end.

At a given point in this process, the believer has walled himself in. Every event he encounters must be processed in terms of his beliefs. Every opportunity must be used to cement his system. At this stage, only authority can produce innovation (pp. 155-56).

Every social movement has its peculiar jargon and symbols that act as unifying factors binding the participants together. The Jesus Movement has its One Way sign, its Jesus cheers, and its favorite expressions like "Praise the Lord," "Jesus Loves You," and "Right On!" Just as the Ku Klux Klan has its elaborate regalia and secret rituals, the Jesus Movement has its own cultic uniforms and unusual activities, such as the silent vigils of the Children of God. The garb, the vigils, the beach baptisms, the bumper stickers, the huge Bibles, the music—these all provide some of the "color" of the movement, and they also serve as a means of positive identification with the movement and as a way of engendering a certain pride in belonging.

In this chapter we have outlined the major characteristics of the Jesus People as a social movement. Although other social movements demonstrate the same traits in different configurations, in the case of the Jesus Movement it must be remembered that its members find divine sanction for practices that ordinarily would be explained at the socio-psychological level only. For example, students of social behavior would seek

to explain the authoritarian leader and his submissive following in terms of the human dynamics of the relationship. But the Jesus People themselves would insist that their obedience to the elder is merely a response to the clear-cut teaching of the Bible. And at every point in a sociological analysis of the movement, its participants would quote the Bible as justification of their actions and attitudes.

Part of the systematic analysis of social movements is an exploration of variables like social class, sex, age, economic status, geographic location, educational level, and racial or ethnic background. Since we conducted no formal surveys of these factors in our research on the Jesus People, we have had to limit ourselves to the impressionistic information that is presented throughout this book. For purposes of summary here, suffice it to say that the Jesus People are a highly diverse group of individuals found throughout the nation, but predominating in California and the Pacific Northwest, coming from virtually all social and economic levels, but including very few Blacks or other minority group members. The fact that few black young people are in the movement is no doubt significant and deserves additional research.

In the final analysis, the Jesus Movement is really an example of what sociologists of religion call "revitalization movements." Such movements involve more than reform or renewal; they can best be understood as revolutionary. Movements of revitalization include a reaching out into the unknown for new patterns, rather than simply a return to the more familiar. As Barbara Hargrove points out, "Revitalization is distinguished by its potential to recombine those familiar elements into creative new patterns" (p. 277).

A number of observers have compared the Jesus Revolution with the Great Awakening of mid-eighteenth-century America. Herberg, for example, feels that the Jesus People, because of their revivalistic pietism, have "placed themselves squarely in the line of 200 years of American revivalism." He continues: "Note how thoroughly traditional their pietistic religion is, even in their anti-establishment posture" (*New Guard*, Nov. 1971, p. 16).

While to some commentators the Jesus Movement may appear to be "thoroughly traditional" and represent a return to a familiar, earlier fundamentalism, upon closer analysis one must conclude that the Jesus Movement demonstrates a new kind of response to the continuing search for ultimate meaning and a transcendent God. It retains elements of the familiar, to be sure. But its distinctions are far more striking and significant. It is for that reason that this chapter has set the Jesus Movement against the background of the culture, for the cultural crisis of our times has left its distinct imprint upon the youth who now make up the Jesus Movement. Thus, though this revival has many similarities in common with earlier religious awakenings in America, the distinguishing features of our times cause close analogies between this and the previous revivals to be inadequate because oversimplification is inevitable.

Is the Jesus Movement a Great Awakening, or is it merely a "Gentle Stir?" Perhaps the answer to that question is found in a statement of Dr. David L. McKenna appearing in the Fall 1971 issue of *United Evangelical Action* magazine:

> At the present time, it is an eddy outside the mainstream of American life. If it is a genuinely spiritual awakening, it will also change the direction or the quality of the stream. That is the long range test of spiritual awakenings that only time can answer (p. 14).

In short, we must wait until more of the evidence is in.

18 Religion and the Search for National Stability

For thou didst form my inward parts; Thou didst weave me in my mother's womb. I will give thanks to Thee, for I am fearfully and wonderfully made . . .

—Ps. 139:13-14

Perils of Politics
Charles Colson

Charles Colson (1931-   ) served as special counsel to President Richard M. Nixon from 1969 to 1973. In 1974 he pleaded guilty to charges related to Watergate and served seven months in prison. Since 1976 he has been chairman of Prison Fellowship, a Washington, D.C.-based organization he founded to minister to the needs of prison inmates. He has authored several best-selling books and writes frequently for magazines and journals. In the chapter "Perils of Politics" taken from *Kingdoms in Conflict* (1987) Colson explores the interplay between religion and politics.

Christian faith may work wonders if it moves the minds and hearts of an increasing number of men and women. But if professed Christians forsake heaven as their destination and come to fancy that the state... may be converted into the terrestrial paradise—why they are less wise men than Marx.

Russell Kirk

[I]n recent years many Christians have urged a more direct approach for bringing needed social change: simply elect Christians to political office. One spokesman has even suggested a religious version of affirmative action; if, for example, 24 percent of the people are born again, then at least 24 percent of the officeholders should be born again. Others have argued that Christians should "take dominion" over government, with those in public office speaking "for God as well as for the American people."

On the surface this shortcut might seem to some an appealing answer to America's declining morality. It is, however, simplistic and dangerous triumphalism. To suggest that electing Christians to public office will solve all public ills is not only presumptuous and theologically questionable, it is also untrue.

Today's misspent enthusiasm for political solutions to the moral problems of our culture arises from a distorted view of both politics and spirituality—too low a view of the power of a sovereign God and too high a view of the ability of man. The idea that human systems, reformed by Christian influence, pave the road to the Kingdom—or at least, to revival—has the same utopian ring that one finds in Marxist literature. It also ignores the consistent lesson of history that shows that laws are most often reformed as a result of powerful spiritual movements. I know of no case where a spiritual movement was achieved by passing laws.

In addition, history puts the lie to the notion that just because one is devout one will be a just and wise ruler. Take the nineteenth-century leader who forged a unified Germany from a cluster of minor states. Otto von Bismarck-Schönhausen was a committed Christian who regularly read the Bible, spoke openly of his devotion to God, and

claimed divine guidance in response to prayer. "If I were no longer a Christian, I would not serve the king another hour," he once declared.

Yet Bismarck was also the ruthless architect of *Deutschland Über Alles* (Germany Over All), a chauvinistic worldview that laid the foundation for two world wars. Historians described Bismarck as a Machiavellian master of political duplicity who specialized in blood and iron.

As we have said earlier, power can be just as corrupting—or confusing—to the Christian as to the non-Christian. And the results in some ways are more horrible when power corrupts men or women who believe they have a divine mandate. Their injustices are then committed in God's name. This is why an eminent conservative historian has suggested that "religious claims in politics should vary inversely with the power or prospects for power one has."

It's a fair distinction: Prophets should make religious claims. Political leaders should not—otherwise they can become ayatollahs.

So the first test for public office should not be a spiritual one. The celebrated claim that "the ability to hear from God should be the number one qualification for the U.S. presidency" is dangerously misguided.

Politicians, like those in any other specialized field, should be selected on the basis of their qualifications and abilities *as well as* on their moral character. Even in Israel's theocracy, Jethro advised Moses to select "capable men . . . who fear God" to help in governing the Jewish nation.

Jethro's advice makes sense. If terrorists were to take control of an airport, would we want policemen who were merely devout Christians handling the situation, or would we choose those who had specialized training in hostage negotiations? Luther had it right when he said he would rather be ruled by a competent Turk than an incompetent Christian.

The triumphalist mindset also fails to make the crucial distinction between a Christian's function as a private citizen and as an office-holder. As private citizens, Christians are free to advocate their Christian view in any and every form. In America that is a fundamental constitutional right. Christian citizens should be activists about their faith, striving by their witness to "Christianize" their culture—not by the force of the sword, but by the force of their ideas.

But Christians elected to public office acquire a different set of responsibilities. Now they hold the power of the sword, which God has placed with government to preserve order and maintain justice. Now they act not for themselves but for all whom they serve. For this reason they cannot use their office to evangelistically "Christianize" their culture. Their duty is to ensure justice and religious liberty for all citizens of all beliefs.

This does not mean they can compromise their faith or their first allegiance to God; they should speak freely of their Christian faith and witness Christian values in their lives. But they cannot use their offices to seek a favored position for Christianity or the church.

A Christian writer has summed this up well: "The 'Christian state' is one that gives no special public privilege to Christian citizens but seeks justice for all as a matter of principle."

At the turn of the century a towering Dutch theologian, Abraham Kuyper, was elected prime minister of the Netherlands. His opponents voiced fears of theocratic oppression. Instead, his administration was a model of tolerance and public pluralism as Kuyper affirmed proportional representation, that the legitimate rights of all be fully represented.

If Christians today understood this distinction between the role of the private Christian citizen and the Christian in government, they might sound less like medieval crusaders. If secularists understood correctly the nature of Christian public duty they would not fear, but welcome responsible Christian political involvement.

But Christians should not unwarily plunge into the political marshlands, thinking they will drain the swamp.

There are traps. I know; I used to set them.

My first assignment as President Nixon's special counsel was to develop strategies for his 1972 reelection. A tough task. He had been elected by only a small margin in the three-way 1968 election against Hubert Humphrey and George Wallace. Not only was the Republican party a minority, but Nixon had inherited an unpopular war and a hostile press. Added to this, he himself projected something less than a charismatic presence for the television imagemakers just beginning to dominate politics.

I studied the political classics, particularly the strategy devised by Clark Clifford for Harry Truman in the 1948 election. I learned that Clifford had curried the favor of disparate special-interest groups, one by one, assembling voting blocks into a surprise majority.

My first memorandum to the president outlined a similar strategy: write off the minorities, but reach out to traditional supporters in business and farm groups; pick off some conservative labor unions; cultivate Southern evangelicals; build a new coalition among Catholic, blue-collar voters of the Northeast and Midwest. I labeled it the "Middle America Plan," later dubbed the "Silent Majority Strategy." It was cynical, pragmatic, and good politics, designed to exploit whatever allies would let us cultivate them.

Nixon loved it. The memo was returned a few days later with his markings all over the margins: "Right. . . . Do it. . . . I agree." It became one of the key documents for the political strategy of Mr. Nixon's presidency.

Setting out to put it into practice, I began by inviting key leaders to the White House, following a scenario staged for maximum benefit.

First, they dined with me in the executive dining room located in the basement of the West Wing. I would escort my guests past saluting guards, down a long corridor lined with dramatic photographs of the president in action, then pause at the door to the din-

ing room, pointing to another door to the right. "That's the situation room," I'd say in hushed tones. They all knew of the legendary super-secret national-security nerve center. The very words conjured up images of map-covered walls, whirring computers, and a bevy of generals studying the movements of Soviet aircraft. (Actually, it was then nothing more than a large, crowded office with some communications equipment and old charts on the wall; the real command centers had been moved to the Pentagon after World War II.)

The executive dining room was paneled in rich, hand-rubbed mahogany, lined with a waiting row of red-jacketed Navy stewards. Seated at the dozen tables, huddled in conversation, would be most of the cabinet and senior staff.

The dramatic effect overwhelmed even the staunchest adversary. One union leader, a lifelong Democrat who had never been to the White House before, blurted out during our first lunch together that he'd be available to help in any campaign. A Chicago alderman strong in the Polish neighborhoods signed up on the spot.

Those who needed more prodding were treated to a walk upstairs after lunch. If the president was out, I'd usher them reverently through the Oval Office; if Mr. Nixon was there, I'd ask (always by prearrangement) if my visitor would like to meet the president. His chin would drop as I led him in the side door, cut almost unnoticeably into the wall, and remarked casually, "Oh, Mr. President. I was just having lunch with Jim here. Could we say hello?"

Nixon was a master at the game. He always gave his dazzled visitor gold-plated cuff links with the presidential seal. The person would be overwhelmed as he left, almost bowing, not more than sixty seconds later. It's not easy to resist the allure of the Oval Office.

I took all kinds of groups to see the president, from friendly cattlemen to sophisticated educators enraged over budget cuts or the Vietnam war. It was always the same. In the reception room they would rehearse their angry lines and reassure one another, "I'll tell him what's going on. He's got to do something."

When the aide came to escort us in, they'd set their jaws and march toward the door. But once it swung open, the aide announcing, "The president will see you," it was as if they had suddenly sniffed some intoxicating fragrance. Most became almost self-conscious about even stepping on the plush blue carpet on which was sculpted the Great Seal of the United States. And Mr. Nixon's voice and presence—like any president's—filled the room.

Invariably, the lions of the waiting room became the lambs of the Oval Office. No one ever showed outward hostility. Most, except the labor leaders, forget their best-rehearsed lines. They nodded when the president spoke, and in those rare instances when they disagreed, they did so apologetically, assuring the president that they personally respected his opinion.

Ironically, none were more compliant than the religious leaders. Of all people, they should have been the most aware of the sinful nature of man and the least overwhelmed by pomp and protocol. But theological knowledge sometimes wilts in the face of worldly power.

I frequently scheduled meetings for evangelical groups, denominational councils, and individual religious leaders. Henry Kissinger's briefings in the Roosevelt Room across the hall from the Oval Office were always a big hit.

The weekly church services Nixon scheduled most Sundays for the East Room provided great opportunities as well. To select the preacher, we determined who would give us the greatest impact—politically, that is, not spiritually. At the time I was a nominal Christian at best and had no way to judge the spiritual. And there were always two hundred or more seats to be filled, tickets that were like keys to the political kingdom.

Then there were invitations to social functions and state dinners. I was allowed a quota for every event and filled it with those whose support we coveted most. It is difficult to resist the allure of that most regal of events, the state dinner, held in honor of visiting world leaders. Each of the twelve tables seated ten of the most influential people in America—Supreme Court justices, senators, ambassadors, film stars, cabinet members—and my targets for political support.

One instance I recall illustrates just how well the system works. We needed several electoral-rich Northeastern and Midwestern states to win the 1972 election—or so we thought. So one spring day I called a prominent Christian leader whose influence was particularly great in that region and invited him for a private dinner cruise with the president.

As we arrived at the Washington Navy Yard, sailors in white dress uniforms lined the gangway at attention and saluted as the three of us boarded the presidential yacht, *Sequoia*. Its mahogany sides and brass fittings sparkled as the grand old vessel eased away from its dock.

The Washington skyline faded into the distance, and the president escorted us to dinner in the main salon. White House china, silver, and crystal appointed the starched white tablecloth; stewards scurried back and forth serving chateaubriand and the vintage La Fête Rothschild.

The dinner discussion was as impressive as the food. When our guest mustered the courage to raise points of concern to the religious community, Mr. Nixon showed an amazing grasp of even the intricate details of those issues (as a dutiful aide, I had briefed him thoroughly that afternoon). Every now and then he would stop and say, "Chuck, I want this done. This man is right. You order the attorney general to take care of that tomorrow morning." Then he would résumé the conversation.

It wasn't all sham, of course. The president meant what he said, and we even thought some of the things might be accomplished. But whatever else happened, that religious leader was convinced that Richard Nixon was on his side.

Before we arrived at Mount Vernon, the president led us to the foredeck and stood at attention as the colors were retired, his hand over his heart. Our guest did the same. When the bugle had faded, we docked; a waiting Marine helicopter took our new friend back to the airport, and another returned Mr. Nixon and me to the White House lawn.

I would be wrong to suggest that this leader was unduly influenced; but even such a wise, honorable, and religious man could not help but be impressed by the trappings of power. He got what he wanted—the president's ear on certain key issues. And we got what we wanted.

Nixon's prominent public friendship with this leader sent a powerful signal to millions of voters. That fall we carried more than 58 percent of the vote in many Northeastern and Midwestern precincts that had never before voted for a Republican.

This is not to suggest that the Nixon White House was engaged in a sinister conspiracy to corrupt the church. It is simply the way political systems work. People in power use power to keep themselves in power. Even if they are genuinely interested in a special-interest group's agenda—or naturally disposed to their position—they will work that relationship for everything they can get out of it.

In totalitarian regimes some officials are so unscrupulous as to feign religious interest simply to ensnare Christians. In Nicaragua, Interior Minister Thomas Borge maintains two offices. When he is receiving churchmen or American visitors, he sits in a Bible-laden office adorned with crucifixes. When he meets with government officials or visitors from socialist nations, he occupies an office displaying Marxist slogans and pictures of such revolutionary heroes as Marx, Engels, and Lenin.

I'm not advocating that religious groups or leaders boycott the White House or the palaces and parliaments of the world. That's where the political action is, and Christians need to influence policies for justice and righteousness. That is the best biblical tradition of Jeremiah, Amos, Micah, Daniel, and a host of others—though many prophets clearly preferred the desert to the palace.

But Christians (and others as well) need to do so with eyes open, aware of the snares. C.S. Lewis wrote that "the demon inherent in every [political] party is at all times ready enough to disguise himself as the Holy Ghost." Tolstoy made a similar point: "Governments, to have a rational foundation for the control of the masses, are obliged to pretend that they are professing the highest religious teachings known to man."

Consider several of the most dangerous pitfalls awaiting the unwary.

The first is that the church will become just another special-interest group.

When President Reagan was challenged by the press during the 1980 campaign for mixing religion and politics by attending a meeting of Religious Right activists, he responded that the church was like any other special-interest group, after all—like a union, for example. Reagan was refreshingly candid, but dead wrong.

The church is not and must never allow itself to become just another special-interest group lined up at the public trough. For in doing so, as one contemporary scholar observes, it would "sacrifice its claim to objective ethical concern which [is the church's] chief political as well as moral resource."

Tocqueville warned that if the church were to become a mere interest group, it would then be measured and honored according to political and not moral criteria. The great strength of the American church, he believed, was that it was not linked to a partisan cause. By way of contrast, he pointed out that in Europe people "reject the clergy less because they are representatives of God than because they are friends of authority."

A second danger is that politics can be like the proverbial tar baby. Christian leaders who are courted by political forces may soon begin to overestimate their own importance. The head of one large international relief agency mistakenly came to believe that heads of state welcomed him because of who he was rather than what he represented. It wasn't long before his work and his personal life failed to measure up to his delusions of power. He left his family and was eventually removed from his position—after doing great harm to the cause he had served for much of his life.

A side effect of this delusion is that rather than lose their access to political influence, some church leaders have surrendered their independence. "If I speak out against this policy," they reason, "I won't get invited to dinner and my chances to minister will be cut off." While such rationalizing is understandable, the result is exactly the opposite; they keep their place but lose their voice and thus any possibility of holding government to moral account.

In this way the gospel becomes hostage to the political fortunes of a particular movement. This is the third and perhaps most dangerous snare. Both liberals and conservatives have made this mistake of aligning their spiritual goals with a particular political agenda.

One Christian New Right leader, when asked what would happen if the Democrats won the 1988 U.S. election, said, "I don't know what will happen to us." After the 1980 election, a Methodist bishop wrote, "The blame [for Reagan's victory] ought not be placed on all the vigor of the Right, but maybe on the weakness of saints." A better day will come, he said, "If the people of faith will be strengthened by defeat and address themselves to the new agenda which is upon us." The implication was clear: if you disagreed with the bishop's partisan politics, you were not among "the people of faith."

Several years ago a prominent leader of a large Christian mission visited a Third World nation ruled by an authoritarian leader. The leader was friendly to the U.S. and held a regal dinner party at the palace honoring the mission executive. The awestruck visitor publicly and effusively praised the head of state. Months later when that head of state was deposed, the Christian's mission work in that country was deposed right along with him.

Inevitably, this kind of political alignment compromises the gospel. James Schall writes, "All successful Christian social theory in the immediate future must be based on this truth: that religion be not made an instrument of political ideology."

Because it tempts one to water down the truth of the gospel, ideological alignment, whether on the left or right, accelerates the church's secularization. When the church aligns itself politically, it gives priority to the compromises and temporal successes of the political world rather than its Christian confessions of eternal truth. And when the church gives up its rightful place as the conscience of the culture, the consequences for society can be horrific.

As we've seen, many German churches in the thirties allied themselves with the new nationalistic movement. One churchman even described the Nazis as a "gift and miracle of God." It was the *confessing* church, not the politically-minded church, which retained its orthodoxy and thus resisted the evils of Hitler's state.

Today's liberation theologians have fallen into this trap, putting ideology ahead of orthodoxy. It began, as did many Christian political movements, with noble intentions. Righteously outraged at injustices to the poor in so-called Christian cultures, priests and church workers began to organize communities for action. So far, so good.

But as those organizations failed to solve problems, frustrations grew; attacks on structures became more strident.

When Christians put economic issues ahead of spiritual salvation, they are embracing economic determinism; it is then but a short step to revolutionary politics, Marxism, and the fatal mistake of believing the Kingdom of God can be ushered in by political means, as Father Ernesto Cardenal, a Nicaraguan government official, well illustrates: "A world of perfect communism is the Kingdom of God on earth."

Does all of this mean that Christians cannot work with political groups? Certainly not. In fact, often Christians must work with coalitions of like-minded people who have different motivations. But as Donald Bloesch has pointed out, "In order to maintain their Christian identity they must inwardly detach themselves from the motivations and ultimate goals of their ideological colleagues."

In World War II, for example, a devout Christian might have fought to stop the evil of Nazism and the Holocaust because he believed God commanded that the state is to restrain evil. Next to him in the same foxhole might have been a soldier fighting solely for national pride or honor. Both would have been shooting at the same enemy, but for different reasons.

Today Christians may find themselves suspect—I have experienced this myself—to the very people on whose side they are fighting. But that is the price they must pay to preserve their independence and not be beholden to any political ideological alignment.

Only a church free of any outside domination can be the conscience of society and, as Washington pastor Myron Augsburger has written, "hold government morally accountable before God to live up to its own claims." And as the amazing events in the next chapter demonstrate, when the church faithfully fulfills this role, even the most determined of tyrants topple.

Abortion and the Conscience of the Nation
Ronald Reagan

Ronald Reagan (1911-   ) was the President of the United States from 1981 to 1989. Early in his life he was influenced by conservative evangelical teachings, though during his presidency "he was not a church goer and gave little more than rhetorical attention to most of the new Christian right concerns," among which was the controversial abortion issue. Reagan used the tenth anniversary of *Roe v. Wade* (1973) as the occasion to address this topic. The Charleston, South Carolina *News and Courier* noted that "it is significant that President Reagan chose the quietude of the printed word to respond to the dictates of his conscience and speak to the conscience of the nation."

The tenth anniversary of the Supreme Court decision in *Roe v. Wade* is a good time for us to pause and reflect. Our nationwide policy of abortion-on-demand through all nine months of pregnancy was neither voted for by our people nor enacted by our legislators—not a single state had such unrestricted abortion before the Supreme Court decreed it to be national policy in 1973. But the consequences of this judicial decision are now obvious: since 1973, more than 15 million unborn children have had their lives snuffed out by legalized abortions. That is over ten times the number of Americans lost in all our nation's wars.

Make no mistake, abortion-on-demand is not a right granted by the Constitution. No serious scholar, including one disposed to agree with the Court's result, has argued that the framers of the Constitution intended to create such a right. Shortly after the *Roe*

v. Wade decision, Professor John Hart Ely, now Dean of Stanford Law School, wrote that the opinion "is not constitutional law and gives almost no sense of an obligation to try to be." Nowhere do the plain words of the Constitution even hint at a "right" so sweeping as to permit abortion up to the time the child is ready to be born. Yet that is what the Court ruled.

As an act of "raw judicial power" (to use Justice White's biting phrase), the decision by the seven-man majority in *Roe v. Wade* has by no means settled the debate. Instead, *Roe vs. Wade* has become a continuing prod to the conscience of the nation.

Abortion concerns not just the unborn child, it concerns every one of us. The English poet, John Donne, wrote: ". . . any man's death diminishes me, because I am involved in mankind; and therefore never send me to

---

The entire essay, written in 1985, is printed here with the permission of Thomas Nelson, Inc.

know for whom the bell tolls; it tolls for thee."

We cannot diminish the value of one category of human life—the unborn— without diminishing the value of all human life. We saw tragic proof of this truism last year when the Indiana courts allowed the starvation death of "Baby Doe" in Bloomington because the child had Down's Syndrome.

Many of our fellow citizens grieve over the loss of life that has followed *Roe v. Wade*. Margaret Heckler, soon after being nominated to head the largest department of our government, Health and Human Services, told an audience that she believed abortion to be the greatest moral crisis facing our country today. And the revered Mother Teresa, who works in the streets of Calcutta ministering to dying people in her world-famous mission of mercy, has said that "the greatest misery of our time is the generalized abortion of children."

Over the first two years of my administration I have closely followed and assisted efforts in Congress to reverse the tide of abortion—efforts of congressmen, senators and citizens responding to an urgent moral crisis. Regrettably, I have also seen the massive efforts of those who, under the banner of "freedom of choice," have so far blocked every effort to reverse nationwide abortion-on-demand.

Despite the formidable obstacles before us, we must not lose heart. This is not the first time our country has been divided by a Supreme Court decision that denied the value of certain human lives. The *Dred Scott* decision of 1857 was not overturned in a day, or

a year, or even a decade. At first, only a minority of Americans recognized and deplored the moral crisis brought about by denying the full humanity of our black brothers and sisters; but that minority persisted in their vision and finally prevailed. They did it by appealing to the hearts and minds of their countrymen, to the truth of human dignity under God. From their example, we know that respect for the sacred value of human life is too deeply engrained in the hearts of our people to remain forever suppressed. But the great majority of the American people have not yet made their voices heard, and we cannot expect them to—any more than the public voice arose against slavery—*until* the issue is clearly framed and presented.

What, then, is the real issue? I have often said that when we talk about abortion, we are talking about two lives—the life of the mother and the life of the unborn child. Why else do we call a pregnant woman a mother? I have also said that anyone who doesn't feel sure whether we are talking about a second human life should clearly give life the benefit of the doubt. If you don't know whether a body is alive or dead, you would never bury it. I think this consideration itself should be enough for all of us to insist on protecting the unborn.

The case against abortion does not rest here, however, for medical practice confirms at every step the correctness of these moral sensibilities. Modern medicine treats the unborn child as a patient. Medical pioneers have made great breakthroughs in treating the unborn—for genetic problems, vitamin deficiencies, irregular heart rhythms, and other medical conditions. Who can forget

George Will's moving account of the little boy who underwent brain surgery six times during the nine weeks before he was born? Who is the *patient* if not that tiny unborn human being who can feel pain when he or she is approached by doctors who come to kill rather than to cure?

The real question today is not when human life begins, but, *What is the value of human life?* The abortionist who reassembles the arms and legs of a tiny baby to make sure all its parts have been torn from its mother's body can hardly doubt whether it is a human being. The real question for him and for all of us is whether that tiny human life has a God-given right to be protected by the law—the same right we have.

What more dramatic confirmation could we have of the real issue than the Baby Doe case in Bloomington, Indiana? The death of that tiny infant tore at the hearts of all Americans because the child was undeniably a live human being—one lying helpless before the eyes of the doctors and the eyes of the nation. The real issue for the courts was *not* whether Baby Doe was a human being. The real issue was whether to protect the life of a human being who had Down's Syndrome, who would probably be mentally handicapped, but who needed a routine surgical procedure to unblock his esophagus and allow him to eat. A doctor testified to the presiding judge that, even with his physical problem corrected, Baby Doe would have a "non-existent" possibility for a "minimally adequate quality of life"—in other words, that retardation was the equivalent of a crime deserving the death penalty. The judge let Baby Doe starve and die, and the Indiana Supreme Court sanctioned his decision.

Federal law does not allow federally-assisted hospitals to decide that Down's Syndrome infants are not worth treating, much less to decide to starve them to death. Accordingly, I have directed the Departments of Justice and Health and Human Services to apply civil rights regulations to protect handicapped newborns. All hospitals receiving federal funds must post notices which will clearly state that failure to feed handicapped babies is prohibited by federal law. The basic issue is whether to value and protect the lives of the handicapped, whether to recognize the sanctity of human life. This is the same basic issue that underlies the question of abortion.

The 1981 Senate hearings on the beginning of human life brought out the basic issue more clearly than ever before. The many medical and scientific witnesses who testified disagreed on many things, but not on the *scientific* evidence that the unborn child is alive, is a distinct individual, or is a member of the human species. They did disagree over the *value* question, whether to give value to a human life at its early and most vulnerable stages of existence.

Regrettably, we live at a time when some persons do *not* value all human life. They want to pick and choose which individuals have value. Some have said that only those individuals with "consciousness of self" are human beings. One such writer has followed this deadly logic and concluded that "shocking as it may seem, a newly born infant is not a human being."

A Nobel Prize winning scientist has suggested that if a handicapped child "were not declared fully human until three days after birth, then all parents could be allowed the choice." In other words, "quality control" to see if newly born human beings are up to snuff.

Obviously, some influential people want to deny that every human life has intrinsic, sacred worth. They insist that a member of the human race must have certain qualities before they accord him or her status as a "human being."

Events have borne out the editorial in a California medical journal which explained three years before *Roe v. Wade* that the social acceptance of abortion is a "defiance of the long-held Western ethic of intrinsic and equal value for every human life regardless of its stage, condition, or status."

Every legislator, every doctor, and every citizen needs to recognize that the real issue is whether to affirm and protect the sanctity of all human life, or to embrace a social ethic where some human lives are valued and others are not. As a nation, we must choose between the sanctity of life ethic and the "quality of life" ethic.

I have no trouble identifying the answer our nation has always given to this basic question, and the answer that I hope and pray it will give in the future. America was founded by men and women who shared a vision of the value of each and every individual. They stated this vision clearly from the very start in the Declaration of Independence, using words that every schoolboy and schoolgirl can recite:

> We hold these truths to be self evident, that all men are created equal, that they are endowed by their Creator with certain unalienable rights, that among these are life, liberty, and the pursuit of happiness.

We fought a terrible war to guarantee that one category of mankind—black people in America—could not be denied the inalienable rights with which their Creator endowed them. The great champion of the sanctity of all human life in that day, Abraham Lincoln, gave us his assessment of the Declaration's purpose. Speaking of the framers of that noble document, he said:

> This was their majestic interpretation of the economy of the Universe. This was their lofty, and wise, and noble understanding of the justice of the Creator to His creatures. Yes, gentlemen, to all His creatures, to the whole great family of man. In their enlightened belief, nothing stamped with the divine image and likeness was sent into the world to be trodden on. . . . They grasped not only the whole race of man then living, but they reached forward and seized upon the farthest posterity. They erected a beacon to guide their children and their children's children, and the countless myriads who should inhabit the earth in other ages.

He warned also of the danger we would face if we closed our eyes to the value of life in any category of human beings:

> I should like to know if taking this old Declaration of Independence, which declares that all men are equal upon principle and making exceptions to it where will it stop. If one

man says it does not mean a Negro, why not another say it does not mean some other man?

When Congressman John A. Bingham of Ohio drafted the Fourteenth Amendment to guarantee the rights of life, liberty, and property to all human beings, he explained that *all* are "entitled to the protection of American law, because its divine spirit of equality declares that all men are created equal." He said the rights guaranteed by the amendment would therefore apply to "any human being." Justice William Brennan, in another case decided only the year before *Roe v. Wade*, referred to our society as one that "strongly affirms the sanctity of life." Another William Brennan—not the Justice—has reminded us of the terrible consequences that can follow when a nation rejects the sanctity of life ethic:

> The cultural environment for a human holocaust is present whenever any society can be misled into defining individuals as less than human and therefore devoid of value and respect.

As a nation today, we have *not* rejected the sanctity of human life. The American people have not had an opportunity to express their view on the sanctity of human life in the unborn. I am convinced that Americans do not want to play God with the value of human life. It is not for us to decide who is worthy to live and who is not. Even the Supreme Court's opinion in *Roe v. Wade* did not explicitly reject the traditional American idea of intrinsic worth and value in all human life; it simply dodged this issue.

The Congress has before it several measures that would enable our people to reaffirm the sanctity of human life, even the smallest and the youngest and the most defenseless. The Human Life Bill expressly recognizes the unborn as human beings and accordingly protects them as persons under our Constitution. This bill, first introduced by Senator Jesse Helms, provided the vehicle for the Senate hearings in 1981 which contributed so much to our understanding of the real issue of abortion.

The Respect Human Life Act, just introduced in the ninety-eighth Congress, states in its first section that the policy of the United States is "to protect innocent life, both before and after birth." This bill, sponsored by Congressman Henry Hyde and Senator Roger Jepsen, prohibits the federal government from performing abortions or assisting those who do so, except to save the life of the mother. It also addresses the pressing issue of infanticide which, as we have seen, flows inevitably from permissive abortion as another step in the denial of the inviolability of innocent human life.

I have endorsed each of these measures, as well as the more difficult route of constitutional amendment, and I will give these initiatives my full support. Each of them, in different ways, attempts to reverse the tragic policy of abortion-on-demand imposed by the Supreme Court ten years ago. Each of them is a decisive way to affirm the sanctity of human life.

We must all educate ourselves to the reality of the horrors taking place. Doctors today know that unborn children can feel a touch within the womb and that they respond to pain. But how many Americans are aware that abortion techniques are allowed today, in all fifty states, that burn the skin of a baby with a salt solution, in an agonizing death that can last for hours?

Another example: two years ago, the *Philadelphia Inquirer* ran a Sunday special supplement on "The Dreaded Complication." The "dreaded complication" referred to in the article—the complication feared by doctors who perform abortions—is the *survival* of the child despite all the painful attacks during the abortion procedure. Some unborn children *do* survive the late-term abortions the Supreme Court has made legal. Is there any question that these victims of abortion deserve our attention and protection? Is there any question that those who *don't* survive were living human beings before they were killed?

Late-term abortions, especially when the baby survives, but is then killed by starvation, neglect, or suffocation, show once again the link between abortion and infanticide. The time to stop both is now. As my administration acts to stop infanticide, we will be fully aware of the real issue that underlies the death of babies before and soon after birth.

Our society has, fortunately, become sensitive to the rights and special needs of the handicapped, but I am shocked that physical or mental handicaps of newborns are still used to justify their extinction. This administration has a Surgeon General, Dr. C. Everett Koop, who has done perhaps more than any other American for handicapped children, by pioneering surgical techniques to help them, by speaking out on the value of their lives, and by working with them in the context of loving families. You will not find his former patients advocating the so-called "quality-of-life" ethic.

I know that when the true issue of infanticide is placed before the American people, with all the facts openly aired, we will have no trouble deciding that a mentally or physically handicapped baby has the same intrinsic worth and right to life as the rest of us. As the New Jersey Supreme Court said two decades ago, in a decision upholding the sanctity of human life, "a child need not be perfect to have a worthwhile life."

Whether we are talking about pain suffered by unborn children, or about late-term abortions, or about infanticide, we inevitably focus on the humanity of the unborn child. Each of these issues is a potential rallying point for the sanctity of life ethic. Once we as a nation rally around any one of these issues to affirm the sanctity of life, we will see the importance of affirming this principle across the board.

Malcolm Muggeridge, the English writer, goes right to the heart of the matter: "Either life is always and in all circumstances sacred, or intrinsically of no account; it is inconceivable that it should be in some cases the one, and in some the other." The sanctity of innocent human life is a principle that Congress should proclaim at every opportunity.

It is possible that the Supreme Court itself may overturn its abortion rulings. We need only recall that in *Brown v. Board of Education* the court reversed its own earlier "separate-but-equal" decision. I believe if the Supreme Court took another look at *Roe v. Wade*, and considered the real issue between the sanctity of life ethic and the quality of life ethic, it would change its mind once again.

As we continue to work to overturn *Roe v. Wade*, we must also continue to lay the groundwork for a society in which abortion is not the accepted answer to unwanted pregnancy. Pro-life people have already taken heroic steps, often at great personal sacrifice, to provide for unwed mothers. I recently spoke about a young pregnant woman named Victoria, who said, "In this society we save whales, we save timber wolves and bald eagles and Coke bottles. Yet, everyone wanted to me to throw away my baby." She has been helped by Sav-a-Life, a group in Dallas, which provides a way for unwed mothers to preserve the human life within them when they might otherwise be tempted to resort to abortion. I think also of House of His Creation in Coatesville, Pennsylvania, where a loving couple has taken in almost two hundred young women in the past ten years. They have seen, as a fact of life, that the girls are *not* better off having abortions than saving their babies. I am also reminded of the remarkable Rossow family of Ellington, Connecticut, who have opened their hearts and their home to nine handicapped adopted and foster children.

The Adolescent Family Life Program, adopted by Congress at the request of Senator Jeremiah Denton, has opened new opportunities for unwed mothers to give their children life. We should not rest until our entire society echoes the tone of John Powell in the dedication of his book, *Abortion: The Silent Holocaust*, a dedication to every woman carrying an unwanted child: "Please believe that you are not alone. There are many of us that truly love you, who want to stand at your side, and help in any way we can." And we can echo the always-practical woman of faith, Mother Teresa, when she says, "If you don't want the little child, the unborn child, give him to me." We have so many families in America seeking to adopt children that the slogan "every child a wanted child" is now the emptiest of all reasons to tolerate abortion.

I have often said we need to join in prayer to bring protection to the unborn. Prayer and action are needed to uphold the sanctity of human life. I believe it will not be possible to accomplish our work, the work of saving lives, "without being a soul of prayer." The famous British member of Parliament William Wilberforce prayed with his small group of influential friends, the "Clapham Sect," of *decades* to see an end to slavery in the British empire. Wilberforce led that struggle in Parliament, unflaggingly, because he believed in the sanctity of human life. He saw the fulfillment of his impossible dream when Parliament outlawed slavery just before his death.

Let his faith and perseverance be our guide. We will never recognize the true value of our own lives until we affirm the value in the life of others, a value of which Malcolm Muggeridge says: ". . . however low it flickers or fiercely burns, it is still a Divine flame which no man dare presume to put out, be his motives ever so humane and enlightened." Abraham Lincoln recognize that we could not survive as a free land when some men could decide that others were not fit to be free and should therefore be slaves. Likewise, we cannot survive as a free nation when some men decide that others are not fit to live and should be abandoned to abortion or infanticide. My administration is dedicated to the preservation of America as a free land, and there is no cause more important for preserving that freedom than affirming the transcendent right to life of all human beings, the right without which no other rights have any meaning.

The Culture of Disbelief
Stephen L. Carter

Stephen L. Carter (1954-　　) is a professor of law at Yale University. Having worked earlier as a clerk to former Supreme Court Justice Thurgood Marshall, today Carter is recognized as a leading expert on constitutional law. The following excerpt is taken from his *The Culture of Disbelief: How American Law and Politics Trivialize Religious Devotion* (1993). The author discusses the recent cultural devaluation of religious devotion and provokes his readers to meet its challenges.

Contemporary American politics faces few greater dilemmas than deciding how to deal with the resurgence of religious belief. On the one hand, American ideology cherishes religion, as it does all matters of private conscience, which is why we justly celebrate a strong tradition against state interference with private religious choice. At the same time, many political leaders, commentators, scholars, and voters are coming to view any religious element in public moral discourse as a tool of the radical right for reshaping American society. But the effort to banish religion for politics' sake had led us astray: In our sensible zeal to keep religion from dominating our politics, we have created a political and legal culture that presses the religiously faithful to be other than themselves, to act publicly, and sometimes privately as well, as though their faith does not matter to them.

Recently, a national magazine devoted its cover story to an investigation of prayer: how many people pray, how often, why, how, and for what. A few weeks later came the inevitable letter from a disgruntled reader, wanting to know why so much space had been dedicated to such nonsense.

Statistically, the letter writer was in the minority: by the magazine's figures, better than nine out of ten Americans believe in God and some four out of five pray regularly. Politically and culturally, however, the writer was in the American mainstream, for those who do pray regularly—indeed, those who believe in God are encouraged to keep it a secret, and often a shameful one at that. Aside from the ritual appeals to God that are expected of our politicians, for Americans to take their religions seriously, to treat them as ordained rather than chosen, is to risk assignment to the lunatic fringe.

Yet religion matters to people, and matters a lot. Surveys indicate that Americans are far more likely to believe in God and to attend worship services regularly than any other people in the Western world. True, nobody prays on prime-time television unless religion is part of the plot, but strong majorities of citizens tell pollsters that their religious beliefs are of great importance to them in their daily lives. Even though some popular histories wrongly assert the contrary, the best evidence is that this deep religiosity has always been a facet of the American character and that it has grown consistently through the nation's history. And today, to the frustration of many opinion leaders in both the legal and political cultures, religion, as a moral force and perhaps a political one too, is surging. Unfortunately, in our public life, we prefer to pretend that it is not.

Consider the following events:

- When Hillary Rodham Clinton was seen wearing a cross around her neck at some of the public events surrounding her husband's inauguration as President of the United States, many observers were aghast, and one television commentator asked whether it was appropriate for the First Lady to display so openly a religious symbol. But if the First Lady can't do it, then certainly the President can't do it, which would bar from ever holding the office an Orthodox Jew under a religious compulsion to wear a yarmulke

- Back in the mid-1980s the magazine *Sojourners*—published by politically liberal Christian evangelicals—found itself in the unaccustomed position of defending the conservative evangelist Pat Robertson against secular liberals who, a writer in the magazine sighed, "see[m] to consider Robertson a dangerous neanderthal because he happens to believe that God can heal diseases." The point is that the editors of *Sojourners,* who are no great admirers of Robertson, also believe that God can heal diseases. So do tens of millions of Americans. But they are not supposed to say so.

- In the early 1980s the state of New York adopted legislation that, in effect, requires an Orthodox Jewish husband seeking a civil divorce to give his wife a *get*—a religious divorce—without which she cannot remarry under Jewish law. Civil libertarians attacked the statute as unconstitutional. Said one critic, the "barriers to remarriage erected by religious law . . . only exist in the minds of those who believe in the religion." If the barriers are religious, it seems, then they are not real barriers, they are "only" in the woman's mind—perhaps even a figment of the imagination.

- When the Supreme Court of the United States, ostensibly the final refuge of religious freedom, struck down a Connecticut statute requiring employers to make efforts to allow their employees to observe the sabbath, one Justice observed that the sabbath should not be singled out because all employees would like to have "the right to select the day of the week in which to refrain from labor." Sounds good, except that, as one scholar has noted, "It would come as some surprise to a devout Jew to find that he has 'selected the day of the week in which to refrain from labor,' since the Jewish people have been under the impression for some 3,000 years that this choice was made by God." If the sabbath is just another day off, then religious choice is essentially arbitrary and unimportant, so if one sabbath day is inconvenient, the religiously devout employee can just choose another.

- When President Ronald Reagan told religious broadcasters in 1983 that all the laws passed since biblical times "have not improved on the Ten Commandments one bit" which might once have been considered a pardonable piece of rhetorical license, he was excoriated by political pundits, including one who charged angrily that Reagan was giving "short shrift to the secular laws and institutions that a president is charged with protecting." And as for the millions of Americans who consider the Ten Commandments the fundaments on which they build their lives, well, they are no doubt subversive of these same institutions.

These examples share a common rhetoric that refuses to accept the notion that rational, public-spirited people can take religion seriously. It might be argued that such cases as these involve threats to the separation of church and state, the durable and vital doctrine that shields our public institutions from

religious domination and our religious institutions from government and state, and I will have more to say about the doctrine later in the book—but that is not what these examples are about.

What matters about these examples is the *language* chosen to make the points. In each example, as in many more that I shall discuss, one sees a trend in our political and legal cultures toward treating religious beliefs as arbitrary and unimportant—a trend supported by a rhetoric that implies that there is something wrong with religious devotion. More and more, our culture seems to take the position that believing deeply in the tenets of one's faith represents a kind of mystical irrationality, something that thoughtful, public-spirited American citizens would do better to avoid. If you must worship your God, the lesson runs, at least have the courtesy to disbelieve in the power of prayer; if you must observe your sabbath, have the good sense to understand that it is just like any other day off from work.

The rhetoric matters. A few years ago, my wife and I were startled by a teaser for a story on a network news program, which asked what was meant to be a provocative question: "When is a church more than just a place of worship?" For those to whom worship is significant, the subtle arrangement of words is arresting: *more than* suggests that what follows ("just a place of worship") is somewhere well down the scale of interesting or useful human activities, and certainly whatever the story is about is *more than* worship, and just suggests that what follows ("place of worship") is rather small potatoes.

A friend tells the story of how he showed his résumé to an executive search consultant—in the jargon, a corporate headhunter—who told him crisply that if he was serious about moving ahead in the business world. he should remove from the résumé any mention of his involvement with a social welfare organization that was connected with a church, but not one of the genteel mainstream denominations. Otherwise, she explained, a potential employer might think him a religious fanatic.

How did we reach this disturbing pass, when our culture teaches that religion is not to be taken seriously, even by those who profess to believe in it? Some observers suggest that the key moment was the Enlightenment, when the Western tradition sought to sever the link between religion and authority. One of the playwright Tom Stoppard's characters observes that there came "a calendar date—a moment—when the onus of proof passed from the atheist to the believer, when, quite suddenly, the noes had it." To which the philosopher Jeffrey Stout appends the following comment: "If so, it was not a matter of majority rule." Maybe not—but a strong undercurrent of contemporary American politics holds that religion must be kept in its proper place and, still more, in proper perspective. There are, we are taught by our opinion leaders, religious matters and important matters, and disaster arises when we confuse the two. Rationality, it seems, consists in getting one's priorities straight. (Ignore your religious law and marry at leisure.) Small wonder, then, that we have recently been treated to a book—coauthored by two therapists, one of them an ordained minister, arguing that those who would put aside, say, the needs of their families in or-

der to serve their religions are suffering from a malady the authors call "toxic faith"—for no normal person, evidently, would sacrifice the things that most of us hold dear just because of a belief that God so intended it. (One wonders how the authors would have judged the toxicity of the faith of Jesus, Moses, or Mohammed.)

We are trying, here in America, to strike an awkward but necessary balance, one that seems more and more difficult with each passing year. On the one hand, a magnificent respect for freedom of conscience, including the freedom of religious belief, runs deep in our political ideology. On the other hand our understandable fear of religious domination of politics presses us, in our public personas, to be wary of those who take their religion too seriously. This public balance reflects our private selves. We are one of the most religious nations on earth, in the sense that we have a deeply religious citizenry; but we are also perhaps the most zealous in guarding our public institutions against explicit religious influences. One result is that we often ask our citizens to split their public and private selves, telling them in effect that it is fine to be religious in private, but there is something askew when those private beliefs become the basis for public action.

We teach college freshmen that the Protestant Reformation began the process of freeing the church from the state, thus creating the possibility of a powerful independent moral force in society. As defenders of the separation of church and state have argued for centuries, autonomous religions play a vital role as free critics of the institutions of secular society. But our public culture more and more prefers religion as something without political significance, less an independent moral force than a quietly irrelevant moralizer, never heard, rarely seen. "[T]he public sphere," writes the theologian Martin Marty, "does not welcome explicit Reformed witness—or any other particularized Christian witness." Or, for that matter, any religious witness at all.

Religions that most need protection seem to receive it least. Contemporary America is not likely to enact legislation aimed at curbing the mainstream Protestant, Roman Catholic, or Jewish faiths. But Native Americans, having once been hounded from their lands, are now hounded from their religions, with the complicity of a Supreme Court untroubled when sacred lands are taken for road building or when Native Americans under a bona fide religious compulsion to use peyote in their rituals are punished under state antidrug regulations. (Imagine the brouhaha if New York City were to try to take St. Patrick's Cathedral by eminent domain to build a new convention center, or if Kansas, a dry state, were to outlaw the religious use of wine.) And airports, backed by the Supreme Court, are happy to restrict solicitation by devotees of Krishna Consciousness, which travelers, including this one, find irritating. (Picture the response should the airports try to regulate the wearing of crucifixes or yarmulkes on similar grounds of irritation.)

The problem goes well beyond our society's treatment of those who simply want freedom to worship in ways that most Americans find troubling. An analogous difficulty is posed by those whose religious convictions move them to action in the public are-

na. Too often, our rhetoric treats the religious impulse to public action as presumptively wicked—indeed, as necessarily oppressive. But this is historically bizarre. Every time people whose vision of God's will moves them to oppose abortion rights are excoriated for purportedly trying to impose their religious views on others, equal calumny is implicitly heaped upon the mass protest wing of the civil rights movement, which was openly and unashamedly religious in its appeals as it worked to impose its moral vision on, for example, those who would rather segregate their restaurants.

One result of this rhetoric is that we often end up fighting the wrong battles. Consider what must in our present day serve as the ultimate example of religion in the service of politics: the 1989 death sentence pronounced by the late Ayatollah Ruhollah Khomeini upon the writer Salman Rushdie for his authorship of The Satanic Verses, which was said to blaspheme against Islam. The death sentence is both terrifying and outrageous, and the Ayatollah deserved all the fury lavished upon him for imposing it. Unfortunately, for some critics the facts that the Ayatollah was a religious leader and that the "crime" was a religious one lends the sentence a particular monstrousness; evidently they are under the impression that writers who are murdered for their ideas are choosy about the motivations of their murderers, and that those whose writings led to their executions under, say, Stalin, thanked their lucky stars at the last instant of their lives that Communism was at least godless.

To do battle against the death sentence for Salman Rushdie—to battle against the Ayatollah—one should properly fight against official censorship and intimidation, not against religion. We err when we presume that religious motives are likely to be illiberal, and we compound the error when we insist that the devout should keep their religious ideas—whether good or bad—to themselves. We do no credit to the ideal of religious freedom when we talk as though religious belief is something of which public-spirited adults should be ashamed.

The First Amendment to the Constitution, often cited as the place where this difficulty is resolved, merely restates it. The First Amendment guarantees the "free exercise" of religion but also prohibits its "establishment" by the government. There may have been times in our history when we as a nation have tilted too far in one direction, allowing too much religious sway over politics. But in late twentieth-century America, despite some loud fears about the influence of the weak and divided Christian right, we are upsetting the balance afresh by tilting too far in the other direction—and the courts are assisting in the effort. For example, when a group of Native Americans objected to the Forest Service's plans to allow logging and road building in a national forest area traditionally used by the tribes for sacred rituals, the Supreme Court offered the back of its hand. True, said the Justices, the logging "could have devastating effects on traditional Indian religious practices." But that was just too bad: "government simply could not operate if it were required to satisfy every citizen's religious needs and desires."

A good point: but what, exactly, are the protesting Indians left to do? Presumably, now that their government has decided to destroy the land they use for their sacred rituals, they are free to choose new rituals. Evidently, a small matter like the potential destruction of a religion is no reason to halt a logging project. Moreover, had the government decided instead to prohibit logging in order to preserve the threatened ritual, it is entirely possible that the decision would be challenged as a forbidden entanglement of church and state. Far better for everyone, it seems, for the Native Americans to simply allow their rituals to go quietly into oblivion. Otherwise, they run the risk that somebody will think they actually take their rituals seriously. . . .